A Concise History of German Literature to 1900

A CONCISE HISTORY OF GERMAN LITERATURE TO *1900*

Edited by
Kim Vivian

CAMDEN HOUSE

Published by Camden House, Inc.
Drawer 2025
Columbia, SC 29202 USA

Printed on acid-free paper.
Binding materials are chosen for strength and
durability.

ISBN:1-879751-29-1 (Cloth)
ISBN:1-879751-30-5 (Paper)

Library of Congress Cataloging-in-Publication Data

A Concise history of German literature to 1900 / edited by Kim Vivian.
  --1st ed.
    p.   cm. -- (Studies in German literature, linguistics, and
culture)
    Includes bibliographical references and indexes.
    ISBN 1-879751-29-1 (cloth : acid-free paper). -- ISBN
1-879751-30-5 (pbk. : acid-free paper)
    1. German literature--History and criticism. I. Vivian, Kim.
II. Series.
PT91.C66 1992
830.9--dc20   92-17763
                                                              CIP

Contents

Acknowledgments

Grateful thanks are extended to the following institutions and individuals:

Augustana College and the Faculty Research Fund for generous support of the project.

To professors Gunther Holst and James Hardin for their support and editorial assistance, and to professors Michael M. Metzger, Jeffrey L. Sammons and other colleagues who provided invaluable commentary on individual essays and the entire manuscript.

To Professor Larry Scott for technical assistance, to Mr. Wayne Wilson for editorial assistance.

Most of all, to Tricia Johnson for her indefatigable efforts in the preparation of the manuscript.

Stuart P. Atkins

zum 75. Geburtstag gewidmet

Preface

*I*f one were to ask non-German-speaking readers with a limited knowledge of world literature to associate a word with German literature before 1900, one might hear responses such as "Goethe," "Schiller," "Heine," or perhaps *"Parzival"* or "Fontane" — all in all a meager response to one thousand years of a major European literature. After the titan Goethe has been acknowledged, one might hear the question: "Is there no Shakespeare in German literature? No Tolstoy, no Flaubert, no Balzac, no Chaucer, no Dante, no Petrarch or Boccaccio, no Milton?" Perhaps not, but these are novas in a crowded, dimly-lit heaven. Besides, can English, French, Italian, or Russian literature boast of a Goethe or Schiller, or Heine or Fontane, or Hartmann, Walther, and Wolfram?

A respectable canon of German literature is available in English translation, though many works that appeared in English decades ago or even in the nineteenth century are no longer in print. Some excellent new translations such as the 12-volume Suhrkamp Goethe edition in English and reprints of older translations such as those of Thomas Carlyle have recently become available, and thus a new audience has to some extent been made aware of the range and depth of German literature, from the first hesitant steps in a new language to the rugged splendor of *Das Hildebrandslied*; of the brilliance of the medieval courtly period with its *Minnesänger* and epic writers and such works as *Parzival, Tristan*, and *Das Nibelungenlied*; in the Renaissance and Reformation period the wit and biting satire of works such as *The Ship of Fools* or *Till Eulenspiegel*, or the strikingly relevant *Ploughman* and the *Faust* chapbook; the thundering cadence of Gryphius's sonnets on eternity and the transience of all things earthly, and the rich humor and earthy wisdom of the first great German novel, Grimmelshausen's *Simplicius Simplicissimus*; the urbanity and humanity of the Enlightenment writer Lessing; the brief but searing flame of the young men of the Storm and Stress with the mover and shaker Goethe in the forefront; the lofty heights of Weimar Classicism, its polished exterior only partially concealing the strains and stresses of emerging modernity; the search for the infinite and the unknown among the Romantics; the politically-charged works of Young Germany and the wistfulness, wit, and bitter irony of Heinrich Heine; the eminently dramatic plays of Grillparzer; the elegant prose of Stifter, and the lyrics of Droste-Hülshoff; the elevation of the novella form to new heights of psychological and artistic subtlety at the hands of Keller, Meyer, and Storm; and the exploratory novels of Fontane and the sophisticated prose of Raabe; to the revolutionary theatre of the Naturalists and Gerhart Hauptmann: literary achievements that deserve the attention not just of Germanists and their students, but students of literature in all languages.

The *Concise History of German Literature* is offered to the above readers as a guide through this library of German literature in English. The authors have attempted therefore to make their presentations as helpful to the reader as possible, to provide translations of all quotations in German, and to assume little or no knowledge of German history and culture on the part of the reader. Hence, the first appearance of a German title is accompanied by its English equivalent, and the suggestions for further reading have been drawn with English readers in mind. The aim of the Camden House *Concise History* is to furnish English-speaking undergraduate and graduate students of German literature with a tool with which they can deepen their knowledge of the background, the authors, and the works of German literature. Finally, it is hoped that even scholars of German literature will find new information in these pages, or at the very least ideas that will lead to lively discussions.

In England and America several notable histories of German literature have appeared in this century; the two standard works were written by Calvin Thomas and J. G. Robertson in the first decades of the century, both of which went through a number of printings. Robertson's work in the revised version of Edna Purdie remains a useful if somewhat dated reference work. In more recent times shorter histories have been written by Henry Garland, and C. P. Magill. Horst Daemmrich's *The Challenge of German Literature* offers stimulating essays dealing with the epochs of German literature, but not a strictly ordered, chronological presentation such as the present volume attempts. James Hardin's *Dictionary of Literary Biography, German Series* in a planned seventeen volumes is not yet complete and has the primary goal of providing discrete biographical and bibliographical articles on individual writers rather than of interpreting and synthesizing the data of German literary history.

The Camden House *Concise History of German Literature* aims at more than literature, which, as we well know, does not exist in a vacuum. The present volume views the authors of twelve periods and their works against the historical, social, cultural, economic, philosophical, and psychological background in which the authors lived and their writings originated. In a limited sense it is intellectual history, but one with a decided emphasis on the evolution of German literature.

The twelve essayists represented here cannot, of course, completely dismiss the intellectual background in which they studied, the influences of previous scholars, or their own view of literature developed over the years. But the editor has striven to give the volume as much of a neutral tone as possible, with the hope that neutral does not connote boring. Although each chapter has been harmonized as to structure, we have not forced the essays to agree in all cases with conflicting judgments by other authors in the work. For example, although Frank Tobin at the end of his essay on medieval literature speaks of a decline from the high standards of courtly literature, Albrecht Classen in his essay on the Renaissance and Reformation urges readers *not* to view post-courtly literature as a decline but as a fresh beginning. Here, then, is a dis-agreement of no small consequence which the editor has not attempted to smooth over.

To divide the history of German literature into twelve periods is, of course, problematical. Even a benchmark year such as 1832, the year of Goethe's death, does not signal an end to the movement of which he was the chief proponent: Weimar Classicism. One need only think of Stifter or Grillparzer to see that Weimar Classicism did not die with its most famous resident. No literature easily allows itself to be classified, but there is a didactic, practical need to do so, for to divide anything into periods is, ideally, to facilitate under-standing, and that is what this *Concise History of German Literature* hopes to achieve.

The overriding editorial principle of this book has been to cover all the periods of German literature from its beginnings to approximately 1900, includ-ing all the major authors in those periods (and a few who normally elude cate-gorization), and to present this wealth of material in a readable, straight-forward manner that illuminates rather than obfuscates. I have attempted to harmonize the spelling, titles, literary schools, periods and other designations throughout the book and to standardize the method of presentation and general structure of each chapter. Any lapses are my responsibility.

To aid the reader of this *History*, indexes have been provided covering authors and their works, and important subjects or concepts. The author's birth and death dates are given, as they are the first time the author appears in the text. Titles of works are listed alphabetically under their German title; anony-mous works are listed in alphabetical order. After each author or work follows the page(s) on which they appear.

Obviously, the editor has made no attempt to impose an ideological viewpoint on the essayists. This freedom provides for a variety of viewpoints, ideas, and positions, with which readers may, of course, take exception. But that too is an aim of this *History*, to stimulate interest in what all twelve writers cherish so much: German literature.

1 The Early Middle Ages: Gothic and Old High German

Richard H. Lawson

Historical Background: Latin and Christian Precedents

arly medieval German literature derives from two broad streams: Latin-Christian-liturgical and Germanic-pagan. Of course, matters are not quite so tidy as our formulation. The poets of pagan Rome are sometimes imitated. Much more frequent, as the streams flow together, is the replacement of the pagan element in the Germanic heritage by the literary precipitate of a gradually encroaching and triumphant Christianity. That accounts for the frequent appearance of doctrinaire Christianity in a literary context that at least at first glance seems pagan, Germanic, and heroic.

Another consequence of the cultural dominance of Christianity was that some German literature was written not in German but in Latin. This phenomenon is most prevalent when the several German languages or dialects lacked the cachet of cultural respectability — which is not necessarily early in the period of cultural conflation but more often later, in the tenth and eleventh centuries. The earliest role of German in a world — a very limited and elite world — of Latin literacy was as a missionary tool. The Latin influence was not at all limited to that emanating from the south, from Rome. Latin was powerfully represented by the Anglo-Saxon and Irish monks who proselytized much of the German-speaking area of the continent and converted it to Christianity.

The threads of an inchoate German literature can first be glimpsed around 800. The Christian and Latin elements of which it is partly comprised go back hundreds of years before that date. Its German components also derive from many centuries previously, not necessarily from a period before Roman-Germanic interaction — that would have to antedate Tacitus and Caesar — but from a period antedating the cultural interpenetration marked by the pope's crowning in the year 800 of the Frankish king Charlemagne (Charles the Great/Karl der Große) as Emperor of the West. Charlemagne's native language was Frankish, a Germanic language. Estimates of his competence in Latin vary; his friendly biographer Einhard declares that he spoke it as well as his native language. In any case, that he was a king and not a chief or a kinglet already bespoke social Romanization.

The Franks, whose earlier homeland seems to have been between the Weser and the Rhine Rivers, and who were an amalgam of much smaller tribal groupings, migrated west and south (thus to present-day northern France, to the Franconia region of Germany, to the Netherlands, and to much of Belgium) in a microcosm of the larger migrations that are called the *Völkerwanderungen,* that is, the migration of the Germanic peoples. On the basis of scattered archaeological, historical, and linguistic data one now believes that the Germanic peoples or tribes — the ancestors of the Franks included — began leaving their Scandinavian homeland in waves probably before 1,000 B.C.

These migratory waves continued to inundate Europe — and parts of Asia and North Africa — for roughly 1,500 years, impinging and being impinged on by each other, by older inhabitants (e.g., the Romans) and by non-Germanic invaders from Asia (e.g., the Huns). Many of the Germanic migrations covered, in the course of the centuries, distances that make the Frankish migrations seem modest. Emerging from Scandinavia in the last century before Christ, the Burgundians, the Vandals, and the Goths began moving east and south in an epic migration that centuries later placed the Burgundians in the south of France, the Vandals in North Africa on the site of ancient Carthage, and the Goths successively by the Black Sea, in Dacia (present-day Romania), in Constantinople, in Italy, in the Balkans, and finally in Spain, where the Visigothic kingdom yielded to Arab military power in 711. All were variously Romanized and Christianized during their settlements in Roman venues. But it was only the Franks who survived to lay the foundations of a modern state — that of France. Their distinction was not merely to become Romanized and Christianized, but in their timely Christianization to become associated with the Catholic church in its rise to power — not, like the Goths for example, to tie their fortunes to what became the Arian heresy. (Arianism, a widely prevalent alternative in the eastern region of Christianity, held that God is completely alone and unknowable, that Christ is not part of the Godhead but a secondary divinity. In the fourth century it was condemned as heresy.)

Literary Origins

That association of the Franks and Catholicism fostered the preservation of the liturgical literature. But what of the non-Christian literature? Although Charlemagne also sponsored a collection of heroic Germanic lays, it has ceased to exist, probably a victim of his less broad-minded descendants on the thrones of his subsequently divided empire. Surviving non-Christian literary remnants are sparse, but from them we are able to draw conclusions about the nature of pagan, Germanic, heroic culture.

The earliest poetry sprang from a communal religion and from the practice of war, celebrating the latter within the framework of the former, reinforced by magic, charms, and curses. It was music as well as poetry, characterized by ceremonial articulation and a heavy, regular stress accent (as distinguished from a pitch accent). End-rhyme was unknown; in its stead Germanic verse originally relied on *Stabreim*, or alliteration, by which the same consonantal phoneme (single sound) recurs in a succession of accented (i.e., root) syllables. Or an initial stressed vowel rhymes with any other stressed initial vowel. Remnants of *Stabreim* still permeate vernacular expression in modern German and modern English: *Haus und Hof,* "hearth and home." As a formal principle in Old High German it looks like this (from *Muspilli* [c. 880]):

> hus in himile, dar quimit imo hilfa kinuok

> A house in heaven, help enough will come to him there

The heavily stressed, strongly aspirated "h" in *hus* rhymes with, is keyed with, is in *Stabreim* with the "h" in *himile* and the "h" in *hilfa.* Words in *Stabreim* do not need to be nouns, as in the illustration, but they do need to be words or word-parts of some importance — that is, normally not particles, nor prepositions, nor verbal prefixes.

The original martial-religious focus of the early poetry led to the creation of heroic lays depicting the valorous and violent deeds of a hero who was half-historical, half-legendary. For example, Theodoric the Great (c. 454-526), Ostrogothic king and successor to the Western emperors in Rome, emerges as Dietrich von Bern (Verona) in what must have been a cycle of heroic lays, *Das Hildebrandslied* (*The Lay of Hildebrand*), a rare surviving example. Such legendary-heroic cycles, well adorned with magic and the supernatural and even a Christian overlay, survived more copiously in epics of the Middle High German literary period, but they must have been plentiful too in the old High German period — only to suffer destruction in the less tolerant Christianity that followed Charlemagne's enlightened reign. (In this connection one thinks chiefly of his son, Ludwig the Pious [der Fromme] — Louis I).

The Goths and Bishop Ulfilas

Terms like Old High German and Middle High German had to do originally not with literature but with language and with language change in the area in which High German was spoken. They have long been applied to the chronologically coinciding literary period as well, however. We will here follow the convention by which Old High German literature extends from 800, the year of Charlemagne's imperial coronation — or even conceivably as far back as 750 — to about 1050, at which point the early Middle High German period begins. But before we consider the literary monuments of Old High German that have been preserved, we need to back up for several centuries — to the fourth century — to consider the earliest extant text in any Germanic language: the Gothic Bible. (This does not consider non-literary inscriptions, which date from about the beginning of the Christian era.)

For their military exploits and the sheer geographical scope of their migrations, the Goths early achieved prominence, well before the Franks, much further west, had coalesced into a force to be reckoned with. The Goths' originally more easterly migrations and warfare — neither was distinct from the other — brought them into contact with, among others, the Romans and Greeks in Dacia and Constantinople. Frequently they entered the Roman service as *foederati*; on the other hand, in the Battle of Adrianople (Edirne in present-day Turkey) they decisively defeated a Roman army. But what is culturally important is not this or that defeat of, or by, the Romans, but the continuing Gothic contact with the Mediterranean and Christian civilization.

The Goths converted to Christianity three or four hundred years before the Franks; not to Catholicism, however, but to Arianism. The Goths' Arianism, when they migrated to Western Europe, served to isolate them from the surrounding cultural streams, though their monarchs in Italy and Spain were remarkably tolerant of the Catholicism of their adversaries/subjects.

The moving force behind the conversion of the Goths in Dacia was their bishop Ulfilas (sometimes also Ulfila or Wulfila). He was born in the Crimea, probably in 311 and not of purely Gothic parentage. He served as ambassador to the court of the Roman Emperor, Constantine the Great, in Constantinople, whence he received the charge to serve as missionary bishop to his Gothic countrymen. As part of his mission of conversion he translated the New Testament from Greek — the language of the Eastern Roman Empire — into Gothic. Substantial preserved fragments of his labors, the so-called Gothic Bible, testify to his linguistic and literary, as well as missionary, talents. He died about 383.

Ulfilas was obliged to construct an alphabet and a grammar for a language not previously written. Reflecting the Greek-speaking environment of his part of the Roman world, he used the Greek uncial alphabet to render most Gothic phonemes. In the few instances where the Greek letters did not suffice, he used the Latin alphabet of letters deriving from the runic alphabet (the magic-related letters used by the Germanic tribes up to about the third century). Ulfilas's translation into Gothic has an expressive quality that approaches poetic, rendering new and — to the Goths — unfamiliar spiritual and intellectual concepts with a flexible resourcefulness.

Besides Ulfilas's New Testament translation into Visigothic, there are a few non-poetic monuments preserved from the kingdom of the East Goths in Italy. The Goths undoubtedly possessed a poetic literature as well. It is reported that heroic songs were presented at the court of the Visigothic King Theodoric II in Toulouse in the fifth century — a century after the conversion — and it is fair to infer that they drew from the Germanic heroic cycles. But in the end little remained either of the Goths or their literature — except for their Bible — and as the Arian Goths waned, the Catholic or soon-to-be Catholic Franks were gathering power and in their way amalgamating with the Roman Christian heritage.

Early Writings in Old High German

The earliest prose in Old High German — we shall be looking first at the prose, then at the poetry, and in the later period at both more or less simultaneously — was of minor artistic merit compared with Ulfilas's Gothic Bible: two dictionaries, the so-called *Abrogans* and the *Vocabularius Sancti Galli* (Vocabulary of St. Gall). The former is not Frankish but Bavarian, having been compiled in Freising around 760 or 765. (Freising stood directly in the cultural stream emanating north from Rome.) It is a Latin-German dictionary, an expansion of the original *Abrogans*, which was simply an alphabetical dictionary of Latin synonyms as used in rhetoric. A monolingual dictionary has become bilingual, still called *Abrogans*, after its initial entry. A sample entry, briefer than most, is:

Elegantia urmari   pulchritudo liuplih

(*pulchritudo* means "physical beauty"). Old High German *urmari* means "excellent," *liuplih* "lovely." Usually, however, the parts of speech do not change interlingually as they do here.

The *Vocabularius*, in which the German is Alemannic dialect, is arranged by subject-groups rather than alphabetically. It cannot be dated more precisely than as of the eighth century. It did not originate in the famous monastery of St. Gall (in present Switzerland), but more likely at Fulda, in the other center of monastic concern with language, which was much more under the influence of missionary monks from England (who in turn reflected Roman influence).

The incidence of linguistic activity — here, the writing of dictionaries to include German — did not occur by chance at the monasteries, effectively Benedictine monasteries. Nor was the Benedictine preoccupation with language rooted in the idea of developing literacy for the public weal — except to the degree that the public weal was equated with religion, with proselytizing, and conversion. Furthermore, the monasteries were the only places to command sufficient literacy for the making of dictionaries and glosses, the other category of religiously effective language work. There were three types of glosses: German glosses of Latin sources, interlinear translations of Latin, and translations in which the Latin and the German are separate from each other.

The problems confronting the translators, the dictionary-makers, and the glossators were essentially those that had confronted Ulfilas. Non-German letters, in this case the Latin alphabet, had to be matched with the often very un-Latinlike German phonemes. German lacked a linguistic standard; the monk-translators naturally tended to favor their own dialects: for example, Frankish, Alemannic, Bavarian, or to approximate with varying degrees of accuracy the regional standard of the dialect region in which their monastery was located. German lacked words for many a spiritual or metaphysical concept — words had to be invented. And naturally a tension inhered in the task of translating or glossing sacred or ecclesiastical texts. Finally — and differing from Ulfilas's presumably solitary labors — the work was often done by teams of monks assigned by and overseen by a preceptor, and some of the monks simply were not very good at translating. To a perhaps rudimentary or uncertain command of Latin, add the feeling that German was of inferior status compared with Latin.

So it is that the St. Gall translation of the *Pater noster* and the *Credo*, Alemannic translations of the Lord's Prayer and the Credo from near the end of the eighth century, are full of mistakes — even in what were two of the most plentifully recited passages in monastic life. To judge from phonological evidence, these two short prayers, incorporated (as written Old High German often was) in a much larger Latin manuscript, are the handiwork of two different translators. They resemble each other, however, in a propensity for a variety of mistakes, which include the gratuitous addition of syllables, failure to recognize a relative clause (or maybe the inability to cope with it in German), nonsensical misspelling, wrong case ending (evidently a Latin ending on a German noun). Altogether not inspiring performances — and yet they surely brought the Lord's Prayer and the Credo closer to the overwhelming majority of people who knew no Latin whatever.

Tatian

A prominent early preceptor and probable preceptor of a team of translators was the monk Hrabanus (or Rabanus) Maurus, born in Mainz around 776, during his middle years abbot of the monastery at Fulda, and later, until his death in 856, Archbishop of Mainz. Hrabanus was a student of the missionary English monk and theologian, Alcuin, and a contemporary of Charlemagne's son Ludwig the Pious, who decisively rejected any scrap of surviving native German, pagan literature — but not the language — and resolutely supported the cultivation of Latin-Christian models. Hrabanus Maurus was the abbot par excellence in seeing to the realization of this latter goal.

Compiled by a team effort at Fulda around 830 during the abbotship of Hrabanus was the East Frankish translation of a sixth-century Latin version of a gospel harmony (*Evangelienharmonie*) originally composed in Greek by a second-century Christian named Tatian — or Latinized, Tatianus. The German translation generally goes by the name of, simply, *Tatian*. (A gospel harmony — the usual way of presenting the New Testament in the second century — consists of extracts from the four gospels, those of Matthew, Mark, Luke, and John, strung together to provide a continuous but reiterative narrative. It is thus ideal for educational and proselytizing purposes.) Hrabanus Maurus himself, it is speculated, may have contributed some of his own translation to the joint effort, but this is at least doubtful; more likely his role was supervisory and editorial. While in general *Tatian* is East Frankish, the contributions of half a dozen, perhaps more, translators can be discerned on the basis of more localized dialect items. It appears that the 171-page (formerly 172) manuscript in the monastery library at St. Gall is removed in time by hardly more than a few decades from the translational endeavor itself. The St. Gall manuscript has the Latin in one column, the Old High German in another. Originally, though, the German was probably written in between the Latin lines, a perhaps more usual — certainly earlier — style of glossing and translating.

Interlinear translation is basically word-for-word, literal translation; and very literal is what Old High German *Tatian* is. It reflects the Latin in a generally slavish way, complete with unlikely German replication of Latin syntactical features. The words, to be sure, are German — which already implies expertise in molding a German lexicon (conceivably via Old English) to suit the needs of Latin semantics and theological precision. But the overall results are doubtful as German. And even where the Old High German seems to show some adherence to a "natural" German tense sequence — as in rendering the Latin present tense *dicit*, "he says," by Old High German *quad* (past tense) rather than *quidit* (present tense) — the reason may well lie in an alternative Latin source that has the Latin perfect, *dixit*.

The Benedictine Rule

Very much in the translational vein of *Tatian*, perhaps just slightly freer, is the Old High German *Benediktinerregel* (*Benedictine Rule*), likewise translated from Latin. (St. Benedict of Nursia founded the Benedictine order as an alternative to extreme monastic asceticism. Work, and increasingly work of a theological and intellectual nature, replaced extreme asceticism. Most German monasteries and nunneries by the time of Charlemagne were Benedictine. St. Benedict propounded his Bible- and common-sense-inspired Rule as the standard of governance for Benedictine houses.) The seventy-five-chapter *Benediktinerregel* in Latin is one of the most widely dispersed documents of its era. The Old High German interlining the Latin original starts becoming more than slightly incomplete as early as chapter 16 or 17. It ceases entirely with chapter 67, by which time we are dealing with no more than isolated words and phrases, in effect a gloss — like many another — meant only to be helpful in difficult places rather than complete.

The Old High German *Benediktinerregel* was written in Alemannic around the beginning of the ninth century. It exists as a St. Gall manuscript, although there is some uncertainty whether it originated in St. Gall or in neighboring Reichenau, both of which monasteries had vigorous traditions of glossing. The lexical glossing style of both houses is reflected in the translated *Regel*. If we proceed, however, to spelling preferences and to the use of certain abbreviations, our judgment tilts toward St. Gall.

The Old High German *Benediktinerregel* is the purest and the most extensive example of an interlinear translation. The German, heavily dependent on word-for-word renditions of the Latin, is hardly comprehensible without the Latin. Still, there are minor supplementations, very much like those evidenced in *Tatian*. For example, the definite article is used even though Latin lacks such, and the Latin gerundive construction is rendered by *ze* (to) plus a suffixed infinitive. Biblical citations are sometimes pithier than the Latin originals. Furthermore, even in the thoroughly Christian scriptorium of a monastery and in translating a work as earnestly Christian as the *Benediktinerregel,* there are apparent remnants (more than in *Tatian*) of the *Stabreim* that comprised the fundamental poetic principle of Germanic heroic verse. Thus in the prologue where there is a citation from Psalms 34:14, the Latin original goes: *inquire pacem et persequere eam,* that is, "seek peace and pursue it." The Old High German runs: *Suahhi fridu indi kefolge den,* in which the emphasized "f's" introducing stressed syllables are in a *Stabreim*-relationship to each other. (The Latin counterpart "p's" are not felt to be in any such relationship.)

Isidor

A less extensive and at the same time a more naturally German translation from Latin — and a few decades before the German *Benediktinerregel* — was that comprised in the fragments of St. Isidore's *De fide catholica contra Judaeos,* that is, *On Catholic Faith against Jews.* Bishop Isidore of Seville, known as Isidorus Hispalensis, wrote etymologies as well as his tract on the nature of Catholic faith vis-à-vis doubts and attacks on the part of the Jews, but it is the latter that made its way into Old High German translation at about the beginning of the ninth century. Some critics give the date as some time after 770; the most recent, citing paleographic evidence, modify this into the final decade of the eighth century.

If its date is uncertain, other descriptions of the Old High German *Isidor* are hardly more definite. Its place of origin was probably a monastery in upper-Alsatian Murbach, although this attribution is spiritedly rejected by a minority (some of whom prefer Tours, France). Others urge Alemannic, Alsatian, or Frankish territory — a range of attribution that could hardly miss but that adds little to the cause of precision. Its dialect in any case is Middle Frankish, but as has been noted, the dialect of the translator and translation often does not coincide with that of the region of the scriptorium in which the work was done — let alone with the locale of the chief surviving copy: in this case, Paris.

The Paris manuscript in its present state consists of eighty-eight parchment leaves, all but one containing twenty-two lines of carefully inscribed and remarkably error-free writing. Apparently some eight pages at the outset are missing. The arrangement of the writing is at first columnar, Latin and Old High German side by side, then only Latin with the right-hand column vacant, and finally Latin covering pages that are no longer columnar.

Isidore's purpose, emergent in his title, is to defend the truth of Christian doctrine against the Jews. One may imagine that the Old High German version served an ecclesiastical-educational goal, perhaps at one of the three synods held under Charlemagne in 792, 794, and 799, having to do with the doctrine of the dual and differential sonship of Christ — as God and as Man — in which Spanish bishops were opposed by Frankish theologians, who ultimately prevailed. On the other hand, one may think of the shift from two-column to single-column format that occurs on page 34 as an indication that the manuscript was prepared by a cleric for his own use. In either case one may further suppose, correctly, that such a tract would be fraught with linguistic complexities. And yet despite the inherent difficulty, the translator is subtly expressive, fully the master of his material in producing a translation in natural — as opposed to Latinized — German, a translation that stood unrivaled for its time and for more than a century after. The only work that comes close at the beginning of the ninth century is the *Monsee-Wiener-Fragmente* (*Monsee-Vienna Fragments*), fragments of a New Testament translation into Bavarian — although the original German version seems to have been in the same language as the Isidore translation, that is, Middle Frankish.

The Frankish Baptismal Vow and *The St. Gall Paternoster and Credo*

There are preserved a considerable number of short prayers and vows from the Carolingian era, of which the *Fränkisches Taufgelöbnis* (*Frankish Baptismal Vow*) and the *St. Galler Paternoster und Credo* (*St. Gall Paternoster and Credo*) may serve as illustrations. The *Taufgelöbnis*, from a manuscript of the latter part of the ninth or the early part of the tenth century, is in the form of an interrogation by a priest — questions and answers. For instance, the first question and answer are:

Forsahhistu unholdun?   Ih fursahu.

Do you forsake the devil?   I forsake.

There are altogether ten such questions and responses, of which the last are:

Gilaubistu lib after tode?   Ih gilaubu.

Do you believe in life after death?   I believe.

The *St. Galler Paternoster und Credo* is in Alemannic of the eighth century. The Lord's Prayer, possibly erring on the early relative clause, begins:

Fater unseer, thu pist in himile.

Our Father, thou art in heaven.

The Credo, as well, offers some deviations, conceivably erroneous, from how one has come to know it in English or Latin.

Psalm Translations

From the ninth to the eleventh centuries there was apparently a lively tradition of — mostly interlinear and mostly prose — psalm translation. Only fragments survive, however, and in most cases fragments of fragments — that is, few of the psalms translated are complete. One such complete psalm is the Middle Frankish — or at least showing some Middle Frankish characteristics but otherwise dialectically diverse — version of the First Psalm. This translation is presumed to date from the ninth century but survives only in a much later non-interlinear manuscript. Of a similar source, age, and completeness is, for example, the Lower Frankish version of Psalm 62 (King James: Psalm 63), whereas the Lower Frankish translations of Psalm 73 (King James: Psalm 74) in the same manuscript is truncated.

A few interlinear Rhine Frankish psalm fragments survive on two parchment leaves of the tenth or eleventh century: Isaiah 38, I Kings 2 (King James: I Samuel 2), Habakkuk 3, and Deuteronomy 32. A somewhat greater number of Alemannic psalms survives — as fragments in all but one instance — in a ninth-century manuscript: Psalms 107 (King James: 108), 108 (King James: 109), 113 (115), 114 (116), 123 (124), 124 (125), and 128-130 (129-131). Only Psalm 129 (130) is complete.

In addition to the mostly incomplete prose translation of the psalms, there is a remarkable poetic paraphrase of Psalm 138 (139). It is from the tenth century, and the language is Bavarian. The sequence of the manuscript lines is doubtfully correct, yet scholars have not been able to agree on a better alternative sequence. Some point to the possible survival of *Stabreim*, typical of pre-Christian verse, in this Christian material — as, for example, in line 20:

De uuider dir uuellent tuon   de uuillih fasto nīdon.

Those who would act against you   them I will hate profoundly.

Others hold that the alliteration occurs purely by chance. Certain is that the end-rhyme is pervasive, although not all instances would pass muster by present-day requirements. One that clearly does so occurs in line 35.

ne megih in nohhein lant,   nupe mih hapet dīn hant.

I cannot get anywhere (attain any land),   unless your hand holds me fast.

The Strasbourg Oath

Not all Old High German prose was of a basically religious or ecclesiastical nature. For example, some bits of the *Lex salica* (*Law of the Salian Franks*) is preserved in East Frankish in a manuscript of the ninth century, although the laws far antedate the ninth-century commitment to parchment. Still more interesting is the *Straßburger Eide* (*Strasbourg Oaths*) of February 14, 842, recited in the presence of their respective troops by two grandsons and partial successors of Charlemagne, making common cause against a third brother. Ludwig the German (der Deutsche [or, the Bavarian]) recited the Old French version before the troops of his brother, Charles the Bald (Karl der Kahle [Charles II of France]), while Charles recited the Old High German in Rhine Frankish in front of Ludwig's army. The whole, complete with Latin introduction and transitions, amounts to little more than thirty lines. It would be a mistake to imagine that these oaths were sworn entirely oblivious to religion, for Ludwig's first words were:

Pro deo amur et pro christian poblo et nostro commun salvament...

while those of Charles were:

In godes minna ind in thes christānes folches ind unsēr bēdhero gehaltnissī...

That is, leveling the slight differences:

For the love of God and the Christian people and our common salvation...

True, the last may refer to military as well as religious salvation, for their brother Lothar was a restive adversary.

The Physiologus

The *Physiologus* exists in two prose versions and one rhymed version, dated from about 1070 to perhaps 1150. The prose versions, based on a probably fifth-century Latin prose model, are respectively Alemannic and Bavarian. The older and more original Old High German prose version, possibly made in Hirsau by two co-translators, is in a manuscript from Carinthia. The *Physiologus* blends medieval "natural science" with religion for religious-didactic purposes. *Physiologus* presents brief prose descriptions of animals, both real and fabulous, from the lion to the unicorn. They are anthropomorphized in such a way that their good — in human moral terms — qualities are said to represent Christ or God, whereas their bad qualities represent the devil and his realm. For example, at the outset we are informed that

> Leo bezehinet unserin trohtin turih sine sterihchi.

> The lion represents our Lord on account of his strength.

It is for this reason that the lion is often mentioned in holy scripture. Whereas, in another section of the *Physiologus*, "the crocodile represents death and hell."

The Wessobrunn Prayer

The oldest spiritual poetry in Old High German — although it turns out to be about one-third prose — is the *Wessobrunner Gebet* (*Wessobrunn Prayer*). Traditionally it is dated as of 814, although some would put it as early as the last decades of the eighth century. In Bavarian, revealing possible traces of an English writer, it is variously attributed to Regensburg or, as its conventional name reflects, the Bavarian monastery of Wessobrunn. It consists of nine poetic lines of moderately well-preserved *Stabreim*, which might properly be termed a hymn, followed by a forty-one-word prayer in prose.

While the style of the pre-Christian Germanic lay is suggested by the intensity of poetic feeling — and critics formerly were given to connecting the Wessobrunn Prayer with the Germanic creation myth, as in the tenth-century Old Norse *Völuspa* — the content is in fact purely Christian, resonating to the sense of the 89th (King James: 90th) Psalm as well as that of Genesis (in any case the *Völuspa* itself was influenced by Christianity). In the fashion of the lay, the heavily accented half-lines separated by a caesura produce a staccato effect, which would be still more pronounced when the poem was read aloud. The poem conveys a picture of primordial chaos in which no natural terrestrial features or beings are to be discerned, only excepting a very Christian God, "the one almighty God, mildest of men," and his heavenly host of angels. This vision having been established in the verse, the supplicant in the prayer that follows asks God to grant him true faith, good will, wisdom, intelligence, and strength — qualities to enable him to withstand the devil and to work God's will.

Heliand and Genesis

The oldest historical form of Low German is contained in the Old Saxon verse epic that was given the name *Heliand* by its first editor, in the nineteenth century (*Heliand*=Saviour). The approximately 6,000-line work is preserved in two manuscripts, one almost complete, the other complete, from the ninth and tenth centuries. It was composed in the early ninth century — date ranges are variously given as 820-830, 822-840, and 822-843, in any case a few decades after the forced conversion of the Saxons to Christianity. Probably it was composed at the behest of Charlemagne's son Ludwig the Pious, with the intention of acquainting the largely illiterate populace with the life and teachings of Jesus and with how one ought to act as a servant of the Lord.

The *Heliand* appears to be based not on the Vulgate Bible but on the Latin version of Tatian's *Evangelienharmonie,* supplemented by Hrabanus Maurus's commentary on the gospel of Matthew and quite likely by Old English commentaries on Mark and Luke. As the Hrabanus Maurus connection implies, it was probably composed at Fulda. The poet is unknown, and even his professional identity has been a subject of critical dispute. One camp held that he was a professional minstrel, a *skop* — in which case the question arises: how did he know all the religious material — even though it is not free of mistakes — that is contained in the epic? Nowadays the view prevails that the poet was a Saxon priest — although a priest with an exceptional poetic talent and a bit of susceptibility to doctrinal error.

Although the *Heliand* is traditionally designated as Old Saxon, it is far from pure — and even farther from spoken and colloquial — Old Saxon. "Bible Saxon" has been suggested as an alternative. It contains an admixture of both Old Frisian and Old English, as well as Old High German elements. For example, it often includes literary and religious words unknown in subsequent Low German but with counterparts in Old High German. In general, but not uniquely, the *Heliand* fits old Germanic words into new Christian concepts. By way of illustration, *wurd,* whose basic meaning was simply "fate," "blind fate," now does duty as the equivalent of *providentia Dei,* literally the "providence of God."

The verse form of the *Heliand* is an attenuated form of *Stabreim* that has parallels in Old English. The long line has two stressed syllables on either side of the caesura; the half-lines are linked by a single alliterative pair. The long line can be extended, however, to accommodate ideas of greater complexity. Indeed — a more important deviation from the continental Germanic verse form — a single idea may occupy more than one long line and may end at mid-line. Furthermore, symbolic numbers in the text appear to function also as determinants of form. More traditionally, a very strong feeling for nature comports with Germanic epic style.

It used to be argued, and sometimes still is, that the *Heliand* represents a Germanization of Christianity, as to both inner and outer form. There are details that seem to support such a view: like swan maidens the angels don feathered garments. But such scattered items do not constitute a persuasive case. Inside, the *Heliand* is completely Christian — and that is true even if some unprincely details of Jesus's life, such as riding on an ass and offering counsel to turn the other cheek, are deleted. The external framework is Germanic: Jesus is the Master, to whom the disciples are bound by an oath of allegiance, that is, a feudal relationship. On the one hand this is a skillful poetic conversion by which the Saxon poet obtains identification from his audience, whereas on the other hand it reflects the naive medieval point of view that has little alternative at hand in depicting past eras and foreign peoples — thus the New Testament scene — in terms of local and contemporary models. War, in any case, is unambiguously wicked — a lesson to the warlike Saxons. And Peter's denial of Jesus is viewed as the consequence of Peter's un-Christian arrogance.

The poet, a resourceful medieval storyteller, is a diligent and skillful teacher of Christianity to a Saxon nation less than perfectly attuned to his message. He re-emphasizes and de-emphasizes in a sensitive awareness of both his audience and his messages. He portrays scenes vividly and with epic fullness, and the messages usually speak for themselves. The result is that the *Heliand*, free of pedantic baggage, moves with a briskness that is quite comfortable to the modern reader.

Surviving in fragmentary form — 337 lines — on pages of a Latin codex (that also contains eighty lines of the *Heliand*) is the *Altsächsische Genesis* (*Old Saxon Genesis*). This poetic paraphrase of Genesis, based on the Vulgate Bible and commentaries thereon, probably dates from the first half of the ninth century. Genesis does not lend itself to the superimposition of a Germanic exterior as well as does the life of Jesus. When an amenable topic is treated, such as the fall of Adam and Eve into sin, the *Genesis* poet proves unusually adept at psychological explanation.

Otfrid's *Book of the Gospels*

The monk Otfrid's Old High German *Evangelienharmonie* (*Book of the Gospels*) ranks with the *Heliand* as a substantial and important poetic work of the ninth century. Its dialect is South Rhine Frankish. Although dwelling on the same general topic, the life, deeds, and words of Jesus, the two poems are otherwise quite different, both as to content and form. Related to, if not largely responsible for, these differences is the fact that Otfrid and his work (the work is often given the name of its author), unlike the *Heliand*, stem from a region that could look back to a Christian tradition already many generations long.

Otfrid studied at Fulda under Hrabanus Maurus from 820 to 830, but he was a native of Weissenburg in Upper Alsace (now the French town of Wissembourg), where he returned to teach in the monastery. What we know of Otfrid is based entirely on the four lengthy and elaborate dedications, traditional in late Roman culture, within his long and discursive poem. While a student at Fulda he formed friendships with several fellow-students, with whom he continued to correspond, so that he had connections at Constance and above all at St. Gall. Around 868 he finished his *Evangelienharmonie* as a rather old man — but still flexible; one can see his adaptability as the work progresses. His work is preserved in four variant manuscripts of the ninth and early tenth century, of which the basic one is not only complete but apparently was corrected and provided with accent marks by the poet himself.

Otfrid's source is the Vulgate Bible, mostly from John's Gospel, but he selected his material and its sequence to accord with his own didactic purposes. He divided his material not into four gospels but into five "books," each of which contains a number of sections with Latin subheads. He interrupts his poetic narrative of Jesus's words and deeds with sections of explanations and interpretations of a moral or allegorical nature derived from the Christian and Neoplatonic theology of his day. His message is: flee the present and commit yourself to heavenly salvation. His virtue does not lie in the direction of originality — not a virtue in his day in any event; nor in his poetic re-creation: it is long-winded and clumsy; rather it lies in the execution of his didactic purpose and in his poetic form in the narrower sense.

Ostensibly his work is a response to a charge placed on him by friends — but that is simply the window-dressing of tradition. We may imagine correctly that his perception of the need for such a work is his own, however common that perception was in church circles. Specifically, vain and repulsive lay songs are said to have become all too popular. What is necessary is a new Christian epic to overwhelm the popular songs, to help root out the lingering remnants of the pagan Germanic popular consciousness. Moreover — to continue paraphrasing the poet — the Franks, given their prominence and power as the leaders of Christendom, should receive the divine word in their own languages rather than in Latin. For God can be invoked in any language; and the Franks are heirs of the Romans. So then, a Christian epic in Frankish! And meant to be declaimed, not sung.

What of his form in the narrower sense? Avoiding Germanic alliteration for the most part, Otfrid has the distinction of being the first to introduce end-rhyme in an Old High German poem of substantial length. End-rhyme was of Roman (and probably Irish) and ecclesiastical origin. In the latter respect it thus suited his Christianizing anti-lay mission — although not ideally, for rhyme is inherently intended to be sung. Actually, his end-rhymes are not at the end of the long lines but within two halves of a long line. For instance:

Oba ih thaz irwéllu   theih sinaz lób zellu

If I choose that,   that I enumerate his praise(s)

But by no means did all of Otfrid's rhymes fall into the category of pure rhyme. He made use of both vocal and consonantal assonance, by which, respectively, *harto* and *worto*, and *ein* and *deil* qualify as rhymes. As to stress, each of his rhyming half-lines contains four stresses as determined by natural word-accent, although not all of the stresses are of equal force. In several of the Otfridian manuscripts some of the primary stresses are marked, but not in a consistent way. As in historical Germanic verse, any number of unstressed syllables may occur. In sum, Otfrid is a tendentious and rather tiresome poet (the poet of the *Heliand* was *not* tiresome), whose signal accomplishment, besides that of composing a very long, didactic, poetic Gospel harmony, was that of adapting end-rhyme to Germanic verse (but end-rhyme broadly construed to include assonance as well as pure rhyme).

Muspilli

Hardly less Christian — despite early critical misperceptions — than Otfrid, but in every other way vastly different is the unknown Bavarian priest and preacher who was the poet of *Muspilli*. The fragmentary, but probably fairly complete, poem runs to just 105 lines. It was found written in an awkward hand, on the margins and on the empty pages of a manuscript presented by Bishop Adabram of Salzburg to Ludwig the German around 825 (when the later monarch was still a duke). The beginning and the end, supposedly written on the inside of the front and back covers of the manuscript, are missing — for the covers themselves are missing. The date of composition is variously given as between 826 and 836, between 830 and 840, and, based on uncertain internal evidence, 827 — in any case after the manuscript was in Ludwig's possession. It has been suggested that Ludwig himself was the poet, but this is refuted by the Bavarian language of the poem: Ludwig's language was Middle Frankish.

Whoever the poet was, he had only a loose command of *Stabreim*. The alliteration often consists of but one word in each half-line. Several lines have end-rhyme, in the broad Otfridian sense of the term. Rhetoric rather than narrative predominates. Dialogue, the staple of epic verse, is totally lacking; all but lacking as well is that other characteristic of Germanic epic verse, the formulaic expression. The stylistic and rhythmic beauty of *Muspilli* seems to lie in the eye and ear of the beholder: whereas one critic can bemoan its awkward style and rhythm, another can see it as a masterpiece of rhetoric. Perhaps the disparity can be at least partially resolved if we resist the temptation to judge it by epic criteria. Again, it is above all rhetorical. It has lines that are more prose than poetry — indeed, the prose of the pulpit with its characteristic turns of phrases.

Muspilli is divided into two only imperfectly joined parts. Lines 1-30 deal in stark terms with the fate of the soul, detached from its body immediately after death, as an object of contention between the army of heaven and that of hell. That contention, the bright heavenly host versus the remorseless cruelty of Satan's troops, may at first sound as if it were derived from the Germanic heroic lay; but in fact it coincides with medieval biblical exegetics. The remainder, lines 31-103 (lines 74a and 99a run the total linage to 105) are a description of Doomsday and the stern judgment awaiting the rejoined souls and bodies, which are judged by their deeds during life. Repentance is forcefully urged, especially in those who in life enjoyed wealth and power.

Central to the Doomsday scenario is a duel — that much is Germanic, but not necessarily from the heroic era — between Elias and the Antichrist. Both fall, at which the cosmos is subject to calamity, movingly presented. The blood from Elias's wounds, for example, turns into an earth-destroying firestorm. That transformation is paralleled only in Russian legends; the world-fire itself is borrowed form Latin sources. The rest of the catastrophe derives ultimately from the book of Apocalypse together with other books of the Bible and commentaries thereon.

The title *Muspilli* (the word has analogues in the *Heliand* as well as in Old English and Old Norse) is of uncertain etymology — although not for lack of suggestions. What seems certain is that it is to be equated with the destruction of the world or with the day when that destruction is to occur. The poem remains, despite its formal imperfections, including the flawed integration of its two parts, the only substantial example of Old High German alliterative religious poetry. The poet's intent appears to have been to wed Christian-religious content with surviving Germanic cultural values; at best, he succeeded only partially.

The Merseburg Charms

The *Merseburger Zaubersprüche (Merseburg Charms)*, so-called because of their modern presence in Merseburg, are the only Old High German poems that in their totality hark back to pre-Christian Germanic culture. (Attempts to link them with Christianity have been generally rejected.) They are not the only incantations that have been preserved. But their antiquity and the unique insight they offer into pagan culture make them the most prominent. In Thuringian dialect, they probably originated in Fulda in the early tenth century. The first one goes:

Eiris sazum idisi,   sazun hera duoder.
suma hapt heptidun,   suma heri lezidun,
suma clubodun   umbi cuoniouuidi:
insprinc haptbandun,   inuar uigandun!

Once the Idisi [wise women, or battle goddesses]   were sitting here and there.
Some secured fetters,   some impeded the army,
Some picked   around the fetters.
Escape from the bonds,   escape from the enemy!

Incantations tend to be of aphoristic brevity and difficulty, but the narration of the first three long lines is the following: a warrior has been taken prisoner (the point of view is his). Three groups of wise women — one thinks of the Valkyries of Norse legend — help him in three ways: putting fetters on captives brought in from the opposing army, contending with that army, and, finally, undoing the bonds of the warrior to whom they are well disposed, setting him free. The fourth line contains the exorcism in the form of the imperative clauses. That reflects the usual proportion in a charm between the narration — sometimes called the example — of several long lines' length, and the exorcism or magic formula at the end, a mere long line or two or three.

In the second Merseburg charm the narration consists of six and a half long lines, the magic formula consists of two. The gods Phol (Balder) and Wodan are riding in the forest when Balder's horse pulls up lame. One or possibly two pairs of goddesses — it is unclear whether their names are distinct or simply in apposition — consecutively cast spells to heal the horse's lame foot. In vain.

Thereupon Wodan casts a spell, as only he can, whether the wound is a dislocated bone, a hemorrhage, or a sprained limb. (The highest god proves to have the requisite power.) Now comes the incantational conclusion:

> ben zi bena,   bluot zi bluoda,
> lid zi geliden,   sose gelimida sin!

> Bone to bone,   blood to blood,
> limb to limb,   as if they were glued!

After Otfrid there were a number of rhymed poems of shorter length. Most are Bavarian or Alemannic. The earliest, from Freising in the ninth century, is the *Petruslied (Lay of St. Peter)*, the first German choral church song. Written by an anonymous cleric, its rhythm is that of a Latin hymn. It consists of three simple two- (long) line stanzas, after each of which occurs the familiar refrain from Greek: *Kyrie eleyson, Christe eleyson* (Lord have mercy upon us, Christ have mercy upon us). The strophes were to be sung by a soloist, the refrain by the people. As often was the case, the words are supplemented by neumes, an early approximation to musical notation. As the name of the song suggests, the text is a prayer to St. Peter that he intervene with God in behalf of the singers.

Christus und die Samariterin (Christ and the Samaritan Woman), on the other hand, is not for singing but for recitation. In popular epic style after several (here six) lines of introductory narration, the rest (twenty-five lines) follows the scheme: speech and response. It is thus removed from Otfrid's style of poetic preaching, but its half-lines, in the Otfridian style, are linked by end-rhymes. In Alemannic with Rhine Frankish undertones (probably it was transcribed by a Rhine Frank), it dates from 909 or later. The poem follows exactly its Vulgate source, John 4:6-20, the first part of the story of *Christus und die Samariterin*.

The Alemannic *Georgslied (Lay of St. George)* is meant to be sung. It is the first preserved (though incomplete) German saint's legend, dwelling in heroic popular style on the miracles performed by the indestructible St. George (the dragon-story is not included). In verse that moves briskly, the Christian hero St. George is praised for surviving his travails, including several varieties of death. The poem probably dates from the end of the ninth or the beginning of the tenth century.

The Lay of Hildebrand

In contrast to the several overtly Christian poems, of which the above three are typical, there stands (along with the *Merseburger Zaubersprüche) Das Hildebrandslied (The Lay of Hildebrand)*. While its martial hero summons the God of Christianity pro forma, the Christian spirit remains untouched. *Das Hildebrandslied* is tough, basic, Germanic heroic poetry, the only survivor of its kind in Old High German. It provides a unique insight by way of Old High German into the spirit and form of the Germanic epic song. It is not, however, part of a longer, epic poem, but an independent poem of more than sixty-eight long lines, if we include a few missing within the poem and at its end.

Originally composed by an unknown secular poet between 750 and 800, our version was copied — not very well — in 820 by (probably) two scribes at the monastery of Fulda, or with connections to Fulda. Its language is a mixture of Saxon and Bavarian (or Saxon and Frankish), which suggests the incursion of the scribal dialect into the poem being copied. The story is as follows: Hildebrand, in accordance with his oath of loyalty, followed Dietrich (the legendary heroic figure derived from the historical Theodoric the Great) into exile, leaving his wife and child behind. Returning thirty years later at the head of an army, he is challenged to a duel by the leader of the opposing army. Hildebrand, on asking the name of his opponent, discovers that he is face to face with his own son, Hadubrand. The latter, having years before been told that his father was dead, is suspicious of treachery (and of Hildebrand's conciliatory approach). He calls Hildebrand a traitor and a coward, which leaves the older man no alternative but to fight. The duel begins — but after a half dozen long lines the manuscript breaks off. From analogues in other Indo-European literatures, we know, however, that the father kills his son. Moreover, stricken by grief, he then commits suicide. There are later — much later — versions with a conciliatory ending, for example *Das jüngere Hildebrandslied* (*The Younger Lay of Hildebrand*), of which there are many fifteenth- and sixteenth-century manuscripts, drawing from the thirteenth century. The derivation of the eighth- or ninth-century *Hildebrandslied* is difficult to establish, in spite of the presence of analogues. A likely sequence is that the material of history was remolded into the (supposed) Ostrogothic heroic lay, which in turn passed into the Bavarian heroic cycle.

The essentials of the action and the narrative background are contained in a series of conversational exchanges between the contrasting figures of Hildebrand (older, masterful, conciliatory) and Hadubrand (younger, more assertive, and aggressive). Their dramatic dialogue encompasses all but the first six lines — the formulaic introduction by the consistently objective poet-narrator — and the final six lines — the duel. The whole poem is rich in heroic-poetic formulas, for example, Hadubrand's *ort widar orte* ("[spear-] point against point"), the essence of the challenge he hurls at his father. Idealization and value-judgment have no place in this heroic environment, in which cause and effect follow an implacable pattern. Similarly, there is no tragic guilt; where cause and effect stand in an unclear relationship, fate and fatalism prevail. The duel is a trial before God; the outcome is in God's hands. Wealth is esteemed equally with martial virtue; esteemed are, for example, physical courage, honor, pride, gold, and armor.

As the poet presides objectively over his material, so his style is blunt, non-reflective, non-discursive, compressed, heavily reliant on formulas. His rhyme is not end-rhyme, but alliteration, *Stabreim*. As copied however, the *Stabreim* is in a deteriorated state. Many half-lines are keyed to each other by only a single alliterating stave on either side of the caesura. A typical line of this kind is Hildebrand's dar man mih eo scerita   in folc sceotantero

where one always assigned me   to the army of shooters

The End of the Carolingian Renaissance

After about 900, the momentum of the so-called Carolingian Renaissance
having weakened under Charlemagne's successors and then expired altogether,
there is for the most part a void in German poetry — and prose as well — that did
not end until about 1050, which traditionally marks the beginning of the Middle
High German period. With the increased ascendancy of the Church, whose
predilection for Latin always redounded to the disadvantage of German, the latter
was in large part relegated to the role of a barbarian language unsuitable for the
expression of serious or cultivated thought.

That rule is proved by the unique exception of Notker the German (der
Deutsche) of St. Gall. Notker not only wrote German when few others did, he
eloquently justifies his doing so. He was also accomplished in Latin. He was not,
strictly speaking, a writer of German literature but rather a learned and dedicated
preceptor who, for the benefit of his students, wrote translations of, and
commentaries on, Latin works. The best known are his texts of Boethius's *De
consolatione philosophiae* (*On the Consolation of Philosophy*) and Martianus
Capella's *De nuptiis philologiae et Mercurii* (*On the Marriage of Philology and
Mercury*), but he also translated Virgil's *Bucolics*, Terence's *Andria*, and a Latin
version of Aristotle. These are not word-for-word translations, such as that of Old
High German *Tatian*, but translations of concepts — and into fluent, unstilted
German. Notker's translation of the psalms reflects his erudite yet sensitive feel for
his native language. He was, moreover, an perceptive and — for his day — a
sophisticated linguist, concerned that his orthography consistently and accurately
reflect the sounds of German. The literary works that this enlightened churchman
translated and commented on, however, give no hint of the courtly literature that
was to dominate a secular literary world — the chivalric court — within eighty
years of his death in 1022.

2 Middle High German

Frank Tobin

Historical Background

At its zenith (1170-1230), German literature in the Middle Ages attained a universally recognized level of quality it would not reach again for many centuries. To understand how this body of considerable literary achievement arose, why it was the kind of literature it was, and why it was followed by a period of relative decline, we must examine it in its political, social, and religious contexts.

A. Political Events

The rise, eminence, and decline of medieval German literature coincided to a great extent with the fortunes of the Hohenstaufen dynasty's first major ruler, Friedrich I (Barbarossa), who reigned as Holy Roman Emperor from 1152 until 1190 when he drowned in Asia Minor while leading the Third Crusade. His brilliant leadership revived the empire as a political force which could provide a counterbalance to the claims of supremacy that the papacy had been asserting since the Cluniac reform. Friedrich's idea of imperial rule stressed its equality with and independence from ecclesiastical authority. Through his election by the princes he viewed imperial authority as coming directly from God, not from the pope. By combining this idealistic vision of the empire with great skill in practical politics, he was able to restore and enhance civil order. Friedrich was viewed by many as embodying the ideals of Christian knighthood, and the festival at Mainz in 1184 celebrating the knighting of his two sons — and attended, it was said, by more than seventy thousand nobles — stands as a symbol of chivalric culture's coming of age.

Though the necessity for a spiritual foundation was never denied, secular culture now attained a legitimacy and a degree of independence from religion that caused it to blossom vigorously within a remarkably short time.

Friedrich's son, Heinrich VI (1190-1197), extended and strengthened the empire, especially in Italy, during his short reign. Because Friedrich II, Heinrich's son and heir, was only four at the time of his father's death, a struggle ensued between Philip of Swabia (1197-1208), Heinrich's younger brother, and Otto IV of Brunswick (1208-1218) of the rival Welf party. When Philip was murdered, Otto became emperor. However, when Otto tried to press his imperial claims in Italy, Pope Innocent III excommunicated him, thus causing the Hohenstaufen party to rebel. Friedrich, after making concessions in Italy to the papacy, received Innocent's support and became emperor in 1215. The savage power struggle between Friedrich II and the papacy (Innocent III, Honorius III, Gregory IX, and Innocent IV) characterized Friedrich's entire reign (1215-1250) and sapped the strength of both sides. A clear decline in courtly culture and literature paralleled the worsening political conditions which resulted from this conflict.

During the next two decades there was in effect no imperial government, and various noble families strove to increase their own spheres of influence at the expense of imperial power. The resulting political chaos gave added impetus to the social and cultural decline. In 1273 the chief German princes elected Rudolf of Habsburg (1273-1291) king and emperor of Germany. He was chosen because he was strong enough to end much of the prevailing lawlessness without, at the same time, having enough power to restrict severely the princes's own dynastic ambitions. Rudolf brought some order into German lands, but, because of the rise of national states in England and France and the emperor's reluctance to undertake adventures in Italy, the Holy Roman Empire now became a central European affair.

The fourteenth century witnessed the continued decline of knighthood as an ideal and of the knightly class as the dominant social force and source of secular culture. More and more the towns and the burghers who ruled them became an important economic base of political power. Towns also became a major source and location for what culture there was. However, the optimism about and enthusiasm for establishing a sound and just order on this earth, or for idealizing it in literature, had largely evaporated. The too obvious signs of further deterioration caused widespread loss of confidence and pessimism about human affairs. The church's prestige and claim to spiritual leadership were seriously compromised by two events. First, through the "Babylonian Captivity" of the papacy at Avignon (1309-1376, a reference to the defeat and deportation of the Jews to Babylon in the sixth century B.C.), the popes, fleeing the turmoil of Italy for the safety of southern France, were reduced to lackeys of the French King, Philip IV (the Fair [1268-1314]). Then followed the Great Schism (1378-1418), during which there were two and later three claimants to the papal crown — each with an international following. And the ravages of the Black Death (bubonic plague) at mid-century only served to underline further the transitoriness and futility of human endeavor.

B. Social and Economic Factors

Although at the beginning of the thirteenth century several towns flourished in German-speaking lands and were, as centers of commerce, a force to be reckoned with, they played almost no role in the thought of the times concerning the nature of society. Medieval society was to a very large extent agrarian and certainly thought of itself as such. Feudalism, the prevailing social and economic system, was based on ownership of land. At the top of the social pyramid was the lord, who had virtually absolute dominion over his lands and the people inhabiting them. In order to gain support for his conflicts against other lords, a lord might grant ownership of some of his land to vassals. Such vassals would then be free nobles exerting dominion over the lands granted them, but on the condition of homage and fealty. The chief duty of the vassal, upon which his position depended, was that he come to the aid of his lord with his resources and knights when the lord justly demanded this of him. In time the system became more complicated. Often, the same person would be both lord with vassals under him and himself vassal to a more powerful lord.

Those providing the labor force for the feudal estates were called serfs. They were the unfree peasant class, owned by their lord and bound to the soil, so that when the land they worked changed hands, they too were subject to a new lord. There were also free peasants, but they comprised only a small minority. An anomalous but important phenomenon in the feudal system was the ministerial. Ministerials were persons arising from the serf class who, because of their talents, rose to positions of prominence in the households of their lords. At times ministerials would even be put in charge of a whole estate. However, because they were not freeborn, they did not hold land as vassals, but merely as administrators for a lord. In time the status of the ministerials as persons of unfree origin changed and they frequently were assimilated into the free nobility. The lower ranks of the knightly class were often ministerials living in the castles of their lords in dependence on him. Many Middle High German poets belonged to the ministerial class.

Feudalism provided the socio-economic foundation for the ethos of the nobility. The system of ethical and cultural values which informed the lives and behavior of medieval nobility is called chivalry. The ideals of the age were to be reached by embracing the life of the knight or the lady. The knight was a member of a warrior class, a fighter on horseback (French: *chevalier*; German: *Ritter*, i.e., *Reiter*) in the service of his lord. The principal virtues which he strove to practice and which determined his behavior both in physical conflict and while serving at his lord's court were clearly defined. Knowledge of these qualities and their importance is indispensable for anyone trying to understand knightly/courtly literature. Toward his lord the knight had to demonstrate loyalty (in Middle High German: *triuwe*), and he could never desert him in times of trial. Bravery or courage (*tapferkeit*) had to distinguish him in battle. Discipline and good breeding (*zuht*) as well as constancy (*staete*) characterized his behavior both in conflict and at court.

Generosity (*milte*) governed his attitude toward wealth, especially in the case of a powerful lord or king. *Mâze*, "having everything in the proper amount," was the virtue by which the knight determined the proper relationship among all other virtues. The practice of these virtues guaranteed the knight's being shown honor (*êre*) by the court. And the reward resulting from full and proper participation in the life of the court with its mixture of heroic deeds and festivals was a feeling of exhilaration (*hôher muot*) which permeated the knight's entire being.

The education or formation of a knight began early. While still a child of seven or more, the young aspirant was sent to the castle of his father's liege lord or some other court of high reputation where he served as page and learned the etiquette of chivalry. At fourteen, the young man, now called a squire, began learning the physical skills required of him, such as racing, jumping, swimming, wrestling, fencing, hunting, archery, and, of course, those combat skills on horseback necessary for his performance on the battlefield and in tournaments. Normally one finished an apprenticeship and was considered ready for knighthood at the age of twenty-one.

The knighting ceremony provided an opportunity to display both the splendor of courtly society and the religious and secular values from which it took its orientation. The squire about to be knighted spent the night preceding the ceremony in prayerful vigil before the altar in the family chapel. In the morning the young man confessed, attended mass, and received communion. Then the attending prelate or priest blessed his sword and urged him always to practice the virtues of knighthood; he should be magnanimous, helpful, courteous, truthful, loyal, and brave; he should aid the church, protect widows, orphans, pilgrims, and the poor and oppressed. Then the one presiding official — be it the king, a prince, the liege lord, the bishop, or some distinguished knight or noble lady — handed over to the squire his shield, sword, and spurs, and carried out the accolade, or three blows on the shoulders, by which knighthood was conferred.

More jovial and spirited pursuits usually followed these solemnities. The tournament offered the new knight and the noble guests a chance to engage in or watch knightly contests of various kinds, with the participants either vying in single combat or as members of opposing armies. Essential to these contests was the presence among the spectators of noble ladies. The hope of obtaining the favor of such ladies spurred the knights on to deeds of prowess. A knight often competed in tournaments wearing the colors of the lady or some token from her, or he entered the competition in order to win a prize from her, such as a garland, a belt, or some such sign of her esteem. Such a token was considered reward enough for the perils and toils of the tournament.

Nothing, perhaps, better illustrates the mixture of religious and secular elements in the conception of knighthood — as well as the enormous gulf separating the ideal from reality — than the crusades (1096, 1144, 1190, 1204, among others). The holy place where the Son of God had been born, lived, died on the cross, and from where He had ascended to His Father were in the hands of the "infidel." Clearly, it was felt in the Christian West, the Holy Land rightfully belonged under

Christian rule. Once this was achieved, pilgrims could safely visit the places where their Savior had trod. As the church made clear, here was a perfect opportunity for Christian knighthood. As a crusader, a knight could devote his soldierly talents to a holy cause, one that would give the ordinarily secular and limited nature of his activity new and absolute value. By vowing to go on a crusade, or "taking the cross," a knight became a special person with a special status in society. If he undertook this obligation for the proper religious motives, he was promised remission of all temporal punishment accruing to him because of past sins. The stature of the enemy provided him with a worthy opponent. Saladin, as the Islamic potentate was frequently called in courtly literature, was much respected as a courtly ruler who shared the ideals of knighthood with his Western opponents. And his warriors were considered highly skilled in knightly pursuits. By conferring chivalrous qualities on their Muslim foe, the crusaders from the West enhanced both their own image and the cause which they were undertaking. Although the crusades often degenerated into something bearing little resemblance to ideal knightly behavior — crusaders at times were nothing more than irresponsible adventurers — it was this idealistic vision which for so long a time caused the idea of the crusade to be attractive to so many. Precisely this idealistic conception of the crusades underlies most of the courtly literature relating to the crusades.

C. Learning and Religion

Although the influence of the church and religion permeated all aspects of medieval life, nowhere was this influence as dominant as in the areas of education and learning. The two possibilities for receiving an education were, in the eleventh and twelfth centuries, monasteries and cathedral schools. The foundation of all education was mastery of the rudiments of Latin; for, with the exception of the vernacular literature which we are about to treat in detail, almost anything considered worth learning or writing down was transmitted in Latin. Once Latin had been mastered to the extent that it could serve as a tool, the pupil proceeded on to the *trivium* (the three ways), a system of studies embracing grammar (the study of classical Latin grammarians, writers, and poets), rhetoric (with stress on such writers as Augustine, Cicero, and Quintilian), and logic or dialectic (based on texts from Boethius, Cassiodorus, and Latin translations of Aristotle, especially from his logic). The traditional continuation of the curriculum, the *quadrivium* (the four ways), which consisted of the study of music, astronomy, arithmetic, and geometry, received less and less emphasis.

Out of the cathedral schools arose one of the crowning achievements of the Middle Ages: the university. The earliest ones, such as Salerno, Bologna, Oxford, and — with a certain pre-eminence — Paris, had developed into important centers of learning by the early thirteenth century. These institutions were exempt from local civil jurisdiction, and the faculty answered only to the pope in matters of theology. Students, who were clerics and had received at least the tonsure, would flock to these centers from all parts of Europe to study liberal arts, theology, law, or medicine. All studies were carried on in Latin, the universal language of scholarship. There were no universities in German-speaking lands until the mid-fourteenth century (Prague, 1348, but the great proliferation came in the fifteenth century), but the intellectual developments at Paris, where the study of philosophy and theology became highly refined academic disciplines, exerted especially great influence on religious thought in Germany in the fourteenth century. The beginnings of scholasticism, as the new systematic approach to philosophy and theology was called, is usually associated with the activity of Peter Abelard (1069-1142). Fresh impetus was given to the scholastic thinkers' exploration of the nature of God, the human being, and the world when the thought of Aristotle, unfamiliar to Western thinkers since classical times, except for his logic, was recovered for the West in the thirteenth century through the mediation of the Arab philosophers. The Dominicans Albertus Magnus (1193-1280) and Thomas Aquinas (1225-1274) were especially diligent in attempting to achieve a synthesis of Aristotelian, Platonic, and Christian thought, while the great Franciscan thinker Bonaventure (1221-1274) continued in the tradition of Christian Platonism.

By the middle of the fourteenth century scholasticism had begun to decline. Two of its later representatives, the Franciscan William of Occam (c. 1300-1349) and the Dominican mystic Meister Eckhart (c. 1260-1328), each in his own way, carried on the scholastic tradition of speculation on divine things while at the same time emphasizing more than his predecessors the limitations of the human intellect in its attempt to grasp God. Eckhart's speculative mysticism influenced later religious thought and found its way into various popular religious movements. However, the next generation of Dominican mystical authors, Johannes Tauler and Heinrich Suso (Seuse), de-emphasized speculative mysticism and gave their thought a more ethical (Tauler) or emotional (Suso) emphasis.

As implied above, the founding and flourishing of the mendicant orders of Franciscans and Dominicans greatly influenced intellectual and religious developments from the thirteenth century on. Earlier, reform movements had taken as a given the Benedictine view of religious life, with its daily routine of community and private prayer, study, and physical labor — all carried out in a rural setting and involving only minimal contact between the monks and those outside their religious community. The Franciscans and Dominicans conceived of life in a religious order in new and revolutionary terms. Members of both orders, called friars (from Latin *frater*: brother) would renounce all but life's most necessary possessions and live from charitable donations. They concentrated their activities around the spiritual and material needs of others, which required their settling in towns. The Franciscans stressed preaching the gospel and imitating Christ in practicing poverty and by aiding the poor, the sick, and sinners. The Dominicans focused on preserving and restoring Christian teaching by preaching and scholarship. However, both orders produced outstanding scholars. Much of the religious renewal in the thirteenth and fourteenth centuries was the result of these orders.

D. The Literature

The wealth of high-quality literature around 1200 did not arise out of nothing. One can often find sources and influences among earlier literary endeavors in Germany. However, what is especially striking for the literary historian is the extent to which this literature stands out against what precedes it and begins to explore new themes, especially those of human love and adventure. Both its authors and its audience were almost exclusively of the knightly/courtly class, a group that felt more solidarity with their fellow knights in other countries than with other social classes within their linguistic homeland. It is especially to France that German knightly/courtly culture turned for its literary sources.

First, a word about the language this literature uses as its medium: Middle High German. It is called Middle High German to distinguish it both from Old High German which begins with the Second Consonant Shift (c. 500-800 A.D.) and extends to about 1050, and from Early New High German, beginning about 1350. The transitions from Old High German to Middle High German to Early New High German are, of course, fluid. Nevertheless, the bulk of documents within this period have a certain linguistic unity not shared with either the preceding or the subsequent period. It is called Middle *High* German because it has the characteristics of the dialects of the south (the high country), such as Alemannic and Bavarian, which were affected by the Second Consonant Shift, and not the characteristics of the dialects of the north (the Low countries), such as Anglo-Saxon and Dutch, which remained unaffected.

The language in which the literature was written never attained the unity or uniformity of, say, present-day High German. Nor was it a reflection of the everyday speech of the period. It was the language of the court further refined and unified for use as a literary medium while, at the same time, showing differences as used by poets from different regions. Middle High German literature, as it generally appears today, gives the impression of much greater linguistic unity than it actually had because most texts have been "normalized," that is, modern editors have removed most of the variations in forms and orthography that one finds in the manuscripts in favor of standardization. While this facilitates the learning and reading of the language, it also gives the texts a uniformity they never had.

Early Middle High German literature falls roughly into four categories: religious poetry, heroic poetry serving the needs of religious didacticism, the so-called *Spielmannsepos* (minstrel's adventure tale), and early courtly literature. The first category, religious poetry, differs from the religious literature of preceeding times in that it less slavishly imitated sources but rather turned fresh religious impulses into devotional literature of genuine literary merit. Some of the most important examples of this religious literature are: *Das Hohelied (c. 1060)*, Williram's version of the *Song of Songs*; *Das Ezzolied (Lay of Ezzo* [c. 1060]), a hymn celebrating the story of human salvation; *Annolied (Lay of Anno* [c. 1085]), a legend in verse treating the life of the saintly bishop Anno set against the background of world history; Heinrich von Melk's *Memento Mori* (c. 1160), a grim reminder of human mortality and the meaninglessness of all earthly values in the face of it; Lady Ava's *Leben Jesu* (*Life of Jesus* [c. 1120]), a lively narrative without theological sophistication; and poetry to and about the Virgin Mary, as exemplified in the priest Wernher's *Marienlied* (*Song of Mary* [1172]), which draws heavily on apocryphal gospels and shows the influence of early courtly poetry, and in the Arnstein *Driu liet von der maget* (*Three Songs on the Virgin* [c. 1180]), which combines praise of Mary because of her merits and privileged position with the request that she come to us in our sinfulness.

Two religiously motivated works which show the influence of French models are Lamprecht's *Alexanderlied* (*Lay of Alexander* [c. 1140]) and Konrad's *Rolandslied* (*Lay of Roland* [c. 1170]). Lamprecht, struggling to translate his French source, portrays the legendary Macedonian ruler as a king with many good qualities but, ultimately, as a heathen. Despite all his power, military conquests, and fabulous adventures — including an attempt to gain entrance into paradise — Alexander serves in the last analysis to show us the vanity of all earthly success in the light of eternity. In the translation of *Rolandslied*, Konrad omits the nationalistic motivation of the original and substitutes instead universal Christian ideals. Charlemagne is given the features of the exemplary Christian ruler and Roland those of the ideal Christian warrior and crusader. In both narratives the heroes embody qualities that will become essential to the knightly/courtly hero.

More light-hearted and refreshing in their single-minded goal of providing entertainment are those tales of adventure known, perhaps misleadingly, as *Spielmannsepen*. It seems unlikely, as the term implies, that these verse narratives were composed and performed orally by wandering minstrels or actors to be passed on to other members of the trade. Such professionals may have had a hand in their origin and performance, but the structure of these stories points to a more careful mode of composition, and their length requires several sittings for a complete recitation. In any case, with their emphasis on action and erotic adventure, they seem to have been a staple of castle entertainment. Most frequently the search for a bride provides the occasion precipitating the hero into a series of adventures. As in the courtly romance which follows them, the hero first gains his bride or achieves his quest without complication. Suddenly, however, his fortunes are reversed and, though he is ultimately successful, he must first face a second, more serious series of perilous encounters. Only a fraction of these narratives have come down to us, often in only fragmentary form and in manuscripts of a much later date. The finest preserved example of this genre is *König Rother* (*King Rother* [after 1152]).

Among the representatives of early courtly literature, Heinrich von Veldeke deserves mention. A native of the Lower Rhine where connections with the more developed French literature were stronger than in the southern areas, he was later well received at the court of Hermann von Thüringen, whose patronage of literature many authors, including Wolfram von Eschenbach and Walther von der Vogelweide, would experience. Heinrich was considered by his contemporaries as the father of courtly literature because of the linguistic refinement and poetic virtuosity of his work. However, the subject matter of his courtly narrative was not the court of Arthur, as in many French works, but rather classical antiquity. His *Eneit* (after 1170) follows Aeneas from the fall of Troy to Dido's Carthage, from there to the underworld, and, finally, to his triumph in Rome and marriage to Lavinia. The direct source for the story was not Virgil, but rather a recently completed French romance. Besides showing courtly refinement in language, Heinrich's narrative displays courtliness in the behavior of its heroes. The poet's chief concern throughout is to glorify exemplary knightly behavior and the irresistible power of love.

Standing in isolation from these different categories is one early example of a type of literature that would become more popular in the following centuries throughout northwestern Europe: the beast epic. About 1180 a certain Heinrich, later known as "*der Glîchesaere*" (the Trickster), composed a short (c. 2,000 lines) narrative *Reinhart Fuchs* (*Reynard the Fox*), basing it on the French *Roman de Renart*. Though occasionally suffering a setback, in most episodes of this finely structured story the cunning and deceitful Reinhart triumphs over his enemies, most frequently over the wolf Isengrin, the representative of brute strength, animal lusts, human greed, and stupidity. Reynard's triumphs are amoral, and they subvert the order of law and justice no less than his less frequent defeats do. No transcendental view of reality emerges from the story, but rather scepticism about human nature. Knightly society, portrayed so idealistically in courtly literature, is shown here as something base and eminently corruptible. Frequently the clergy and the institution of monasticism become the object of ridicule. Heinrich skillfully uses the satirical mode of the beast epic to uncover the flaws in society and to provide keen insight into everyday life in the world around him.

The High Courtly Period. 1: Narrative

A. Arthurian Knighthood

Since many of the finest examples of courtly narrative are set in the world of King Arthur, some comments about this fabled ruler and his world can provide orientation. Though King Arthur existed in bits and pieces both in history and in legend much earlier, it was the French *trouveur* Chrétien de Troyes (c. 1140-c. 1190) who turned this material into a consistent whole, thereby creating an ideal world of gallant chivalry and courtly splendor far removed from history and the everyday drabness of rural life which was most often the lot of the knight of the times. Symbolic center of this world and arbiter of its values is King Arthur himself. Freed from the necessity of further proving himself through knightly endeavor, Arthur assumes his place among his knights as *primus inter pares* (first among equals). The knights assemble at the festive Round Table, whose shape symbolizes equality among its members. To be accepted as a member of the Round

Table is reward and distinction enough, for one is then a member of an international elite that has no ranks and recognizes no national boundaries.

The Arthurian world exists in the tension between its two poles: the *aventiure*, or quest, and the court. The nature of the quest is that of the game; more particularly, the game of chivalry. The knight rides forth from Arthur's court to perform chivalric deeds. As the word *aventiure* implies (from Latin *advenire*: to come upon, to happen upon), there is an element of chance in the way the knightly encounter comes about. One does not seek out a specific encounter or foe. One suddenly finds oneself confronted with a situation where knightly deeds cannot honorably be avoided. These deeds are valuable in themselves and are carried out for their own sake. In Hartmann's *Iwein* (ll. 524-549), Kalogrenant's explanation of the quest to the strange creature he meets in the forest reveals both its grandeur and its questionable side. Overcoming a knightly foe brings one honor and makes one a hero. No further reason for the contest is required. Succeeding in knightly endeavor is an end in itself and ennobles the one who succeeds. The celebration honoring the returning hero takes place at court, where he is publicly praised for his success in the quest by King Arthur, his fellow Round Table knights, and the courtly ladies. These ladies are an essential element of the court. Like chivalric deeds, the beauty of the lady is a value in itself; and her radiant presence at the courtly feast, along with her approbation and praise of the knightly triumph, is a confirmation and enhancement of all that the Court of Arthur represents.

The structure of the Arthurian romance is an elaboration and a refinement of the bipartite structure of the *Spielmannsepos*. The knightly protagonist rides out, overcomes all obstacles in his path by sheer prowess, and wins the prize — usually a wondrously beautiful and noble bride. Soon thereafter, however, he suffers a reversal which shows his triumphs to have been only apparent successes and his grasp of the true nature of knighthood to have been superficial and incorrect. A much more arduous series of *aventiuren* ensues. The encounters are more serious and more perilous. The hero finally emerges victorious, with a much more profound understanding of the values of true knighthood. His honor and future now rest secure.

B. Chief Authors and Works

1. Hartmann von Aue

To Hartmann belongs the distinction of being the first major high-courtly narrator in German. A Swabian by birth and persuasion, he belonged to the knightly class as a ministerial. Certain features of his works lead us to believe that he enjoyed a good education in a monastery school. He is highly praised by the discriminating Gottfried von Strasbourg for the literary skill with which he weaves his tales and for his *cristalline wortelin* (crystal-like diction). Aside from some lyric poetry of high quality, Hartmann's major works are *Erec* (c. 1180-1185) and *Iwein*

(c. 1200), two Arthurian romances adapted from the French versions of Chrétien de Troyes and the finest examples of pure Arthurian literature in German, and two shorter non-Arthurian works, *Gregorius* (c. 1187-1189) and *Der arme Heinrich* (*Poor Henry* [c. 1195]).

Both *Erec* and *Iwein* raise questions about the nature of knighthood and about the proper balance among the knightly virtues upon which achieving the ideal depends. Erec, Arthurian knight and son of the King of Karnant, wins the poor but noble and beautiful Enite after he triumphs in a series of knightly adventures. They return to his kingdom where, preoccupied with his bride and their love, Erec neglects knightly activities, thus bringing shame on his court. He first becomes aware of his situation when he overhears Enite lamenting their shame to herself. He immediately orders their horses prepared for a journey. After many perilous adventures together, Erec and Enite return home, now in possession of a true understanding of all that their roles as knight and lady entail. Erec's fault had been that of *verligen*: he had so completely given himself over to the demands of *minne* (love) for Enite that he lost the proper balance that should govern chivalric existence. He did not pursue quests. Love should have motivated him to seek knightly encounters. This is part of love's proper role: to urge on to knightly activity that increases honor. Only when love has been integrated into the totality of the knightly ideal can Erec and the long-suffering Enite take up their lives again and rule in Karnant.

Gregorius, a shorter narrative with many of the characteristics of the *Lives of the Saints*, calls into question the possibility of harmony between the chivalric and divine orders. Its hero, born of incest between brother and sister, is set adrift, like Moses, by his mother. The smiling infant is found by monks and brought up by foster parents near the monastery under the fatherly eye of the abbot. By far the most gifted in the monastery school, Gregorius seems destined to become a monk when he chances to discover that he is not the child of his foster parents. The possibility that he is of noble birth fires his imagination, and he resolves to leave the monastery to become a knight despite the warnings of the abbot who, in a final attempt to dissuade him, reveals to Gregorius that he is indeed noble, but is also the product of incest. Though troubled by the shameful aspect of his origin, he acts solely on the basis of the good news and sails off from the monastery in search of knightly deeds. Unknowingly, he arrives at the land ruled by his mother, overcomes in combat the duke oppressing her, and marries her. After a period of blissful ignorance, they are shattered when by chance they discover the shameful truth. Gregorius, after urging his mother/wife to embrace a life of penance, goes off into the wilderness and chains himself to a desolate rock in order to devote himself completely to a life of self-castigation and penitential renunciation. After enduring legendary hardships there for seventeen years, he is visited by two emissaries from Rome who have been told in miraculous dreams to seek as the new pope a man chained to a rock in these regions. After much protest Gregorius relents, goes to Rome, and becomes a pope renowned for holiness. When his mother journeys to

Rome to confess to the saintly pontiff, he reveals his identity. She, too, then remains in Rome where they both lead exemplary lives until their deaths.

It is difficult to know to what extent *Gregorius* is intended as a criticism of chivalry. Hartmann chooses the other-worldly genre of legend or life of a saint for his narration with its demands from the protagonist of heroic and even superhuman sanctity. Because of his fateful, almost deterministic double involvement in incest, one is reluctant to consider the hero simply as everyman. He has been singled out, divinely chosen. Yet it also remains true that by pursuing the path to chivalric perfection and glory the hero becomes enmeshed in unspeakable shame. At the very least we are given a stern warning not to assume that the values of knighthood completely coincide with the absolute and divinely ordained values by which one's eternal destiny is determined.

The subsequently written *Der arme Heinrich* again treats the relationship of knightly and absolute values — this time, in spite of the physical suffering and depression of the hero, in a more light-hearted and optimistic fashion. Indeed, the story has many elements of a fairy tale. The hero, described to us as the epitome of knightly perfection, finds himself stricken with leprosy. He withdraws from courtly life and takes shelter with the family of a freeborn peasant whom he has treated generously. There his suffering is lightened by the delightful young daughter of the peasant who, in contrast to the others, is not put off by his offensive malady and spends much of her time entertaining him. He, in turn, playfully calls her his bride, giving her small gifts. In a moment of near despair he unburdens himself to the family. He has been told that he can only be cured by blood from the heart of a young maiden who sacrifices herself willingly. Assuming it impossible to find such a person, he falls victim to a mood of hopelessness. Hearing what can cure him, the young girl resolves to sacrifice herself and save him. At first her intention is passed off as a childish whim. Such is her tenacity of purpose and power of argument, however, that first her parents and then Heinrich reluctantly and sadly acquiesce.

Finely attired upon a palfrey and accompanied by Lord Heinrich, she rides off to Salerno where the operation is to be performed. As with the others, she soon convinces the incredulous doctor of her steadfastness. With Heinrich locked outside, the eager girl undresses and is strapped to a table. As the doctor is whetting his surgical knives, Heinrich looks through a crack in the door and sees the beautiful young creature on the table. He suddenly realizes the incongruity of what is about to happen and prevents it. The girl, her heroic act frustrated, is inconsolable, and she showers abuse and accusations of cowardice upon poor Heinrich. God, seeing their charity and compassion, miraculously restores Heinrich's health and youth. Upon his triumphant return home, his counselors urge him to take a wife. Heinrich agrees and chooses the girl, who is freeborn. We are assured that after a long and pleasant life they attained eternal happiness.

In *Der arme Heinrich* we are again faced with the question of how the values of knighthood and the court, values which admittedly have moral implications and perfect one as a human being, relate to the absolute values inherent in the divinely ordained order. Heinrich has all the qualities of the perfect knight, and yet he contracts leprosy, which was often seen as a sign of divine displeasure. But the somber and threatening tone of *Gregorius* does not predominate here. Nor does the resolution of the conflict depend upon having the hero and heroine lead purely spiritual lives.

When Heinrich, the flower of knighthood, is suddenly stricken, the narrator refrains completely from criticizing his life or conduct, nor does he rail against "worldly" values. He stresses, rather, the fragility and transitoriness of the knightly existence, good though it may be in itself. Early in the story Heinrich struggles to at least a partial insight about the true state of affairs, even though at this point he neither acts upon it nor is it able to dispel his gloom. He admits that his misfortune is well deserved. Why? Because he did not see that his former good fortune was not at all his own doing but was rather utterly and completely a gift from God. In his arrogance he had thoughtlessly assumed that he himself was the cause of his former good life and that he had possessed it independently of God's favor.

The story does, however, provide in the figure of the young girl an eloquent spokesperson for a much more negative view of the world. Despite her freshness and charm, in her uncompromising rejection of the world she has many of the features of the legendary saint. She sees the world as fraught with dangers to the soul. She fears to live in it one day longer than necessary. Its pleasures are like a silk cloth hiding a dungheap beneath. She yearns to leave it while still young and not yet drawn by its pernicious delights that lead to hell. Instead of taking an earthly peasant for a husband, she wishes to become the spiritual bride of Christ, whose fields are not visited by killing frosts and hail and who alone promises constancy and eternal bliss.

That the reader is not supposed simply to embrace the girl's point of view becomes evident when one reflects on the spirit in which she advocates it, its internal inconsistencies, and how it conflicts with the resolution of the story. Although we can understand how her pious parents might assume that her yearnings to sacrifice herself for Heinrich and thus gain heaven can only be the work of the Holy Spirit, the fanatic single-mindedness with which she relentlessly refutes all "merely human" misgivings should give us pause. Beneath her thoughts of self-immolation lurks a headstrong egocentricity that will brook no interference. Her childish tantrum, when Heinrich refuses to allow her sacrifice, is evidence enough that her heroism is not without its flaws and should not simply be attributed to divine inspiration. In addition, her grand plan to save both Heinrich and herself is lacking in logic. If everything she says about life in this world is true, then by enabling Heinrich to resume his place in it she would be placing his soul at risk while selfishly saving her own.

One must also question the wisdom in Heinrich's consenting to her sacrifice in the first place. Should one not rather stand aghast at the very thought of it? Despite the girl's assertion that Heinrich's health will ensure the continued well-being of her parents and their children, can Heinrich's initial decision to regain his health at the expense of her young and vibrant life be justified? Is this decision not monstrous and unnatural? How would we view the story if the girl's wishes had ultimately prevailed?

Finally, the circumstances of Heinrich's change of heart refute the girl's point of view. It is precisely the physical beauty of her naked body that causes him to see the absurdity of the situation and to undergo a spiritual conversion whose authenticity is confirmed when he echoes those words which are the ultimate measure of correct spiritual orientation: "Thy will be done." Heinrich, with divine assistance, liberates himself from egotism and allows love, a strange mixture of *eros* and *agape*, to determine his fate. This, together with the girl's enduring compassion for his suffering, frees God's hand to work the miracle of restoring Heinrich's health and youth. That the would-be bride of Christ becomes Heinrich's bride, that they spend a long and happy life together in this world, and that they are subsequently received into eternal beatitude is all made possible by Heinrich's sorely gained insight that courtly values, though good, are, like all good things of this world, contingent and a gift of God. Once one accepts this and lives by it, one's life, both courtly and in its totality, rests on an unshakable foundation.

2. Wolfram von Eschenbach

In Wolfram we are confronted with a gifted poet and storyteller of great originality. Proud of his knightly station and lack of much formal education, Wolfram fashioned in *Parzival* (c. 1200-1210) a chivalric romance with cosmic implications. Its unusual popularity, despite its length — of Russian-novel proportions divided into sixteen "books" — is vouched for by the large number of extant manuscripts. A native of the surrounding area of Ansbach in Franconia, Wolfram spent some time after 1203 at the court of Hermann von Thüringen. Besides a small number of lyric poems — mostly dawn songs — and his masterpiece *Parzival*, he is the author of two other narratives: *Willehalm* (c. 1215) and *Titurel* (after 1215).

Parzival can well be said to represent the culmination of the medieval Arthurian tradition. At the same time, it transcends this tradition, as its hero leaves the Arthurian world behind because he has been destined to enter into and rule the mysterious Kingdom of the Grail whose knights practice a heightened and spiritualized kind of chivalry. Wolfram's chief source for *Parzival* is generally assumed to be Chrétien de Troye's unfinished *Perceval le Gallois ou Le conte du Graal* (*Perceval the Gaul or the Tale of the Grail* [c. 1180]), even though Wolfram himself generally denies this and claims he follows the version of a certain Kyot. Most scholars consider Kyot to be a fiction created by Wolfram in response to criticism that he does not use the Parzival material properly. If Wolfram's creative innovations in the story disturbed his colleagues, his wilfully eccentric style did so no less. In contrast to Hartmann's measured sentence structure and controlled courtly vocabulary, Wolfram presents an undisciplined richness that is at times overwhelming. His syntax is often complex and unclear, leading to ambiguity and occasionally rendering passages incomprehensible. He chose his vocabulary from a wide range of sources, expanding linguistic horizons while most of his contemporaries were bent on purifying the language. One finds neologisms and new combinations, dialect expressions, and terms from the works of pre-courtly heroic poetry, as well as a large influx of French. His imagery, drawn mainly from daily life and from the world of knightly pursuits, is earthy and concrete even when it is baffling. Because of his lack of orthodoxy both in his use of sources and in his style, he earned the ire of Gottfried von Straßburg who calls him a "vindaere wilder maere" ("inventor of chaotic tales").

In contrast to the purely Arthurian tale which takes place in a never-never land untouched by historical events, Wolfram gives his hero roots by tying him to two worlds existing apart from the world of Arthur. For Wolfram, as for his contemporaries, one's character and nature were greatly influenced by one's family origins. In Parzival's parents we find much of the hero and his story preformed. Independently of Chrétien, Wolfram devotes the first two books of his romance to the story of Parzival's father Gahmuret, who wishes to serve only the most powerful ruler in the world. This restless urge for chivalric perfection leads him, a Christian knight, into the service of the Baruch, supreme ruler of Islam. It is also the source of much sadness for him and for others. First, it causes him to desert his first love, the black pagan queen Belicane, by whom he sires Feirefiz, Parzival's half brother. Later, because of it, he takes leave of his Christian wife Herzeloyde, Parzival's mother. Finally, it results in his untimely death. From the father he never knows, Parzival inherits all the manly qualities a knight must possess as well as his capacity for love and infinite desire. On his mother's side he is related to the kings of the Grail, the current Grail king Anfortas being his uncle. From Herzeloyde also comes his capacity for suffering (Herzeloyde=heart's sorrow, suffering), for his birth takes place in the shadow of his absent father's death.

Grieving for her husband, Herzeloyde retreats with her child and household to remote Soltane, a rural setting, where she hides from her son his knightly origins as well as all suffering. Parzival's childhood, his boyish pursuits, his natural inclination for hunting, his instinctive grief at causing the death of a bird that had just sung so sweetly, the sorrow and restlessness which these singing messengers of another world awaken in him — all are portrayed with freshness and vigor. However, the peace of Soltane is shattered when Parzival encounters knights on a quest and mistakes them for gods, so impressed is he by their splendorous appearance. Now nothing can stop him from pursuing the life he was meant to lead. His mother, hoping that adversity will cause her son to return to her, clothes him as a fool and provides him with a shabby horse. At the same time, she gives him sound advice: to avoid dark (and therefore deep) fords, to accept advice from those with experience, and to strive to win the ring and greeting of a woman. After he rides off, she dies of grief.

In his simplicity he follows his mother's advice to the letter, refusing to cross a streamlet whose trickle is dark because it is in the shade, and wresting a ring and forcing a kiss from Jeschute, a lady whose knight is away. The shame and sorrow he brings to her, like the fatal grief he caused his mother and like much of the pain and sorrow he inflicts on others later, is chiefly the result of ignorance and naiveté, but is not less real for that.

Parzival happens upon the court of Arthur and is given to understand that knighthood will be granted him if he conquers Ither, the Red Knight, who is challenging the Round Table. In ignorance and violation of knightly rules of combat, he kills Ither, despoils his body of its armor, dons it himself, and thus becomes known as the Red Knight. Next he comes to the castle of Gurnemanz, whom his mother's advice lets him see as a wise mentor. Under Gurnemanz's tutelage Parzival learns basic knightly skills and behavior, at least the externals, even if he does not yet always grasp the spirit. Off he rides again, unaware of the sorrow his departure inflicts on Gurnemanz and his daughter Liaze.

Parzival comes to the besieged land of Queen Condwiramurs, conquers her enemies, and marries her. Again off to pursue knightly adventure, he chances upon Munsalvaesche, the Grail castle. He is received with great hospitality and, at a wondrous feast, is presented with a sword by the ailing King of the Grail, Anfortas. Parzival, dazzled by the festivities, notices his host's indisposition but, mindful of Gurnemanz's advice not to ask too many questions, does not inquire about his host's condition. He goes to bed, awakens after a night of fitful sleep to find the castle empty, and rides off hearing behind him the voice of a squire who curses him on behalf of the castle's inhabitants for not having asked about the Grail king's condition. Parzival rides to Arthur's court and takes his place among the knights of the Round Table only to be decried by the sorceress Cundrie as a disgrace to the Round Table for not having taken pity on Anfortas by asking about his health, a question that would have freed the Grail king from his affliction. Parzival, confused and angered by her charge, asks how God, if He is good and just as one says of Him, could allow such a thing to befall him. With a mixture of despair and defiance in his heart, the hero blindly rides off. The story leaves the hero for a time to follow the path of Parzival's counterpart, Gawan. Of Parzival's exploits we hear only rumors.

Traditionally, commentators consider Book Nine the turning point. Here Parzival meets Trevrizent, the hermit brother of the Grail king Anfortas and his own uncle and, while staying with him, is given basic orientation — this time, however, not, as at the castle of Gurnemanz, about knighthood, rather, Trevrizent instructs the hero on a cosmic level, narrating for him the history of salvation and the history of the Grail. Concerning the latter, Parzival admits that it was he who visited Munsalvaesche and failed to ask the crucial question. At first even the other-worldly Trevrizent is disturbed by this news, though he stresses more the hero's guilt for the fate of his mother and for killing the Red Knight. Finally, he bids his noble nephew go in peace.

Again through several books we follow the exploits of noble Gawan, the perfect Arthurian knight, as he triumphs in perfect Arthurian manner, until the story focuses again on Parzival as he returns first to the Arthurian court and then to the

Castle of the Grail where he inquires after Anfortas's health and frees him from his malady. And so Parzival, re-united with his wife and united with his half brother Feirefiz, finally assumes the role to which he has been predestined: King of the Grail.

Much in the story is mysterious and has invited a variety of interpretations. It has been seen both as propounding in code the doctrine of a secret brotherhood and as a *roman à clef.* We can be content here to follow a few traditional lines. Particularly intriguing is Wolfram's conception of the Grail and its knights. Traditionally, the Grail is the chalice used by Jesus at the Last Supper. Not so for Wolfram. It is a magic stone that provides food and drink, and it bestows continuous youth on all who gaze upon it. It can only be transported by a chaste virgin. Indeed, celibacy is required of both its knights and ladies. Only the Grail king is permitted to marry and thus both sustain with his progeny the family line and provide through his sons kings for countries needing them. The Grail is invisible to pagans, and one arrives at Munsalvaesche only if one does not consciously seek it. The grail's power is renewed on Good Friday when a white dove descends from heaven and deposits a host upon it. From time to time the name of the future Grail king appears upon it.

In departing from tradition, Wolfram has set up a world of the Grail that both transcends and stands in contrast to secular Arthurian chivalry. The Kingdom of the Grail is a religious world; that is, it provides a foundation for the absolute orientation of human and knightly endeavor which Arthurian knighthood lacks. Arthur's world is a law unto itself but does not point to a reality beyond itself. It is a closed or immanent system, ideal in itself but cut off from larger issues. It tries only to answer the question of what the knight should be, without raising the question of how knighthood relates to the nature and duties arising out of one's simply being a human and intelligent creature of God. Wolfram has his hero enter a world of religious or absolute values. However, while Christian, the Kingdom of the Grail seems consciously set apart from the Christianity of the thirteenth century. Noticeably absent are any members of the clergy. Even the saintly and ascetic Trevrizent has no ecclesiastical connections. We should by no means assume an anticlerical posture on the part of Wolfram because of this. Rather, just as the Arthurian world was created as an idealization of the actual knighthood of the times, so Wolfram, critical of the shortcomings of the Arthurian world, created a new idealization of knighthood, one that established its relationship more clearly both to human nature as such and to its infinite and supernatural goal.

Wolfram's juxtaposition of Parzival's path to that of Gawan helps clarify his intentions. Gawan, the exemplary Arthurian knight, endures the usual chivalric struggle and reaches the usual Arthurian goals of honor and love. He accepts the system and thrives when measured by it. Parzival, on the other hand, misunderstands and misuses the system in his naiveté; on the other, his desires, strivings, and predestination drive him beyond Arthur's court to the Castle of the Grail. It is not that Gawan is not a Christian knight. God is as much a given for him as is Arthurian knighthood. When Parzival is chastened by Cundrie for disgracing the court of Arthur, Gawan tries to console him and says: "Friend, I know very well that your path will not be free of strife. God give you good fortune in battle!" This is typical of Gawan. God is an unquestioned presence for him. His wish is both sincere and a cliché. Parzival's reply characterizes his own position as well: If God is powerful, he would not have placed me in such disgrace. If He hates me, then I shall bear His hatred. For Parzival, God, like knighthood, is something he must struggle with before proper integration is achieved. However, once Parzival has been successful in this struggle, his grasp of both knighthood and God far surpasses what Gawan can ever hope to attain.

Finally, there is the question of Parzival's guilt. As we have mentioned, he inflicts needless suffering and death on several innocent victims. And yet he never does so out of malice, but somehow out of a combination of incredible ignorance and attractive naiveté. He does not fail to ask the question of Anfortas because he lacks compassion, but because he has not been able to assimilate correctly Gurnemanz's advice. His mother dies of sorrow because Parzival is ignorant of the depth of her love for him. His savage killing of Ither occurs because of his ignorance and misunderstanding of the knightly code. His defiance and hatred of God stems from his ignorance of who God is and what the human creature's relationship to Him must be. Parzival overcomes his ignorance slowly and painfully for all concerned. His ignorance was a serious problem, but the nobility of his character aided by divine grace allows him ultimately to overcome it and to compensate for most of the suffering he has caused.

Willehalm, Wolfram's other major narrative work, which exists as a long and almost complete fragment, relates the conflict between French knights and the Saracens. Wolfram's source is a French *chanson de geste*, and much in the story shows marked similarity to pre-courtly narrative, for example, in its reliance on historical events and figures. Willehalm, the grandson of Charles Martel (c. 689-741), goes off to the wars leaving his castle to be defended by his wife Gyburg, a baptized pagan. Marital love and fidelity overcome differences of religion. Saracen knights are respected for their valor, and Rennewart, a noble pagan prisoner of Willehalm, wins the respect of his Christian lord and the affections of Alice, King Louis' daughter. The whole work breathes the spirit of tolerance and the superiority of human virtue to specific religious faith.

Titurel exists only in two short fragments and, as the only courtly romance in strophic form, narrates the history of the Grail family prior to the Parzival material. Wolfram seems to use no sources for the story which was probably intended to focus on Sigune and Schionatulander, secondary figures in *Parzival*, and the tragic outcome of their love.

3. Gottfried von Straßburg

Gottfried is the antithesis of Wolfram in several ways. Whereas Wolfram proudly proclaims himself a member of the knightly class and an advocate of the chivalric ethos, Gottfried was almost certainly not of the nobility but rather a burgher in the service of the town of Strasbourg or a cleric serving a bishop. And while his hero Tristan displays courtly culture and refinement of the highest order, knightly deeds are downplayed. In contrast to Wolfram's professed lack of formal schooling, Gottfried's knowledge of classical and foreign literatures, as well as his familiarity with contemporary philosophical issues, give clear evidence of a thorough and advanced education. He is by far the most refined stylist among the Middle High German narrative poets and consciously employs classical rhetorical figures with great virtuosity.

Except for a few lyric poems of doubtful authenticity, the story of *Tristan* is the only work by Gottfried we possess. The Tristan material had already been treated in German at least once by Gottfried's time in Eilhart von Oberge's *Tristrant* (c. 1170-1190). Eilhart's version is in the same tradition as that of the French author Béroul (fl. 1190), according to which Tristrant, at the outset an exemplary knight, and Isalde, the betrothed of his uncle Marke, fall victim to an overpowering passion for each other through the workings of a magic potion they unwittingly drink together. In the author's view this love is degrading and puts the lovers at odds with the social order. Such love is foolish, irrational, and, in its blindness to the values with which it conflicts, destructive. Its victims are to be pitied and their passion to be considered a sickness, an aberration.

Gottfried's *Tristan*, as we have it, is a fragment comprising well over half the story as it exists in the tradition of Thomas of Britain, whom Gottfried praises as the only teller of the "true" tale of the lovers. Only parts of the French version written by Thomas have survived, principally sections of the story which follow where Gottfried's version breaks off. However, because a Norwegian version (1226) of Thomas's whole work also exists, we can verify that Gottfried's assertion that he is sticking very close to Thomas's version is generally quite correct. New in Gottfried's work are his substitution of a critique of Middle High German authors in place of Tristan's knighting ceremony and his allegorization of the episode of the lovers' stay in the grotto of love.

Regarding Tristan and Isolde's love one can clearly see Gottfried's adherence to Thomas and his rejection of Eilhart. In Gottfried's view, as his elaborations in the prologue make especially clear, love in its purest form is an ennobling force and not the unfortunate and crippling experience portrayed by Eilhart. Gottfried professes his unqualified allegiance to the kind of love his story will describe. However, this is no ordinary love nor is his story intended for an ordinary audience. It is for "noble hearts," those refined enough to appreciate the love of Tristan and Isolde. Only such hearts will be willing to embrace this love in all its aspects, accepting the suffering along with the joy. For this qualified audience, however, he intends this story of their love, life, and death to be sustenance. Indeed, Gottfried states that their life and death is bread for noble hearts. This startling comparison of his story to the sacrament of the Eucharist would not have been lost on his audience.

Though the story unfolds in the usual episodic manner of the courtly romance, the plot can be simply told. Tristan (French *triste*: sad), an orphan born of tragic love and raised by a vassal loyal to his parents, is kidnapped but finds his way to the court of Marke in Cornwall. Tristan becomes the court favorite, especially after Marke learns that Tristan is his dead sister's son. Tristan fights and slays the Irish giant Morold on behalf of Cornwall but receives a poisonous wound which only Queen Isolde of Ireland, Morold's sister, can cure. Tristan travels there in the guise of a minstrel, is cured, ingratiates himself to all through his music and courtliness, and becomes a tutor to the queen's daughter, also called Isolde. They are attracted to each other by learning and art, not by love. Tristan takes his leave and returns to Cornwall. Marke has named him his heir, and this arouses jealousy in many at court. Marke's barons urge the king to take young Isolde as a wife, and Tristan undertakes the task of pressing Marke's suit. After perilous adventures Tristan successfully wins Isolde's hand for Marke. Before they leave Ireland, the Queen Mother Isolde gives to Brangaene, young Isolde's companion, a magic love potion which Marke and Isolde are to drink on their wedding night. This will guarantee their everlasting mutual love. On the ship, when the day becomes unbearably hot, Tristan and Isolde drink the potion, unaware of what it is. Brangaene, discovering what has happened, is distraught as she watches the potion take effect, and the lovers struggle against it. Finally, they confess the true state of affairs to each other and consummate their love. Brangaene becomes their confidante and it is she, still a virgin, who must help in the deception of Marke by becoming his partner on his wedding night.

From this point on the story alternates between the lovers' secret meetings and their endured separations, between short experiences of bliss and extended periods of longing. Marke, vacillating between blind love for Isolde and suspicion, finally banishes Tristan from court and forces Isolde to prove her integrity by undergoing the ordeal of the hot iron. She and Tristan plot to turn the ordeal to their advantage. Tristan, disguised as a pilgrim, helps her off the boat where the ordeal is to take place. He stumbles and they tumble to the ground together. Thus Isolde can truthfully swear that she has only lain in the arms of her husband and this poor pilgrim. She then takes up the hot iron and is not burned, which seems to be a sign of complicity in their love by some supernatural power. All three are soon together again at court, but Marke cannot free himself from his doubts and banishes them both.

The lovers retire to a grotto in the wilderness where they pass the time celebrating their love. Gottfried describes the grotto in allegorical terms. Since in medieval times only churches were described allegorically, Gottfried thus seems to imply that their love has value similar to the absolute claims of religion. Marke, while hunting, discovers the grotto, peers in, and sees them sleeping, separated by Tristan's unsheathed sword. He interprets this as proof of their innocence. His passion for Isolde is renewed and the lovers are permitted to return to court. Soon thereafter Marke again discovers the lovers sleeping together, and Tristan flees to

Arundel where in his loneliness he meets and is attracted to Isolde of the White Hands.

Here Gottfried's poem breaks off. In Thomas's version Tristan marries Isolde of the White Hands but puts off consummating their marriage. He receives a wound that only his former lover can cure. Isolde comes, the ship bearing her carrying a white sail, a prearranged sign that she is on board. But the jealous Isolde of the White Hands informs her husband that the ship's sail is black. Tristan dies. Isolde, arriving and seeing him dead, herself falls dead over his body.

Because of its subtlety and sophistication, Gottfried's *Tristan* lends itself to a wide range of interpretations. We would do well to view it as Gottfried urges us to view it: as a love story, albeit an unusual one. In contrast to Eilhart's version where the lovers regret having unwittingly drunk the love potion and lament its effects on their lives, Gottfried's Tristan welcomes the change in his life the potion has brought. When Brangaene reveals to him that his new all-consuming passion for Isolde is the result of the potion and that it will be the death of them both, Tristan replies that he willingly accepts the potion's effects and asserts that, if this love is their death, he would gladly try to gain "eternal death." Here, as in Eilhart's version, this adulterous love conflicts with the values of society. However, Gottfried does not condemn it for this reason. He describes their love as far superior to the married love of Isolde and Marke. It is an ideal, a special love that claims value in its own right despite its destructiveness in society.

This love differs from the ideal of chivalrous love as portrayed by Hartmann and Wolfram. It is not earned by knightly deeds. It simply happens to the lovers, and the lofty value of their love is a result of their own worth as persons of cultural refinement and courtliness. Their love derives its great value from their being worthy vessels of love. In contrast to *Erec, Iwein,* and *Parzival,* marriage does not offer a solution to the lovers' dilemma. Isolde's marriage to Marke is less an obstacle to the love between her and Tristan than its necessary condition. The pangs of longing the separated lovers endure can be said to be more essential to their love than its occasional fulfillment and union. If Gottfried were to remove all social and ethical obstacles for the lovers, he would also be changing the nature of their love. Like Romeo and Juliet, they, too, cannot marry and settle down to a life of marital bliss and contentment. This is not the kind of love Gottfried wishes to celebrate.

Since Gottfried's version remained unfinished, one wonders how he would have treated Tristan's relationship with Isolde of the White Hands. Would he portray Tristan as remaining true to the first Isolde in spite of his marriage, as Isolde had been true to Tristan in spite of her marriage to Marke? Or would Tristan's relationship to Isolde of the White Hands signal a defection on his part from the lofty and ideal love that existed between him and the first Isolde? Any answer we might give would remain in the realm of the hypothetical. What is evident is that the question of how Gottfried might have ended his tale cannot be answered by examining how Gottfried's continuers, Ulrich von Türheim (c. 1240) and Heinrich von Freiberg (c. 1285), brought their versions to a close. They represent rather a return to the ideas of Eilhart and seem oblivious to what Gottfried was trying to accomplish.

4. The Nibelungenlied

The *Nibelungenlied*, the last major narrative work of the classical period under discussion here, has its roots in a tradition completely different from that of the courtly romances discussed thus far. Certainly there are elements of courtliness (for example, how the poet describes Siegfried's love for Kriemhild), and Rüdiger, an obviously recent addition to the *Nibelungenlied* material, clearly represents an ideal Christian knight. Also, in no other literary work of the time do we gain so much knowledge of actual courtly protocol (i.e., etiquette, legal procedures, etc.) as we do here. Because of the somber mood pervading much of the story and the tragic outcome of events, one could make the case that the author is presenting us with an anti-courtly view of the "real" court around 1200, and that he wishes to present a realistic view of politics and society to counter the happy-end optimism of Arthurian romance. In any event, stripped of its courtly veneer and one seriously Christian figure, the *Nibelungenlied* is particularly to the art and ethos of Germanic heroic poetry of earlier centuries.

In contrast to the courtly romances which were composed in rhyming couplets with four stresses per line, this poetic narrative is written in strophic units of four lines called the *Nibelungenstrophe*. It can be schematized as follows:

1. _´_ _´_ _´`_ / _´_ _´_ _´_ ( ) a

2. _´_ _´_ _´`_ / _´_ _´_ _´_ ( ) a

3. _´_ _´_ _´`_ / _´_ _´_ _´_ ( ) b

4. _´_ _´_ _´`_ / _´_ _´_ _´_ _´_ b

The first half of each line usually ends with a feminine cadence while the second half usually closes with a masculine cadence and rhyme. However, the second half of the final line is expanded to four full stresses. This tends to slow down the action in bringing the four-line unit to a close. Frequently the slowing effect of the final line is used by the poet to express one of his dire predictions or forebodings.

The poet who about 1205 authored the Middle High German version we possess remained anonymous. Because of his obvious familiarity with the area along the Danube and his sketchy knowledge of geography in areas to the north and west, he is assumed to have been from this area, Passau being the best guess of several scholars. Determining which strands of Germanic lore went into this version was long a focal point of scholarship, but it is sufficient to know that the Middle High German version consists of two main stories, which themselves are amalgamations of mythical and quasi-historical Germanic heroic material that have been joined — not to every critic's satisfaction — into one narrative.

The first part tells the story of Siegfried, how he came to Worms first challenging the Burgundians under King Gunther, how he then became their ally and champion, how he helped woo the mythical Queen Brunhild, how he himself wooed and won Gunther's sister Kriemhild, how Brunhild and Kriemhild quarrel, and how, because of this, Siegfried is treacherously killed by Gunther's powerful vassal Hagen. The second part narrates Kriemhild's later marriage to Etzel, King of the Huns, and how she lures her brothers Gunther, Gernôt, and Giselher, as well as her archenemy Hagen and the rest of the Burgundians, to Etzel's court to take her revenge on them. The Burgundians die to a man, but Kriemhild also dies, slain by Hildebrand, officer of visiting King Dietrich, so appalled is he by the actions of this vengeful "she-devil" (l. 2371).

The two main characters whose mutual antagonism provides the strongest thread of unity to the story are Kriemhild and Hagen. It is Hagen in the first part whose murder of Siegfried turns the lovely but haughty Kriemhild into the monomaniacal seeker of revenge of the second part. It is also Hagen who assumes the moral leadership of the Burgundians as they journey to the land of the Huns to be slaughtered at Kriemhild's instigation, a catastrophe Hagen knows will happen but cannot prevent. The dramatic confrontation in the heroic tradition between the two, with which the story ends, ranks as one of the most gripping passages in medieval literature.

That the struggle between Kriemhild and Hagen will emerge as a central and unifying aspect is not at all obvious as the story begins. The focus is rather on Siegfried, a super-human and virtually invulnerable hero from the realm of myth, and his entrance into the world of mortals. The differing value systems represented by Siegfried and the Burgundians immediately clash when Siegfried travels to the land of the Burgundians and offers them a challenge in the heroic mode. He demands that they do combat with him, their lands against his. The Burgundians are mystified by such behavior. In their world, dominion is determined by quite different norms. King Gunther and his brothers reply that they have inherited their lands justly and rule them well. They reject the idea that dominion should be determined by brute force. The Burgundians are able to resolve this disturbing confrontation with another world by offering Siegfried princely hospitality. He accepts and, through the shrewd manipulation of Hagen, is soon putting his superior strength at their service, successfully leading their forces against the attacking Saxons.

Siegfried's love for the as-yet-unseen Kriemhild provides the occasion for the introduction of the second mythical figure into the story: Brunhild. Gunther wishes to win this Amazon-like queen as his bride and begs Siegfried to aid him. Siegfried agrees to help, provided Gunther allow him to wed Kriemhild. Brunhild can only be won if a suitor defeats her in three prescribed physical contests. Unsuccessful suitors must die. Since hapless Gunther is no match for her, Siegfried, made invisible by a magic cloak, takes his place and wins the contests. The deceived Brunhild submits to becoming "mighty" Gunther's bride. However, their wedding night, described with great humor, hardly fulfills Gunther's fondest hopes. Brunhild refuses to consummate the marriage until Gunther explains why he has allowed his sister Kriemhild to accept a dishonorable marriage with Siegfried, whom she has been led to believe is an unfree vassal. Gunther, his mind otherwise occupied, wants to get on with the matter at hand. However, the virgin queen prevails, and dawn finds the marriage as yet unconsummated and Gunther hanging from a nail in the wall. Siegfried must again be called upon. He subdues Brunhild in bed before turning her over to Gunther so that the marriage can be consummated. Brunhild, again thinking she has been conquered by Gunther, offers no further resistance.

The quarrel between the queens, which ultimately causes Siegfried's death, arises when, watching their husbands engaging in chivalric sport, each claims that her husband is better. Brunhild, still believing that Siegfried is socially inferior, argues that Gunther is better. Kriemhild takes the position of the heroic tradition: Siegfried is better because he is superior in strength and prowess. The quarrel ends with Brunhild's complete humiliation when Kriemhild produces Brunhild's ring and bridal girdle, which Siegfried had taken from Brunhild while subduing her on the second wedding night, and claims that Queen Brunhild is really Siegfried's concubine, since it was he to whom she surrendered her virginity.

Hagen hears of the matter from Brunhild and decides Siegfried must die. Views differ on what motivates him. Does he wish to get his hands on Siegfried's treasure? Is he jealous of Siegfried? Does he blame Siegfried for Brunhild's humiliation? In any case, he considers Siegfried a danger to the Burgundian state and, though merely a vassal, he knows that any decisive action will have to be initiated by him. Gunther, the legitimate ruler of the Burgundians, has too often proved to be ineffectual and inept as a ruler, not to mention his failures as a suitor and husband. Indeed, a major theme underlying the story is the deleterious effects caused by weak leadership. In poetry of this kind one must not be misled by the laudatory expressions the poet heaps upon all characters. To judge people and events, one must observe actions, their causes and effects. Judged by his actions or rather at times by his inability to act, Gunther simply does not measure up. Hagen, shrewdest and most powerful of the Burgundian nobles and completely devoted to the best interests of the land, is keenly aware of the power vacuum at the top and knows it is he who must fill it. No deed is too base for him, as his treacherous slaying of Siegfried makes clear, if Burgundian interests are at stake. On the other hand, no one equals Hagen's nobility and eminence, as he assumes actual and moral leadership of the Burgundians on their journey to Etzel's court, protecting them where he can and preparing them to die like heroes when their doom proves to be inevitable.

It is the heroic stance of the Burgundians as they face certain death that most clearly reveals the Germanic core of the *Nibelungenlied*. Unlike the Arthurian romances where all conflicts are resolvable and ultimately are resolved once the necessary insights have been achieved, there is no possible solution to the conflict at Etzel's court. Things have gone too far. Much as Hildebrand in *Das Hildebrandslied (The Lay of Hildebrand* [810/820]) sees that he simply has to accept his predicament and face it unflinchingly to retain his heroic integrity, so, too, the only insight possible for the Burgundians is that their destiny is tragic and must be met with the courage of heroes if they are to wrest moral victory from physical defeat. We are left with a sense of waste and human loss at the end, much as in a tragedy like *Hamlet*. Rather than consider how things might have been, we are overwhelmed by how things are; and we can only agree with the judgement the poet draws from the events he narrates, profound in its simplicity: *nach liebe leid* (after joy and pleasure come sorrow and suffering).

Appended to the *Nibelungenlied* in all complete manuscripts is the so-called *Nibelungenklage (Lament)* which narrates the events which follow the slaughter at Etzel's court — how the combatants are buried and how the news of the tragedy is received along the way in Bechelaren (Rüdiger's home), Passau, and Worms. Written in couplets, it in no way approaches the poetic level of the *Nibelungenlied*. That the two poems are so consistently paired causes one to wonder about the poetic sensitivity of those commissioning the manuscripts.

2. Lyric Poetry

Lyric poetry up to and, with the notable exception of many poems by Walther von der Vogelweide, through the classical period of medieval German literature is almost exclusively poetry about love between man and woman. It can most conveniently be divided as follows:

1. Pre-courtly love poetry, characterized by a relationship between the man and woman which is equal or in which the woman especially shows her vulnerability (c. 1150-c. 1190).
2. The poetry of courtly love or *hohe minne*, with the man being a suppliant and the woman idealized and distant — to be described more in detail below — (c. 1170-c. 1230).
3. Anti-courtly love poetry, best represented by Neidhart von Reuental (fl. after 1210).
4. Late love poetry, characterized by playful virtuosity with formal elements, especially with rhyme.

While fitting chronologically into the main period of courtly love poetry, Walther von der Vogelweide defies classification, both as to his love poetry and because he applies his poetic genius to other traditional and non-traditional subjects.

In the case of the pre-courtly love poetry especially, but also later, a large number of the poems can be arranged according to definite traditional types or "objective" genres. The most important of these, which sometimes exist in combination in an individual poem, are the following:

1. The so-called *Wechsel* (exchange) consists of a series of strophes spoken alternately by the man and the woman. The speakers do not address each other directly as in a dialogue. They speak rather in monologue-like fashion or perhaps to a messenger. Each expresses a point of view about a shared love experience or relationship. It is this common bond which provides the unity of the poem.

2. In the dialogue properly speaking, the lovers address each other directly.

3. The monologue spoken by the woman usually as a *Frauenklage* (complaint). Here the woman laments her separation from her lover, desertion, or the envy and spite of other parties.

4. In the *Botenlied* (address to or by the messenger), one or both of the lovers sends a message to the other, or the messenger addresses to one of them the words spoken by the other.

5. The *Tagelied* (dawn song) takes as its point of departure the coming of day after the lovers have spent a blissful night together. Perhaps one of the lovers awakens the other, or they are awakened by a watchman on the castle rampart announcing daybreak, or by the early song of the birds. In any case, the focus is not on the joy of the night shared by the lovers but on the sorrow their imminent separation will bring.

6. Finally, the *Kreuzlied* (crusading song) does not, as one might expect, usually center on a knight's going on a crusade as such, but rather on the conflict between the duties and spiritual intentions required of himself as a crusader and the longing for and duties to his beloved whom he must leave. Hence the knight is presented as torn between these two poles.

Elements of these genres occur in poems that do not fit the categories completely, as poets used these genres in different ways in order to transcend them.

Since the romantic notion of the poet as a creative genius was largely absent from medieval poetics, much of the imagery in this lyric poetry is traditional. So, for example, the use of nature, especially at the beginning of a poem, often has the well-established function of evoking or symbolizing the feelings of the poet. Descriptions of winter call his sadness or grief to mind, and summer represents his joyful mood. The vocabulary for nature is also quite standard. Realism, or nature described for its own sake, is entirely absent. Simile and metaphor are frequent, as in personification, especially regarding the lover's heart, soul, and body (*lîp*). Personification combined with apostrophe often occurs when the poet addresses *Minne* (Lady Love), *Frouwe Werlt* (Dame World), or gives some other abstract value personal characteristics. Besides images taken from nature — sun, moon, stars, fire, as well as images from falconry, bird-snaring, and the hunt — images concerned with knightly combat and feudal relationships are also frequent.

We shall dispense with a discussion of the metrics of this lyric poetry which, in any case, was based on stress and generally imitated normal speech accents. However, acquaintance with the basic strophic form prevalent after the pre-courtly period (a form from which both the sonnet and sonata derive) should prove helpful. Although it exists in many variations, the basic structure of by far the most common strophe was tripartite in nature. The first two parts, called *Stollen*, were the same. The third part differed from the *Stollen* in rhyme pattern and possibly also in its metric pattern. The two identical *Stollen*, taken together, form the *Aufgesang*. The third part is called the *Abgesang* or *cauda*. As these terms imply, this strophic form had implications for the melodies to which the poems were sung. In the *Aufgesang* a melody was introduced which coincided with the first *Stollen* and was then repeated in the second *Stollen*. A new melody accompanied the *Abgesang*. Thus the strophe might look like this:

```
Wie sich minne hebt daz weiz ich wol;    (a)
                                       〉 1. Stollen
wie si ende nimt des weiz ich niht.      (b)
                                                    〉 Aufgesang
ist daz ichs inne werden sol             (a)
                                       〉 2. Stollen
wie dem herzen herzeliep geschiht,       (b)

so bewar mich vor dem scheiden got,      (c)

daz waen bitter ist.                     (w)        〉 Abgesang

disen kumber führte ich ane spot.        (c)
```

New melodies were not composed for every new poem. A melody borrowed from another poem or poet which was then joined to a new poetic text is called a *contrafactum*.

Although it seems likely that love poems existed in German much earlier, the first such poems we have date from around 1150 at the earliest. They arose in the German-speaking area around the Danube (Bavaria and Austria). Of the poets, e.g., Der von Kürenberg or Dietmar von Aist, to whom the poems are attributed in the manuscripts, we know nothing. Although some concepts and terms of courtly love occasionally appear in these poems, they seem to have arisen independently of the courtly love poetry which clearly owes its origins to French influence. These early poems are not as carefully stylized regarding the posture of man and woman; they employ only a few of the same terms and conceits; and their strophic patterns are quite dissimilar. On the other hand, they do not reflect the simple eroticism of Latin goliard poetry. Longing and fulfillment on the part of both the man and the woman are essential elements. Feelings are expressed simply and directly.

In the last decades of the twelfth century a new type of love poetry became popular in Germany, the poetry of *hohe minne* (courtly love) which had come into

Germany from the troubadours, lyric poets of the south of France writing in the *langue d'oc* (Old Provençal). Simply put, the poetry of courtly love goes as follows: the poet or speaker in the poem is a member of knightly/courtly society. The task he sets himself in his poetry is to declare his undivided love for his lady. The lady, who cannot be named, is socially of a higher station than the poet and is married. She is perhaps the mistress of the castle where the poet is in service. The poet himself might be married as well. The poet has been in love with this lady since childhood. Through his poetry he hopes to win her favor, even wildly imagining the possibility of secret moments together and fulfillment. The lady, however, is viewed by him as the essence of all that is good and beautiful. She is like the sun, the moon, a goddess. The poet is unsure about the feelings of the lady toward him. He hopes that his love is in some sense reciprocated and asks for some sign or token that his poetry is not in vain. However, both must be on guard against those jealous members of the court seeking to uncover and thereby destroy their love. In any case, the lady is distant, perhaps impervious to his words of yearning. Yet it is the poet's duty to persist in this state of doubt and tension, waiting for a sign or greeting that may come.

Many of the conventional terms of this poetry are those of feudalism. The exalted lady is called *frouwe*, i.e., the female equivalent of lord. The poet is her *man* (vassal). His relationship to her is viewed as *dienest* (service), through which he hopes to win her *hulde* (favor), *genâde* (grace), or some kind of *lôn* (reward). The service of love brings about a state of *hôher muot* (exaltation or exhilaration) in the poet, but because of all the problems of *huot* (supervision at court), *merkaere* (spies), and the basic unfulfilled and unfulfillable nature of his love, there is also much *truren, kumber, leit, sorge*, and *ungemüete* (sadness, worry, and dejection), causing him many sleepless nights and driving him to the brink of insanity. Such love is, as its theoretician Andreas Capellanus (fl. c. 1200) tells us in his treatise on courtly love, *De Arte honeste amandi* (*The Art of Courtly Love*), a *passio*, i.e., suffering. It is that passion or suffering that comes over one at the sight and nearness of the beloved. Paradoxically, though this love seems adulterous in intent and would be clearly so if the yearnings found surcease in fulfillment, the principal effect of this love on the poet/lover is to make him morally and humanly better. For to be a proper lover and worthy of his beloved, the poet must strive constantly to improve himself in the sight of God and his fellow human beings. When Albrecht von Johansdorf (fl. 1180-1209) pleads with his lady, asking her, in a rare moment when they can speak freely, what good all his poetry and service have been, she replies simply: they have made him more worthy and have elevated his spirit.

A. Walther von der Vogelweide

Although there were many lyric poets of great talent and accomplishment during the classical courtly period, Walther von der Vogelweide far surpasses the rest because of the wide range and originality of his poetry. Other poets of courtly love were, perhaps, his equal in virtuosity of form and language. What distinguished Walther from the rest was his ability to turn the rarefied ideas and conventions of the poetry of *hohe minne* into a broader, more human concern with love. Nor did he confine his efforts to love poetry, but broke new ground by taking the tradition of the *Spruch* (folk wisdom in verse) and modifying it to comment on the political events of the day. Indeed, Walther can be said to have originated the genre of political poetry, at least in Germany. Finally, his religious poems are remarkable for their directness, profundity, and common sense. Two qualities much in evidence throughout his poetry are humor and irony. At times he combines them, with humor softening the blows of irony. At other times his irony expresses deep bitterness and turns into searing sarcasm. One scholar has commented that, despite the paucity of facts about Walther's life, we know no medieval poet as well as we know Walther because he has put so much of himself into his poems.

Walther was born around 1170; the place of his birth is uncertain, although most indications would make him Austrian. Early in his career he was at the court in Vienna when the older and more established poet Reinmar von Hagenau was also there. Walther learned from Reinmar, but the role of disciple did not suit his independent nature, and Walther's verse shows evidence of his satirizing and parodying Reinmar. In 1198 he left Vienna and spent some time at the courts of Hermann von Thüringen (d. 1217) and Dietrich von Meißen (fl. 1195). A document from 1203 shows him in the service of the bishop and lord Wolfger of Passau. Walther's itinerant lifestyle was probably determined by necessity rather than by choice. He was most likely a poor knight of the ministerial class who literally had to sing for his supper. He had to go where poetry was esteemed, at least to the extent that poets were there given some remuneration, little though it might be.

In his political poetry Walther is quite willing to take a position and devote his talents to furthering it. Early on we find him supporting the Hohenstaufen faction whose leader was then Philip of Swabia. Both Philip and Otto of Brunswick, of the opposing Welf party, claimed, each with some legitimacy, to be emperor. When Philip was then murdered in an unrelated matter, Walther threw in his lot with Otto, although his support did not necessarily imply a personal liking and admiration of the man.

What remained consistent in Walther's changing allegiances was his opposition to the pope's meddling in secular politics, especially in affairs of the empire. He shared the view that the emperor's power to rule in secular matters was not in the least dependent on any spiritual power the papacy might have. Since the days of the struggle between Emperor Heinrich IV of the Salian dynasty and Pope Gregory

VII, the idea that the pope as spiritual leader was superior to the emperor, the ruler in temporal affairs, had been a cornerstone of papal policy. Walther, along with those supporting the imperial party, would have none of this and castigated the pope for the negative effect of his interference in German affairs. His diatribes do not focus on the institution of the papacy but rather on the malicious conduct of the pope as an individual.

Friedrich II became undisputed emperor in 1215 and in 1220 became Walther's benefactor, presenting him with a small fief near Würzburg. Walther celebrates this event warmly in a poem contrasting sharply in tone with the somber mood of most of the poetry of his later years. Since there is a strong tradition that Walther was buried in Würzburg, many scholars assume that his last years were spent on his property, his material needs no longer an existential concern.

Although it is true that we learn much about Walther from his poems, one should not assume, especially in his love poetry, that the various views expressed reflect personal experiences or different periods of his life. Both his poems of courtly love and those poems taking issue with it are creations quite independent from his personal life, and more likely represent idealized postures rather than personal ones. The principal complaint about courtly love in his poetry is the inequality it requires. He objects that the burden of such love is not shared fairly, that love should be a mutual relationship. In contrast to the usual view of *frouwe* (lady) and *man* (vassal), Walther introduces the term *friunt* (friend) with its implications of equality to describe his view of what this relationship should be like. In contrast to *minne*, the conventional term for this love, he posits the more inclusive *liebe*. Walther's chief contribution to the genre is to relieve it of some of its stiff conventionality by introducing more directness, simplicity, and common human emotion.

Walther also broadened the scope of love poetry with his so-called *Mädchen-lieder*, poems in which the woman addressed is not a *minnecliche frouwe* (esteemed lady of the court), but rather a *herzeliebez frouwelin*, a simple young woman. By showing the young woman the respect due a courtly lady, Walther ennobles her and, by combining aspects of the Latin goliard erotic poetry with aspects of courtly love, creates a refreshing new kind of love poetry with both feeling and refinement, and yet also with a humor which creates distance and objectivity without robbing the love of its seriousness and authenticity.

As his poems of social and religious comment make clear, Walther was quite capable of pausing in his poetry to ponder life's purpose and the ubiquity of human folly, weakness, and even malice. "Ich saz ûf eime steine" ("I Sat Upon a Rock") reveals Walther's particular genius and point of view in approaching a problem that also preoccupied other noteworthy poets: knightly honor, human love, and material possessions all seem to be worthy goals of human striving. But can one so arrange one's life that the pursuit of these inner-worldly goals does not conflict with one's ultimate transcendental goal of pleasing God? Hartmann, especially in *Der arme*

Heinrich, and Wolfram, as his concluding comments to *Parzival* show, both struggle with the problem and through their poetry propose solutions to the conflict of worldly and spiritual goals.

Walther, too, poses the problem, articulating it with characteristic simplicity: how can one get honor, possessions (which are often in conflict), and God's favor all safely locked up in one cabinet and in a single heart? But for Walther the emphasis lies elsewhere. In his view such metaphysical and religious issues cannot begin to be solved until the proper environment of a just social order exists. Without *frîde* (peace) and *reht* (justice) to provide an armed escort, these other values are too vulnerable on the road of life.

Underlying much of the poetry of Walther's mature years are a greater seriousness and a more reflective manner. Social change, political insecurity, and religious indifference seem to be at the root of his melancholy. He complains that life at court has lost much of the elegant spirit and the moral refinement it used to have. The struggle between pope and emperor, culminating in the latter's excommunication by the former with its negative effects on the political and moral orders, weighed on him as well. The beauty of Lady World reveals itself to him as a moral danger. The devil is the innkeeper, the world his inn. The poet wants to settle his account and move on to more secure quarters. One cause, however, that he can still unequivocally endorse is a crusade. In two late poems, *"Palästinalied"* ("Allerêrst lebe ich mir werde" ["Now really for the first time do I live"]) and his so-called "Elegy" ("Owê war sint verswunden" ["Alas, where have they disappeared"]), he rouses the spirits of his fellow Christians to take part in this spiritual quest. Through unselfish commitment to this spiritual task the Christian knight can revive and redirect his idealism. Through the orientation a crusade provides, he can realize his true human potential and overcome the moral ambiguities of his earthly existence.

B. Post-Courtly Poetry

Lyric poetry following the classical period of courtly love poetry was of two main kinds. Neidhart von Reuental struck off in a new direction by applying the conventions of courtly love to peasant life, though by satirizing both. Much is puzzling in this poetry, but Neidhart's virtuosity, as he combines the language of the court and its lofty idealism with that of peasant-class realism for purposes of caricature, is evident and won him many imitators. Other later poets, such as Ulrich von Liechtenstein and Heinrich von Meißen, also called *Frauenlob* (praise of women), carried on the tradition of courtly love poetry by devoting their efforts to the further refinement of the formal elements of their verse. Their poems are characterized by extravagant play with strophic structure, rhyme, and the proliferation of rhetorical devices. As courtly love became less and less a real concern of the court and sank ever more deeply into pure conventionality, it seemed to be able to justify its existence only by being the occasion for the poet and his audience to indulge themselves in displays of formal linguistic artistry.

C. Literature After the High Courtly Period

As both the late poetry of Walther and the innovations of Neidhart show, the political turmoil and cultural and moral decline of the nobility was beginning to be reflected in the literature. Nowhere is the change in society and how knighthood and courtliness were perceived as starkly portrayed as in the short verse narrative *Meier Helmbrecht*, composed between 1250 and 1280, by an author at home in the Bavarian-Austrian Inn district who identifies himself only as Wernher der Gartenaere (the Gardener). Because of the frequent contemporary metaphor and the didactic intent of the story, many have considered the author to be a cleric. As is clear from the story, he is also conversant with courtly life and literature.

The protagonist is Helmbrecht, son of Meier (farmer) Helmbrecht, who wishes to leave home and rise above his station by becoming a knight. His father strongly urges him to remain, but the son, backed by his doting mother and his sister Gotelind, wins out. The relenting father sells some livestock to provide him with a good horse and dandified clothing. He joins a band of plundering knights and with them wreaks havoc on the local peasantry. After a year he returns home so changed in manner, speech, and appearance that no one can believe it is he. His affectation and jumble of foreign phrases dumbfound the simple parents. Nevertheless, they receive him with joy into their house.

In what is perhaps the best-known passage, the father, reminiscing about visiting the court when young, paints a picture of courtly virtue, refinement, and entertainment which reflects the idealized courtly life portrayed in classical courtly literature. He then asks his son to describe what he has experienced of life at court. Young Helmbrecht obliges with tales of riotous drinking bouts, deceit, intrigue, and crass behavior of every kind. Despite the pleas and warnings of his father, young Helmbrecht returns to his plundering knightly companions, taking the admiring Gotelind with him. At her wedding to one of her brother's boon companions, the judge and his deputies suddenly appear. Helmbrecht's nine companions are summarily hanged. He, as the tenth, is blinded and has a hand and a foot severed. He finds his way home only to be rejected and cast out by his father. Finally, he meets his end when he is caught and hanged by peasants he had robbed and abused.

Despite the obvious moralistic intent, *Meier Helmbrecht* is a well-crafted narrative, so that the message (or messages) flows from the story and does not strike the reader as an appendage. One clear concern of the author is to chronicle the decline among the nobility, many of whom descended or were reduced to robbing and pillaging the peasantry for their livelihood. Perhaps a more central concern of the poet is to portray the social order as divinely ordained. It is folly and arrogance for a peasant boy to abandon his class and attempt to rise into the knightly class. It is also against God's commandment to disobey one's father. Helmbrecht's disobedience to his father is portrayed as the principal reason for his severe punishment.

Wernher intentionally makes several allusions to the parable of the Prodigal Son in the story. Helmbrecht, in a sense, takes his inheritance when he leaves home, and he is welcomed with warm love upon his first return. However, the conclusion to the story is all the more harsh because of its contrast to this classical Biblical example of mercy and forgiveness. The author thereby seems to stress that God is also a God of justice. Young Helmbrecht's failings were not as innocent as those of the younger son in the parable: Helmbrecht had disobeyed his father and had scorned the life which God had chosen for him; he had not squandered, but had become the savage scourge of the peasant class to which he rightfully belonged. The story serves as a grim admonition to an age and a society grown unaccustomed to subtlety and refinement.

D. Medieval Drama

Drama in the Middle Ages is a completely original phenomenon. The drama of ancient Greece and Rome had no influence on it whatsoever. One consequence of this is that medieval drama cannot successfully be analyzed according to Aristotelian poetics. It has, rather, many characteristics of what we have come to call epic theater. Granted that the Roman playwright Terence was read in medieval times, his plays were never staged; and Hrotsvitha von Gandersheim, a Benedictine nun of the tenth century who wrote Latin dialogues based on lives of the saints in the style of his plays, did so in order that pupils would have something to read in place of this pagan author. Hrotsvitha's dialogues were not meant to be staged, nor did she have any followers who might have influenced medieval drama.

In contrast to narrative and lyric poetry, medieval drama is not characterized by clear national traits from one vernacular language to another. It is much more an international form of literature with its roots in church liturgy, which was the same throughout western Europe and with its earliest expression in the universal Latin language. As best we can assess, Latin liturgical plays were being staged in Germany long before German plays were attempted. Besides plays completely in Latin or German, there were also plays written in a mixture of the two languages.

Religious drama preceded secular drama by centuries. The earliest plays were Easter Plays which developed from the Easter liturgy. Later religious drama also embraced plays on the Passion, the Christmas liturgy, the Last Judgement, parts of the Old Testament, and indeed the whole history of salvation. The original purpose of these productions was to offer the viewers a vivid re-enactment of central events having to do with the Christian view of salvation, thereby instructing them in their faith. However, the introduction of material peripheral to this purpose, that had dramatic, especially comic, potential, reveals that already in its beginnings drama tended, at least in some ways, to seek its own goals. Very early the theatrical aspects began to dominate over the basic liturgical texts, and the number of actors required rose into the thirties and forties. This expansion required that members of the lay congregation be added to the clerics who originally had been the sole actors. The plays were moved outside the church, being staged either in front of the church or sometimes, if the two places were not the same, in the marketplace. In some places they were performed at ground level, in others on raised wooden platforms constructed for the occasion. Different parts of the stage functioned as different settings. Props often became quite elaborate.

The earliest German medieval drama extant is the Easter Play of Muri (Switzerland) which dates from about 1250 and exists only in fragmentary form. (Most Easter Plays seem to have been written in the fifteenth century.) In contrast to later versions, the Muri play shows similarities to the language and verse forms of courtly literature. In instructing the faithful about this central event of their faith, this Easter Play stresses the complete triumph of Christ over the powers of darkness and the impotence of earthly power when confronted by the divine.

Secular drama arose about 1350 and from its beginnings existed only in the vernacular. Three main types of plays were:

1. *Fastnachtspiele* (Shrovetide Plays), which, as their name implies, became part of the festivities preceding Ash Wednesday and the beginning of Lent. The earliest version takes the triumph of the anti-Christ in this world as its point of departure, and in the form of satire criticizes the emperor for mismanagement and both the nobility and the clergy for their selfishness and greed.

2. "Plays of the Seasons," which treat the question which of the seasons should be preferred. Extant material is slim. However, the contest between the seasons in a Dutch version was in the form of a dispute between Summer and Winter about which season was better for love. German versions seem to have involved dance and pantomime.

3. "Neidhart Plays," in which this poet, having become a legendary figure, and the buffoonish lads who are his traditional enemies, attempt to get the better of each other through various pranks.

E. Mystical Literature

Mystical literature, as understood here, differs from religious literature that is basically instructional in nature, such as catechetical works, as well as from strictly theological works, that is, writings whose purpose is to further the academic discipline of theology as taught at the universities. Mystical literature is less didactic than catechetical writings and generally less rigorous than theological treatises. It focuses on the relationship of humans to God. The goal of the mystic is to achieve as nearly perfect a union with God as possible. Because of this stress on the personal relationship between the person, or soul, and God, other traditional and more visible elements of religion, such as the mass, the sacraments, and the church-approved structure of religious orders often seem to receive less than their due, as though the mystics thought that such things were merely unnecessary external trappings. Such assumptions on the part of orthodoxy, sometimes well-founded and sometimes not, have often brought mystically oriented religious movements into conflict with ecclesiastical authorities. Also, in describing the union which they claim to experience with God, mystical writers often speak of it in ways that exclude any differentiation between God and creature, which again raises the suspicion of heresy. Most medieval mystical orthodoxy was never questioned. A few mystics, however, like the Dominican Meister Eckhart, did run afoul of authority because their formulations were so daring.

In the fourteenth century along both the Upper and Lower Rhine there was much religious ferment with mystical overtones. This activity was broadly based in both the religious orders and among the laity. However, some of its most visible proponents were the so-called beghards and beguines. These were, respectively, men and women, sometimes living in communities, who lived a life quite similar to that led by members of religious orders but, as independent of these, were not under direct ecclesiastical jurisdiction. They often supported themselves by cottage-industry type work or by begging. Because of their independent status and lack of church supervision, they often, rightly or wrongly, came under suspicion of heresy. Often their uneasy situation was alleviated if they developed close relationships with religious orders and received guidance in spiritual matters from Franciscan or, more often, Dominican friars. Frequently communities that had begun as a group of beguines later received permission to incorporate themselves into the Dominican order. The combination of beguines and the new religious orders was the principal impetus providing new vigor to religious activity in northern Europe.

The language of mysticism is based on the premise that God is ineffable. If mystics speak of some personal experience of union with the divinity, they consistently emphasize the utter inadequacy of language as a medium to describe such experiences. So, too, mystical theologians, in discussing the ability of human language to grasp the reality of God, deny that language expresses anything positive that really exists in God. God and union with Him are simply beyond human comprehension. Since, however, mystics do try to describe God and mystical union with the divinity, their language is marked by the tension between this striving and its ultimate frustration. As a result, they employ figures and devices of inadequacy and indirection. Since one cannot say what God is, they employ negation, saying what he is not. He is not material (spiritual); he has no limits (infinite); he does not exist in time (eternal). Or they resort to paradox and call him the being, or the nothing beyond being. Through dialectic — applying contradictory terms to God — they try to transcend the limitations of single concepts predicated of Him. Their use of metaphor — that God is the sun of justice or the bridegroom of the soul — assumes language's inability to describe God directly. Thus mystical expression often operates at the frontiers of language and through the task it sets for itself has been, as here, responsible for many new linguistic and poetic impulses.

Mechthild von Magdeburg, a beguine who spent the evening of her life in a Cistercian convent in Helfta, near Eisleben, that was under the guidance of Dominican friars and known for its intense mystical activity, composed in *Das fließende Licht der Gottheit* (*The Flowing Light of the Godhead* [1250-1282]) a wonderfully lyrical mystical work that defies literary classification. Originally written in Low German, it has only come down to us in a Latin translation and an excellent Middle High German version. Mechthild employs several literary genres, such as short narrative, legend, dialogue, inspired utterances, revelations, visions, prayers, hymns, and warm lyricism, to express an affective mysticism of love between God, the lover, and his beloved, the soul.

In the midst of all the mystical ferment along the Upper Rhine, three figures stand out prominently — all of them Dominicans: Meister Eckhart, Johannes Tauler, and Heinrich Suso (Seuse). Meister Eckhart distinguished himself as a university professor in Paris, as a provincial superior of his order in Germany, and as a preacher of great renown. He wrote theological treatises in Latin of great acuity. However, he is best known for his vernacular sermons preached for the most part later in life, probably in Strasbourg and certainly in Cologne, two centers of religious fervor. His last years were clouded by ecclesiastical investigations of his orthodoxy, and several of his statements were ultimately condemned as heretical. Eckhart is usually called a speculative mystic because he applies the academic discipline of scholastic thought to a mystical examination of God's ultimately unknowable nature and his oneness with the soul. No other mystic of the time explored these unchartered and unchartable regions of the spirit with such theological and linguistic daring.

Johannes Tauler's works consist entirely of vernacular sermons. These lack the theological sophistication of Eckhart, even though echoes of him are frequent. Tauler centers less on the divine aspects of the soul and more on the necessity for self-knowledge, humility, and asceticism as necessary conditions of union. The reality of sin and its effects, the centrality of Christ's role as redeemer, especially through his suffering and death, and the importance of suffering for spiritual progress — all of which receive little emphasis in Eckhart — are central concerns. His forceful and lucid expression of moral issues affecting the soul's union with God earned him a reputation as a safe and practical spiritual guide. His sermons enjoyed wide and lasting popularity.

If one can characterize Eckhart as a speculative mystic and Tauler as emphasizing the moral prerequisites of mystical union, Heinrich Suso's (Seuse's) works are significant for their contribution to affective mysticism. After an attempt in an early work (*Das Büchlein der Wahrheit* [*The Little Book of Truth*]) to defend the thought of his former teacher Eckhart from heretical interpretations, Suso abandons the field of speculative theology and lays emphasis on union through feeling and intimacy with Christ in His humanity. *Das Büchlein der ewigen Weisheit* (*The Little Book of Eternal Wisdom*), in which the soul is given guidance in meditating on Christ's passion, consists principally of dialogues between the servant (Suso or reader) and Jesus or His mother. Through an empathetic reliving of Jesus's suffering, a union of God and the soul is achieved, a union of feeling. The Latin version of this work, *Horologium Sapientiae*, was the second most popular book of the later Middle Ages. Perhaps more interesting for the literary scholar is his *Vita* or *Life*, which is the first autobiography in the German language. One must be careful not to measure it by completely modern notions of autobiography. Because he wishes its protagonist to serve as a model for the spiritual progress of others (even though his mistakes and failings are described as well as his pious practices), it also possesses several characteristics of hagiography.

Conclusion

The close of the Middle Ages and the dawning of the age of the Renaissance and Humanism, whose spirit, viewed centuries later, differs so clearly from that of the medieval period, actually came about almost imperceptibly. Certainly the eruption of religious, national, social, and cultural changes, which we know as the Reformation, marked a clear turning point. But its causes lay in large measure in the gradual cultural decline of the late Middle Ages. The volume of literary works composed after the classical period increased significantly. However, there is general agreement that, in quality, the literature of the fourteenth and fifteenth centuries cannot compare with what writers of the previous period, especially the major figures of the time between 1170 and 1230, had achieved. Tales of knights tended to become rigidly formalistic as chivalric culture declined further. Didactic verse propounding homey morality became a favorite literary pastime for reader and writer alike. What narrative talent manifested itself reflected in its hardy realism the men-

tality of the townsfolk. An age had passed, whether people were aware of it or not; and it would be quite some time before a constellation of circumstances would again arise which would provide an environment suitable for literary creativity of such high quality.

3 Late Middle High German, Renaissance, and Reformation

Albrecht Classen

Historical Time Frame

Whereas the western kingdoms of England and France experienced a steady rise in power, political unity, and centralized government during the twelfth and thirteenth centuries, the German Empire, later to be called *Das Heilige römische Reich deutscher Nation* (The Holy Roman Empire of the German Nation) experienced the very opposite and broke into many different and largely independent political units. As early as 1231 the Hohenstaufen Emperor Friedrich II had given the territorial dukes their relative sovereignty, which was later confirmed and cemented in 1356 (*Goldene Bulle* [Golden Bull]) by Emperor Karl IV (1316-1378) from the Luxemburg dynasty. After Karl's death in 1378 only weak personalities occupied the German throne. Once the Habsburg family took control of the imperial crown with Albrecht II in 1438, the emperors' political concerns were directed more toward the south and southeast of Europe and not toward developing and unifying the central parts of Germany. Thus, predominantly territorial politics dominated the public sphere of Germany throughout the later Middle Ages. The archbishops of Trier, Mainz, and Cologne, the King of Bohemia, the Count Palatinate, the Duke of Saxony, and the Margrave of Brandenburg, among others, vied for power and influence. This allowed many new political forces to come into play.

Many cities sprang up during the thirteenth and fourteenth centuries and soon established formidable alliances (e.g., the Hanseatic League, in place since the late twelfth century), against which the dukes and princes had little say. Powerful merchant families such as the Fuggers and Welsers in Augsburg and the Hirsch-vogels in Nuremberg spanned the world with their trade. In 1488 the Swabian Alliance was formed uniting cities, knights, and princes of southwest Germany. The nobility aligned itself in new political orders such as the Society of St. George, the Society of St. William, and "The Order of the Lion." The Czech Hussites, followers of the reformer Jan Hus (c. 1369-1415), fought bitter and successful battles against the German imperial armies after their leader had been burned at the stake at the Council of Constance in 1415 for his allegedly heretical belief. Eventually Bohemia was lost to the German crown when George Podiebrad was elevated to the throne in 1458. Somewhat later, around 1500, the Swiss Federation was bolstering its independent role within Europe. Large parts of the former German Empire were lost to Hungary (since 1457 under the rule of King Matthias Corvinus), Poland, and Burgundy. Moreover, since 1471 the Turks began to attack the heartland of central Europe. When the Low Countries passed on to Spanish rule with Emperor Karl V's resignation in 1556, an unrelenting battle for their independence ensued (1568-1648). The *Feme*, a secretive alliance of peasants and noble-men, which had its origin in Westphalia and soon spread to all parts of the old Empire, took it upon itself to prosecute criminals and to bring to trial heretics and other major offenders. Law and order was not sufficiently enforced by the princes, and thus this powerful organization attempted to keep chaos at bay.

Throughout the fifteenth century imperial diets met for the purpose of fighting anarchy, but the political center was absent, and the German nobility was opposed to any central rule by the Emperor. The sixteenth century did not bring a solution to this chaotic state of affairs; on the contrary, the political turmoil intensified. With the emergence of Martin Luther's (1483-1546) Reformation the political strife between individual leaders assumed a religious pitch which soon led, after several bitter wars, to the Thirty-Years' War (1618-1648). First, the peasants staged a desperate, unsuccessful uprising against their aristocratic lords (Peasant War, 1524/25), then the Protestant dukes fought against their Catholic counterparts in the War of Schmalkalden (1546/47); many local disputes ensued before the Thirty-Years' War which left Germany in shambles, because the Empire existed in name only. In the peace treaty of Münster and Osnabrück (*Westfälischer Frieden*) in 1648 both the Netherlands and Switzerland were recognized as independent nations, Sweden and France received large parts of Germany, many territories were redistributed, the Habsburg family finally lost its last spheres of influence in the heartland of Germany, and the foundations were laid for the vigorous development of Brandenburg-Prussia.

At the same time, a multiplicity of cultural developments characterized life in Germany. Intellectual life was influenced by the Italian Renaissance and by humanists, such as Erasmus of Rotterdam. The beginning of this influence can be marked from the middle of the fourteenth century when Petrarch had close contacts with Emperor Karl IV in Prague and his chancellor Johann von Neumarkt (c. 1310-c. 1380). The first German university was founded by Karl in the same city in 1348, followed by the university of Vienna in 1356. Urban culture reached a new apogee in Germany, where the patrician class along with the craftsmen guilds participated in the art form of the Meistersänger. In architecture, the late-Gothic style mixed with an early form of Renaissance, and in painting Albrecht Dürer (1471-1528), Matthias Grünewald (1460/70-1528), and Hans Holbein the Younger (1497-1553) dominated a populous field.

When Johann Gutenberg (1399-1468) invented the printing press in the 1450s, he revolutionized the world. Literary productivity soon picked up and reached unforeseen levels as early as the turn of the century. To some extent Gutenberg's invention made it possible for the writings of Martin Luther to be read and heard all over Germany and Europe in a very short time, this following the posting of his 95 theses on the doors of the Wittenberg castle chapel in 1517. The Reformation spread quickly and established itself, beginning in the 1520s, in the form of a new church. Splinter movements also emerged, and thus independent church organizations were formed by Ulrich Zwingli (1484-1532) in Zurich in 1519, John Calvin (1509-1564) in Geneva in 1541, and by Thomas Müntzer (c. 1490-1525) and Andreas Karlstadt (c. 1480-1541) in Thuringia and Franconia in the 1520s, not to speak of the various Anabaptist groups all over the south and southwest of Germany. The Frisian Menno Simon (1492-1559) became the founder of the Mennonites who later emigrated to Prussia, then to Russia, and, in the seventeenth century, to the United States.

Philosophical Framework: Renaissance and Humanism

Traditionally, we consider Italy to be the birthplace of the Renaissance, a movement aimed at the renewal of classical antiquity. This could either mean the rediscovery of classical learning and of the classical languages Greek and Latin, or it could mean the re-orientation toward the self and the refocusing on humankind as the center of the universe, determined through the reception of philosophical treatises from antiquity. Both trends did indeed begin in Italy and spread all over Europe from the thirteenth to the seventeenth centuries, but it would be erroneous to believe that the one must be identified with the other. Moreover, the Renaissance was not only limited to the Mediterranean countries, but also affected northern Europe quite early. The degree to which the Renaissance was received in Germany, and when, is still a matter of debate. But there is a high degree of probability that many of the contacts, such as between Petrarch and Emperor Karl IV and his chancellor Johann von Neumarkt, and between Aeneas Sylvius Piccolomini (1405-1464), the later Pope Pius II, and Niklas von Wyle (c. 1410-c. 1478), for instance, had an impact, even though a Renaissance as we are wont to define it — according to the characteristics which it had assumed in Italy during the fourteenth and fifteenth centuries — might not be detectable in Germany.

The renewed interest in classical studies led to a new fascination with realism and the individual. The subordination of the individual to God was not abandoned, but the relationship between individuals and their environment assumed new

Dürer, Aus dem Marienleben

dimensions, giving the former an unforeseen predominance. This can be observed in literature as well as in sculpture and painting. Many Italian Renaissance thinkers travelled to Germany, such as Poggio Bracciolini (1380-1459) or Cardinal Branda Castiglione (1350-c. 1429). In turn, German scholars, poets, merchants, and clerics visited Italy and thus came into immediate contact with the Renaissance world. The so-called Bohemian Renaissance under Emperor Karl IV and his chancellor Johann of Neumarkt was probably no more than a brief interlude, but it was a spark that inaugurated many new developments.

With the rise of the German cities, a wealthy bourgeoisie replaced the aristocracy as the leading class in society and provided the socio-economic foundation for the tremendous intellectual changes in the fifteenth century. As printing presses were set up in the cities, a growing reading public was ready to accept the new visions and ideas engendered by the Italian Renaissance.

The influence of the Italian Renaissance first became apparent during the two great Church Councils of Constance (1414-1418) and of Basel (1431-1440), both meeting places of scholars, churchmen, and politicians from all over Europe. These councils were constituted to end the Schism; as a result, the end of the dominance of the Catholic Church in all aspects of daily life in Europe brought about the liberation of individual thinking both in secular and spiritual realms. The councilary movement placed the intellectuals within the church and thus indirectly paved the way for the Reformation itself.

During the long decline of the German Empire the relatively independent ducal territories emerged as prototypes of centralized modern states. Such states have always been in need of a well trained bureaucracy, and thus a large number of universities were founded to supply city and state governments with clerics able to handle the administrative demands of the new political structures. Among these universities were: Freiburg im Breisgau (1457), Basel (1459), Ingolstadt (1472), Trier (1473), Mainz (1476), and Tübingen (1477). The intellectual foundation for the university graduates was different from the one in Italy, however, because life at court or in the cities was still dominated by a medieval system of rules and laws, of which the guild system and the class structure (*ordo*) were the most visible signs. The large merchant families (patricians) strove, however, to develop international contacts and trade, particularly with Italy, the Netherlands, and Flanders. They were thus well suited as ambassadors and in turn brought back new intellectual concepts and ideas. Other channels were those of university students and scholars who travelled throughout Europe and thus returned with exciting new information and ideas. But the aristocratic culture did not disappear altogether; rather it experienced a late blooming at such courts as Rottenweil (near Stuttgart) with Mechthild of Austria (1418/19-1482), in Saarbrücken with Elisabeth von Nassau-Saarbrücken (1379-1456), in Innsbruck with Duke Sigmund der Münzreiche (1427-1496) and his wife Eleonore, and in Vienna with the Habsburgs, especially Maximilian I (1459-1519). But most of the big cities along the Rhine and in the southwest of Germany, such as Augsburg, Regensburg, Ingolstadt, and Nuremberg became major centers of bourgeois culture. The peasantry, on the other hand, never played any major role except in such areas as Tyrol and Switzerland, where important religious plays dealing with the common people were written in the fifteenth and sixteenth centuries.

Among the leading Renaissance philosophers of German origin are Nicholas von Cues (1401-1464), Johannes Reuchlin (1455-1522), Rudolph Agricola (1443-1485), Conrad Celtis (1459-1508), Willibald Pirckheimer (1470-1530), Agrippa von Nettersheim (1485-1535), Paracelsus von Hohenheim (1493/94-1541), and Jacob Böhme (1575-1624). They formed the crucial catalysts between German and Italian Renaissance thinking, and they stood at the forefront of humanistic scholarship north of the Alps.

In the realm of philosophy, an actual break with the Middle Ages already took place in the fourteenth century when William of Occam (1280/85-1349/50) spread his philosophy of nominalism. Occam believed that speech was nothing but convention, an agreement among people, and thus the human mind was not forced any longer to detect the predetermined meaning as given by God, but could create its own thoughts and concepts (*nulla substantia est universalis* [no matter is universal]). From this ensued the thought that everything was individual, unique, and needed to be established by individuals. Occam disinvested the Church, all religious and political institutions, and social arrangements (*ordo*) of God and the cosmos, and called upon people to determine their own destiny and morality. In this sense, Occam opened up an avenue for the modern subject to determine the path toward the future, independent from God's, the Church's, or the Emperor's decisions. God was removed from the world and considered an infinitely remote, incomprehensible, and unimaginable entity within the universe. As a result of his philosophy, Occam was banned by the Pope, fled from Avignon, and then found refuge at the court of Emperor Ludwig of Bavaria. For the next centuries his thought was to influence German intellectuals, among them Jan Hus and Martin Luther.

The Turn of the Century (1400)

Around 1400 several major authors appeared who are now considered prominent but who enjoyed very little success during their lifetime. Hugo von Montfort (1357-1423), Oswald von Wolkenstein (1376/77-1445), the Monk of Salzburg (fl. 1400), Johannes von Tepl (Saaz) (c. 1350-1414), and Heinrich Wittenwiler (fl. 1400-1414) all composed their works in close chronological proximity. Because of their limited popularity the writings of these men have come down to us in a small number of manuscripts, and sometimes in only a single manuscript. Their works reveal, however, modern trends unbroached by their literary predecessors and contemporaries. Indeed, this modernity might have been one reason for the scant reception of these writers.

Exceptions to this phenomenon are Johannes von Tepl, whose dialogue *Der Ackermann aus Böhmen* (*The Ploughman*) met with great enthusiasm (although practically all manuscripts written in Bohemia vanished during the Hussite Wars when the Czech followers of Jan Hus burned and destroyed what they felt represented German culture), and the Monk of Salzburg, whose works are documented in more than one hundred manuscripts.

The Monk of Salzburg

The so-called Monk of Salzburg has yet to be identified. The name could simply be a collective title for a whole group of authors of approximately one hundred religious and secular songs which were quite popular and subsequently found their way into a number of song books dating from the middle of the fifteenth century. We do know, however, that these works were written in Salzburg under Archbishop Pilgrim II, to whom several of the songs are dedicated (indicated by acrosticha). Pilgrim ruled over a luxurious and art-loving court from 1365 to 1396. During his reign he considerably expanded his rule over neighboring countries. We assume that his court was like that of other secular princes at the time, which explains the inclusion of so many secular love songs in the work of the Monk. The Monk's poetry is important to us for the extant musical notations that accompanied the writing, a rarity since most medieval notations have been lost or were never written down. The themes of these songs do not differ markedly from those espoused by the late medieval *Minnesang* of the Swabian school: the lover offers his service to the lady, he suffers when she does not listen to him, he beseeches her to accept his love, etc. The Monk's so-called "*Kuhhorn*"("cow-horn") dawn song (*Tagelied*) is important in the history of this genre as a continuation of the medieval song of Steinmar, where a farm hand and a maid make love in the shed and lament the coming of the dawn. The Monk also favors a more sensuous concept of love and talks about it in a frank manner. Other themes include loyalty, New Year's greetings, and descriptions of the physical beauty of the mistress.

Whereas his contemporary Oswald von Wolkenstein used many melodies from French and Italian sources and adapted them in his songs, the Monk refrains from this technique and does not compose so-called *contrafacta* (i.e., a new text for an old melody). His music reveals novel aspects and techniques within the current German practices, among them polyphony and the pentatone. Many of his secular songs are composed to accompany a dance and thus follow the model of the *tanzwise, reie, ballade, virelai,* and *rondeau.* In the Monk's works and in other documents from the court in Salzburg we can observe early forms of a German Renaissance culture in which traditional chivalric ideals coalesce with novel intellectual concepts from Italy to create forms of expression. The court life becomes an expression of art itself, for which the Monk's poetry serves as a prime example.

Oswald von Wolkenstein

Oswald von Wolkenstein is one of the very first German poets whom we can identify both through his lyric poetry and from a large number of historical documents (more than one thousand have come down to us). In two of his three manuscripts (A, B, and c) remarkable portraits of the author are included. The one in ms. B was carried out, in all probability, by the Italian Renaissance painter Antonio Pisanello or by one of his disciples. Oswald's songs encompass a large spectrum of themes and are remarkable by their idiosyncratic structure and content. Many of his songs are autobiographical in nature, although the term autobiography itself might be misleading since the poet does not abstain from irony and satire. His songs represent a combination of fact and fancy, and yet many aspects heretofore held to be fanciful have been corroborated over the last fifteen years. Practically unknown to us until about 1960, when literary scholarship rediscovered his lyric *oeuvre*, Oswald is now considered to be one of the greatest lyric poets of the late German Middle Ages. Some researchers even believe that he reflects early forms of the Renaissance in his work, as many deliberate self-references and a remarkable metapoetic discourse betray. The focus rests on himself, even when the poet laments his sad fate first at the hands of a disloyal mistress, then of angry peasant neighbors, and even of his duke, Friedrich IV of Tyrol (1382-1439).

The remarkable aspect about Oswald's work is the ease and technical perfection with which he employs the whole range of medieval lyric genres. His dawn songs are perhaps equalled only by Wolfram von Eschenbach. His crusade songs (*Kreuzlieder*) rival those of Hartmann von Aue and Albrecht von Johansdorf, and yet they display novel realistic elements and a sense of *curiositas,* such as when he has Italian sailors detail in their local dialect their passage from Venice to Palestine. His love songs (*Minnelieder*) contain all the major literary motives from the Middle Ages, but they reveal a more acute interest in sensuality. Oswald composed several *pastourella* in which women characters possess a much stronger voice than in those by the medieval troubadours. Vivacity and realism permeate his verses, and he does not shy away from openly discussing his feelings of sexual frustration, as in dawn song Kl 33, which portrays the singer lying in bed alone at night and lamenting the absence of his wife. Instead of the traditional *Minnedame* (courtly lady), the poet usually refers to Margareta von Schwangau, whom he had married in 1417.

Politics also play a major part in Oswald's work, although he discusses them from a very personal perspective. Oswald traversed large parts of Europe during his youth and served Emperor Sigismund as a diplomat and translator. Thus he came into contact with major political leaders of his time and was highly regarded by local and national governments as an advisor and lawyer. In several of his songs he claims to know ten languages and to have visited all parts of Europe and even some areas in the Near East (Kl 19, Kl 44).

As Oswald's songs of repentance and penitence, his Marian-songs (*Marien-lieder*) and songs of old age indicate, Oswald's work must still be placed within the Middle Ages. His social and political perspectives were closely modelled after the medieval *ordo* (Kl 112), and he vocally expressed his anger at the rise of the burghers with all their money (Kl 25). But irrespective of those traditional elements, Oswald did open up German lyric poetry to the Renaissance, even if his work does not at all show the signs of learned poetry typical for that period. His one reference to Petrarch does not prove his familiarity with him, and his open antagonism against Duke Friedrich IV of Tyrol, who successfully centralized government and subdue the independent landed gentry, places him within the context of conservative politics of his time. Oswald remains a complex figure. Depending on the perspective and methodology employed, modern interpreters have come up with very diverse opinions about his work. There is no doubt that Oswald introduced polyphony and aspects of the *Ars nova* into German lyric. He also excelled with his polyglot poetry and his amazing linguistic flexibility. His language represents a mix of both classical Middle High German and typical Tyrolian dialect (Ladinian). Much of his idiom has remained enigmatic, which again highlights his intellectual independence and modernity. It comes as no surprise that his reception was rather limited. Of his 132 (133?) songs and didactic poems, only ten were later copied by various editors and poets. They do not, however, represent his major literary texts and thus underline even more how little his contemporaries comprehended his work. Obviously Oswald perceived his songs as a medium for expressing himself and for coming to terms with his fears, hopes, anxieties, expectations, anger, and frustration. Thus the autobiographical aspect dominates his *oeuvre*, although it remains a literary device and does not allow us to see the historical personality behind the mirror of his language. This literary strategy connects Oswald with many other European lyric poets of his time, such as Charles d'Orléans (1394-1465), Thomas Hoccleve (1368/69-1425?/1450?), François Villon (c. 1431-c. 1463), Antonio Pucci (c. 1310-1388), Michel Beheim (1416-c. 1474), and others. At the same time, Oswald made extensive use of poetic texts from French, Flemish, and Italian sources. But he was also well aware of the German tradition of Walther von der Vogelweide, Neidhart, and Wolfram von Eschenbach. Some of his *contrafacta* are of extraordinary complexity both in musical and textual terms. He could be compared to Geoffrey Chaucer in regard to his literary versatility and scope of themes, strategies, devices, and images. Like Chaucer, Oswald reveals a number of affinities with the Renaissance, but demonstrates in the end that his true intellectual home was the later Middle Ages.

Hugo von Montfort

Hugo von Montfort does not equal Oswald in expressiveness or theme, but he stands on his own concerning his poetic awareness and interest in the literary process. As a representative of the Habsburgs, Hugo was one of the most important politicians in the Steiermark and Vorarlberg. We also know a great deal about his personal life, as a large number of historical documents attest to his activities and experiences as administrator and politician. Like Oswald, Hugo attended the

Council of Constance, although we do not know whether the two knew each other. It remains equally obscure what literary sources he used to create his lyric poetry. Recently, a link between one of his *Lieder* (songs) and the *Roman de la Rose* has been claimed, but apart from this thesis no direct evidence has been produced which would place Hugo either in the literary milieu of his own time or within the literary tradition of the *Minnesang*. Most of his songs are based on traditional themes and images; thus we hear the lonely lover lamenting his destiny, exchanging love letters with his mistress, or moralizing to his audience. An interesting aspect surfaces when Hugo addresses one of his wives (he was married three times) and thus makes clear that for him love is to be considered as marital love. Many of his forty poetic texts (songs, dances, didactic poetry [*Spruchgedichte*], et al.) are allegorical in tone and didactic in their content. Hugo is one of the first German poets to state that his songs came about through the help of a musician, Bürk Mangolt, who composed his melodies. In addition, Hugo displays a considerable fascination with his own learning process, thereby revealing his ability to read and write, these skills not always being a prerequisite for a songwriter at this time. Hugo's work has come down to us in a single manuscript; thus we must assume that he did not even experience the limited reception which Oswald von Wolkenstein enjoyed.

Heinrich Wittenwiler

Heinrich Wittenwiler's *Der Ring* also appears to have had limited success. Now, however, his peasant satire and encyclopedic work, composed either around 1400 or shortly after 1414, is considered to be a literary masterpiece. We can only speculate who the author was and what he intended with his work. He uses the colors red and green to show which parts of his work are to be taken seriously and which ones not, but the author either erred himself in his color distribution, or he deliberately tried to mislead his readers since the color lines often seem to be in the wrong place. Two historical references to a Wittenwiler have been discovered, but the one to a citizen of Constance, who was a learned lawyer, seems to be the most likely. The allusions to Swiss localities would make good sense, as does the cultural context of the city of Constance where the author would have found a more receptive audience for his work.

The *Ring* is based on a wide range of literary traditions, among which the Neidhart songs play a major role. Medieval encyclopedia such as the *Lucidarius*, Hugo von Trimberg's (1230/1240-after 1313) *Der Renner* (*The Runner*), and Ulrich Boner's (fl. 1324-1350) *Edelstein* (*The Jewel*) were influential as well. The narratives *Metzen hochzît* (*Metzen's Wedding*) and Wernher der Gartenaere's (fl. 1250) *Meier Helmbrecht* might also have been models upon which Wittenwiler built his satire.

The theme centers on the couple Bertschi Triefnas (Bertschi with the Dripping Nose) and his mistress Mätzli Rüerenzumph (Mätzli Touch the Penis), both peasants, who form a marital union. Along with the other members of their village they prove to be fools, committing foolish acts from the first wooing to the final wedding celebration. When a fight breaks out and all the people from Bertschi's village are killed, he alone survives when the opponents withdraw from their siege of his barn. Realizing his and the world's foolishness, Bertschi abandons his worldly existence and becomes a hermit in the Black Forest.

Many diverse aspects surface in this work. The author includes teachings on the knightly tournament, courtly love, marriage, raising children, Christian beliefs, warfare, and medicine, among others. But the practical application proves that people are not able to act in a rational manner because they are fools. The setting of the peasant world is only a thin veil for human existence in general. Grotesque aspects such as gluttony, sexual perversions, breaking of all kinds of taboos, and transgressions of social and ethical norms permeate this narrative which foreshadows, in a certain way, the Rabelaisian narrative and its obsession with enumerations, amplifications, and the total reflection of the world through poetic language. The final battle, completely unmotivated, contains a strong parody of traditional heroic epics as famous knights of the past, giants, and dwarfs participate on both sides. The *Ring*, however, proves to be a moralistic satire and a call to order in a world that has gone awry. It would be difficult to accept an interpretation of Bertschi as an anti-hero who illustrates a moral conversion. The poet aimed, rather, at portraying his reality in its totality, which might not be characterized as overtly pessimistic, although the ending is rather anarchical. Whether we can detect some elements of the Renaissance or of Nominalism in this narrative remains a question for debate. But the *Ring* unquestionably represents one of the major literary works of the early fifteenth century.

Johannes von Tepl

In *Der Ackermann aus Böhmen* (c. 1400/01), Johannes von Tepl's prose dialogue between Everyman and Death, some elements appear which Oswald von Wolkenstein and Hugo von Monfort also considered. Tepl, probably a disciple of the erudite Chancellor of Bohemia, Johann von Neumarkt, composed one of the most important early modern German prose texts. He started his career as a member of the Prague Chancellery, was appointed city notary of Saaz around 1373, and entered the same position for the Prager Neustadt in 1411, in all likelihood as Johann von Neumarkt's successor. Both Tepl and Neumarkt developed an intricate rhetorical style filled with alliterations, antithetical structures, rhythmical narrative, anaphora, nominal composita, verbal nouns, metaphors, amplifications, abbreviations, variations, and many others narrative techniques.

The immediate reason for writing the dialogue was allegedly, as Tepl claims, the death of his wife Margareta on August 1, 1400. A letter to his friend Petrus Rothers written many years later seems to suggest, however, that the *Ackermann* had been nothing more than a literary exercise to practice his rhetorical skills. And the debate between the poet (*Ackermann* is only a *nom de plume*) and Death seems to corroborate this statement. Death and Everyman argue over the value of life, marriage, love and death, but not until the middle of the text does the Ploughman begin to listen to Death's arguments. Up to that point the grieving husband excessively laments his wife's demise and praises her beauty and virtue. Death, in contrast, ridicules the Ploughman's earthly desires and value system. Death presents his function in life and illustrates the temporariness of human existence. His logical argumentation seems to assign him victory in this debate, as God himself proclaims at the end, in the 33rd chapter: "Therefore, complainant, I bestow honor on you! Death, you have won because every person is obliged to give his life to death, his body to the earth, and the soul to me."

Contrary to older scholarship, however, a different view of this narrative is possible. Certainly death displays his superior intellectual abilities and ridicules Everyman's call for revenge, his laments about his wife's death, and his demands that his young wife should have been exempted from natural law. But death also espouses a very medieval view that all joy is followed by sorrow (ch. 12), that death in the early years prevents one from suffering from old age (ch. 14), and that life is nothing but a function of death (chs. 20 and 22). The Ackermann, on the contrary, reveals a novel admiration for marital life; he adulates his beloved wife, he insists on the value of human existence, and is, in clear opposition to Death, willing to overcome his pains and to listen to his opponent's arguments (ch. 19). And against Death's appeal to exert moderation in his love for life and to understand human mortality, the Ackermann embarks on a glorious and triumphant defense of human dignity, both in its earthly form and as God's creation (ch. 25).

At this point Death has lost the debate because he cannot argue against this claim. Whereas before he had requested from the Ackermann that he exert his intellect and rationality in understanding Death's role in life, from now on he denigrates human science and knowledge, and scoffs at the seven arts, thus undermining his own defense, which had initially been founded on those very criteria. Even his criticism of marriage is met with bitter opposition by his enemy who quotes Boethius as the highest authority (ch. 29). But the Ackermann's strongest point rests in his argument that Death in itself is nothing but the total negation of all existence. Once life disappears, death would also no longer exist (ch. 31). Although God then intervenes in favor of Death, the actual winner remains the Ploughman.

Aeneas Sylvius Piccolomini

The promising development of the Bohemian Renaissance, of which the *Ackermann* was a remarkable representative, soon suffered a complete defeat, however, in the Hussite Wars. The only observable continuity of the cultural world of Prague rested in the passing on of the imperial administration to the Viennese chancellery of the Habsburg family where Aeneas Sylvius Piccolomini, later Pope

Pius II, was active after the middle of the fifteenth century. He mediated between Italy and Germany and was directly responsible, in 1451/52, for the first lectures on classical authors at the University of Vienna and for the appointment of Peter Luder at the University of Heidelberg in 1456 as a teacher of *studia humanitatis*. Piccolomini had a particular influence on the Esslingen town-clerk Niklas von Wyle who collected his letters and published them in 1478 as a monument to humanistic thinking.

Niklas von Wyle

Born in Bremgarten in the Swiss canton of Aargau, near Zurich, Niklas von Wyle soon emerged as a leading poet in the German south and southwest. He profited considerably from his close relationship with the Countess Mechthild of Austria (1418/19-1482) who established during her widowhood an important literary circle at her castle in Rottenburg near Tübingen. His appointment as chancellor in 1469 by the Duke of Württemberg also heightened his awareness of international cultural developments, of the Renaissance, and of humanism in general. Among his friends were Gregor von Heimburg and Felix Hemmerlin (1388-1458), not to mention Aeneas Sylvius Piccolomini. Wyle's major contribution to German literature consists of his translations from Latin texts (*Translatzen*) written by Italian poets such as Boccaccio, Aeneas Sylvius, and Poggio Bracciolini, and even one German, Hemmerlin. Among their themes are love, whether an old man should marry again, the virtues of a *pater familias*, the value of humanistic studies, happiness and misfortune, and nobility. In his prologue to the *Translatzen*, Wyle develops, for the first time in the history of late medieval German literature, a theory of translation. He strongly favored a close word-by-word rendering of the original into German because the use of the classical Latin by his contemporaries in Italy was to be favored over the crude German. Niklas also translated Piccolomini's novella *Eurialus and Lucretia*, which was one of the most popular texts of its time.

Heinrich Steinhöwel

In contrast to Wyle, his contemporary Heinrich Steinhöwel (1412-1482) favored a translation technique which aimed at the meaning of a sentence or a word, not at a literal rendering. His translations include Boccaccio's novellas *Griseldis* and *Guiscardo and Sigismunda*, his *De claribus mulieribus* as *Von den sinnrychen erluchten Wyben* (*Of the Ingenious and Famous Women* [1473]), and, above all, Aesop's (c. 620-560 B.C.) and the Spaniard Petrus Alphonsus's (d. 1106) fables, and Poggio Bracciolini's (1380-1459) *Fazetie*. Interestingly, Steinhöwel was a medical doctor and practiced his profession after 1450 in Ulm, where he gained both wealth and a great reputation for his art.

Boccaccio's *Decamerone*

An intriguing character is hiding behind the pseudonym Arigo (Italian for Henry) who translated the complete *Decamerone* by Boccaccio and edited it in 1472 or 1473 in Ulm. His work did not receive the attention that one might expect, but he succeeded in introducing the Italian Renaissance poet to a German audience, although a sustained reception did not begin until a new edition of the work appeared in 1535.

Albrecht von Eyb

Albrecht von Eyb (1420-1475) was another major literary figure. From an old noble family, Eyb was a university-trained lawyer and canon in Eichstätt, Bamberg, and Würzburg. After a residence of more than fifteen years in Italy, he facilitated the transmission of Renaissance texts to Germany. His major literary achievement was the *Ehebüchlein* (*Little Book on Marriage*), published in Nuremberg in 1472, which enjoyed considerable popularity and was reprinted many times. In contrast to typical Renaissance treatises and poems on the same subject matter, Eyb espoused a rather bourgeois ideology, favoring marital love over free love, and thus defended the morality of the urban burghers. However, in one of his earliest texts, *Tractatus de speciositate Barbarae puellulae* (*Treatise on the Physical Beauty of the Young Girl Barbara* [1452]), the author stressed an eroticism freed of bourgeois moral considerations. The *Ehebüchlein* revoked his earlier theses and argued for the rite of marriage and for marital loyalty; it also defended women as supporters of their husbands, and added a number of practical recommendations for child raising and household economy, among others.

To illustrate his points Eyb included the legend of Griseldis, Marina, and a novella about Guiscardus and Sigismunda. In his *Spiegel der Sitten* (*Mirror of Manners*) from 1474, but not printed until 1511, he offered a florilegium of moral advice. Although Eyb again showed that he was rooted in medieval didacticism, he also appended prose translations of two comedies by Plautus, *Bacchides* and *Menaechmi*, and a German version of Ugolino da Pisa's comedy *Philogenia*, all of them rather erotic in tone and somewhat contrary to the original intention of his work. In one of his early Latin treatises *Oratio ad laudem et commendationem Bamberge ciuitatis* (*Oration and Encomium on the City of Bamberg* [1451/52]), Eyb clearly showed his indebtedness to his Renaissance teachers. A comparison of his text with those of his German predecessors and contemporaries reveals that Eyb possessed a new eye for his surroundings and knew how to appreciate life in a freer world.

Minor Poets

Much more traditional in style, themes, and ideological outlook are the minor poets such as Hermann von Sachsenheim (1366/69-1458), who wrote nostalgic chivalric romances such as *Die Mörin* (*The Black Woman* [1453]), *Der Goldene Tempel* (*The Golden Temple* [c. 1455]), *Des Spiegels Abenteuer* (*The Adventure of the Mirror* [c. 1452]), and *Das Schleiertüchlein* (*The Veil* [after 1453/55]); Jakob Püterich von Reichertshausen (1400-1469), who composed the significant *Ehren-brief* (*Letter of Honor* [1462]) in honor of Archduchess Mechthild of Austria, who resided in Rottenburg on the Neckar; and Ulrich Füetrer, a younger friend of Püterich, born c. 1420 in Landshut and a painter of coats of arms and furniture. He authored the *Buch der Abenteuer* (*Book of Adventures* [1490]) and a *Prosa-Lanzelot*. Whereas older scholarship mostly disregarded this type of literature, it has received new attention since the early 1980s and is now considered an interesting testimony to late medieval culture in German-speaking countries. Although few vestiges of Renaissance thinking can be discovered in these works, the authors dealt with themselves as authors in a highly sophisticated manner and thus transformed their seemingly old-fashioned and ridiculously amplified chivalric texts into literary media for a self-reflexive process. The amount of literary texts re-utilized and re-fashioned by Füetrer, for instance, and the enormously complex nature of *Buch der Abenteuer* leave us as modern readers rather baffled, but it does not allow us to denigrate it as inferior simply because the author only looks back to the Middle Ages and not further to Antiquity. One possible avenue for the interpretation of this type of romance may lie in the viewpoint that these authors did not distinguish between history as fact and literature as fancy, and thus sought to combine both as glorious manifestations of medieval chivalry, which still could be evoked at a time when a whole culture was quickly disappearing and the bourgeoisie emerging as a threat to chivalry and to the aristocracy in general.

The Court

Not surprisingly, several major courts emerged where traditional poetry was strongly supported. Whereas Niklas von Wyle, Heinrich Steinhöwel, and Albrecht von Eyb gathered at the court of Mechthild of Austria, Georg von Ehingen (1428-1508), Konrad Stürtzel (1433/35-1508/09), and Hermann von Sachsenheim were more or less connected with the court of Duke Sigismund of Tyrol in Innsbruck, and Johann Hartlieb (c. 1400-1468), who wrote mostly *Fachprosa*, that is scientific and scholarly texts on astronomy, hagiography, and mnemonic techniques, with the court in Munich. Johannes von Soest (1448-1506) composed his works, such as an autobiography and an adventure novel, *Die Kinder von Limburg* (*The Children of Limburg*), in Heidelberg at the court of Friedrich the Victorious (der Siegreiche [1425-1476]).

Another center of late medieval courtly literature was the court of Elisabeth von Nassau-Saarbrücken. After the death of her husband she assumed the government from 1429 to 1438. She had close familial ties with the courts in Heidelberg, Rottenburg, and Nancy, France, and thus stood at the forefront of the French-German literary exchanges of the fifteenth century. Elisabeth translated several French *Chansons de geste* into German prose, such as *Herpin* (c. 1437), *Sibille* (c. 1437), *Loher und Maller* (before 1437), and *Huge Schepel* (1437). All of these works deal with Charlemagne and his battles against the Arabs, unjustly accused women, and with love affairs. In contrast to the medieval versions of these texts, Elisabeth infused them with a considerable degree of realism and a sense of human limitations and of rationality. Often the heroes experience an unfair destiny, and fighting back against their misfortunes they regain their previous status in life and find happiness. The combination of traditional and modern elements made these works very popular among both the aristocratic and bourgeois audiences. Almost all of Elisabeth's romances found entrance to chapbooks (*Volksbücher*) and thus continued to be read for a long time thereafter.

Eleonore of Austria (1433-1480), wife of Duke Sigismund of Tyrol, allegedly translated the French *Pontus and Sidonia* (version A). It is a model romance that paints the picture of an ideal couple that is supposed to represent the duke and his wife. The identity of the translator and author has been questioned, however, and also the character of Sigismund's court as a literary center.

Chapbooks

Romances or *Volksbücher* (chap-books), or *histori*, as the authors often called them, proved to be extremely popular and quickly found their way to the printing press. Among them we find Thüring von Ringoltingen's (1415-1483) 1456 translation of the French *Melusine* (c. 1401-1405) by Couldrette from Poitou. Later, the work was repeatedly reprinted and soon became a popular literary text; even Goethe referred to it in his autobiography *Dichtung und Wahrheit* (*Poetry and Truth*). The anonymous *Fortunatus* was of equal importance; it was first printed in 1509 in Augsburg. Like the *Faustbuch*, this is one of the few German chapbooks that was not based on foreign literary sources. In turn, it was

Illustration for the Magelone *Volksbuch*

often copied and imitated by English, French, Spanish, Italian, Polish, and other

Ein kurtzweilig lefen von Dyl
Dlenfpiegel gebore oß dem land zů Buupßwick. Wie
er fein leben volbracht hatt, ycvi. feiner gef.hichreit.

Titlepage of Till Eulenspiegel
chapbook

Slavic writers in the sixteenth, seventeenth, and eighteenth centuries. It is also the first work in German literature where the topic of money and its impact on the destiny of the individual plays a major role.

In 1527, Veit Warbeck (c. 1490-1534) composed *Magelone*, also based on a French source, which told the saga of Bishop Maguelone near Montpelier in southern France. Other *Volksbücher* included *Reineke Fuchs* from 1498, *Wilhelm von Österreich*, *Tristrant und Isalde*, *Wigalois*, *Ernst von Bayern*, *Florio und Bianceflora*, *Barbarossa*, *Olivier und Artus*, and *Haimonskinder*. Some were based on medieval subjects and even followed them quite closely; others used French and Italian sources, and still others relied on Greek and Latin texts which had become familiar throughout Europe during the Renaissance.

In the category of chapbook belong some of the famous adventure stories of fools and jesters, such as *Lalebuch* (*Schildbürger* [*Gothamites*]) and *Till Eulenspiegel*. The latter, probably written about 1500, might have been the work of the Braunschweig author Hermann Bote, as recent scholarship has pointed out, but the attribution remains somewhat disputed. It stands firmly in the tradition of such jester literature as the Stricker's (fl. 1215-1250) *Pfaffe Amîs*, Franco Sacchetti's (c. 1335-1400) *Trecento novelle*, and Poggio Bracciolini's *Fazetie*. In *Till Eulenspiegel* (c. 1500), however, the focus of the narrative rests on the life of one protagonist and the many tricks he played on people. Many of the episodes strongly satirize the false use of words and language, attack false intellectuals, pretentious behavior, arrogance, and social (dis)order, and make fun of all sorts of various social classes. The hero Till Eulenspiegel creates chaos but never leads in the criticism of the economic and political structures of his time. He is no social revolutionary, nor do his pranks have specifically sexual overtones; they do, however, often border on the scatological. Till rebels against many taboos, but does not point the way towards a better comprehension of our world. The reader is nevertheless led to sympathize with him and to laugh at those whom he has fooled. Despite being rooted in the literary tradition of jester literature, most of the short chapters in the book are based on original material. The reception of this work was enormous and in fact continues today. In 1895 Richard Strauß created a tone poem based on Till Eulenspiegel, and the number of modern German editions, not to speak of the numerous translations around the world, reaches into the hundreds.

Faust

Perhaps best known among German literary texts from the sixteenth century is the anonymous *Volksbuch Historia vom D[r]. Johann Fausten, dem weitbeschreyten Zauberer vnd Schwartzkünstler* (*History of Dr. John Faustus, the Well-known Sorcerer and Magician*), published by Johann Spies in Frankfurt in 1587. There is some historical truth to the text because a Dr. Faust, an alchemist and natural scientist, did indeed exist in the sixteenth century, but the chapbook also continues the tradition of "devil-literature" popular during the Reformation. Dr. Johann Faust lived from c. 1480 until c. 1540. He was

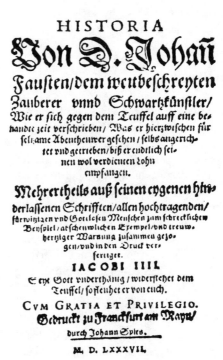

Titlepage of the *Faustus* Chapbook

the son of a Württemberg peasant and achieved fame as a medical doctor, astrologer, fortune-teller, and magician. According to the testimony of Luther, Erasmus, Melanchthon, and other humanists, he was well known all over Germany. In the *Historia* Faust receives his doctorate degree in Wittenberg and sets out to explore all parts of heaven and earth. He concludes a pact with the devil and experiences with his help all aspects of learning and study; he even visits hell, sees all the major cities and countries of Europe — here the text closely follows Hartmut

Schedel's *Weltchronik* (*World Chronicle* [1493]) — ridicules the Pope, presents a lecture on Homer at the University of Wittenberg, and has classical heroes appear live in the lecture hall. The devil even helps him rediscover the comedies of Plautus and Terence and thus quite unwillingly supports the development of modern philology. At the end, however, in a surprising and horrifying analogy to Christ's Passion, Faust dies at the hands of the devil, after having said good-bye to his students and celebrated the Eucharist with them. Enigmatically, he calls himself both a good and a bad Christian because he repents his acts, but he does not believe in his rescue through God.

The *Volksbuch* was soon imitated by Georg Rudolf Widmann (1599), and Johann Nikolaus Pfitzer (1674), and dramatized by Christopher Marlowe (before 1593). English comedians presented a theater version on their many tours through the mainland in the seventeenth century. The fascination with the subject is evident in later centuries in works by such writers as Goethe, Heine, Lenau, and Thomas Mann, just to name some.

Maximilian I

Maximilian I, crowned German Emperor in 1493, represents one of the last major writers of the later Middle Ages. He attempted to introduce reforms in administration, law, finances, and the military which would help Germany recapture a sense of political unity and regain its position as the center of medieval Europe. But despite many attempts to establish a glorious court in Vienna, no major breakthrough in intellectual spheres was achieved, the general political quagmire continued, and along with it the disintegration of the Empire.

Maximilian was called the last knight because he attempted to restore a past chivalric glory. His influence and inspiration were great, but in the end he left nearly all of his major projects unfinished. Several of his writings document his restless activities and cultural ambitions. Beginning in the 1490s he undertook a project in the form of an autobiography for which he received extensive help from a large group of hired artists, writers, and scribes. In this *Weißkuning* (*The White King*) he included 251 woodcuts and other illustrations, but it remained a fragment. It did not appear in print until 1775. In this work the Emperor depicts himself as a new Messiah who was eventually to overcome the Turks — a lifelong dream which he could never realize. Although designed as an autobiography, Maximilian composed, with the help of his staff, an allegorical description of his family and its history, of the political events of his time, and of his dream to solve the problems of his generation. He might have been familiar with Karl IV's Latin autobiography, and he certainly tried to combine traditional and humanistic aspects in his work.

Another fragmentary autobiography was the Emperor's *Freydal*, also a courtly depiction of the author's life as a young man; also autobiographical in nature was *Theuerdank*, from 1517, his only completed work. 118 superb woodcuts by, among others, Hans Burgkmaier the Elder (1472-1531) and Leonhard Beck (c. 1480-1542) enrich this unique bibliophilic masterpiece in which the protagonist, Maximilian himself, again in the form of an allegory, strives for the hand of his lady Ehrenreich (full of honor), but initially every time he embarks on his journey to visit her he encounters dangers and has to defend himself, ultimately never reaching his goal. Behind the figure of the lady stands Mary of Burgundy, Maximilian's wife; the enemies are Fürwittig (juvenile impetuosity), Unfalo (misfortune), and Neidelhart (envy), each of whom leads Maximilian into life-threatening adventures (in the sense of medieval courtly epics). Finally, he overcomes all hindrances, reaches the court of his lady, and marries her. The allegorical text has to be read as a statement on how threatening the world had become for the sixteenth-century individual. Fortune determined daily life, and no rational approach could prevent disasters (cf. the chapbook *Fortunatus*). Maximilian is said to have compared himself with Christ insofar as he claimed that no man since Christ had suffered as much. The dangers which the hero encounters represent separate stages of his life from youth to old age, and each time God intervenes to rescue him from his dilemmas because he is the chosen one. Interestingly, no medieval monsters, dwarfs, or giants appear in this work. The figures of one devil and one angel, apart from the allegorical opponents who are personifications of vices and dangers in real life, remind us of the fictional character of *Theuerdank*. The considerable number of editions of this book after the Emperor's death in 1519 demonstrates its extensive popularity. Even Goethe, in *Götz von Berlichingen* (1771), was to mention *Theuerdank* as worthwhile reading material.

Sebastian Brant

In 1494, a few years before Maximilian's autobiographies appeared, one of the most influential writers of the late Middle Ages, Sebastian Brant (c. 1457-1521), a highly respected city clerk in Strasbourg, composed his *Narrenschiff* (*Ship of Fools*). The humanists of southwest Germany greeted the Alsatian work with great enthusiasm, and a broader reading audience responded very positively as well. We know of thirty editions of the work before 1630, and it was translated into almost all major European languages. Brant had studied law in Basel and strongly defended the political unity of the German Empire. He received considerable inspiration from thinkers and writers such as Johannes Heynlin von Stein (c.1428/31-1496), Geiler von Kaisersberg (1445-1510), Johannes Trithemius (1462-1516), and Jakob Wimpfeling (1450-1528). When Basel separated from the Empire in 1499, Brant returned to Strasbourg where he soon began his political activities as imperial councillor. Emperor Maximilian liked to receive advice from him and summoned him to Vienna on several occasions. Brant supported the development of a centralized government in Germany and its hegemony in Europe, although to no avail.

The *Narrenschiff* consists of 114 chapters which contain a broad array of comments on people, attitudes, ideas, costumes, habits, vices and virtues, death, morality, usury, indolence, sloth, women, star-gazing, marriage, God, dancing, begging, etc., all written in blunt, rhymed verse. Brant perceived fools everywhere, and every social class reveals the many fools among its ranks. The *Narrenschiff* is not so much a satire as a social critique of misbehavior, vices, wrongdoing, and moral shortcomings. Judges are reminded of God's own Day of Judgement (ch. 2), and greedy people of the true purpose of wealth, that is, to give alms and to help the poor and thus to honor God (ch. 3). Brant admonishes his readers that God will exert His power as eternal judge and will not let mercy take the place of justice (chs. 8 and 14). Although wealth counts here on Earth, it will not help the rich enter heaven (ch. 17). Referring to Cicero (106-43 B.C.), Demosthenes (c. 385-322 B.C.), and Aeschines (389-314 B.C.), he advises his neighbors to guard their tongue and not to be loquacious in the manner of fools (ch. 19). Brant often relies on his knowledge of classical antiquity and recommends that his contemporaries heed the examples from that age. He ridicules the medieval university system and scholasticism as useless babble. Students should study seriously, and teachers should apply common sense to what they pass on to their students (ch. 27). Parents should be model examples to their children (ch. 49), and fallen women should be heeded by men, although Brant tempers contemporary misogyny by reminding his readers that there are good women as well (ch. 64).

The *Narrenschiff* has heretofore often been labelled an indiscriminate collection of moral advice, but more recent scholarship has discerned that Brant closely followed classical models by Horace (65-8 B.C.) and particularly Juvenal (c. 60-c. 140), and the rules they established for writing satirical texts. Brant's contemporary Johannes Trithemius, Abbot of Spondheim, even called the *Narrenschiff* a *Divina Satyra*, and it was often recommended for school use. The major emphasis rests in the teaching of wisdom to those who are willing to listen and to approach God after being admonished. At the same time, Brant is not simply a religious writer; he follows rather the lead of humanists all over Europe, copying textual strategies from classical antiquity and adapting classical lore to current conditions. This characterizes him certainly as a humanist, but his treatise remains medieval in style, subject matter, and morality as well. Its contemporary popularity can be deduced from the fact, for instance, that Geiler von Kaisersberg preached on several chapters of the *Narrenschiff* in Strasbourg in 1498/99. Many of the woodcuts accompanying the text were carried out by Albrecht Dürer and other leading masters of the time, thus enhancing its popularity.

Late Medieval Poetry

Before we turn to the age of the Reformation we need to focus on some of the lyric poets of the fifteenth century. Although modern philologists have almost exclusively concentrated on Oswald von Wolkenstein, Hugo von Montfort, and the Monk of Salzburg, there was a great number of lesser poets active throughout the later Middle Ages whose work represents to a great degree the culture of their time.

Most of them were city dwellers and wrote about military, political, religious, and amorous topics. By the fifteenth century many nobles had relocated to the cities, and thus we find both aristocrats and bourgeois among the poets. The genre of *Volkslied* (Folksong), in which themes of general concern could be expressed, developed at this time.

We have, for the first time in the Middle Ages, a plethora of *Liedersammlungen* (song collections) and *Liederbücher* (songbooks) such as *Limburger Chronik, Sterzinger Miszellaneenhandschrift, Mondsee-Wiener Liederhandschrift, Lochamer Liederbuch, Augsburger Liederbuch, Liederbuch der Klara Hätzlerin, Frankfurter Liederbuch, Glogauer Liederbuch,* and *Rostocker Liederbuch.* This interest in the lyric genre continued well into the sixteenth century when, for instance, Aegidius Tschudi (1505-1572), a Swiss historian and politician, collected historical songs in his *Chronicon Helveticum (Swiss Chronicle* [before 1556]). The song was a practical medium for the illiterate audience to participate in the political and military events and thus fulfilled more or less the function of modern newspapers in disseminating information. The *Liederbücher* were, furthermore, a testimony of the degree to which aristocratic poetry had become palatable to a bourgeois, patrician, and even rural population. The *Rostocker Liederbuch,* for instance, mainly written in 1465 for the University of Rostock, contained, apart from traditional *Minnelieder,* Latin verse, religious poetry, and several poems by Oswald von Wolkenstein and the Monk of Salzburg. In the famous *Liederbuch der Klara Hätzlerin* (1471) we find lyrical pieces such as dawn songs, spring- and winter-songs, didactic verses, and wine- and eating-songs.

Michel Beheim

One of the more prolific lyric poets of the later fifteenth century was Michel Beheim (1416-c. 1474), a precursor of the *Meistersänger.* Neither a court poet in the traditional sense, nor an urban citizen, he wandered from one court to the other throughout his life, crisscrossing Germany and Austria. His songs are mostly *Sangsprüche* (song-poetry), that is, rhymed chronicles, accounts of his life, political reports and reflections, descriptions of warfare, religious meditations, moralistic admonishments, idealizations of marital love, and satirical and ironic pieces. Apart from various chronicles such as the *Buch von den Wienern (Book about the Viennese),* he wrote an extensive historical poem about the cruel Woiwod Vlad II Drakul (1386-1434), and about the sieges of Vienna and Trieste. He also alluded to Jan Hus, Johann Hunyadi (c. 1385-1456), Sultan Mehmed II (1430-1481), and the war of the Palatinate in his *Pfälzische Reimchronik (Rhymed Chronicle of the War of the Palatinate* [after 1471]). Beheim tried his hand at virtually all traditional lyric genres and displayed an amazing facility in composing verse while discussing a wide range of topics. In writing poetry he assumed the roles of the poet as artist, philosopher, teacher, and theologian. Many of his works were set to music. Although not touched by any Renaissance thought, and far from humanistic learning, Beheim impresses us in his lyrical *oeuvre* by his considerable self-consciousness as poet and by his critical self-reflection.

Hans Rosenplüt

The other important fifteenth-century poet who has been largely ignored is Hans Rosenplüt (c. 1400-c. 1470). We do not know whether his name is a pseudonym for Hans Schneperer (or vice versa), or whether he deliberately changed his name once he had established himself as a craftsman in Nuremberg. He emerged, in his role as poet, as a leading spokesperson for his city and found wide reception in more than sixty manuscripts and early prints. The breadth of his literary work is considerable. It includes *Fastnachtspiele (Shrovetide plays)*, *Spruchgedichte* (didactic poetry), *Priameln* (short didactic poems), *Schwänke* (a type of *fabliau*), political and moralistic poetry, and the remarkable *Lobspruch auf Nürnberg (Encomium on Nuremberg)*. Rosenplüt was one of the first to defend Jews against the anti-Semitism of his fellow-citizens (*Die fünfzehn Klagen* [*The Fifteen Laments*]) and took the side of the peasants against the nobility (*Müßiggänger* [*The Loafer*]). Similarly, poor people are represented in his poetry, although this endangered his own position in the city where the patricians exerted a tight censorship. In *Die Lerche und die Nachtigall* (*The Lark and the Nightingale*) the poet ridicules the cultivated lifestyle of the rich and the aristocracy; he intensifies this criticism in his Shrovetide plays *Ritterspiel* (*Chivalric Game*), *Fastnachtspiel von Kaiser und Ritter* (*Shrovetide Play of the Emperor and the Knight*), and in *Des Türken Fastnachtspiel* (*The Turk's Shrove-Tide Play*).

In many of his songs Rosenplüt attacked the various enemies of the city of Nuremberg and glorified its military successes. But he also witnessed the pitiable defeat of the German imperial armies by the Hussites and warned his contemporaries of the imminent danger of the Turks attacking southeastern Europe. Rosenplüt did not call for a social utopia or for a revolution against the city government, but he used his free speech to highlight social failures, squalor, and poverty within the city. In his political poetry he displays a remarkable identification with the imperial city (one that is subject only to the Emperor) and its urban community. Similar to Beheim, Rosenplüt proves to be a strongly self-conscious poet who explicitly deals with his own art and his position as poet within the city.

Comparable also to Sebastian Brant's *Narrenschiff*, his many *Schwänke* (facetious stories with a moral) deal with virtues and vices and portray his compatriots' shortcomings and foolish behavior. Some of them contain strong sexual and scatological undertones, but this was not at all unusual for the later Middle Ages. Rosenplüt is considered to be the creator of the epigrammatic genre of *Priameln*, short poems of four lines in which the speaker jokingly discusses problems of political and moral nature. It is characterized by the combination of contrary terms and thus reveals the faults in society.

Meistersänger

With the rise of the cities in the thirteenth and fourteenth centuries, a new group of poets emerged whom we call *Meistersänger*. Their *Meistergesang* experienced its widest expansion in the sixteenth century and had its major centers in such cities as Augsburg, Nuremberg, Ulm, and Memmingen, but it also extended to Austria, Silesia, Danzig, Hesse, even to Switzerland.

Meistergesang arose from lay fraternities whose members were trained by clerics in the seven liberal arts and sang at funerals and public events. From the beginning, new participants were recruited from the guilds, and soon the art of the *Meistersänger* was considered to be the highest skill among all the crafts. Accordingly, the competitive singing was organized in concordance with the guild-structures. One challenger would initiate the event with his song, which was then judged by his fellow singers and the audience. The highest criteria for their art was the following of strict rules of composition. In the fourteenth and early fifteenth centuries the *Meistersänger* closely imitated the melodies provided by the twelve medieval masters: Frauenlob, Regenbogen, Mügeln, Walther von der Vogelweide, Wolfram von Eschenbach, Reinmar the Elder, the Marner, Klingsor, the Chancellor, Boppe, Stolle, and Heinrich von Ofterdingen. In order to become a master, one had to pass through various stages of the *Meistersänger* guild. Initially the music was borrowed from the Gregorian chant, but new melodies were then invented and set down as strict models for all singers. Later, after a decisive reform around 1480 by the Nuremberg poet Hans Folz (1435/40-1513), only those singers who were able to invent their own *Ton* (melody) were called *Meister* (master).

The entire song was called *Bar* and had to consist of at least three stanzas, called *Gesätz*. The rhyme scheme was the *Gebänd*, and the musical form the *Ton*, which again was divided into two identically structured stanzas (*Aufgesang*) and a third differently organized stanza (*Abgesang*). The exact counting of syllables per verse was of particular importance and only changed in the seventeenth century when the natural stress of the syllables gained preponderance. The texts of the *Meistersänger* were not allowed to be printed, but they have come down to us in large quantities of manuscripts. Although traditional scholarship has largely condemned the *Meistergesang*, we are today aware of its considerable socio-political function in the burgeoning cities of the later Middle Ages. The musical character of the *Meisterlieder* does not appeal to us chiefly because the natural stress of language has been lost (the verse structure is called *Knittel*), but it would be inappropriate to use the term "epigonal" for this large body of literature which reveals little influence from humanism. Instead, it relied heavily on the Bible and the medieval seven liberal arts. The *Meistersänger* perceived their art as an expression of a divine confirmation of the guild members, their theological and secular training, and their ideal way of living. In this sense *Meistergesang* is a social expression and a mode of self-assertion and has to be evaluated by social and historical criteria, less by aesthetic literary ideals from the twelfth and thirteenth centuries, let alone from the eighteenth and nineteenth.

Hans Sachs

The most important *Meistersänger* were Hans Folz (c. 1450-c. 1515), Lienhard Nunnenpeck (d. c. 1515), Sixt Beckmesser (c. 1500-c. 1539), Ulrich Wiest (fl. 1450), Onoferus Schwarzenbach (d. 1574), and, above all, Hans Sachs (1494-1576). Sachs, a shoemaker by profession, learned the art of singing from Nunnenpeck and travelled widely in Bavaria, Franconia, and the Rhineland. Beginning with the *Meistergesang* "Gloria patria: lob und ehr" ("Glory to the Fatherland: Praise and Honor") in 1514, Sachs produced a massive body of literary texts (c. 6,169 items) which included practically all medieval genres and revealed an amazing breadth of topics garnered from the Bible, classical antiquity, and from medieval and contemporary literature. Sachs considered his roughly 4,200 *Meisterlieder* as his main achievement, whereas modern scholarship deems such *Fastnachtspiele* as *Der farend Schüler ins Paradeiss* (*The Itinerant Student who Goes to Paradise* [1550], *Das heiss eysen* (*The Hot Iron* [1551]), or *Der baur in dem fegfewer* (*The Peasant in Purgatory* [1552]) to be his best works. His dramas, that is, tragedies and comedies, on the other hand, seem to have relevance only in conjunction with the Reformation and its reception among the urban population. But whereas Sachs could follow literary tradition in his Shrovetide plays, he entered a completely new field with his dramas and can be credited with inventing or rather recreating this genre in the German language.

In 1520 Sachs stopped all poetic productivity for about three years, after which he published the religious dawn song *Die Wittembergisch Nachtigall* (*The Wittenberg Nightingale*), openly praising Martin Luther for his reformist activities and condemning the representatives of the Church of Rome for its moral decline. In his four *Prosadialoge* (1524) he expressed his fervent support of the Reformation. In *Disputation zwischen einem Chorherrn und Schuhmacher* (*Dispute between a Prebendary and a Shoemaker*), for instance, the craftsman proves that an ordinary lay person can be much more capable of grasping the truth of the Bible by actually reading it than a prebendary who relies on scholastic learning and ignores the study of Scripture. With wit and undeniable logic the lay person ridicules the cleric and thus shows to the public that the Church has outlived itself.

In his many other works Sachs adapted a wide range of themes from classical antiquity and the Italian Renaissance. He had become familiar with Boccaccio's *Decamerone* through Steinhöwel's translation and helped to popularized the work in Germany. He was also familiar with the writings of Plautus, Terence, Ulrich von Hutten (1488-1523), and Reuchlin, and a number of humanists and Latin poets of his time. The *Schwank*, a witty and short genre, proved to be his favorite literary genre and one in which he excelled. His themes centered on his contemporaries' foolishness and naivete, as in *Das Schlauraffenland* (*Fool's Paradise* [1530]), *Sanct*

Peter mit der gaiss (*Saint Peter with the Goat* [1555]), and *Der Bauer mit dem bodenlosen sack* (*The Peasant with the Bottomless Bag* [1563]). There is little political or erotic material in his work, either because he avoided it deliberately or because the Nuremberg city government suppressed any form of free speech after 1527.

In a certain sense Sachs's work sums up the late Middle Ages, and yet it was also the starting point for modern German literature, since the poet lived in Nuremberg where humanists such as Willibald Pirckheimer (1470-1530), sculptors such as Adam Kraft (c. 1455/60-1509) and Peter Vischer (c. 1460-1529), and, above all, the painter Albrecht Dürer resided. Whereas the Baroque poets tended to ignore him, he did receive attention from Christian Thomasius (1655-1728), Johann Christoph Gottsched (1700-1766), and, above all, from Goethe and Friedrich Schiller (1759-1805), who admired his wit and language skills. Goethe employed Sachs's *Knittelvers* in portions of *Faust*, as did Schiller in *Wallenstein*.

Martin Luther

Martin Luther certainly deserves a central position within the literary history of the sixteenth century. Not only did he translate both the New (1522) and the Old Testament (1534), thus laying the foundation for the Protestant Church as well as the development of the New High German language, but because he also composed a large body of church songs and other literary texts. Initially Luther was hesitant in pronouncing a new church as such and was bypassed by the social revolutionary Thomas Müntzer (c. 1490-1525) in his outline of a German liturgy (*Deutsches Kirchenamt* [*German Church and Ministry*]). In 1523, however, when Luther heard of two Belgian reformers who had been burned at the stake, he took to the pen and published a famous poem, a unique

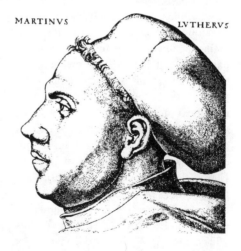

MARTINVS   LVTHERVS

paean to the Reformation, "Eyn newes lied wyr heben an" ("Here Shall be Begun"), in which he combined the religious message with the genre of the broadsheet. Instead of praising the two victims, Luther claims their death to be symbolic of God the Son himself who was persecuted by the Roman Church. Many more songs were to follow which soon formed an integral part of the church service, not supplanting the sermon, but serving as a literary medium for confession, announcements, and praise of God. The most famous of Luther's thirty-six church songs is probably his "Ein feste Burg ist unser Gott" ("A Mighty Fortress is Our God") from c. 1527 or 1529, which in the nineteenth century Heinrich Heine (1797-1856) labelled the "Marseillaise of the Reformation." With few exceptions, almost all of Luther's songs are translations, rephrasings, or expansions of older models. He relied heavily on the Bible, such as in his songs based on Psalms. In "Aus tiefer Not schrei ich zu dir" ("From Trouble Deep I Cry to Thee") he formulated an expressive image of the believer searching for God. Luther's success rests in his simple language, intense earnestness, and heartfelt piety, as in his masterpiece of hymnal poetry, "Von himel hoch da kom ich her" ("From Heaven High I Come to You"), from c. 1524.

Luther's *Tischreden* (*Table Talks*) and his many letters both in Latin and German are remarkable in their straightforwardness and wit. Of great importance are his theoretical essays, published in the form of pamphlets: *An den Christlichen Adel deutscher Nation* (*To the Christian Nobility of the German Nation*), his Latin treatise *De captivitate Babylonica ecclesiae praeludium* (*Prelude to the Babylonian Captivity of the Church*), and *Von der Freiheit eines Christenmenschen* (*The Freedom of a Christian*), all from 1520.

In *Sendbrief von Dolmetschen* (*On Translating: An Open Letter*) from 1530, and *Summarien uber die Psalmen, Und ursachen des dolmetschen* (*A Defense of Translation of the Psalms*) from 1533, Luther outlined his basic principles of translation. Luther's contribution to the development of German literature remains, however, to be fully investigated, particularly if his writings are not seen exclusively from a religious-historical point of view. Luther deeply influenced the development of the drama, the fable, the proverb, and the church song. He was often rivalled in his Bible translations, especially by Catholic writers such as Berthold von Henneberg (d. 1549), Thomas Murner (1475-1537), with whom he carried on a famous feud in numerous polemics, Hieronymus Emser (1478-1527), Georg Witzel, and Johann Eck (1484-1543), but his work continued to

be the most influential source of the intellectual, religious, and literary development in Germany for centuries to come.

Women Writers

In the wake of the Reformation emerged a number of women poets who argued both for and against the Reformation. Some of them composed poetry, but most of them employed the prose essay or the broadsheet to defend their case. The best known were Argula von Grumbach (1492-c. 1563), Katharina Zell (1497/98-1562), and Caritas Pirckheimer (1466-1532). We know much too little of women's literature in the late Middle Ages in Germany, but it is certain that within a short period female authors gained access to the book market and were widely read in southern and southwestern Germany. Margarete Peutinger (1481-1552), for instance, was known from her Latin treatises as *uxor docta* (learned wife), the reference being to her famous husband Conrad Peutinger (1465-1547); Magdalena Behaim (1555-1642), wife of the Nuremberg merchant Balthasar Paumgartner (1551-1600), exchanged a large number of remarkable letters with her husband while he was on business trips. Private in nature, they reveal a noteworthy woman writer of the sixteenth century. But apart from these few names, the history of German women's literature in the later Middle Ages still needs to be researched and written.

Georg Wickram

Georg Wickram (c. 1505-1554) founded the Colmar *Meistersängerschule* in 1549 and acquired for it the famous *Colmar Liederhandschrift*. In 1554 or 1555 he became city clerk of Burkheim. Wickram explored a very different field of German literature. In his collection of short stories (or novellas) *Das Rollwagenbüchlein* (*The Little Stage-Coach Book*) from 1555 he borrowed both from late medieval narratives and from the humanistic tradition of Boccaccio's *Decameron* and Poggio Bracciolini's *Fazetie*. The title itself indicates the purpose which Wickram pursued: to be of entertaining value for travellers. The majority of the stories deals with burghers and peasants and illustrates their lack of intelligence or how they are outsmarted by other people. Sometimes Wickram included events from his own environment, such as a horrible murder story (55). Sometimes we encounter a simple-minded person who proves his superior ability in handling a catastrophic situation, and this much better than his learned and noble fellow-travellers. In the 58th story a peasant is travelling on a ship during a dangerous storm. Whereas all the other passengers either cry or pray, the peasant takes a piece of bread and eats it along with a lot of salt. Asked after the storm why he did that, he explains that he intended to be sufficiently thirsty before they went under and he had to drink all the water. In other stories, where a strong anti-clericalism comes through, the protagonists often ridicule the rich and powerful. In a certain sense the *Rollwagenbüchlein* resembles Chaucer's *Canterbury Tales*, but Wickram is much more realistic and aimed almost exclusively at entertaining his readers. His stories remained very popular and were often reprinted, up to the middle of the seventeenth century. Other writers such as Jakob Frey (1556), Martinus Montanus (1557), Michael Lindener (1558), and Valentin Schumann (1559) imitated his model.

More importantly, however, Wickram composed a number of novels, dramas, and Shrovetide plays. He is remembered, above all, for such novels as *Ritter Galmy vss [=aus] Schottland* (*Knight Galmy from Scotland* [1539]), *Der jungen Knaben Spiegel* (*The Young Boys' Mirror* [1554]), *Gabriotto und Reinhard* (1551), *Von guten und bösen Nachbaurn* (*Of God and Evil Neighbors* [1554]), and *Der Goldfaden* (*The Golden Thread* [1557]). In contrast to other novels by contemporary writers, his works were composed rather independently of earlier models and followed the outlines for narrative fiction as developed by the humanists, especially Erasmus of Rotterdam. *Der Goldfaden* is considered to be the first freely invented prose novel in the history of German literature, and was adapted in 1808 by Clemens Brentano (1778-1842). Wickram combines, in all of his works, traditional concepts of love relationships with bourgeois motives. The medieval "ordeal" plays as much a part in *Ritter Galmy* as does in *Der Goldfaden* the late-medieval theme of a young hero of nobel descent who grows up among peasants, later finds his wife, a countess, and re-enters the world of nobility. *Der Knabenspiegel,* closely following the model of the Biblical Prodigal Son, presents the consequences of a virtuous yet idle and wasteful lifestyle. The loyal peasant boy Friedbert rises to the position of chancellor at the Prussian court, whereas the noble Wilbaldus loses his previous rank and has to work with pigs. Later he repents his evil lifestyle and is accepted back home, whereas his seducer Lottarius is hanged. In a sense, Wickram's heroes represent the emerging Protestant ethic since they can climb the social ladder if they work hard enough. Economic success is achieved through industriousness, parsimony, and mutual help (*Nachbaurn*). The author depicts a bourgeois world and idealizes its Protestant ethic. With Wickram the author becomes an educator for the general public.

Other Prose Works

Between 1569 and 1575 the successful printer Siegmund Feyerabendt (1528-1590) published in Frankfurt a German translation of the highly popular novel *Hystorien vom Amadis auß Frankreich* (*Tales of Amadis from France*) which was based on the Spanish *Amadis de Gaula,* which in turn had been adapted from an anonymous novel by Garci-Ordonnez de Montalvo in 1508. It had already been translated into French in 1540 and now began its triumphant march through Germany. The novel combines many medieval elements from *Lancelot, Pontus und Sidonia,* and *Floire und Blanscheflor.* In the tragic love story a multitude of narrative structures are interwoven and project a novel narrative cosmos in which lovers meet and lose each other, where sons strive for reunification with their families, and where knights and ladies fight for good against evil. Underlying *Amadis* is the emerging territorial and centralized court culture, an early stage of

the absolute monarchy with its typical seventeenth-century culture. The protagonists use the ceremonial language of the later Baroque courts and stress the
greatness of the ruler. This new ceremonial style was already evident at the court
of Maximilian I and had found expression in his autobiographies, and in other
novels such as *Magelone* or *Pontus und Sidonia*.

Johann Fischart

Another translation from a Romance language was Johann Fischart's (1546/47-
1590) *Geschichtsklitterung (Patchwork of History)*. Fischart was born in Mainz and
received a thorough humanistic education in Worms from Kaspar Scheidt (d. 1565),
who was himself a poet. He travelled all over western Europe, acquiring a wealth
of experience, an important source for his later literary works. While translating
François Rabelais's *Gargantua et Pantagruel* (1533-1553) into German in 1575,
Fischart created his own masterpiece. It quickly becomes clear that the French
model only serves as a literary vehicle for Fischart's own ideas. The German
Gargantua is about three times as long as the French and describes in the form of
a parody the growing up of the giant Gargantua who thoroughly enjoys grotesque
eating habits and transgressions of all sorts. The work is filled with sexual and
scatological elements, but the author worked hard to attain an amazing linguistic
artistry unprecedented in German literature. The stringent rules of behavior from
the world of chivalry are set aside, and the free enjoyment of lust, sensuality, and
orgies replaces the traditional world of virtues and vices.

The novel deals with the history of the giant Gargantua, son of King Grand-
goschier, his fight against King Bittergroll, and the founding of the abbey Willig-
muth. Following the plot is often made difficult by the seemingly endless chains
of words, descriptions, images, and references, later rivalled only by Jean Paul
(1763-1825) in his satirical texts. Borrowing linguistically from French, his local
Alsatian dialect, and other specialized idioms of German law and academia,
Fischart often erects word barriers that impede a simple understanding of his work,
which has some scholars believe that his true intention rests with language as such,
not with a narrative plot. The scene involving the drinking spree, for instance,
consisting in Rabelais of a few pages, is here expanded to thirty, on which nothing
is recorded but the shouts, exclamations, and language of a drunken party. The
critic Max Wehrli compares it with a piece of modern *poésie automatique*, but the
image of a linguistic carnival seems to be more fitting.

Some have labelled Fischart's *Geschichtsklitterung* a play with language, a play
in which all traditional values are parodied, satirized, and placed in a topsy-turvy
world. His work epitomizes *Grobianismus*, a form of literary crudeness deliberately
employed for the purpose of ridicule and parody. Although based on Rabelais's
Gargantua et Pantagruel, the *Geschichtsklitterung* is really a panorama of Fischart's time and culture and thus stands at the forefront of German literature in the
sixteenth century.

Other works from him include his satire against Jacob Rabe and the Jesuits, *Nacht Rab oder Nebelkrähe* (*Night Raven or Hooded Crow* [1570]), a collection of treatises by Plutarch, a dialogue by Erasmus, other fragments in German translation, *Philosophisches Ehezuchtbüchlein* (*Philosophical Book on Marital Discipline* [1578]), a German version of a Dutch Calvinist satire by Philipp Marnix, *Binenkorb des heyl[igen] römischen Imenschwarm* (*Beehive of the Holy Roman Swarm of Bees* [1579]), a narrative poem *Das glückhafft Schiff* (*The Fortunate Ship* [1576]), and other shorter works and translations.

Drama

The development of the drama illustrates well the phenomenon of continuity and diversity vis-à-vis the Middle Ages. Around 960, Hrotsvitha von Gandersheim was the first to write legendary dramas in which she adapted the models provided by Terence to express a Christian message. Goliards in the twelfth century continued this tradition, but they met with much criticism from the Church. From the beginning, however, the church service itself contained dramatic elements in its presentation of the Easter *tropus* and in the Christmas plays. The first play in the German vernacular was the Benediktbeuren Passion Play from around 1200. From the fourteenth and fifteenth centuries we have the plays *Theophilus*, *Das Spiel von den zehn Jungfrauen* (*The Play of the Ten Virgins* [first performed in 1322 in Erfurt]), and *Frau Jutta* (*Pope Joan* [c. 1480]). The drama gained strong momentum in the fourteenth century with Shrovetide Plays, and in the fifteenth century with Passion Plays from Tyrol and other parts of Austria, along with Christmas plays from Hesse. *Neidhartspiele*, which focus on the battle between a poor knight and boorish peasants, gained wide popularity in the south as well. Hans Sachs also adopted this subject. Many *Meistersänger*, such as Hans Rosenplüt, Hans Folz, and Niklaus Manuel tried their hand at dramas as well. Whereas the medieval drama can be called a collective enterprise in which sometimes the whole population took part, the Renaissance and Humanist dramas assumed a more individual character. In Riga, Burkard Waldis (c. 1490-c. 1556) composed *De Parabell vam vorlorn Szohn* (*Parable of the Prodigal Son*); Joachim Greff (c. 1510-c. 1550) produced a number of plays with biblical themes; and Tiebolt Gart's (d. after 1554) *Joseph* (1540) is considered one of the best Bible plays of the sixteenth century. The popularity of the religious plays lasted well into the seventeenth century. Other dramas, actually comedies, were written by Nicodemus Frischlin (1547-1590), Duke Heinrich Julius von Braunschweig (1564-1613), and Ludwig Hollonius (c. 1570-1621); Paul Rebhun (c. 1505-1546) composed many important Protestant school dramas.

Conclusion

The later Middle Ages and the Age of the Reformation did not end with these works, even though features of the coming era, the Baroque, are noticeable in them. As with many other literary and intellectual periods, the "New Age" did not begin in a certain year, and one can argue either in favor of continuity or of discontinuity. The hymn on life and on the human being as God's greatest creation, as developed by Johannes von Tepl in his *Ackermann*, was an early signal, but Hans Jacob Christoffel von Grimmelshausen's *Der abenteuerliche Simplicissimus* (*The Adventures of Simplicissimus* [1669]) would certainly suggest a turning away from idealizing human existence while lamenting the temporariness and frailty of human life. Similarly, Renaissance or humanism are concepts which are not easily pinned down to an age, a culture, a country, a poet, or to a literary work. Does familiarity with Petrarch, Boccaccio, and Poggio Bracciolini, to mention three names at random, immediately mark the poet or a work as belonging to the Renaissance? Hans Sachs was without doubt as aware of the power of the word as Johann Fischart, but they differ in degree to what end they employed language. Jörg Wickram obviously borrowed from Italian novellas, and Oswald von Wolkenstein referred specifically to Petrarch, and yet both are closer to the Middle Ages than to the Renaissance with regard to their style, outlook, and opinions regarding life, death, and a personal relationship with God. The Reformation unquestionably changed German literature, and the emergence of Baroque courts again heralded the coming of a new age. Yet popular literary motives continued to be borrowed from the Middle Ages, and the new genre of novels relied heavily on the Arthurian romances, the *Chanson-de-geste* cycles, and the *Matière de Bretagne*.

In general, we can confirm that literary productivity did not decline in the later Middle Ages, including the fifteenth and sixteenth centuries. Although scholarship has often ridiculed this literature as epigonal and secondary in quality, modern studies have revealed its considerable growth as literature and the importance of its writers. To measure the late Middle Ages with criteria garnered from an earlier age would lead to misconceptions and misinterpretations. Many of the poets whom we now consider superb representatives of their time, such as Oswald von Wolkenstein, Michel Beheim, and Hans Rosenplüt, as well as Sebastian Brant, Paul Rebhuhn, and Hans Fischart, have received adequate attention only in the last two decades. Many names remain hidden or still exist only in the footnotes of standard literary histories. It is quite likely, for instance, that future feminist critics will discover women authors from the fifteenth and sixteenth centuries of whom we know little or nothing at the moment.

Certainly, the Renaissance did not have the same chance in Germany as in other European countries, which is in part because of the Reformation, but also in part to a rich tradition independent of foreign sources. The large collections of short narratives for an urban audience, the renewal of chivalric romances, drama, and other religious texts, church songs, and historical and political songs are aspects of the tremendous variety which characterizes late medieval German literature. In this sense, John Huizinga's dictum of the "Waning of the Middle Ages" should not be heeded in a too dogmatic sense. To be sure, the Middle Ages gave way to the Age of the Reformation and Humanism, but the path through this transition period was paved with a large number of complex, sophisticated, and exquisitely embellished and structured literary works. Although the period cannot boast of a Wolfram von Eschenbach, Gottfried von Strasbourg, Walther von der Vogelweide, or Hartmann von Aue, we do find excellent writers such as Johannes von Tepl, Hans Sachs, Martin Luther, and Jörg Wickram. Obviously, a solitary group of four "classical" authors gave way to a large number of vocal, expressive, and literate poets who, among many others, make up the voices of a much louder choir than the Middle Ages had ever known.

4 Baroque

Judith P. Aikin

The literature produced in German-speaking areas in the seventeenth century, still usually referred to as "Baroque" in spite of criticism of the term, exhibits great variety and a progression of sub-styles within a fairly unified and easily discernable period style: highly graphic, rich in figurative language, a melding together of the traditional and the original, often even the bizarre. The seventeenth century saw a continuation of the proliferating production and dissemination of printed books to an ever widening audience of avid readers, but it should be pointed out that many texts, particularly those of a literary nature, continued to be appreciated orally and in a social context in a household, at a royal court, or in a salon, by a group of persons who listened to one of their members reading aloud. Additionally, many texts were designed to be sung, either as a performance or as a social activity (love songs, hymns and other religious meditations, chamber and grand operas). Even literary texts with a pictorial basis — common in this period — were probably shared by a group, a mode of reception which is delightfully documented in Georg Philipp Harsdörffer's (1607-1658) *Frauenzimmer-Gesprächspiele* (*Conversation Games for Women*) of 1644.

Martin Opitz and German Verse Reform

During the first decade of the seventeenth century, literature continued to exhibit a split personality: texts for the general reader, written in German, were rustic, often coarse, with a relaxed attitude toward versification, generic labels and generic characteristics, and stylistic levels; self-styled poets, those with literary pretensions, on the other hand, usually wrote in Latin and conformed to strict rules deriving from antiquity and from Neo-Latin poetic production in other areas of Europe. While a few poets were trying to write poetry with a more literary tone in the German vernacular (most notable is Georg Weckherlin [1584-1653]), the true breakthrough toward a vernacular poetry occurred in the *Buch von der Deutschen Poeterey* (*Book about German Poetics* [1624]) of Martin Opitz (1597-1639). In 1617 Opitz had already sounded the clarion call for a new vernacular literature in his *Aristarchus. Sive de contemptu linguae Teutonicae* (*Aristarchus, or On the Contempt for the German Language*) and had published some German-language poetry of his own. In this treatise he contributed to the new literary style primarily in three areas: verse reform, language building and cleansing, and genre definitions.

In the first quarter of the century German versification still depended almost exclusively on the sixteenth-century *Knittelvers* derived from folk usage — a verse

Opitz's influential poetic,
Buch von der deutschen Poeterey

form which normally counted four accented beats, but had complete freedom in the number and distribution of unaccented beats. An extreme example appears in a parody from mid-century, Andreas Gryphius's (1616-1664) comedy *Absurda Comica, Oder Herr Peter Squentz* (1658); of the title character's line "Dieses Spiel habe *ich*, Herr Peter *Squentz*, Schulmeister und Schreiber zu *Rum*pelskirchen, selber ge-*macht*," another character says, "This verse has an awful lot of feet." (I have emphasized the probable accents in a four-beat *Knittelvers* rendering.) Neo-Latin poetry, on the other hand — like French and Italian literature — based versification on syllable-counting and on rhythms of varying syllabic length. Opitz's breakthrough, derived from his study of contemporary Dutch literary theorists, consists in pointing out that the syllable-counting technique of the Romance literatures was at least as unsuccessful for the German language as the old *Knittelvers* had been. He follows the Dutch poets in basing German versification on the regular alternation of accented and unaccented syllables; the verse patterns he promotes, iambic and trochaic, are analogous to those of the same name in Latin or French, but take into account a basic difference in the sound systems of the languages. Thus the iambic Alexandrine verse Opitz suggests for epic poetry and for tragedy, derived from the French verse of the same name, is in German a line of six accented syllables (beats), each preceded by a single unaccented syllable, with either masculine or feminine end-rhyme, and with a caesura (pause) in the middle.

Opitz's *Buch von der Deutschen Poeterey* also addresses vocabulary, ornament, and tone. German language poetry, in his view, needed to go beyond the stylistic level of Martin Luther's (1483-1546) Bible translation (1522 ff.) — the implicit model for style previously — and create a new literary style. Thus he suggests that poets ought to create new words, not by borrowing them from other languages, but by manufacturing them out of existing German roots, suffixes, and prefixes, and particularly by uniting two (or more) roots in a compound word (he suggests "Hertzen-dieb" and "kriegs-blut-dürstig," heart-thief and war-blood-thirsty, for example). Opitz emphasizes that a literary language is not an unadorned language, but one which employs a variety of ornamental or "rhetorical" devices which can be divided into two major types: *tropes* (tropes, devices involving imagery) and *schemata* (figures, structural patterning). These devices are not new inventions of Opitz or of the seventeenth century, but instead derive from the poetic and rhetorical treatises of antiquity (especially Quintilian [c. 35-c. 100]) and the Renaissance. A list of the most frequently used rhetorical devices of German Baroque literature should help not only in evaluating individual literary texts, but also in understanding the aesthetic taste of the period.

Tropes: simile, metaphor, metonymy, synecdoche, hyperbole, ironia, litotes, periphrasis, personification, onomatopoeia, synaesthesia, oxymoron, tropical epitheton.

Figures: ellipsis, zeugma, isocolon, acrostichon, anagram, antithesis, inversion, enumeratio, paired synonyms, geminatio, reduplicatio, redditio, anaphora, and epiphora.

The last five figures, in particular, describe patterns: *geminatio* is the pairing of two instances of the same word, one right after the other, generally in the middle of a verse line; *reduplicatio* repeats a word or phrase at the end of one line and at the beginning of the next; *redditio* re-uses a word or phrase at the beginning and end of a single line; *anaphora* repeats a word or phrase at the beginning of two contiguous lines; and *epiphora* does the same at the end of two contiguous lines.

Opitz also addresses the question of stylistic level or tone. In general, he promotes an elevated tone for all texts with literary pretensions, but he also differentiates stylistic levels by genre according to a hierarchical schema. The most elevated tone is appropriate for epic poetry and tragedy, both of which deal with the deeds of persons of the highest social status; a more rustic tone belongs to the "lower" literary form dealing with the common people, comedy; satirical and pastoral poetry and lyric poetry have their own appropriate styles.

Opitz distinguishes the various standard literary genres not only by their appropriate stylistic levels, but also by their content and structure, thus offering simple rules for applying generic labels and for avoiding a mixture of generic types. One genre he defines and lauds, the heroic (verse) epic, never finds an author in Baroque Germany; another which he never mentions — probably because he does not consider it quite literary — is the novel, a genre which flourished during the period but which had to wait until late in the century for any theoretical acknowledgement of it as a literary genre with its own internal logic. Tragedy, comedy, and the various lyric forms defined by Opitz as literary genres, however, thrive throughout the period (as did a variety of mixed-genre forms which Opitz would probably not have been so pleased to see).

At least as important as the *Buch von der Deutschen Poeterey* in furthering the development of German Baroque literature were Opitz's translations from literary works in French, Italian, Latin, and Dutch which he viewed as models for similar original works in German. Chief among these, after the lyric poetry samples in his treatise and his poetry collections, are the Alexandrine tragedies from Sophocles's *Antigone* and Seneca's *The Trojan Women*, the prefaces of which further define their genre. He also translated two Italian opera libretti, *Daphne* and *Judith*, thus providing models for a fashionable new verse form, the madrigal or recitative. All of these translations by Opitz served as models for generic types, for an adorned German language, and for an elevated poetic style. Few literary works after 1625 show ignorance of, or disregard for, the norms established, in theory and in model texts, by Martin Opitz.

Historical Background

It is often said that the seventeenth century in German-speaking areas of Europe was a time of strife, uncertainty, and anxiety. In the wake of the Protestant Reformation and the Catholic Counter Reformation, uncertainty about religious truth on the one hand, and participation in various forms of spiritual extremism on the other, were to be expected. Religion colored all aspects of German culture: poetry, science, history-writing, musical forms. The religious divisions contributed to the dominant event of the first half of the century, the Thirty Years' War (1618-1648), during which time foreign (Spanish and Swedish) and German armies ranged over Germany, killing, plundering, destroying everything in their path. With the movement of armies and refugees, great epidemics also ravaged the land; the producer/consumer economy was disrupted, as were normal trade connections. No principality, no town, no landowner, no farmer, no individual could feel entirely secure about what tomorrow would bring. The second half of the century saw an end to the great war, but armed strife continued between various German principalities and with other nations, particularly France under Louis XIV (1638-1715). Furthermore, the Turks were once more advancing in the Balkans, conquering as they came; great battles were fought in Hungary in the 1660s, and by 1683 they would be at the very gates of Vienna.

Politically, there was no "Germany" in the seventeenth century, but instead a variety of political entities, large and small, ranging from the traditional and modern powers (the Holy Roman Empire and Prussia, respectively) to the dozens of tiny duchies and counties, plus the numerous semi-independent city-states. Then, too, the German-speaking area extended further east than it does today: dominant in the German-speaking cultural life of the time were Silesia (now in Poland) and Königsberg in East Prussia (now in the Soviet Union); German was also an important cultural language at the courts in Copenhagen and St. Petersburg (although Italian dominated as the language of culture in German-speaking Munich and Vienna). The old patriarchal feudal system was gradually giving way during this century to more centralized absolutistic forms of government in which a single prince did not share his power with lesser hereditary nobility, but instead rewarded educated bureaucrats to carry on the business of governing while he retained the reins of government in his own hands. The rigid social class system of the Middle Ages continued its metamorphosis into a more mobile system in which education and expertise could better be rewarded; it is from the rising upper middle class of educated public servants and professionals that most of the poets of the age derive. Many became teachers themselves in the burgeoning schools; others served as ministers, secretaries, librarians, or advisers to the princes, and their duties, implicitly or explicitly, included the provision of occasional and honorific poetry and perhaps plays for the various festive events celebrating the vitality of the ruler and his dynasty; some served similar functions for semi-independent municipalities like Nuremberg or Breslau. The poetic-minded among these schoolmen and civil servants banded together in societies for the advancement of the German language and German literature (*Sprachgesellschaften*, the most famous of which were the *Fruchtbringende Gesellschaft* in Saxony, the *Elbschwanen* in Hamburg, and the shepherds of the Pegnitz river [*Pegnesischer Blumenorden*] in Nuremberg.)

Authors of the German Baroque

Following in the footsteps of Martin Opitz, the other literary figures who dominate the Baroque period are the dramatists Andreas Gryphius, Daniel Casper von Lohenstein (1635-1683), and Christian Weise (1642-1708); the novelist Hans Jakob Christoffel von Grimmelshausen (c. 1621-1676); the pastoral poets of Nuremberg, especially Georg Philipp Harsdörffer (1607-1658), Sigmund von

Birken (1626-1681), and Johannes Klaj (1616-1656); the lyric poets Simon Dach
(1605-1659), Paul Fleming (1609-1640), Christian Hofmann von Hofmannswaldau
(1617-1679), and Caspar Stieler (1632-1707); and the religious and mystic poets
Friedrich von Spee (1591-1635), Catharina Regina von Greiffenberg (1633-1694),
Paul Gerhardt (1607-1676), and Angelus Silesius (= Johannes Scheffler [1624-
1677]). Andreas Gryphius figures as one of the most important lyric and religious
poets, in addition to his place as foremost author of tragedies and comedies. In
recent years, much attention has been extended to the satirical novels of Johann
Beer (1655-1700) and to the courtly novels of Lohenstein, Duke Anton Ulrich von
Braunschweig-Lüneburg (1633-1714), and Philipp von Zesen (1619-1689), as well
as to the tragedies of Johann Christian Hallmann (c. 1640-1704 or 1716) and the
romantic comedies of Caspar Stieler. Brief biographies of most of these authors are
to be found in Roy Pascal's *German Literature in the Sixteenth and Seventeenth
Centuries* (see Books for Further Reading).

These German Baroque literary figures derive from the various classes in the
social hierarchy of the time, from prince to peasant, and in many ways their own
positions in the social hierarchy, together with the social class of the audience or
readership for which they designed their works, are more significant than any
biographical details from their individual lives. Yet brief biographies of several
representatives from each social class will provide useful background for an
understanding of the socially determined nature of the literary efforts of the period.
Furthermore, what is known about the lives of these poets can serve as typical
accounts of individuals caught in those chaotic times. Since, from this perspective,
the major figures did not necessarily lead the most interesting lives, this list will
be augmented by the addition of several poets whose lives were extraordinary or
who played significant roles in historical and cultural events. Following the usual
method of organization still traditional in the seventeenth century, these biographical vignettes will begin with the highest ranking aristocrats and proceed
downward through the social scale.

Duke Anton Ulrich von Braunschweig-Lüneburg, a younger son who was a
much more capable and talented individual than his elder brother, assisted his
brother with governance of the Duchy after their father's death in 1666, a situation
which was officially recognized in 1685 when he was made co-regent. He ruled
alone after his brother's death in 1704. His upbringing was typical of princely
houses: he had tutors of outstanding scholarly and literary reputation (Justus Schottel [1612-1676] and Birken), he participated in festive performances of the musical
dramas written by Schottel and set to music by his talented stepmother, Sophie
Elizabeth, and he travelled widely on his "grand tour" (his Parisian stay was
particularly influential for his own later literary production). He wrote pious poetry,
musical dramas and *"Sing-ballete,"* and immensely long courtly novels (*Aramena*
[1669-1673] and *Die römische Octavia* [1685-1707]). His conversion to
Catholicism late in life is thought to have been politically motivated. Among the
many poet-princes, he figures as both the most powerful politically and the most
talented and productive.

A number of women from the highest social classes — duchesses, countesses — produced literary works, although usually limited to pious (often pietist) lyric poetry. Typical were the countesses Ludaemilia Elizabetha von Schwarzburg-Rudolstadt (c. 1632-1672) and her sister-in-law Aemilia Juliana von Barby (1637-1692), who, together with their former tutor Ahasverus Fritzsch (1629-1701), formed a lay congregation modelled both on the secular *Sprachgesellschaften* and on the lay religious groups established by Philipp Jacob Spener (1635-1705), founder of German Pietism. The lesser noblewoman Catharina Regina von Greiffenberg (1633-1694), a pious Lutheran with mystical leanings in Counter Reformation Austria, lived through a period of religious persecution which, coupled with the suffering in her personal life (she was coerced into a marriage with her uncle she considered incestuous), is vividly reflected in her spiritual poetry. Near the end of her life, after the death of her husband, she found a congenial refuge in Nuremberg, where she was aided by her long-time literary patron and correspondent, Sigmund von Birken. She died there, an impoverished refugee, at the age of 61.

Andreas Gryphius suffered along with his upper middle class Lutheran family from the religious persecutions, dislocations, epidemics, and devastations of the Thirty Years' War. Like many Silesians, he studied at the University of Leiden in the Netherlands, which offered a calm harbor for intellectual and literary activity. His legal preparation there paved the way to a series of important positions in the government of his hometown and region. His poetic works — primarily sonnets and dramas — eloquently reflect the suffering and chaos of his life and times. Two younger Silesians, Daniel Casper von Lohenstein and Christian Hofmann von Hofmannswaldau, both from the educated patriciate in Breslau, similarly found careers in local and regional government, although their duties also took them on diplomatic missions to the imperial court in Vienna in the post-war period of negotiation and recovery.

The son of a town councillor and butcher, Martin Opitz is a typical example of the upward mobility of members of the middle class with outstanding talents. His academic successes as a classics scholar both in his home town, Bunzlau (Silesia), and in the higher schools in Frankfurt (an der Oder) and Heidelberg led him to positions with various powerful princes, both Catholic and Lutheran (Opitz himself seems to have abandoned the Lutheranism of his childhood for Calvinism). He travelled widely in Northern Europe as a diplomat and — probably — a spy. His death at the age of 42 from one of the plagues which periodically swept war-torn Germany cut short an immensely productive and influential output of literary and theoretical works. Somewhat similar is the life of Paul Fleming, son a Lutheran pastor. He studied medicine at the Universities of Leipzig and Leiden, but also entered diplomatic service. His travels in this capacity took him much farther than Opitz: Moscow and Persia. He, too, died young of an epidemic illness, just as he was about to settle down in Hamburg to pursue a medical career. His lyric poetry, some of it written as love letters to his two fiancées, was always a leisure-time activity.

Like Opitz of slightly lower social class origins, Caspar Stieler came from a long line of Lutheran pharmacists. His academic precociousness led him to study

law (and poetics) at various universities. However, his mischievous personality led
to his expulsion from one university (Giessen); a document gives the reasons as
dueling, resisting arrest, and escaping from custody. His university career was cut
short when he ran out of funds; he joined a Prussian army as a sort of secretary and
legal clerk for a period of time, then took positions as companion and guide to
various young gentlemen on the grand tour. In this way, he was able to finance
travels to Holland, Paris, Rome, and Switzerland which otherwise would have been
beyond the means of a son of a pharmacist. At one point, while in France, he again
had to enlist in an army in order to support himself, and he ended up as a prisoner-
of-war for several months. His visit to Rome included a papal audience, in spite of
his Lutheranism. Upon his return to his home town, he fell in love and, wishing to
find the means to marry and settle down, quickly finished his legal degree and
found a position as secretary to a small principality. His growing family forced him
to change employers frequently and to write profitable books of instruction on the
side, but he also produced a respectable body of poetry and dramatic works. The
death of his wife in childbed (with their seventh child) was so devastating that he
was rendered unfit to continue his work for nearly a year and lost an excellent
position. It took him several years to recover his spiritual equilibrium and financial
security, but by the end of his long life, he was able to support himself on the
royalties from his books.

     Johannes Klaj, born to a Lutheran family in Meissen, studied theology and
poetics in Wittenberg, but had to flee for religious and political reasons. He found
a refuge in Nuremberg, less touched by the war, and a patron in fellow poet Georg
Philipp Harsdörffer, who took the penniless young refugee under his wing. Klaj,
with the help of Harsdörffer, found employment first as a teacher, then as a pastor
in Nuremberg. Together with his patron and other Nuremberg poets, Klaj penned
much pastoral poetry. Most notable for his biography is the *Pegnesisches
Schaefergedicht*, a long mixed-genre narrative co-written with Harsdörffer, which
includes a pastoralized and fictionalized account of his flight and arrival in
Nuremberg.

     In Grimmelshausen we have the only major poet representative of the lower
classes: his father was a Protestant baker and innkeeper; some of his relatives were
apparently peasants. At the age of around fourteen he was carried off by soldiers
during a raid which destroyed his home; like many such conscripted laborers and
soldiers during the Thirty Years' War, the vicissitudes of the war pulled him first
to one side in the conflict, then to the other. He was entirely self-educated (an
indulgent superior having given him access to his library), but his intelligence
quickly gained him a more responsible and secure position as a regimental
secretary in the Imperial army. After war's end, he held various positions which
recognized his abilities. His great novel *Simplicissimus* (1669) is thought to contain
considerable autobiographical material. His conversion in 1669 to Catholicism
made official a tendency already clear in his earlier writings.

     The Baroque period and its authors are often delineated and distinguished
according to sub-periods (Early, High, and Late Baroque; First and Second Silesian
Schools), regional centers (Königsberg, Leipzig, Breslau, Nuremberg, Hamburg,

Dresden, Wolfenbüttel), stylistic level (*Kunsttragödie* [art tragedy] — as opposed to school drama or the melodramatic *Haupt- und Staats-Aktionen* (feature plays, often on political themes, of the itinerant professional theater), or religion (generally Protestant or Catholic, but designations such as Lutheran, Calvinist, Jesuit, Pietist, and Messianic may also have applications). Sometimes useful distinctions, such designations might tend to obscure or neglect the more important differences between individual poets, not to mention the cross-fertilization through travel and reading.

The political upheavals, societal changes, and resultant anxieties of the times influence the literary production in the Baroque in perhaps a more extreme manner than in many other historical periods. This impact is easily perceived in the antithetical themes which dominate the literary texts: war and peace, *carpe diem* and *vanitas*, earthly and heavenly love. Other characteristically paradoxical aspects of the literary production also echo this historical background: emphasis on traditional forms and imagery (topoi [topos = a motif reused over a long period by many poets]) coupled with a drive towards originality and experimentation; the equal emphasis placed on non-mimetic imitation (fiction, the non-realistic) and historical-biographical factuality; the question of subjectivity and conventionality for lyric poetry; the use of secular, even sexual imagery to describe the most intangible religious experiences; the dichotomy of literal and figurative (allegorical) levels of meaning in each literary text. Discussion of these themes and aspects can serve to characterize the concerns of the Baroque poets.

The Theme of War

Literary accounts of the sufferings of war are perhaps less numerous than might be expected, given the historical circumstances. Those poems and passages which do dwell on the horrors of war or plead for peace express an exhaustion of inner resources, but also a passionately proclaimed urgency to bring the conflict to an end. Andreas Gryphius's sonnet "Tränen des Vaterlandes/ anno 1636" ("Tears of the Fatherland, 1636") is perhaps the best known. After a generalization in the first line, "We are now totally — indeed more than totally — wiped out by armed combat" (the last word could also imply "overrun by armies"), the poet conjures up the horrors of war: the uncivilized and destructive conduct of the soldiers, the spilled blood flooding streets and ditches, the corpses clogging rivers and streams, the ruined and flaming buildings, the murders and rapes, and everywhere the deafening sounds of warfare. The three types of ruined buildings he names — fortifications, churches, and city halls — represent the destruction of the three kinds of authority and stability once to be found in Germany — military (in the sense of the old *Wehrstand*, the nobility), religious, and civil. Gryphius speaks for all Germans, Catholic and Protestant, as he laments, "Everywhere we turn, we see only fire, plague, and death, which pierce us to the heart." As he counts the years of continued bloodshed, he could not know that the three-times-six years of war leave another twelve to go! The poem is not merely the lament of a war-torn land, however, for the point the poet makes in the last three lines — the location of the *pointe* or summation of nearly every German sonnet of the seventeenth century — is that the worst result of the war is the loss by so many individuals of their chance for eternal bliss ("that so many have been forced to give up their eternal soul"). Perhaps an allusion to the fact that many were constrained at the point of the sword to convert to a different religion, this line may also be an observation on the effect of warfare on the behavior and the moral judgment of the individuals caught up in it.

A personal and detailed account of the war and its effect on an individual survives in the greatest (and best known, then as now) novel of the age, Grimmelshausen's *Simplicissimus*. The protagonist, Simplicius Simplicissimus, twice orphaned by the war, weaves his precarious way through the great events of his time, tossed back and forth between two armies and two allegiances, witness to countless horrendous and cruel actions and perpetrator of others less harmless only in degree, victim of man's inhumanity to man and conscienceless deceiver of himself and others. Perhaps the most memorable passages are the vivid and uncomfortably realistic portrayal of the destruction of the homestead when he was a boy (Book I, chpt. iv) and the fantastic dream of the tree representing the old German social hierarchy (*Ständebaum*) whose branches are filled with the representatives of the various social classes and military ranks, each fighting to climb to the top — always at the expense of another who must lose his grasp on a branch (Book I, chpts. xv-xviii). Thus Grimmelshausen depicts not only the horrors of war in its effect upon a single individual and his family, but also the ruinous influence of the long civil war on the social system and on the very moral fiber of the German people. Yet for the novelist, cessation of war alone is not the answer; it will also be necessary to revive the political, ethical, and religious ideals which have succumbed under the pressures of circumstance.

One of the many copperplates that contributed to the
popularity of *Simplicissimus*

Carpe Diem and *Vanitas*

Under the influence of the war and its aftermath, in the midst of the insecurities about physical and spiritual survival, the main thrust of German Baroque poetry is perhaps the concern with time and eternity, that is, with the stark contrast between the anxieties and insufficiencies of life on earth and the joys of eternal life in the hereafter, or — a related theme — the call to "seize the day," coupled with the acknowledgment that life is short, moments of happiness within it rare. The rich poetry on the *carpe diem* theme and, in much larger quantity and probably with greater emotional power, the body of poetry on the theme of the vanity and senselessness of human life and human concerns, dominate the poetry collections by individual authors even more than they do the anthologies of Baroque literature created by later scholars.

Representative for the *carpe diem* poetry of the period is Martin Opitz's song beginning "Ach Liebste, laß uns eilen. . . wir haben Zeit" ("O beloved, let us hurry — we have time"), in which he uses the threat of decay and aging as the rationale for enjoying love now. He lists the various "gifts of beauty" which are transient: the color of cheeks and hair, the sparkle in the eyes, the youthful shape of the mouth, the whiteness of the hands, youth itself. "Thus let us now enjoy the fruit of youth/ Ere we must pass away with the passing years," he urges. We have time, but time is short; thus let us make the most of it. In other poems Opitz proposes drink and song as answers to transience and the brevity of human life.

A more problematical example of a poem on the *carpe diem* theme is Christian Hofmann von Hofmannswaldau's "Die Wollust" ("Sensual Pleasure"). Most of the statements in this poem proclaim "seizing the day," indulging in sensual pleasure: "Lust, in spite of everything, remains the treat of earthly life," "the highest good of human existence." The final strophe seems adamant:

Anyone who doesn't consider Epicurus his teacher
has lost his love-of-life, and all his wits...
Such a person must be inhuman, a monster in this world.
While most teachers offer rules and suffering,
What Epicurus once taught still titillates the heart.

Yet the whole poem is suffused with a subtle irony: lust is the treat "dieser Zeit," of this kind of time, of the here-and-now; he who does not appreciate pleasure is a monster "dieser Welt," of this world, among those whose orientation is strictly worldly. The implication is always that in another time and another place — the hereafter — lust and pleasure count for nothing, and the one who rejects them, although unnatural and unusual in this life, will be welcomed in the next.

Thus the *carpe diem* theme is transformed here, and in most German Baroque poetry, into a statement on the transience and vanity of earthly existence coupled with the hope of attaining eternal life. Two sonnets by Andreas Gryphius are the finest expressions of the *vanitas* theme: "Menschliches Elende" ("Human Misery") and "Es ist alles eitel" ("Everything is Vanity"). In the first, Gryphius contemplates the meaninglessness of human activities and of earthly existence: in answer to the question he poses in the first line, "What are we human beings, anyway?", he responds with a list of metaphors for transience: a dwellingplace of horrible suffering, a ball tossed by inconstant Fortuna, a will-o'-the-wisp of this earthly existence, a stage set where bitter anxiety and cutting sorrow dominate the scene, snow soon melted, candles soon burned to the socket. Life is likened to chatter and jokes, to dreams, to a stream that flows on out of sight, to smoke in a brisk breeze. Those who die (those who have discarded the cloak that is the weak body, in Gryphius's circumlocution) are quickly forgotten; any who breathe must soon leave the air behind; those who come after us must follow us into the grave. In this poem Gryphius speaks to his readers, but also to himself: "we," "us" are the pronouns throughout, as "we" are the persons in need of his pronouncement on the transience of earthly life.

In the second poem, "Es ist alles eitel," Gryphius extends this theme of transience by contrast with what is lasting, and thus establishes the vanity of earthly concerns in the face of eternity and God. The poem begins with a generalization: "You see, wherever you look, only vanity on earth!" The poet then enumerates, in a series of contrasting scenes, examples of what "you," the reader, might be likely to see: what one man builds, another tears down; where cities stand today will eventually be a meadow where a shepherd boy frolics with his sheep; what blooms

Andreas Gryphius

will be trodden down; what strives and fights will soon be bones and ashes. "Nothing that exists is eternal — not even bronze or marble," the poet states, implying that even the monuments to great men and great deeds will decay and disappear; indeed, even the greatness will soon be put in doubt by events to come: "The fame of great deeds will fade like a dream./ How then can the plaything of time, the human being, be expected to live on?" He sums up the human condition and criticizes the behavior of his contemporaries: those things that concern us most today are as trivial and insubstantial as a shadow, as dust, as wind, and no one anymore contemplates what is eternal. In the course of this sonnet, Gryphius's pronouns metamorphose — he first addresses "you," the reader, then includes himself as he addresses "us"; at the end he generalizes to include all humankind. His poem is a sermon about the human condition and the behavior of his contemporaries, but it is addressed to the reader and, ultimately, even to himself, who also needs to hear this lesson.

Gryphius's concerns are echoed in innumerable poems by his contemporaries: Hofmannswaldau's "Die Welt" ("The World") adds these answers to the question wind, an exploding firework. Georg Philipp Harsdörffer's metaphors are similar in his "Das Leben des Menschen" ("Human Life"): seasonal foliage, dust in a wind, a flower, fragile glass, froth on a wave, a purchase which we soon regret.

Caritas and *Amor*

It may strike us as odd that the same period which produced so many literary texts on the themes of transience and vanity should also have been a time when sensual love poetry had its first flowering in German-language literature since the Middle Ages. Three light-hearted kissing poems are exemplary: Paul Fleming's "Wie er wolle geküsset sein" ("How He Would Like to Be Kissed"), Caspar Stieler's "Der Haß küsset ja nicht" ("Hate Doesn't Kiss"), and Hofmannswaldau's "Auf den Mund" ("On the Mouth"). Fleming instructs his innocent beloved in the art of kissing, Stieler celebrates the kiss his beloved has shared with him, Hofmannswaldau wittily pleads with his hard-hearted lady to be allowed to place a kiss upon her mouth, just as he has written a poem upon it (a pun on the title of the poem). In each the joy in (or hope for) reciprocal and physical love, the open pleasure in a sensual pastime, and the fun to be had in dwelling publically on a private activity all contribute to the conclusion that in these poems, in these moments, at least, this life, too, can be rewarding and sufficient.

The most witty of the sensual love lyrics, usually veiled pleas for sexual consummation, are often termed "galante Dichtung," gallant poetry. Much of the love poetry of Caspar Stieler, published in 1660 in his collection *Die Geharnschte Venus oder Liebeslieder im Kriege gedichtet* (*Venus in Armor, Love Poems Penned in Wartime*), can be seen in this light. An excellent example is his "Ehren-Griffe" ("Honor-Blots, literally "Honor-Touches"), which begins:

> Why do you jerk away
> When this my hand
> Wants to try its luck?
> Does it venture too far astray,
> Rosille, when it touches
> What you maidens keep covered up?

He offers all sorts of arguments to convince her that it is not improper for his hand to touch her everywhere. In the sixth strophe he finally mentions the concept in the title, now clearly a reference to the one part of her anatomy he most wishes to touch, euphemistically referred to as her "honor":

The skin loses nothing
And is not besmirched
Even if a finger ever
Wanders out across it.
No one will be able to tell
Whether the honor has been touched!

He then adds the twist: don't resist my touching your "honor," for after all a caress is minor compared to what will be done to it soon, by someone or something else.

Hofmannswaldau's "An Lauretten" ("To Lauretta") is one of his many contributions to gallant poetry. In the first strophe he urges:

Lauretta, are you always stone?
Shall your angelic beauty never
be coupled with some sympathy?
Come, come, unveil your lap
and let us both, unclothed and bare,
intertwine our souls and arms.

Each strophe evokes the sexual act, and the poem culminates in the climax and death-like collapse into satiation and oblivion — and the resultant pregnancy — in the second-to-the-last strophe. The final strophe veils an insult (the supposedly hard-hearted Lauretta is actually promiscuous) in its seeming praise: anyone who wishes to love you after this and hears of my "death" will say: "whoever collapses thus/ and dies in a cushioned lap/ has achieved a gentle death indeed."

Such overt sexuality, with its scarcely veiled double entendres, flourishes also in the *Heldenbriefe*, the *Heroic Letters* of Hofmannswaldau and Daniel Casper von Lohenstein, which tell the tales of famous lovers in world history; the scenes of explicit sexual encounters in Lohenstein's tragedies are equally frank, perhaps more provocative and lascivious in vocabulary, but lack the wit, irony, and humor to be found in the lyric poetry of Stieler and Hofmannswaldau.

Indeed, sexual imagery and sexual sensations are so powerful for the seventeenth-century German poet that they are also the stuff of the most ecstatic religious poetry, paradoxical though that may seem. Such poetry is often termed "Jesus-Minne" (Jesus-Love), and involves the female soul (soul, "die Seele," is feminine in German) wooing Jesus in language borrowed from the biblical *Song of Songs* or even from secular love poetry. Important exponents are the Jesuit Friedrich von Spee (e.g., "Die Gespons Jesu klaget ihren Herzenbrand," ["The Spouse of Jesus Laments Her Burning Passion"]) and Johannes Scheffler (= Angelus Silesius) in his "Heilige Seelen-Lust, Hirtenliedern der in ihren Jesum verliebte Psyche" ("Holy Joy of the Soul: Pastoral Love Songs of Psyche the Soul to Her Beloved Jesus"). One poem from the latter collection begins:

Title copperplate for Lohenstein's
monumental novel *Arminius*

May he kiss me with the kisses of his mouth
And nourish me with the fluid from his breasts,
For they taste sweeter than wine!
And his mouth
Makes at once
A soul to be joyful.

One is reminded of Giovanni Bernini's (1598-1680) contemporary sculptural depiction of the visionary ecstasy of St. Theresa of Avila as a woman in orgasmic posture with a cupid-like cherub standing over her, arrow poised to pierce her.

In most usages in German Baroque literature, of course, sensuality and earthly love instead signify an earthly orientation, as opposed to love of God, heavenly orientation: *amor* as opposed to *caritas*. This opposition is particularly clear in Gryphius's *Catharina von Georgien* (c. 1647), a martyr tragedy in which the title figure, a Christian queen, rejects the offer of marriage and earthly delight with her besotted Muslim captor in order to unite in spiritual marriage with her divine bridegroom, Jesus Christ — a union hastened by her acceptance of suffering and martyrdom. In the foreword to the reader, Gryphius provides this statement on the opposition of the two kinds of love: "Honor, death, and love compete in her heart for the victory, a victory won by love — not, to be sure, earthly and worthless love, but holy and eternal love — with the aid of death." These partners in her martyrdom, (spiritual) love and death, appear as personifications in the chorus of the fourth act, where each claims supremacy during an argument which culminates in stichomythic (epigrammatic) statements:

Death: What is stronger than death?
Love: Love takes the prize!
Death: Death puts an end to sorrow and suffering.
Love: Love provides the eternal crown of honor.
Death: Death brings everything to a close!
Love: Everything but love.
Death: He loves truly who loves until death;
Love: He who dies lovingly is untouched by death.

Catharina has successfully resisted the blandishments of earthly love, embracing a terrible death in order to express her love for Christ. The female protagonists in two plays by Lohenstein, on the other hand, *Cleopatra* (1661) and *Sophonisbe* (1680), are examples of illicit love, in that these two characters commit adultery as they use their sexual allure to manipulate political outcomes. Comparison with Shakespeare's treatment of Cleopatra in his *Antony and Cleopatra* (1623 [c. 1606]) makes it clear that Lohenstein finds far less to admire, and much more to abhor, in his heroines.

Not only the sensual side of earthly love, but even romantic love receives a critique from the pen of Andreas Gryphius. His *Cardenio und Celinde* (c. 1647), the tale of two unhappy lovers, could hardly be more different from Shakespeare's

Romeo and Juliet (1597 [c. 1595]). Cardenio loves Olympia, who, in spite of her love for him because of his youthful follies, marries his rival Lysander. Even as he seeks to kill Lysander and rendezvous with Olympia, Cardenio has a brief affair with Celinde and kills her lover — a Templar Knight — in a duel. Celinde, crazed with love for Cardenio, is informed by a witch that if she wishes to win Cardenio's regard, she will have to cut out the heart of her dead lover. In the tomb, as she prepares to do the grisly deed, she is confronted by the ghost of her lover and sinks to the floor in a faint. Cardenio is led into the tomb by an apparition he takes to be Olympia, and he, too, falls into a swoon as it metamorphoses into a skeleton. Both awake, recognize their sinful behavior and the unworthiness of their loves, and renounce romantic love and earthly concerns altogether. The romantic love of the ill-fated lovers Piramus and Thisbe in Gryphius's play-within-a-play in *Herr Peter Squentz* fares even worse: amateur players make a travesty of the tragic plot, thereby ridiculing the validity of romantic love. It is probable that *Herr Peter Squentz*, a short *satyra* or satyr play with plot and characters deriving indirectly, at least, from Shakespeare's *A Midsummernight's Dream* (1600 [c. 1595]), was intended to be performed following *Cardenio und Celinde*.

Yet this double attack on romantic love is rare in the seventeenth century, and even Gryphius contributes to a larger group of plays — heroic or "romantic" comedies — in which romantic love and the resulting marriage or reconciliation are elevated to allegorical ciphers for divine love and the *unio mystica* or mystic union with God often expressed as marriage to the eternal bridegroom, Christ. Typical of these girl-meets-boy, girl-loses-boy, girl-gets-boy-again plots with religious allegorical significance are Gryphius's double comedy *Verlibtes Gespenste/ Die gelibte Dornrose (Besotted Ghost/ Beloved Dornrose* [1661]), Stieler's *Die erfreuete Unschuld (Innocence Rewarded* [1666]) and *Der betrogene Betrug (Deceit Deceived* [1667]), and Weise's *Die triumphirende Keuschheit (Chastity Triumphant* [1668]). Romantic Comedies can also make political statements, laud princes, or even contain political allegories, as in Stieler's *Der Vermeinte Printz (The Supposed Prince* [1665]) and *Die Wittekinden (The Wittekinds* [1666]).

Religious Poetry

Religious poetry of the time exhibits an enormous variety of approaches, but two of these are perhaps most typical for the period, and also most distinct from the religious poetry of other centuries: 1) the meditation on an event or image, whether biblical or from everyday life, and 2) the mystical, usually paradoxical expression of the relationship to God or Christ. Representative of the first is Paul Gerhardt's hymn "An das Angesicht des Herrn Jesu" ("To the Visage of the Lord Jesus," better known by its first line, "O Haupt voll Blut und Wunden" ["O head with blood and wounds"]), used and made famous by Johann Sebastian Bach (1685-1750) as a chorale in his *St. Matthew Passion* of 1719. This text is a deeply empathetic meditation on the image of the face of the crucified Christ, addressed to the tortured head as if it were present and alive. Typically, the meditation begins with a detailed visualization of the subject: bleeding, wounded, crowned with a garland of thorns, spat upon, pale, the eyes dimmed, the cheeks and lips deprived of color. Then the hymn moves to the consequences to the poet/speaker/singer/congregation ("I myself was guilty of the sins for which you suffered"), thus personalizing and actualizing those distant events in Christian history. The hymn ends with a return to the vision of Christ's image and its place in the worshipper's life (and death):

Appear to me as my shield,
As consolation at my time of death,
And let me see the image
Of you crucified!
Then will I look to you,
then will I, filled with faith,
Press you to my heart:
Whoever dies thus, dies well.

Gryphius's meditations on Heaven and Hell in his two sonnets "Ewige Freude der Auserwählten" ("Heavenly Bliss of the Chosen") and "Die Hölle" ("Hell") are vicarious experiences of those two eternal realms, spoken from the point of view of a saved soul and a damned soul, respectively. The latter is particularly evocative, as its first strophe shows:

Sorrow and Misery!
Murder! Torture! Pain! Fear! Execution! Martyrdom! Worms! Plagues!
Hot Tar! Punishment! Hangman! Flames! Stench! Ghosts! Cold!
Trembling!
O faint away!

"Who can bear the pain?" cries the damned soul who speaks from the depths of the fiery pit to those still outside. He turns directly to his reader and instructs: "O Man, suffer there, in order not to suffer here!"

Everyday images, encountered in the course of an average day, can also evoke such meditation. A case in point is Sigmund von Birken's poem, "Wann du ein frisch Hemd/ oder etwas neues anziehest" ("When You Put on a Clean Shirt or New Garment"), which begins:

Lord, remove my old garment of sin
that I might be created a new man in your image.
Tear this one off, for it is of the earth.
The one you dress me in will last for eternity.

He asks for Jesus's "pure garment of sinlessness," and paradoxically notes that it is necessary to wash it in Christ's blood in order to remove the stains of sin. He thus relates a trivial detail of real life, putting on a fresh shirt, to the concept of the clean white garment worn by the soul at the Last Judgment (Revelation 3:4-5) in a meditation to be recited while getting dressed for the day.

At the other extreme are the mystical paradoxes of Angelus Silesius and the messianic rantings of Quirinus Kuhlmann (1651-1689). Johannes Scheffler, who took the name Angelus Silesius along with his vows (he was a Catholic convert and priest), is best known for his epigrammatic paradoxes on the nature of God. Several examples will suffice:

"The Noblest Prayer"

The noblest prayer is when the person praying
Becomes that in front of which he kneels.

"I am like God and God like me."

I am as large as God, He is as small as I:
He can't be above me, nor I below Him.

"God doesn't live without me."

I know that without me God can't live a moment;
if I am no more, He will have to give up His spirit.

"Man is Eternity."

I myself am eternity, when I leave time behind
and myself in God and God in myself combine.

Kuhlmann, who ultimately believed himself the Messiah as well as His prophet, combined the eternal bridegroom imagery with messianic views of world events in his ecstatic calls to participate in the Millennium.

Conventionality and Autobiographical Truth

One of the great questions about Baroque literature, especially lyric poetry, has always been whether the poets' voices are their own — whether their poetry is subjective, reflective of their inmost feelings, determined by autobiography as much as is (we assume) the lyric poetry of the period from the late eighteenth century to the present. To assume so on the basis that we expect as much of modern poets, that we now so define lyric poetry, is clearly fallacious, anachronistic. The evidence against such a view is compelling: Baroque poetry is tremendously derivative in the sense that it adheres to traditional images and structures for traditional subjects. Love poems, even declarations of love in drama, nearly always employ the Petrarchistic catalogue: the beloved has skin as white as alabaster or snow, eyes like stars, teeth like pearls, lips like coral, and so on. Names for the beloved woman derive from pastoral poetry (Marnia, Leonora, Lesbia, Anemone); the woman, like the proud cruel mistress of medieval poetry, is usually disinclined to listen sympathetically to the laments of the love-sick poet. Yet such topoi participate in the particular kind of originality which the aesthetic sense of the times demands: recombination and permutation, offering novelty and piquancy for each reuse. Thus Hofmannswaldau in his poems "Beschreibung vollkommener Schönheit" ("Description of Perfect Beauty") and "Vergänglichkeit der Schönheit" ("Transience of Beauty") uses the Petrarchistic catalogue ironically, in the former poem to contrast his lady's beauty with her cruelty, and in the latter to demonstrate in addition the worthlessness of beauty because of its eventual destruction by the passage of time. And Caspar Stieler, in his "Amor der Wiedertäufer" ("Cupid the Renamer"), excuses his variety of names for his beloved in a witty poem designed to laugh at his own use of a convention of love poetry. Yet, if we are to believe Stieler in this poem, there is always a real person behind each conventional usage (for him, his girlfriend Barbara, "Buschgen," even if he terms her Melinde, Rosilis, Mele, or Dorinde). The use of topoi, figures of speech, and rhetorical schemata should not necessarily be taken as an indication of a lack of real feeling, although in view of the contrast between two poems on the death of a beloved woman by David Schirmer (c. 1623-1683) (his "Marnia") and Caspar Stieler (his wife, Regina Sophie), it is hard to resist seeing the former as "merely" conventional, the latter as heartfelt. Schirmer's sonnet "Als seine Marnia gestorben" ("Upon the Death of his Marnia") dates from 1663:

O letter! O thunderbolt! my pretty love is gone.
What shall I do with myself? with myself, O with my poor self?
Who will sympathize with me tomorrow, as she was wont to do?
I shall die, I shall die, too, that I might be with her always.

Here you have, Marnia, here you have my mind.
Here you have my spirit, 'tis precious, 'tis still warm.
Here you have my courage. Here you have [my] pain and [my] lament.
Here you have me, yours entirely, you denizen of Heaven.

Out, heart, out, after her! Out! follow your beauty.
Out, soul, out, and upwards! Seek her charm.
Go to Elysium, and shorten there her hours.

This only is my consolation, this only my desire:
Even if you live not, Marnia, you still live on in me.
And even if I don't die now, I'll still die in you.

Schirmer's stuttering imitation of sobbing certainly saves his poem from the
ordinary, but the parallels and repetitions in the second and third strophes, together
with a classical allusion and a series of passionate outcries in succession to his dead
beloved, to his heart, and to his soul, seem contrived, and his paradoxical
consolation in the final strophe somehow falls flat. The stilted Alexandrine sonnet
form furthers the impression that the poem does not come from the heart. How
natural, in comparison, do the lines of Stieler to his deceased wife sound in his
"Madrigal" of 1676:

> My darling, you are slipping from my grasp
>   and leaving me alone
>   and my seven little ones
> Who are no less your own.
> We poor [survivors]; alas, most poor; remain here.
> O! take me along, my heart!
> Wait! I'm ready to follow.
> It's no use; she hears no more. Now, Sorrow!
> Enter here to take her place! Joy is dead.
> Let me and my seven little ones,
> Until we (alas, when will that be) meet again,
> Cry out our pain.

Stieler's madrigal, with its freer rhythms evocative of free verse, its scattered
rhymes, and its broken sentence structure, seems heartfelt in the modern sense. His
oblique allusion to the Orpheus myth, in which the singing poet follows his wife
into Hades in the attempt to rescue her, adds a dimension which the comparatively
vague reference to Elysium in the Schirmer poem fails to do.

Some poems are clearly based on personal experience. For example, in his
sonnets "An sich selbst" ("To Himself") and "Tränen in schwerer Krankheit"
("Lament in Time of Severe Illness"), Gryphius describes in realistic detail his
physical appearance and suffering during a serious illness. But in other poems he
blithely make statements which we know to be false. A famous example is
Gryphius's sonnet "Der Autor uber seinen Geburts-Tag den 29. September" ("The
Author on his Birthday, the 29th of September"). Gryphius was actually born
October 2, but in this poem claims September 29 since the patron saint of that day
is seen as especially helpful for a person with his particular worldview and
problems. Grimmelshausen's novel *Simplicissimus* is in part demonstrably based
on the author's early experiences, in part unrelated to his own life, and in part
totally unrealistic and improbable. The question of autobiographical veracity and
"real" feeling must remain open; yet it is probably desirable to ask anew of each
individual text of the period the extent to which it is "merely" conventional.

Tradition and Originality

Simply because Baroque aesthetics appreciated the use of topoi and other traditional elements does not mean that the period lacked innovation and originality. All across the German-speaking region, poets were exploring and experimenting with their language, but such innovative approaches reached their zenith between 1640 and 1680 in Nuremberg. The poets Georg Philipp Harsdörffer, Sigmund von Birken, and Johannes Klaj experimented with irregular forms, onomatopoeic nature poetry, and concrete poems (in the shape of a cross, a heart, an anvil, a garland); they merged narrative, dramatic, and lyric genres into a single form, the Pastoral; they wrote poems about writing poems; they combined poetry with music and the visual arts. Word-building, advised by Opitz, was even more dominant in their works than in those of most other poets of the time.

Another highly original poet was Catharina Regina von Greiffenberg, an Austrian Protestant whose devotional poetry is so ecstatic that it always seems to burst out of any traditional restraints. Her word-building is truly astonishing; her use of imagery, a mixture of the extraordinary and the everyday, is highly original. Her sonnets often lose their form, as eight-beat lines replace the normal Alexandrines, or as a poem which apparently begins as a sonnet overruns the limits and creates its own organic shape. Her "Uber das unaussprechliche Heilige Geistes-Eingeben" ("On the Inexpressible Holy Spirit-Infusion") is extremely difficult to translate:

You unseen flash, you dark-bright light,
You heart-filled power, yet ungraspable being.
There was something divine in my inmost being
That moved and aroused me: I feel a seldom light.

The soul does not itself to itself give light.
It is a miracle-wind, a spirit, a weaving being,
The eternal breath-force, itself the arch-being,
Which lights up in me this heaven-flaming light.

You color-mirror-glance, you wonder-multicolored shining!
You shimmer here and there, are unimaginably clear.
The spirit's dove-wingbeats are in the truth-sun shining.

The God-stirred pond is, even muddied, clear!
First the spirit-sun will shed upon the moon its shining,
The moonlight in turn is earthward also clear.

Using neologisms, striking compound nouns, unusual verbs and images, Greiffenberg expresses the inexpressible, gives concreteness to the ineffable in her poetry. Even as she uses a standard Baroque sonnet, she extends its limits: her refusal to use different words for end-rhyme, her repetition of key words, help to express the *unio mystica*, the mystic and absolute union of all things tangible and intangible in God.

Originality can also consist in the reduction of language, of a word or concept, to its lowest common denominator, at the same time that it expands its meanings to encompass both itself and its opposite, by the use of a conceit — an elaborate and bizarre play on words. Paul Fleming's "Gedancken über der Zeit" ("Thoughts above Time" — a pun on the conventional title, "Gedanken über die Zeit," "Thoughts about Time") is an excellent example. The poet begins, "You live in time and yet you know not time." In this eighteen-line poem, he uses the word *Zeit* seventeen times; each instance expands its field of meaning: finite time, earthly life, time passing, timelessness, eternity. Some lines resemble Silesius's paradoxes: "Time is something and nothing, humankind the same,/ Yet what that something and nothing is, no one can explain," or "Time dies within itself, and begets itself out of itself." Others employ inversion: "Time is what you are; you are what time is," "Man is in time; time is in man, too." All participate in a network of antithesis, contrast, paradox, and contradiction in order to illuminate the dual nature of that all-encompassing concept, and, by extension, of all that exists. This dual nature is perhaps the predominant structural characteristic of Baroque literature (and thought); it is also the underlying theme in most German Baroque texts, as life is confronted by death, time is opposed to timelessness, earthly concerns are relativized by juxtaposition with eternal values.

Emblem and Allegory

This dual nature, this perception of an underlying eternal significance for every historical event or thing, this intended double structure in the literary text in emulation of the biblical text, has been termed "allegorical" or "emblematic" in scholarship. The assumption is that each text conceals — and reveals to an observant reader — a hidden meaning which is likely to be religious or moral truth. In some cases, echoing a real political situation is instead the underlying purpose. The imbedding of one or more layers of hidden religious meaning in a secular-appearing text is usually accomplished by means of an analogy — events in the drama or novel parallel those of a biblical story or of the entire *Heilsgeschichte* (history of universal salvation) recounted in the Old and New Testaments. Seventeenth-century theory (particularly from the pen of Sigmund von Birken) makes it clear that contemporary poets intentionally structured their works in this way; pagan mythology, however, was also seen to hold such a hidden Christian truth. Birken's own discourse on the Daphne-myth in his *Programma Poeticarum* makes this clear: the nymph Daphne, who flees the amorous advances of Apollo and turns into an evergreen laurel tree just as he seizes her, is the human soul who, touched by her Eternal Bridegroom, Jesus Christ, becomes eternal. Grimmelshausen, at the beginning of his *Continuatio* to *Simplicissimus* (usually published as the sixth book and explicitly intended as commentary to help his readers discern the underlying religious meaning), uses two images which figure traditionally in explaining this dual nature of literary texts: the nut (the nourishing kernel is inside the shell) and the sugar-coated pill (the bitter-tasting medicine to cure the soul is inside).

One of the most productive ways to look at and describe the dual nature of Baroque literary texts is the emblematic perspective. An emblem — collections of them were very popular in the sixteenth and seventeenth centuries — consists of a motto (*subscriptio*), a mysterious picture (*pictura*), and an explanation (*explicatio*). This structure — imagery in need of, and often accompanied by, explication — can be seen to dominate Baroque literature. Most obvious is the tendency of Baroque works to carry two titles, one descriptive, the other explanatory or even interpretive (e.g., Catharina of Georgia, or Proven Constancy; The Armored Venus, or Love Poems penned in Wartime). The chorus of the Baroque tragedy has often been termed the *explicatio* of the *pictura* provided in the preceding act. Allusions to well known emblems may figure in poetic works as metaphors and incidences of intertextuality. Most novels and collections of shorter poetic texts have pictorial frontispieces, of which that for Grimmelshausen's *Simplicissimus* is probably the most intriguing (and most studied) example:

Frontispiece
Der abenteuerliche Simplicissimus Teutsch (1669)
Yale Collection of German Literature, Beinecke Library

Some poems likewise include an engraved image as part of the text; others are printed on the page in the shape of a dominant image (concrete poetry); still others reflect emblematic structure verbally.

Sigmund von Birken's poem in the shape of an inverted heart is a prime example of a concrete poem: (Body,/ pass away!/ The heart shall remain here./ I will inscribe its image/ in this tree bark./ What its outline contains,/ Zephir knows, who carries my sighs/ along with his. The sense that inflames me/ shall merge with me into a pointed flame.// Look here and read;/ the heart is/ itself the/ mouth.// Deeply is it divided;/ much deeper/ the/ wound.)

The poet, in the time-honored way of lovers, carves his words of love in the outline of a heart into the bark of a tree. But here the heart, a metaphor for love in the poem, becomes the dominant visual and verbal image. The shape of the heart is equated to a flame (which perhaps explains the inverted image, allowing the pointed, flame-like end to be on top), a traditional image for passion, then to a mouth (both for kissing and for lamenting). Finally, love's destructive power is revealed: the very shape of the heart, divided into two lobes, reveals the wound dealt it by love. Thus this poem borrows the union of image and lettering characteristic of graffiti in order to comment self-consciously on its own richness in (verbal) imagery and on the nature of the verbal expression of feelings.

Leib/
reise hin!
das Herz soll
hier verbleiben.
Jch will sein Bild in
diese Rinden schreiben.
was aber ist in selbes eingeprägt/
weiß Zephrus / der meine Seufzer trägt
Mit seinen hin. Der Sin/ der mich macht sroiße/
soll noch mit meinem eine Flamme spißen.
Schau hier u. lis;   Tief ists getheilt,
das Herz ist   viel tieffer
selbst der   ist die
Mund.   Wund.

From
Floridans des Pegnitzschäfers Niedersächsische Letze (1648)

One example of a totally verbal emblem is Georg Greflinger's "An eine vortreffliche, schöne und tugendbegabte Jungfrau" ("To an Excellent, Beautiful, and Virtuous Young Lady"). The first three strophes catalogue her physical beauty in Petrarchistic terms, beginning with the top of her head and moving, part by part, downward as far as her breasts: the *pictura*. The last two strophes offer both an *explicatio* (the poet identifies the image not as a living woman, but as a portrait bust — "life-like alabaster" — which forms a monument to her many virtues and to her effect upon the viewer) and a *subscriptio* (the last line and *pointe* of the poem, much like a placard placed on a portrait bust, states: "You have wrested my heart away from me."). Naturally, since a portrait bust has a heart of stone, the lady's virtue is well defended.

Similarly, Hofmannswaldau's sonnet "Auf den Einfall der Kirchen zu St. Elisabeth" ("On the Collapse of the Church of St. Elizabeth") begins with the vivid depiction of the falling church building in the two quatrains, then draws the moral in the tercets, beginning:

O man! This is a curse from Heaven above,
Which has struck this church and awakened your conscience.

He completes the emblem with a *subscriptio*:

If your heart is stone and your conscience dead,
Then these dead stones will have to be your teacher.

The ultimate in this dualistic structure is perhaps the tendency to combine an abstract concept with a concrete image in a compound noun or noun pair, as in *Gnadenfrucht* ([God's] Grace-Fruit) or *Schatten der Sünden* (Shadow of Sin). This dual nature of Baroque literary texts at every structural level, from the most detailed to the most general, provides, for example, that the dramatic plot of an imprisoned woman's acceptance of cruel martyrdom rather than marriage to her captor can signify, on another level, the sufferings of the soul in the captivity of the body and its release from earthly bonds at the hands of death. Or a novel about a boy who leaves behind the naive faith of his boyhood spent in the woods with a hermit to enter the world and experience its joys and sorrows, only to return to a utopian hermit's existence in old age, can signify the Fall of Mankind, the expulsion from the Garden of Eden, the earthly life of mortality and sin, and the entrance into Paradise at life's end. Such repetitive allegorization would be tedious indeed, were it not for the vivid concreteness of the images, the plots, and the scenes the Baroque authors conjure up for their readers: as in an emblem, the meaning underlying the picture is only one of the multiple elements structuring the whole. In any case, the seventeenth-century reader seems to have delighted in the process of decoding the texts, of uncovering the hidden meaning.

Perhaps because of the graphic realism and detailed historicity of the dramas and novels of the period, particularly, such texts contain "key" scenes — that is, scenes which are keys to the underlying meanings. At such points — usually choruses, a series of adages, dreams, or visions in drama, dreams or supernatural incidents in novels — the submerged *explicatio* emerges briefly, often as another and analogous *pictura* rather than as explication *per se*, then once again dips beneath the surface of the historical or quasihistorical events which form the plot. In *Simplicissimus* the most obvious of these "black holes in the text," as one might term these links between two very different dimensions, are the so-called "Ständebaum" scene (the dream of the tree in Book I), the words of the madman who thinks he is Jupiter (Book III, chpts. i to vi), and the Mummelsee episode (the hero visits a utopia at the center of earth where, despite lacking any possibility of an afterlife, the subhuman denizens worship God and practice virtue to an extent unknown by their human counterparts who would have so much more to gain, Book V, chpts. xii to xvi). While most of Gryphius's choruses in his tragedies seem to be strictly explanatory, some of Lohenstein's offer instead a second *pictura*; the audience or reader is to interpret each based on the perceived analogy between them (the best example is the "Hercules at the Crossroads" chorus in *Sophonisbe*).

Psychology and Human Nature

It is often asked what relation *Simplicissimus*, the story of a character who develops from the naive attitudes of early childhood to the wisdom of an old man, might have to the *Bildungsroman* (developmental novel). While there is some validity in seeing a parallel, that parallel is only superficial at best, for Simplicius Simplicissimus is a character without individual characteristics, truly a man without personal qualities, at least from our Post-Enlightenment perspective. For in the Baroque an individual is measured by the sum of his virtues and vices, by the worthiness, in short, of his soul as it appears at death before the Divine Judge. Thus Jakob Bidermann's (1578-1639) Jesuit play *Cenodoxus* (Latin 1602, German translation published 1635), culminates in scenes of Divine Judgment during which the protagonist, now merely called "the spirit," is accused before a Heavenly Tribunal, convicted of leading a sinful life, and sentenced to eternal hellfire. In the scenes leading up to this judgment, Cenodoxus was always accompanied by "characters" who were visible to him and to the audience, but not to the other persons in the play: his guardian angel, various demons, and personifications of his besetting sins (Hypocrisy and Self-Love). This fracturing of a single personality into representations of various aspects and potentialities is typical of psychological conceptions of the time; a similar device, in fact, occurs in *Simplicissimus* as the protagonist is flanked, in Books II to IV, by his two alter egos, Herzbruder and Olivier, the potential for good and the potential for evil, respectively. Indeed, Grimmelshausen's view, like that of his countryman Bidermann sixty years before, is that each person, "everyman," is a soul with freedom of the will, freedom to choose between good and evil. Unity of personality is irrelevant, and thus motivations and actions do not derive from a single personality, as they do in the plays of Shakespeare or Friedrich Schiller (1759-1805), but instead from the various fragmented and opposed aspects which flank, bedevil, or aid the soul during its sojourn on earth. Psychology in the seventeenth century, still focused on a religious, teleological view of human nature, was truly involved with the soul (*psyche*), not the personality, and thus the aspects we might take as individual characteristics were often passed over as unimportant.

Set up in opposition to the freedom of the will, to the freedom to choose between good and evil, are the outside forces which form the human condition, and again they were usually seen from a religious perspective: Divine Providence, the Divine Plan for history, even the stars were seen to determine (or at least foresee) lives, events, outcomes. Thus Lohenstein's historical tragedies, especially, establish a frame for historical events that is cosmic and providential (e.g., the four-monarchies choruses of *Cleopatra* and *Sophonisbe*). Such teleology always has implications for the viewer's present, as for the depicted events of the recent or distant past: every life, every fate is tied to *Heilsgeschichte*, the history of universal salvation.

Rather than focusing on the configuration of personality traits of each individual, seventeenth-century German psychology emphasized the study of emotions, the "affects," and their relationship with reason, the primary exponent of the free will. Thus it should not surprise us that literary theory (and practice) of the time, following one aspect in Aristotle's (388-324 B.C.) *Poetics*, stressed the arousal and manipulation of emotions, usually culminating in the call on reason. Harsdörffer's theory of tragedy speaks of bringing about in the audience the "cold sweat of anxiety" upon viewing the punishment for vice or sin in another, and Sigmund von Birken inverts Aristotle's two tragic emotions, pity and fear, in order to explain the effect of serious comedies with happy endings: joy and hope. This arousal of emotions was not the end, however — any more than it was for Aristotle — but the means. Seventeenth-century German poets, novelists, and (especially) dramatists wished to affect their audiences and readers, alter their behavior, make them change their lives. Thus we can speak of an "affective" theory of literature in a double sense — "affecting" the audience through arousal and manipulation of the emotions, the "affects." Unlike Aristotle in his theory of tragedy, however, "catharsis" of and through the emotions is not the goal for seventeenth-century German theorists and dramatists, for purgation obviates the necessity for changing one's behavior or life. Thus Gryphius and Lohenstein, especially, manipulate the emotions of their audiences — make them feel sympathy or empathetic fear, pain, or even passion, make them identify with the protagonists — only to recall them, by means of some of the same alienation (distancing) techniques used centuries later by Bertolt Brecht (1898-1956), to detached, reasonable judgment of both characters and actions. In *Simplicissimus* the novelist uses an older-but-wiser first-person narrator who looks back critically on his foolish behavior, even as he recounts it in a gripping and often sympathetic manner as if from the viewpoint of his younger self, in order to provide periodic detachment from any tendency to empathize too completely with the protagonist. Lyric poetry often similarly begins with the personal, individual, subjective reaction (you or I), then proceeds to include both poet and reader, only to shift perspective once more to a general-ization: every human being (as in Gryphius's "Es ist alles eitel"). Such shifts in perspective occur also in drama, when characters suddenly stop participating in the illusionistic action and turn to address the audience directly (as at the end of Gryphius's "tragedy" *Cardenio und Celinde*, and frequently by the fools or clowns in the plays of Caspar Stieler and Christian Weise). In all genres, these shifts in perspective serve on the one hand as distancing devices, but on the other as bridges between text (or play) and reader (or audience), thereby establishing the inclusivity of shared insight.

Genre and Medium

Opitz's distinctions among the genres on the hierarchical bases of social class of the protagonists (for drama) and stylistic level (for all literary forms) were destined to dominate Baroque literature only briefly; by mid-century the distinctions in stylistic level were blurred, and the genres had intermingled in countless ways from small intrusions to entire, theoretically-grounded mixed genres that had not existed before. Even the established and continuing genres evolved subgenres: tragedies of two distinct types, the martyr tragedy (e.g., Gryphius's *Felicitas* and *Carolus Stuardus*) and the tyrant tragedy (e.g., Lohenstein's *Agrippina*) existed side-by-side and were sometimes even merged into a single play (e.g., Gryphius's *Catharina von Georgien* and Hallmann's *Mariamne*) in which the persecutor/tyrants Chach Abas and Herod, their wavering and their divine punishments, receive as much or nearly as much emphasis as the martyred innocence of their victims. Four separate manifestations of comedy had evolved by the 1680s: satirical, heroic-romantic, allegorical, and pastoral comedies all flourished. Novels, too, might be satirical or courtly, or a combination of these and other qualities. Comic relief found its way into the tragic and serious plays of Caspar Stieler, Christian Weise, and even Andreas Gryphius (the doorkeeper scene in *Cardenio und Celinde*), and a few Germans began to use the term *Mischspiel* (mixed play, tragicomedy) for plays which intermingled tragic and comic elements or which began seriously and ended happily. The pastoral "poems" of the Nuremberg poets were actually prose narratives with large quantities of interspersed lyrical poetry; even *Simplicissimus* employs a few imbedded poems or songs. Dramas used lyrical poetry (often set to music) not only in the choruses, but also in imbedded songs which characters sing as part of the plot.

The most extraordinary innovation in the arts in the seventeenth century, in Germany as well as in Italy, was the birth of opera, the total union of text (of several kinds), music, and visual effects. Here, the tendency toward mixing genres achieves the destruction of generic boundaries on a grander scale: the combination of disparate media into a single spectacular event. In Germany, this effort began with Opitz's translation of the first opera, *Daphne*, from the Italian, set to music (now lost) by Heinrich Schütz (1585-1672), and performed in 1627 for a marriage festivity at a small Saxon court. Other German-language contributions to this development include Simon Dach's operas of the 1630s and early 1640s, Harsdörffer's *Seelewig* of 1644 (the only German-language opera before 1670 to survive with its score intact), Gryphius's *Verlibtes Gespenste* of 1661, Caspar Stieler's *Die Wittekinden* (1666) and translation of the Viennese grand opera *Il Pomo d'oro* (*The Golden Apple* [1669]), and the anonymous *Floretto* (1683, probably also by Caspar Stieler; one of the earliest texts of the Hamburg opera, the first commercial German opera company). Important also in this regard were the many plays with substantial vocal music interspersed which, together with the fully musical operas, were termed *Singspiele* (singing plays). (This term has since altered its meaning to include only those musical plays which use both spoken and sung text.) Another type of hybrid which originated in the seventeenth century, the oratorio (spiritual opera without the visual aspect), utilized the verse forms — recitative and aria — which by 1680 formed the basis of the German-language opera libretto. While German literary production had faltered by 1700, producing few texts of lasting significance during the period from 1690 to 1750, German opera continued to flourish in Hamburg and elsewhere, and the German oratorio rose to magnificent heights during the first half of the eighteenth century; but it is the composers' names which now live on, not those of the poets who penned the texts.

An End and New Beginnings

Still, the masterpieces of the Baroque continued to be read and savored well into the next century, until, in 1730, Johann Christoph Gottsched (1700-1766 founded his new neo-classical, enlightened style upon his vituperative assaults against the style which preceded it (in his *Versuch einer critischen Dichtkunst* [*Attempt at a Critical Poetics*] — 1730). The exuberance of the Baroque style, originating in the need to invent an elevated, ornamented language for literary production modelled on that of antiquity and the other national literatures, was now condemned as *Schwulst*, a cancerous tumor which deformed rather than adorned the language. Gottsched also lashed out at mixed genres and at the mixed-media triumph of the age, opera; at the excesses in emotionality and violence; at the reliance on visual imagery; and implicitly, at least, at the existence of covert layers of meaning.

At a time when "Baroque" music and architecture were still flourishing — indeed, reaching their zenith — in German culture, Baroque literature was thus officially pronounced dead. Yet some of the most important figures in later German literature — Goethe, Schiller, Heinrich von Kleist (1777-1811), Ludwig Tieck (1773-1853), Franz Grillparzer (1791-1872), Hugo von Hofmannsthal (1874-1929), Brecht — were to return to Baroque literature to find inspiration for their own works and to borrow techniques which would contribute to their own visions of what a literary text should do and be. One might even use the term "neo-Baroque" for Schiller's *Wallenstein* trilogy (the tragedy of a Thirty Years' War general), Tieck's comedy *Die verkehrte Welt* (*The Upside-Down World* [1800]), Grillparzer's play *Der Traum ein Leben* (*The Dream, A Life* [1840]), Hofmannsthal's plays *Jedermann* (*Everyman* [1911]) and *Der Turm* (*The Tower* [1925]), and Brecht's *Mutter Courage* (*Mother Courage* [1941] — likewise set in the Thirty Years' War). Yet — perhaps unfairly — only the novel *Simplicissimus*, the farce *Herr Peter Squentz*, and a few sonnets by Andreas Gryphius have so far entered the canon of world literature, while the contemporary works of Calderón (1600-1681), Lope de

Vega (1562-1635), Jean Racine (1639-1699), Peter Corneille (1606-1684), Molière (1622-1673), Tasso (1544-1595), Giovanni Guarini (1538-1512), Shakespeare, John Donne (1572-1631), Gianbattista Marini (1569-1625), and Góngora (1561-1627) have found assured places in the list of acknowledged masterpieces.

5 Enlightenment

John Van Cleve

Philosophical Determinants

*T*he term "Enlightenment" has two meanings in discussions of German literature. It refers to the literary period in German-speaking Europe that began around 1720 and ended in the late 1780s. But it also refers to the European movement in philosophy and related disciplines that was well developed by 1700 and that supplied the literary period with many of its theoretical reflexes. Whereas the Storm and Stress is largely an indigenous movement, the German Enlightenment is derivative. René Descartes (1596-1650) formulated the most famous dictum of the movement: "Cogito ergo sum" ("I think, therefore I am"). At the time, this constituted a radical departure from the traditional, Christian view of the world, which, if similarly reduced to a few words, could have been formulated as "I believe, therefore I am." Descartes argued that thought, specifically the reasoning faculty, the understanding, is the subject most worthy of study. Pierre Bayle (1647-1706) asserted that revelation and reason are two opposing stimuli of human behavior. But, at a time when the development of the empirical method was producing one scientific breakthrough after another, Bayle's peers tended to accord reason greater significance.

The Enlightenment first emerged as a movement in thought in England after the Glorious Revolution of 1688-1689. There many human rights were granted for the first time, while others already in place were extended. The result was an intellectual climate in which John Locke (1632-1704) could write one of the principal works of the Enlightenment, *An Essay Concerning Human Understanding* (1690). In Locke's epistemology, observation produces experience in the soul, which in turn creates sensations and ideas. Because observation relies on the senses, Locke concluded: "Nothing is in the mind that was not previously in the senses." David Hume (1711-1776) took this philosophical empiricism all the way to sensualism when he asserted that happiness, as a response that originates in the senses, is the goal of all human activity. This temporal reason for being — for a society as well as for an individual — later was cited by the American colonists in their *Declaration of Independence*. "The pursuit of happiness" as social policy was far from the glorification of God that earlier times had considered the proper work of humanity.

In Germany, Immanuel Kant (1724-1804), whose classic studies of reason and judgment carried Enlightenment philosophy into the realm of philosophical idealism, offered the best analysis of the movement in his short essay *Was ist Aufklärung?* (*What is Enlightenment?* [1784]). Kant answers that Enlightenment is humanity's departure from a state of immaturity for which it has only itself to blame. The path to this formulation had been cleared by Gottfried Wilhelm Leibniz (1646-1716), Christian Thomasius (1655-1728), and Christian Wolff (1679-1754). It was Thomasius who in 1688 first used the German language for university lectures in philosophy. The academician's practicality and commitment to reason were evident in his campaign against witch hunts. Leibniz offered an atomistic description of the universe in the hope that it would satisfy man's reasoning faculty while not offending the impulse to believe in that which reason cannot approach, i.e., God. Leibniz called his units "monads" and asserted that each was an independent living mirror of the universe. While Leibniz's cosmology is largely rationalistic, it allows for the presence of the irrational — particularly during creative acts. It was Leibniz who first suggested an idea that was to be of great significance to the Storm and Stress movement, the idea that the artist is a "second creator," that is, second to God. Wolff converted Leibniz's philosophy into what he hoped would be an ethical system of universal applicability. The optimism of the Enlightenment is nowhere more apparent than in Wolff's belief in his ability to help his fellow being cultivate human understanding. He identified virtue as the source of happiness in life and thus instigated a preoccupation with virtue, the virtues, and virtuous behavior that makes some Enlightenment literature tedious for the modern reader.

By the middle of the eighteenth century, Enlightenment philosophers had ceased their increasingly feeble attempts to defer to religious belief. They came to be known as deists — those who deny the participation of the Creator in the laws and processes of the universe. Typical was Voltaire (1694-1778) with his emphasis on social morality. He believed in the concept of justice as a means of making tolerable the imperfections of the world. Montesquieu (1689-1755) declared that justice would be best served in a state that divided its governing power among three clearly separate branches: a legislature, an executive, and a judiciary. His was one of the many Enlightenment ideas that were to be enshrined in the *Constitution of the United States*.

Reliance on reason and dedication to ethical behavior based on the concept of virtue rather than on Christian doctrine — those intellectual postures were advocated in a type of publication widely popular in eighteenth-century England and Germany: the moral weekly (*die moralische Wochenschrift*). These serials appeared monthly, several times per month, or at irregular intervals. Whereas the English moral weeklies discussed political and social issues, their German analogues offered short works of literature and discussions of ethical and aesthetic questions. The first phase of the literary Enlightenment began in the 1720s, when moral weeklies were published in three cities by editors committed to the growth of the movement. Zurich's periodical was edited by Johann Jacob Bodmer (1698-1783) and Johann Jakob Breitinger (1701-1776), Hamburg's by Barthold Heinrich Brockes (1680-1747), and Leipzig's by Johann Christoph Gottsched (1700-1766). Gottsched went on to publish a poetics that he hoped would provide a theoretical basis for a completely new tradition in German literature, a tradition dedicated to the teachings of Enlightenment philosophy.

Gottsched, Brockes, and Haller

Born in Königsberg, Gottsched fled his native Prussia for fear that his imposing physique would attract the attention of army recruiters. He settled in Leipzig, where in 1725 he began to lecture on literature and Wolff's philosophy. Ten years later, he married Luise Adelgune Victorie Kulmus (1713-1762), who later wrote comedies for his literary journal. In the 1730s and 1740s, Gottsched collaborated with the theater troupe of Johann and Caroline Neuber (1697-1760) to eliminate from the German stage all elements of the native farce. Gottsched's *Versuch einer Critischen Dichtkunst vor die Deutschen* (*Attempt at a Critical Poetics for the Germans* [1730]) asserts that literary creativity is a rational, not emotional process. Phantasy is to be controlled by "healthy reason." A writer must bear in mind the educated "good taste" of his audience. Settings, characters, and plots are to proceed from the imitation of nature, but by nature Gottsched understood not physical reality with its grandeur and its harshness but only the beautiful in nature, the depiction of which would lead the reader to the practical moral lesson that each work of literature was to contain.

Gottsched set clear boundaries for the major literary genres. He was particularly concerned about the drama because he believed that the Baroque tragedy and the native farce had led to a severe deterioration in quality. He demanded strict adherence to the Aristotelian unities of time, place, and action. Long monologues, the improvising clown, song, and ghosts and other supernatural phenomena were banned from the stage as incompatible with verisimilitude. Accordingly, both the opera and the works of Shakespeare were found wanting. Tragedy was to be restricted to aristocratic characters and themes; comedy was to be largely bourgeois. The former was to employ verse, the latter prose. Gottsched's aggressive and judgmental writings earned him mocking recognition as the "literary pope" of the Early Enlightenment.

Brockes produced a large body of lyric poetry that depicts the beauty of objects in nature, however small they may be. His multi-volume life's work *Irdisches Vergnügen in Gott, bestehend in physikalisch- und moralischen Gedichten* (*Earthly Delight in God; Composed of Physical and Moral Poems* [1721-1748]), seeks to illuminate the grandeur of God through the examination and observation of nature. Brockes's worldview was teleological in that he believed both in divine reason as the cosmic ordering principle and in the ultimate purposefulness of all that is and happens in nature. A typical Brockes poem details the beauty of a flower in order to magnify the flower's Creator.

Similar themes and attitudes can be found in the poetry of the better-known Albrecht von Haller (1708-1777). But in Haller's famous long poem *Die Alpen* (*The Alps* [1732]), the Bern professor also criticizes the supposedly dissolute customs of his fellow city-dwellers against the backdrop of the simple virtuous patterns of life he finds among the inhabitants of the ruggedly beautiful mountain valleys. The accuracy of Haller's descriptions of nature reflects his training as a botanist.

J. C. Gottsched
(copperplate of 1753)

Anacreontic and Rococo

Nature was presented in a strikingly different fashion by the Anacreontic poets. The few surviving works by the poet of ancient Greece, Anacreon (c. 572-c. 488 B.C.), offer a highly polished celebration of the pleasures of life. Eighteenth-century followers of Anacreon also admired the cheerful odes of Horace (65-8 B.C.) and Catullus (c. 84-c. 54 B.C.). The themes of Anacreontic poetry are Epicurean: the praise of wine, camaraderie, and the power of love. The sundry virtues — physical as well as moral — of the woman loved are extolled in stylized verses that create a pastoral setting complete with names and situations borrowed from classical mythology. Bacchus, Venus, and Cupid often appear. The term Rococo has been used to describe this movement, and the landscapes associated with Anacreontic poetry teem with the babbling brooks, sunny meadows, hidden grottos, and shady groves of French Rococo paintings.

In aesthetics as well as in ethics, Enlightenment principles still prevail among Anacreontic poets, but the rigorous rationalism of Gottsched no longer underlies every utterance. The tone of these sophisticated lyrics is both light and knowing, both sensual and tasteful, both undeniably erotic and transparently reasonable. The resultant tension is apparent in the poem "Anakreon" (1747) by Friedrich von Hagedorn (1708-1754), who has the ancient poet cite his theme of wine, women, and song as the stanzas begin. But, at each halfway point, the poet places a heavy-footed conjunction meaning "however" and then asserts that he has always venerated the gods and those who serve the gods, even when he has been jesting. For that reason he has earned the epithet Anacreon the Wise. Of course, Anacreon speaks for Hagedorn, who held that the style of poetry he introduced to Germany offended neither the traditional Christian God nor the new god of the eighteenth century: reason. Wisdom supposedly lies in the ability to mediate between the dictates of reason and the need for pleasure. Joy in youthful energy, wine, and love is extolled in "Der Tag der Freude" ("The Day of Pleasure" [1740]). In its final line they are brought together in a toast to the love of a latter-day shepherdess.

The members of the *Hallenser Kreis* (Circle of Halle) followed Hagedorn's lead; among them were Johann Wilhelm Gleim (1719-1803), Johann Peter Uz (1720-1796), and Johann Nikolaus Götz (1721-1781). Anacreontic poetry can be superficial, whether as the voyeuristic dream of Uz ("Ein Traum" [A Dream — 1743/1744]) or as the noisy ejaculations of Gleim's "Trinklied" ("Drinking Song" [1744/1745]). Uz leers at the bather in her diaphanous gown only to awaken just as she is about to disrobe. He closes with the sighing acknowledgment that by the time he could fall asleep again, she would be in the water and hidden from his view. Later in life, Uz turned away from teasing sensual poetry and toward a serious tone reminiscent of Brockes. But the ability to describe nature as in a poem such as "Gott im Frühlinge" ("God in the Springtime" [1763]), is significantly inferior to that of the earlier poet. Gleim's "An Doris" ("To Doris" [1744/1745]), with its series of hypothetical subjunctives, begins as a daydream equivalent of the salacious Uz poem. But here reality proves to be preferable. Unlike a work of art, a model can kiss. While still a young man, Gleim went on to serve on the side of Friedrich II (the Great) of Prussia (1712-1786) in the Second Silesian War.

The Seven Years' War

War poetry such as Gleim's "Bei Eröffnung des Feldzuges 1756" ("Upon the Commencement of the Campaign of 1756") achieved a broad popularity that had eluded the somewhat professorial literature of the Enlightenment. It also constituted early stirrings of tendentiousness in literature, the impulse to comment on or participate in political and social discussions of the day. Songs written in support of war opened up war as a topic for poetry, which in turn made possible songs written against war and the policies of war. Ironically enough, Heinrich Heine's vilification of the imperial eagle of Prussia in *Deutschland. Ein Wintermärchen* (*Germany: A Winter's Tale* [1844]) was made possible in part by Gleim's glorification of the same bird a century earlier. With his poem, Gleim hoped to heighten patriotic fervor as the Seven Years' War (1756-1763) was beginning. In sharp contrast, the ode "An den Frieden" ("To Peace" [1760]) by Karl Wilhelm Ramler (1725-1798) was a plea for an end to years of war, a plea that bespeaks the courage of its author: Ramler was himself a Prussian. His characterization of war as a murderer and a destroyer who should be locked in hell for all eternity was written while his country's army was still in the field.

Ramler was noted by his contemporaries for his mastery of the ode, a genre cultivated by the ancient Greeks who used it to give dignified, even majestic expression to a mood of earnest reflection or celebration. Although only tangentially involved in the Anacreontic movement, Ramler shared with it and with Gottsched a preference for classicistic literature, that is, literature that returns to the forms and subject matters found in the literature of ancient Greece and Rome.

During the eighteenth century, debates raged not about the wisdom of producing classicistic art but about the degree of fidelity to the ancient models that modern works were to emulate. The Early Enlightenment demands strict fidelity; later in the century, theoreticians turn to contemporary national traditions for models and re-evaluate the examples set during classical antiquity.

Sentimentality

The first indication that the iron discipline of Gottsched and his followers could not long dominate the literary tradition was provided by a movement within the literary Enlightenment that soon was known as *Empfindsamkeit* (sentimentality). In broadest terms, *Empfindsamkeit* offered a forum for the expression of emotional responses to the philosophical and ethical positions taken by the Enlightenment and to the tensions that would arise in any attempt to assert those positions in everyday life. The attitude that such expression was permissible, even commendable outside of the privacy of one's home, came from the great religious revival movement of the seventeenth century, Pietism.

Within the middle class that gave the Enlightenment most of its writers and the largest part of its audience, one emotion was particularly strong: frustration. More and more burghers had attended the university and, whether as businessmen — women were not yet admitted to the university — or as professionals, had vested interests in social issues and economic policies. But in the absolutist German states, they were denied political power. Their intellectual energies were forced to find other channels in family life, community service, and in the arts. They formed reading circles and learned societies; they joined the new Free Masonry movement, and they participated in the religious fundamentalism of their time. The middle class also purchased and discussed new works of literature, particularly if that literature depicted bourgeois conditions and problems, or if it conjured forth imaginary worlds in which a person's education and intelligence — rather than accident of birth — dictated the position in society. As a result, some works examined relationships within and among families — extended families as well as nuclear families — while other works offered utopian escapes from an unsatisfactory political and social reality. Both options legitimized the expression of an effusive emotionalism that today seems somewhat saccharin, sometimes maudlin, and often contrived. *Empfindsamkeit* displayed a love of the illusory German state and a hatred of tyranny, both of which were to emerge full-blown in the literature of the Storm and Stress.

Pietism owed much to medieval mysticism with its emphasis on contemplation as the path to individual salvation through direct contact with God (*unio mystica*: mystical union). But, whereas mysticism had coexisted, to a large degree, with the Catholic Church, Pietism concurred with the Enlightenment's rejection of orthodoxies and dogmas. In the course of an intensely personal process that combined revelation, reason, and the emotions, the believer was to be "re-born." The founders of Pietism, Jakob Spener (1635-1705) and August Hermann Francke

(1663-1727), expressed themselves in terms that would be understood and appreciated by "born-again Christians" in the United States. The followers of Spener and Francke formed small prayer and meditation congregations that met in private homes. The influence of these congregations on German society and culture lasted until the end of the century. One of the formative experiences in the life of the young Johann Wolfgang Goethe was his relationship with the Pietist Susanna von Klettenberg (1723-1774) from 1768 to 1770.

Sentimentalist literature was largely untouched by the classicistic subject matter and forms of the Early Enlightenment. The dominant influence was the English novel that featured dedication to virtue and honor in the face of emotionally trying circumstances. The epistolary novels of Samuel Richardson (1689-1761) are awash in the tears of heroines whose chastity is tested severely. Every weepy response is then subjected to such extensive examination that plots pale in importance. Attentiveness to feelings was later carried to comic extremes by Laurence Sterne (1713-1768) in his novels *Tristram Shandy* (1760-1767), and *Sentimental Journey through France and Italy* (1768).

A contrasting, melancholy sentimentality also came from England in the form of *Night Thoughts on Life, Death and Immortality* (1742-1745) by Edward Young (1683-1765). Young's examinations of insecurity, anguish, and fear were appreciated by bourgeois Germans suffering under social and political oppression. The same hostile world awaits trusting young women in Richardson's *Pamela* (1740) and in *Das Leben der schwedischen Gräfin von G*** (*The Life of the Swedish Countess of G*** [1747-1748]), a novel by Christian Fürchtegott Gellert (1715-1769). The countess and her extended family must come to terms with bigamy, incest, rape, imprisonment in Siberia, and even death by a lightning bolt. The only safe haven is to be found in a type of familial love that transcends social stratification. From a twentieth-century perspective, the decision of Gellert and Richardson to place a woman at the center of a plot that moves from one emotional response to another seems patronizing and even sexist. But at the time, the very inclusion of women among subjects appropriate for literary treatment was a step forward.

One of the many pastors' sons who became men of letters in the eighteenth century, Gellert was raised and educated in Electoral Saxony. He spent his adult years in Gottsched's Leipzig and therefore participated in many discussions led by and then directed against the great theoretician. Gellert wrote a collection entitled *Fabeln und Erzählungen* (*Fables and Short Tales* [1746/1748]) that was famous in German-speaking Europe during the eighteenth and nineteenth centuries. Each fable had a moral that taught self-sufficiency, self-control, or happiness as goals for the virtuous person. Gellert criticized common character flaws ranging in importance from fashion-consciousness to impiety. In both his dramaturgy and in his drama, Gellert championed the so-called "lachrymose comedy." Originally a French contribution to European literature, the *comédie larmoyante* reduced the amount of pure humor in comedy while adding elements calculated to evoke pity and commiseration within audiences. The spectator went to a performance of such a piece expecting "a good cry" and a happy ending. The comedies of Nivelle de la

Chaussée (1692-1754) had a particularly strong influence on Gellert. Gellert's work enjoyed great popularity, and the writer himself was admired because of his kindly, thoughtful personality. Spectators and readers often wrote to him for advice concerning personal problems, and his extensive correspondence suggests that he usually responded.

Klopstock and the *Göttinger Hainbund*

If Gellert was the most beloved writer of *Empfindsamkeit,* Friedrich Gottlieb Klopstock (1724-1803) was the most admired. Klopstock was the son of a wealthy attorney, and as such received an excellent education from instructors who also imparted their Pietist beliefs. At the University of Jena, the young man studied theology briefly, but he soon decided to pursue a career as a professional poet. In 1750 he paid an extended visit to Bodmer in Zurich, but disagreements with the renowned Swiss led Klopstock to develop his own agenda. As a mature writer, he did not belong to circles of poets nor did he speak for movements. He lived out his days in Hamburg and in death was paid a degree of spontaneous homage unique in the annals of German literary history. At the time, Germans considered Klopstock their

Klopstock as a young man in a silhouette of the time

greatest national poet. This perception was widely shared despite the fact that his single great work *Der Messias (The Messiah* [1748-1773]) rarely was read — even during the poet's lifetime.

Der Messias is a biblical epic of twenty cantos in hexameter; it intersperses the martyrdom of Christ with subjective, Pietistic observations and with visions of metaphysical realms. Klopstock consciously tried to produce a work that would stand comparison with Homer and Milton. *Der Messias* made Klopstock famous. But it was his loose, rhapsodic style in lyric poetry, his innovative sentence structures, and his memorable neologisms that made him the most influential poet of the Enlightenment. Many understood his frequent demonstrations of the plasticity of the German language as an implicit rejection of the insistence on correctness and appropriateness in expression demanded by Gottsched.

Klopstock wrote as though he were recording experiences he was just having. In effect, the reader is able to experience the world through Klopstock's heightened senses and vivid imagination. Every strophe of the poems "Der Zürchersee" ("Lake Zurich" [1750]) and "Die Frühlingsfeier" ("A Celebration of Spring" [1759]) vibrates with an excitement most clearly evident in the many exclamation points. Klopstock often is described as the first to practice what has come to be called *Erlebnisdichtung* (poetry of experience), that is, literature that conveys the individual's subjective response to the surrounding environment. German lyric poetry before Klopstock is less personal and more utilitarian: it is used to teach correct responses to a flawed world or to offer the prospect of a better life after death. Klopstock's rambling lines set the stage for the disciplined but equally experiential poetry of the young Goethe, which is to say that Klopstock made possible what many consider the finest lyric poetry in German. In defense of what may seem to be intemperateness of expression on Klopstock's part, it can be argued that extraordinary themes (for instance, direct contact with God in "Die Frühlingsfeier") are best served by extraordinary means of expression.

Reverence for Klopstock led in 1772 to the formation of a circle of poets in Göttingen. Among the members of the *Göttinger Hainbund (Grove of Göttingen)* were Ludwig Christoph Heinrich Hölty (1748-1776) and Matthias Claudius (1740-1815). The forest grove had served as a forum for poets in the distant Germanic past. Many of the poets of the new "Grove" studied at the University of Göttingen, where students were beginning to reject the francophile literary reflexes of the Early Enlightenment. The young poets followed Klopstock in his transcendence of strict rationalism. They questioned social and cultural conventions and affirmed freedom as the highest ideal for poetry and for life. They espoused a new ethics that emphasized common decency, friendship, patriotism, and opposition to all forms of oppression. Their favorite genre was lyric poetry and specifically the ballad. Here they were greatly influenced by the melancholy Celtic songs published by Thomas Percy (1729-1811) as *Reliques of Ancient English Poetry* (1765). The simple sad poem with close ties to nature and the lives of simple people unaffected by modern civilization — that poem recurs in the later works of Klopstock himself, for instance in "Die frühen Gräber" ("Early Graves" [1764]) and "Die Sommernacht" ("Summer's Night" [1766]).

The mildly confrontational posture of the *Hainbund* is apparent in Claudius's "Der Schwarze in der Zuckerplantage" ("The Black Man at the Sugar Plantation" [1773]). A black slave laments his fate without cursing the whites who have made it so harsh. If he spoke for a movement that was more sharply critical of social injustice, the slave would be called a slave, and he would not describe the whites as "smart and handsome."

Hölty's poem "Das Landleben" ("Life in the Country" [1777]) sings the praise of one who has turned his back on modern urban culture and has lived in nature. Conventional faith is unnecessary to one who can make a shady thicket into a temple. Through the *Hainbund*, sentimentality entered lyric poetry. The contemplative subjectivism of Claudius's "Abendlied" ("Evening Song" [1779]) or his commemorative "Christiane" (1798) would have been unthinkable before

Klopstock. Claudius's "Der Mensch" ("Man" [1783]), with its swirl of conflicting actions and motivations, indicates that the belief of the Early Enlightenment in reason and virtue as the two guideposts for life has been left far behind. The rational and the sentimental, the simple and the complex were beginning to mingle. The resultant complexity in literary expression is first evident in the two writers of international stature to emerge from the German Enlightenment: Gotthold Ephraim Lessing (1729-1781) and Christoph Martin Wieland (1733-1813).

Gotthold Ephraim Lessing

Lessing was a pastor's son who grew up in Saxony and enrolled at the University of Leipzig in 1746. In 1748 he changed his field of study from theology to medicine, but he was already far more interested in the city's bustling literary life. Lessing was an enthusiastic supporter of the Neuber theater troupe and a participant in gatherings of writers. Late in 1748 he moved to Berlin to pursue a career as a journalist and writer. There he wrote for the city's major newspapers and founded one of Germany's earliest literary journals. Financial hardship necessitated subsequent moves back to Leipzig and again to Berlin. In 1758 he edited *Briefe, die neueste Literatur betreffend* (*Letters Concerning the Most Recent Literature*) with two other noteworthy members of the Enlightenment, Moses Mendelssohn (1729-1786) and Friedrich Nicolai (1733-1811). In 1767 he was called to the new German National Theater in Hamburg to serve as resident critic, adviser, and playwright. Soon after the failure of the National Theater, he was appointed librarian in the town of Wolfenbüttel, then under the rule of Braunschweig-Lüneburg. Lessing married Eva König in 1776, but she died in childbirth just over a year later. In his final years Lessing was involved in a prolonged dispute with one of Hamburg's leading Lutheran pastors, Johann Melchior Goeze. What began as tension between a representative of the Lutheran orthodoxy and a representative of the deistic Enlightenment soon became a discussion of religious tolerance.

Lessing began writing dramas in the late 1740s when Gottsched's dicta still held sway. Hence, the young writer's first efforts are comedies that attack faults common in the middle class depicted on stage. His first significant work, *Miss Sara Sampson* (1755), represented a break with Gottsched in that it is a prose tragedy that treats bourgeois, not aristocratic themes. Germany's first *bürgerliches Trauerspiel* (bourgeois tragedy) was another step taken by the Enlightenment to move literature from the aristocratic control exercised during the seventeenth century and toward the middle-class control in place by the end of the eighteenth century. The play fails a modern reader because of its weepy sentimentality. But, even if the play is rarely performed, it occupies a prominent place in the history of German drama.

Miss Sara Sampson heightened Lessing's visibility in the literary community just before the appearance of *Briefe, die neueste Literatur betreffend,* which solidified his position as Gottsched's heir. Lessing set the agenda for the final phase of the German Enlightenment. The most famous of the *Briefe* is the seventeenth; in it he attacks Gottsched and seventeenth-century French Classicism, which Gottsched long had praised as a tradition that German writers would do well to emulate. Lessing rejects French Classicism for having falsified classical antiquity and proposes that the recent English tradition and especially Shakespeare would serve as far better models. In *Laokoon oder Über die Grenzen der Malerei und Poesie* (*Laocoon or Concerning the Boundaries between Painting and Literature* [1766]), Lessing points to Homer as the master of the technique of describing beauty in nature through the use of plotting techniques and through the presentation of the effects of beauty on others. He cites Homer's description of the effect of Helen's beauty on the old men of Troy. Lessing's championing of Homer and Shakespeare was readily accepted and further developed by the Storm and Stress.

As a drama critic, Lessing can be mentioned in the same breath as Aristotle based on the theories and notes contained in the *Hamburgische Dramaturgie* (*Hamburg Dramaturgy* [1767-1769]). Lessing refers to Aristotle's *Poetics* as he elucidates principles

Emilia Galotti.

Ein Trauerspiel

in

fünf Aufzügen.

Von

Gotthold Ephraim Lessing.

Berlin,
bey Christian Friedrich Voß, 1772.

exemplified in English, French, German, and Spanish works; he devotes particular attention to plays from his own century. The *Dramaturgie* reduced the prestige of French Classicism even as it provided a theoretical basis for the drama canon that Lessing believed his contemporaries capable of producing. At the same time, Lessing cautioned against reliance on formulas when writing: for example, attention to the three unities of time, place, and action, so important to Gottsched, should be focused on the unity of action alone.

The *Hamburgische Dramaturgie* began to appear in installments in the spring of 1767, the year Lessing published *Minna von Barnhelm*. Lessing had been working on the comedy since the early 1760s; it is set at the end of the Seven Years' War and depicts the halting romance of a wealthy Saxon noblewoman and a wounded, impoverished Prussian officer. The Saxon Lessing had served Prussia as an adjutant during the war, and his play attempts to reduce tensions between two nations that had begun the war as enemies. Goethe commented that the kindliness and charm of the Saxon lady conquer the intransigence, the sense of dignity, and the dedication to a code of honor in the Prussian Tellheim. It was a victory on the stage for Saxony to balance its capitulation in 1756. Major Tellheim's rigid adherence to his beliefs brings his relationship with Minna to the brink of tragedy. The plot, with its intrigue concerning a ring, was hardly new at the time, but Lessing's unique, three-dimensional characters constituted a break with the use of positive and negative human "types" in earlier Gottschedian comedy.

Lessing returned to the bourgeois tragedy with the publication of *Emilia Galotti* in 1772. He took the idea for the plot from the Roman historian Livy, who relates the story of the death of Virginia at the hands of her father Lucius Virginius in 449 B.C. Livy describes how the decent, upright man acts to save his daughter's honor from the sexual advances of Appius Claudius, leader of the *decemviri*, or council of ten. Livy uses the tale to contrast the strict morality of Rome's early days with the degeneracy he finds rife among his contemporaries. Like Virginia, Emilia Galotti is engaged to one man but pursued by another, who is ready to use the power he possesses as a ruler to get what he wants. The Prince of Guastalla is served by one of the more sinister figures in German literature, the scheming courtier Marinelli. He stages an attack on the coach carrying Emilia and her fiancé, and during the struggle the groom-to-be is killed. Emilia is led off by "rescuers" to Guastalla's pleasure palace where the prince can begin to win over Emilia's affections by offering protection and comfort. Emilia's father Odoardo understands what is happening and finally stabs his daughter at her behest. The play observes the Aristotelian unity of time, but its changes in setting helped legitimize the freedom in the use of structural elements demanded by the Storm and Stress. Lessing showed courage in depicting not only the tyrannical, exploitive reflexes of German absolutism, but also the anger of the middle class. At the play's conclusion, Odoardo must force himself not to kill the one responsible for his daughter's death — his own prince.

Lessing's greatest contribution to world literature is his "dramatic poem" *Nathan der Weise* (*Nathan the Wise* [1779]); its message of religious tolerance was intended as a final response to Pastor Goeze. Lessing sets the piece in Jerusalem at the time of the Crusades. Both Moslems and Christians play major roles in the complicated plot, but the dominant figure is the old Jewish merchant Nathan, whose resilient humanity earns the respect of others regardless of confession. By the play's conclusion, Nathan, the Sultan, and a young Knight Templar are able to resolve the conflicts that have separated them. The embracing as the final curtain falls symbolizes Lessing's hope for reconciliation and understanding within the fractious family of man. Lessing's friend the Jewish philosopher Moses Mendelssohn may have provided a model for Nathan. Mendelssohn's writings examined the nature of feelings and the supposed immortality of the soul. Both the man and his *oeuvre* influenced the perception of Judaism held by Kant, Georg Friedrich Wilhelm Hegel (1770-1831), and their followers.

Nathan der Weise is best remembered for the "Parable of the Ring," which is told by Nathan in response to the Sultan's demand that the Jew indicate which of the three religions represented in Jerusalem is correct. Lessing found the parable in the *Decamerone* of Giovanni Boccaccio (1313-1375). Nathan tells the story of a ring that enabled its owner to discern the truth in matters of faith. The ring passed from one generation to the next within the same family until it came to a man with three sons whom he loved equally. He had two identical copies made. Since then, the original ring still has the power to bring the grace of God to an owner who practices his faith. But only by the conduct of an owner can the genuineness of his ring be determined. In like fashion, it is impossible to describe one of the three religions as correct. The amount of truth in a given religion will be manifest in the actions of its adherents. Christians, Jews, and Moslems should in fact compete with one another in demonstrating the truth of their respective beliefs.

Christoph Martin Wieland

Christoph Martin Wieland's popularity has risen and fallen more dramatically than Lessing's, to a great extent because he has been associated with the Rococo and its French origins. The movement itself was considered frivolous and "un-German" by the German Romantics, who made Wieland a target of their hostility toward the cosmopolitanism of the Enlightenment. Since Romanticism, Wieland's prestige has suffered during periods of nationalistic fervor.

Wieland, like Lessing, was born into a pastor's home. During his later teens he received an education that had a strong Pietist admixture. A university career that included humanistic studies at Erfurt and readings in law at Tübingen was broken off so that the young man could devote himself to literature. From 1752 to 1754, Wieland stayed with Bodmer in Zurich, as Klopstock had done a few years earlier. He subsequently worked as a private tutor. In 1769 he accepted an invitation to join the faculty at the University of Erfurt as a professor of philosophy. He moved to Weimar in 1772 when the Duchess Anna Amalia asked him to take over the education of her two sons. Wieland lived in and near Weimar until his death in 1813. He married Dorothea von Hillenbrand in 1765, and the couple had fourteen children. Wieland also "fathered" much of the discussion of literature in late eighteenth-century Germany through his editorship of the first literary journal of "national" significance, *Der Teutsche Merkur* (*The German Mercury*). It was a unique, highly visible position that Wieland held from 1773 until 1810; his support helped build an audience for the works of Lessing, Goethe, Schiller, and the Romantics.

Whereas Lessing asserted his positions in an energetic, pugnacious, confrontational manner rooted in the philosophical optimism of the Enlightenment, Wieland gave expression to the cheerful fatalism of the Rococo. Less the analytical thinker, Wieland mastered the playfully ironic epic style that made full use of his prodigious linguistic abilities. His epic narrator chats with the reader while telling a story in a sympathetic but distanced, good-humored but gently moralizing fashion. In light of his beginnings as an admirer of Klopstock and a student of Bodmer, it was predictable that Wieland would eschew the cool rationalism of Gottsched in favor of Gellert's openness to emotional response. But Wieland moved beyond his Pietist, sentimentalist beginnings toward a cosmopolitanism marked by a devotion to and an obvious enjoyment of philosophical sensualism.

Typical of Wieland is the juxtaposition in a narrative of an ascetic lifestyle appropriate for the disciplined dedication to virtue with a mild, frivolous eroticism. The later German Enlightenment rejected much of its seventeenth-century legacy: not only French Classicism but also the stylized lyric poetry with its simple message of contempt for worldly things, and the high tragedy with its remote aristocratic characters and their lesson of stoic forbearance. The long Baroque novel was seen as a formless array of moral tales cast in a second-rate medium — prose. One of the great services performed for German literature by Wieland was his legitimation of the novel as worthy of the attention of the educated reader having breeding and good taste.

Wieland accomplished the feat with his first novel *Die Geschichte des Agathon* (*The History of Agathon* [1766-1767]), which simultaneously created a new subcategory, the *Bildungsroman* (novel of development). Wieland supplied the form that his contemporaries had found wanting in the Baroque novel by fashioning a plot that revolved around the hero's development from childhood to maturity. Of course, Grimmelhausen's novel *Simplicissimus* (1669) already had brought picaresque adventures in such a form, and, long before, Wolfram von Eschenbach's *Parzival* (1200-1210) had traced the life's path of the Christian knight. But, in the wake of empiricism in both science and philosophy and under the influence of Pietism with its attention to the play of emotions, Wieland was able to depict emotional as well as educational and intellectual maturation. The individual's psyche is analyzed as it becomes more sharply defined, as it changes in response to changing external influences and in response to physical growth and aging.

The Athenian dramatist Agathon lived at the time of Plato (427-347 B.C.) and is mentioned in the *Poetics* of Aristotle, but most of his *oeuvre* has been lost. Plato sets his *Symposium* in the house of Agathon. Wieland's novel does not attempt to fill in the details of the life of a poet in ancient Greece but instead uses only the most general characteristics of this noted friend of Plato and Euripides.

As a young man, Wieland's Agathon soon proves to be highly intelligent, sensitive, and, naturally, naive. During a turbulent life, he encounters both truth and deception in remote Delphi and in political Athens. He rises to the leadership of an army, falls from the heights into piracy and slavery. Wieland ends the novel with his character at Tarentum among members of the extended family of the sage Archytas. In the course of discussions with the latter, Agathon attains a degree of self-knowledge that enables him to make sense of the events in his life. Archytas and the mature Agathon embody intellectual independence, humaneness, enlightened morality, and an aesthetics with a moral dimension. Lessing asserted that *Agathon* was the first and only novel for a thinking man with classical tastes. The literary theoretician Friedrich von Blanckenburg (1744-1796) went so far as to write that the German literary public was too immature to appreciate Wieland's first novel.

That Wieland was himself aware of the gulf that separated participants in the Enlightenment from the greater part of society was evident in his next major work, *Die Abderiten, eine sehr wahrscheinliche Geschichte* (*The Abderites, A Highly Probable History* [1774-1780]). The comic novel is set in the town of Abdera in ancient Thrace, a town whose inhabitants were renowned for their foolishness. Wieland's main character is the philosopher Democritus, a contemporary of Socrates who lived around 450 B.C. The many extant fragments of his writings show that he was a man of extraordinary intelligence and creativity; he made contributions in areas of knowledge as diverse as ethics, medicine, phonology, physics, agriculture, and poetry. The empiricism that served as the basis for Democritus's methodology already stood to make him attractive to eighteenth-century intellectuals. Wieland built his novel on the comic tension between the parochial Abderites and their well-travelled and broad-minded son. The townspeople mock Democritus, whom they consider an outlandish fool. For his part, the philosopher maintains a posture of cheerful resignation as he watches the Abderites thrust themselves into one impossible situation after another. The novel is episodic: it begins with short tales of everyday occurrences and passes on to longer stories about the visits of Hippocrates and then Euripides, the self-debilitating legal system of Abdera, and the ultimately destructive zealotry of the Abderites' official religion.

Die Abderiten satirizes the smug, self-satisfied, intellectually somnolent townspeople whom Wieland had known in Germany and Switzerland. Book Four contains Wieland's best-known story, the case of the donkey's shadow. A teamster denies his customer the right to sit in the shadow of a donkey on a hot summer day. The customer sues, claiming that he who rents the donkey also rents the shadow. The Byzantine legal process that ensues gives birth to political parties — the "Donkeys" and the "Shadows" — that finally come to blows. The rioters ultimately vent their fury on the mangy donkey as the putative cause of the turmoil and tear the hapless beast to bits. Thus, the case is rendered moot. Here, as elsewhere in the novel, Wieland is skeptical of the Enlightenment's ability to educate the general citizenry, but he is always sympathetic to human weaknesses.

In the romantic heroic poem, Wieland may have found the genre best suited to his literary abilities and philosophical positions. In 1780 he published *Oberon* with its fourteen cantos in ottava rima. As sources he used the anonymous French heroic novel *Huon de Bordeaux* (1216-1229), Chaucer's "Merchant's Tale" from *Canterbury Tales*, Shakespeare's *Midsummer Night's Dream*, and the *Thousand and One Nights*. He tells interwoven tales about the long-suffering knight Huon and his beloved Rezia and about the estrangement and reconciliation of the elfin couple King Oberon and Queen Titania. Oberon helps Huon and learns to value the fidelity that unites the mortal couple and that endures even when they face a bitter death. The king of the elves is no longer the free earth spirit of folk tales but a servant of God. Wieland's work won great acclaim. Goethe called it a masterpiece, and there were many imitations and translations. The first American to translate the work was no less a figure than John Quincy Adams, the sixth President of the United States, who served as minister to Prussia during the administration of his father, John Adams. While working in Berlin, young Adams read *Oberon* and then rendered it in English verse by the spring of 1800.

Conclusion

In Lessing and Wieland, the German Enlightenment produced two writers whose significance has all too often been measured in terms of the literature that immediately followed them: in particular, the lyric poetry of the young Goethe and the *oeuvre* of German Classicism. Lessing and Wieland have been viewed as "forerunners." But the artistry of *Nathan der Weise* and *Die Abderiten* stands on its own merits. In order to appreciate it, one need not attempt to read history backward — an exercise of dubious worth. The message of tolerance, good-naturedness, and simple decency embodied in Nathan and Democritus is as vital now as it was two centuries ago.

6 Storm and Stress

Kim Vivian

The Movement and Historical Background

*L*iterary movements do not appear or disappear abruptly, but represent rather a certain unity within a larger historical context while echoes from earlier literary periods linger on — sometimes very distinctly — and birth cries from incipient movements begin to be heard. Wedged chronologically between the Enlightenment and Classicism, the short-lived Storm and Stress, named after Friedrich Maximilian Klinger's play *Sturm und Drang* (1777 — originally called *Wirrwarr [Chaos]* but re-titled by the *Genieapostel* [apostle of genius] Christoph Kaufmann [1753-1795]), represents at once a revolt against many tenets of the Enlightenment but also a continuation and advancement of some "enlightened" ideals.

In the autobiographical novel *Anton Reiser* (1785/1790) by Karl Philipp Moritz (1756-1793), the sixteen-year-old titular hero immerses himself in the Enlightenment critic and dramatist Johann Christoph Gottsched's oft-criticized *Erste Gründe der gesamten Weltweisheit (Basic Tenets of the Entire World's Wisdom)* — which underwent seven editions after its publication in 1734 — and this in 1772, when the Storm and Stress was already under way — at least regarding theoretical if not poetic works. Johann Wolfgang Goethe (1749-1832), in his autobiography *Dichtung und Wahrheit (Poetry and Truth* [1811/1814]), relates how he, as a young student in Leipzig from 1765 to 1768, experienced the grandeur of an "enlightened" Rococo culture. It was in Leipzig, incidentally, this "little Paris," that Goethe came under the influence of the artist Adam Friedrich Oeser (1717-1799) and, through him, of the art historian Johann Joachim Winckelmann (1717-1768), both of whom later played a significant role in the shaping of German Classicism. In fact, a neo-classical vein runs throughout the Storm and Stress — as it does the entire eighteenth century — as is evident from the titles of two of Goethe's early poems ("Prometheus" and "Ganymed," both 1774).

The continued dominance of the Enlightenment on the theater can be seen from the repertoire of the Enlightenment writer Gotthold Ephraim Lessing's *Hamburgische Dramaturgie (Hamburg Dramaturgy* [1767/1769]) and from the titles of plays which the young Anton Reiser and his classmates perform in the early 1770s. It was not until later in that decade and early in the next that the plays of the young writers of the *Sturm und Drang (Stürmer und Dränger)* began to be performed with regularity, and even then the stage was dominated by the works of minor and foreign Enlightenment authors. As late as 1780, Friedrich II (the Great), King of Prussia (1712-1786), in his work *De la littérature allemande* (*On German Literature*) denigrated the *Stürmer und Dränger* and attempted to restore to German literature the ideals of French Classicism.

Since Johann Georg Hamann's early writings contain many of the central ideas of the Storm and Stress, one can designate the publication date of *Sokratische Denkwürdigkeiten* (*Socratic Memoirs* [1759]) as the starting point of the movement. Real impetus was given in 1770-1771 when Johann Gottfried Herder, a former student of Hamann and the philosopher Immanuel Kant (1724-1804) at Königsberg, who had already published several works critical of Enlightenment thought, went to the Alsatian town of Strasbourg for medical treatment and met with Goethe who was studying at the university. Their exchange of ideas culminated in the manifesto *Von deutscher Art und Kunst* (*Of German Nature and Art* [1773]) which contained among its five essays two by Herder (on Shakespeare and Ossian) and one by Goethe (on architecture, especially the Gothic cathedral in Strasbourg). While Goethe studied in Strasbourg he came to know other young writers who shared his and Herder's revolutionary ideas on such matters as Shakespeare, folk poetry, and genius; these included the novelist Johann Heinrich Jung(-Stilling [1740-1817]) and the dramatists Heinrich Leopold Wagner (1747-1779) and Johann Michael Reinhold Lenz (1751-1792). The *Stürmer und Dränger*, however, did not on the whole form localized groups as the Romantics were later to do, but did keep in contact through visits and letters.

The zenith of Storm and Stress came with the publication of Goethe's *Die Leiden des jungen Werther* (*The Sorrows of Young Werther*) in 1774. By the time the young writers entered their late twenties and took up other careers, the movement had begun to exhaust itself. One must remember that it was nearly impossible for a writer at this time to live solely from the pen. Goethe's call in 1775 to the court at Weimar signals a change. Although important works by him and other authors appear throughout the late 1770s, including those of the famous "drama year" 1776, these works often reveal a self-critical and parodistic tendency. Friedrich Schiller's social-critical play *Kabale und Liebe* (*Intrigue and Love* [1784]) and

Goethe as a young man

Moritz's *Anton Reiser* are the last important literary works of the movement. Goethe's trip to Italy in 1786 heralds a new epoch in German literature.

The Storm and Stress evolved against a backdrop of absolutism in government, a growing middle class and its restless sons who attended the university and welcomed the new writings, increasing skepticism regarding organized religion, and an optimistic sense of mission inherited from the Enlightenment.

Germany in the eighteenth century was made up of a conglomeration of sovereign states numbering over 300. If one includes all the independent governments, the number approaches 3,000, a phenomenon called *Kleinstaaterei* (particularism). The Holy Roman Empire, as the saying goes, was neither holy, nor Roman, nor an empire. It had ceased to be important long before Napoleon (1769-1821) finally dissolved it in 1806. (Goethe satirized it in *Faust*.) Because of particularism, no unifying force existed in Germany. The court of the empire, the *Reichskammergericht*, which had been founded in 1495, proved ineffective as a result of the states' unwillingness to relinquish power or be governed by others. "Germans" not only did not share a

Kabale und **Liebe**

ein

bürgerliches Trauerspiel

in fünf Aufzügen

von

Fridrich Schiller.

Mannheim,
in der Schwanischen Hofbuchhandlung,
1 7 8 4.

Titlepage of Schiller's famous middle-class tragedy

unified government, but were also divided by customs, dress, coinage, and religion, the latter dividing the country in half (in Johann Martin Miller's *Siegwart* [1776], a student studying in Ingolstadt, Bavaria, is not allowed to read such Protestant writers as Friedrich Gottlieb Klopstock [1724-1803] and Ewald Christian Kleist [1715-1759]). A myriad of dialects as well as regional pride even hindered the emergence of a common spoken idiom — similar to the regional opposition to *Lutherdeutsch* during the Reformation — although ever since the *Sprachgesellschaften* (language societies) of the Baroque a standard *Schriftsprache* (written language) had slowly gained acceptance.

The princes who ruled the states of Germany often vied with each other in opulence and decadence. Usually the best the people could hope for was a benevolent despot or enlightened ruler, such as Duke Karl August (1757-1828) in Weimar, Goethe's long-time patron. (Thus the theme of an honorable nobleman versus a corrupt one runs through the entire period.) More often than not, however, these petty princes resembled Duke Karl Eugen of Württemberg (1728-

1793) who imprisoned the poet Christian Schubart (1739-1791) and whose academy (*Karlsschule*, which Schiller attended) was notorious for its rigid discipline. Many states emulated the court of Louis XIV of France (1638-1715) in language, architecture, and pomp. To a large degree, Germany had become "Gallicized" (*französiert* — parodied in Lenz's plays *Der Hofmeister* [*The Tutor*] and *Pandämonium Germanicum*, and in Miller's *Siegwart*). Friedrich the Great spoke French at his court and wrote his multi-volumed works in French; he reserved German for his dogs. The *Stürmer und Dränger*, like the members of the Baroque language societies before them, reacted strongly against foreign influence and called for a return to things German.

In 1770 Friedrich the Great and Joseph II of Austria (1741-1790) formed an alliance against Russia, but only two years later the three powers took part in the first partition of Poland. Taking an example from Friedrich and Prussia, the petty princes and dukes ruled with an iron hand and left little room for dissent. In two scenes (I, 1, 8) in *Emilia Galotti* (1772), Lessing draws a portrait of a ruthless ruler for whom any means justify the end; but the setting of Lessing's play is in Italy, not Germany. A year later, Goethe, in his drama *Götz von Berlichingen*, cloaked criticism of contemporary despots in late-medieval garb. Prolonged, overt criticism of the government was hardly possible, and it is significant that the most scathing attack against oppression comes at the end of the Storm and Stress, in Schiller's *Kabale und Liebe*.

Despite the advances made in many areas during the Enlightenment, Germany in the eighteenth century still lagged far behind England and France, politically, economically, and culturally. Protectionist trade policies and high tariffs prevented the wholesale export of goods which was needed in an economy where three-fourths of the population made a living from agriculture. Many of the peasants lived in poverty, starvation was not uncommon after bad harvests — particularly before the introduction of the potato — disease was rampant — between one-fifth and one-third of all babies died before their first birthday — and a rigid class system was just starting to loosen. Serfdom still existed in eastern Germany and was not abolished until the nineteenth century. As late as 1775 a purported witch was burned at the stake in Bavaria.

Predecessors Inside and Outside of Germany

Historically, especially before Romanticism, German literature has always drawn heavily from foreign sources for inspiration. Even though the *Genies* of the Storm and Stress deemed themselves "originals," their movement was in large part predicated on models from France and England where more advanced social conditions had led sooner to a bourgeois literature. Early eighteenth-century German literature, meanwhile, was still freeing itself from courtly ties.

During the Baroque, German letters had been dominated by France. This influence continued into the Enlightenment under its chief proponent Johann Christoph Gottsched until it received a ringing challenge from two Swiss writers,

Johann Jacob Bodmer (1698-1783) and Johann Jakob Breitinger (1701-1776), who rejected Gottsched's classical French models and proposed as better examples English authors who were, they argued, more akin to the German spirit. In the ensuing decades, English literature supplanted French as a model for German writers, especially for the *Stürmer und Dränger* whose praise of English literature and scorn for French mirrored their adulation of the British political system and their disdain for the monarchical, "Gallicized" states of Germany.

In philosophy, the empirical school of John Locke (1632-1704) and David Hume (1711-1776) posited experience as the source of ideas in opposition to rationalism. A direct line can be drawn from this philosophy to Hamann and Herder's theories on religion and genius and an indirect one to the young Goethe's *Erlebnisdichtung* (poetry of experience). Also of importance, particularly for Heinrich Wilhelm Gerstenberg (1737-1823) and Herder, was the philosophy of altruism and harmony of Shaftesbury (Anthony Ashley Cooper [1621-1683]).

In aesthetics, Edward Young's *Conjectures on Original Composition* (1759) rejected classical rules ("crutches") and emphasized feelings, the creative power of imagination, and genius, all key words of the Storm and Stress. Robert Wood's *Essay on the Original Genius and Writings of Homer* (1769), reinforced the idea of the primacy of genius and helped make Homer a symbol of a more natural, patriarchal culture as we see in Goethe's *Werther* and Moritz's *Anton Reiser*. As early as 1749 Henry Fielding wrote in *Tom Jones*: "many rules for good writing have been established which have not the least foundation in truth or nature, and which serve for no other purpose than to curb and restrain genius..."

With James Macpherson's forged *Fragments of Ancient Poetry* (1760), collected in 1765 with the epics *Fingal* (1762) and *Temora* (1763) as *The Works of Ossian*, there appeared a new kind of character, one who wandered deep in thought over a foggy, mysterious, northern (as opposed to southern, classical) landscape. This landscape reflected the hero's inner turmoil (as we see in *Werther* and Gerstenberg's *Gedicht eines Skalden* [*A Scald's Poem* — 1766]) and competed with the traditional pastoral Anacreontic scenery. At the same time, Thomas Percy's *Reliques of Ancient English Poetry* (1765) showed that songs rooted in folk tradition had value and should be imitated over fossilized classical forms. Herder's *Volkslieder* (*Folk Songs* [1778/1779]) sought to discover for Germany what Percy's had for England, and in doing so influenced Goethe, Lenz, Bürger, and the poets of the Göttingen *Hainbund*. Thomas Gray's *Elegy Written in a Country Churchyard* (1753) evoked a melancholy, romantic contemplation of death and helped usher in the "graveyard poetry" that became popular in Germany in the 1770s (cf. Bürger and Ludwig Christoph Heinrich Hölty [1748-1776]).

Beginning with Samuel Richardson's *Pamela* (1740), English writers dominated the novel. The novel grew to encompass the broadening complexities of society. A deeper psychological insight into human nature was presented by Richardson and fellow novelists Henry Fielding (*Tom Jones* [1749]) and Laurence Sterne (*Tristram Shandy* [1760-1767]). Sterne's *A Sentimental Journey* (1768) unleashed a flood of sentimental travel novels. (Lessing translated sentimental as *empfindsam* and thus provided the name that scholars later attached to a literary period.) Oliver Goldsmith's *The Vicar of Wakefield* (1766) idealized pastoral life and influenced Herder and Goethe. (While riding to the ball Werther and Lotte share their feelings about the book.) It and other English novels were immediately translated into German and enjoyed tremendous popularity. An indication of the influence of the English novel can be seen in the subtitle to Johann Timotheus Hermes's *Miss Fanny Wilkes* (1766): "as good as translated from the English."

In drama, the word was Shakespeare. During the Baroque, Andreas Gryphius (1616-1664) had adapted aspects of Shakespeare, and in 1740 Bodmer had praised Shakespeare over French theater, which prompted Gottsched to rise in defense of Neo-Classicism. In the "17. Literaturbrief" ("17th Literary Letter") from 1759 Lessing had argued how Shakespeare's dramas were truer to the spirit of Greek drama than was the classical French theater. Soon thereafter followed Gerstenberg's encomium to Shakespeare in *Briefe über Merkwürdigkeiten der Literatur* (*Letters on Curiosities of Literature* [1766/1770]) and Herder's essay *Shakespeare* (1771). The drama of the Storm and Stress is not imaginable without Shakespeare; indeed, as one can see in the original version of Goethe's *Wilhelm Meister* [1776] and Moritz's *Anton Reiser,* Shakespeare's influence even penetrated into everyday activities.

Despite the dominance of English letters, French literature still exerted considerable influence in Germany, in particular the works of Jean-Jacques Rousseau (1712-1778). Rousseauism ran at fever pitch in the late 1760s and 1770s, and no writer of the Storm and Stress remained untouched. Rousseau's political thought, as represented in his two *Discours* (1750, 1755) and *Du contrat social* (1762), challenged the self-satisfied Enlightenment tenet of the progressive betterment of society and revealed the abyss that existed between the individual and society and government. Rousseau praised the inherent goodness of the individual and criticized society as corrupt and corruptive. This social-critical theme resonated in Herder's early travel diary *Journal meiner Reise im Jahre 1769*, dramas by Klinger (*Das leidende Weib* [*The Suffering Woman* [1775], *Sturm und Drang* [1777]) and Johann Anton Leisewitz (*Julius von Tarent* [1776]), as well as in Wilhelm Heinse's utopian novel of unbridled life in the Greek islands (*Ardinghello* [1787]), and in Schiller's poem "Rousseau" (1778) and his drama *Kabale und Liebe* (1784).

The sentimentality, passion, and idyllic Alpine setting of Rousseau's novel *Julie ou la Nouvelle Héloïse* (*Julie or the New Heloise* [1761]) made readers all across Europe ecstatic. Its influence can be found in Goethe's *Werther* and Heinse's *Ardinghello.* Coupled with the pastoral theme popularized by James Thomson's *The Seasons* (1730) — treated in Germany by Albrecht Haller (1708-1777), Ewald Christian von Kleist, and Salomon Geßner (1730-1788) — and the dark, brooding scenery of Macpherson's *Ossian,* a new awareness of nature evolved that can be seen in Goethe's early poetry and in *Werther.*

Rousseau's pedagogical novel *Émile* (1762) helped establish the theme of children in literature and influenced Goethe's *Götz von Berlichingen* (1773), Wagner's *Die Reue nach der Tat* (*Remorse After the Deed* [1775]) and the novels of Moritz and the educator Johann Heinrich Pestalozzi (1746-1827). In daily life too, as evidenced in Herder's correspondence with his fiancée Caroline Flachsland, the subject of *Émile* came up regularly. As with Shakespeare, one feels Rousseau's presence everywhere, in literary works as well as in letters, in almost every facet of the Storm and Stress.

A sufficient corpus of German literature had been established during the first half of the eighteenth century to exert considerable influence on the next generation of writers. Goethe's *Dichtung und Wahrheit*, Moritz's *Anton Reiser*, and Miller's *Siegwart* testify to the indebtedness of the young *Stürmer und Dränger* to the writers of the Enlightenment. Even the oft-criticized Gottsched could be praised for helping establish a "German" theater; the same applied to the much maligned Christoph Martin Wieland (1733-1813) who gave German literature a model prose style, pride in the German language, and with his translations of Shakespeare new impetus for the theater.

The two most influential German writers of the Enlightenment for the Storm and Stress were Lessing and Friedrich Gottlieb Klopstock (1724-1803). The *Stürmer und Dränger* regarded Lessing as the father of German literature. His critical works were a model for Herder, Goethe, and Schiller and his endeavors in the theater helped prepare the stage for the dramatic works of the Storm and Stress. Klopstock showed the *Stürmer und Dränger* how expressive an instrument the German language could be. He gave German poetry feeling, and the indebtedness of the young Goethe and Schiller and particularly the Göttingen poets, who viewed Klopstock as a mentor and patron, is great.

The atmosphere of the Rococo that pervaded the 1750s and 1760s can be seen in the early works of the Stürmer und Dränger, particularly in the light, playful poetry of the young Herder, Goethe, Lenz, and the Göttingen poets. A new feeling in religion spread rapidly in Protestant Germany, whence the *Stürmer und Dränger* came. The questioning of heretofore sacrosanct church tenets and the proliferation of new and old sects (e.g., Pietists, Quietists, Quakers, Anabaptists) deeply affected the writers of the 1770s and left its imprint on much of their work. Hamann and Herder's writings, Goethe's autobiography, and the novels of Moritz and Jung-Stilling attest to the important role of religion during the Storm and Stress.

The Writers

Most of the *Stürmer und Dränger* were sons of Protestant ministers or studied Protestant theology at the university. In the eighteenth century the Protestant clergy did not enjoy high social standing — particularly when compared with their Catholic counterparts — and the idyllic picture painted by Goethe in *Werther* and *Hermann und Dorothea* (1797), by Johann Heinrich Voß (1751-1826) in *Luise* (1783/1784), and by their English predecessor Oliver Goldsmith in the *Vicar of Wakefield* (1766) does not quite correspond to reality. Pastor Adams in Henry

Fielding's *Joseph Andrews* (1742) offers perhaps a more realistic portrait, although it too tends to caricature.

At the university the discipline of theology drew the neediest students, in contrast to law — Goethe's field of study — and medicine. For these students a parsonage somewhere in the country, in itself no lucrative employment, represented an escape from even poorer conditions. In the late seventeenth and early eighteenth century sons from the middle classes had begun to receive higher education. Now, for the first time, large numbers of young men — women were not admitted to the university — from the lower classes, having received some kind of earlier education, good or bad, flocked to the university to seek a better life, though the Dickensian description in Moritz's *Anton Reiser* of a rigid, impoverished school life does not seem in the least appealing.

Poorer students were often forced to live in miserable accommodations, often sharing cramped quarters with one or more other students, seek a *Freitisch* (free meal) wherever possible, sometimes under degrading circumstances, work at menial jobs, and suffer the whims of schoolmasters and principals. While still in school or right after graduation many of the students had to take on the occupation of *Hofmeister* (private tutor) to children of well-to-do parents. From Herder and Lenz to Friedrich Hölderlin (1770-1843) and Georg Wilhelm Friedrich Hegel (1770-1831), the job of *Hofmeister* most often resembled that of a glorified but poorly-paid, babysitter. Lenz's play *Der Hofmeister* carries the ironic subtitle "Advantages of a Private Education," and the scenes in act one where the tutor's salary is gradually whittled down by the father of the family must have been all too real for many of these young men. Numerous references, for example in Klinger's *Das leidende Weib*, Lenz's *Der Waldbruder* (*The Hermit* [written 1776, published 1797 in Schiller's *Die Horen*]), and in letters, attest to the misery of this position. But it was a necessary profession, for at this time it was almost impossible for writers in Germany to live from their works. No copyright law existed, and best-sellers were soon pirated, yielding no income for the author. Goethe co-financed his best Storm and Stress play, *Götz von Berlichingen*, and lost money.

In *Dichtung und Wahrheit* Goethe depicts the other, happier side of university life — as does, to a lesser extent, Miller in *Siegwart* — and for many students who were financially well-off, life at the university must have been entertaining if not rigorous. In the correspondence of young men from the early 1770s one senses their excitement as they prepared to change the world. Following the "back-to-nature" call, these writers strove for a simpler, more natural life. They disdained the wigs of their elders and began to wear their hair unadorned by powder, usually in a queue. They took clothes more suited for the outdoors — leather pants and top-boots — and wore them indoors as a sign of their earthiness. They sought God in nature, not in the heavens, and called for natural religion. In general, they were fighting against what they viewed as the arid philosophy of the Enlightenment and a rigid social order imposed from above.

Criticism

In eighteenth-century Germany no sharp division existed between the writer as poet and as critic. Nearly all the *Stürmer und Dränger* were prolific essayists, writing not just about literature but about all facets of human knowledge: religion, aesthetics, politics, language, the sciences, nature, and, of course, literature. While Enlightenment essays tend to be formal and logical, those of the Storm and Stress often lack a rigid structure; the style is rhapsodic, and the context formed from associations, free-flowing. Specialization was an incipient trend, and the *Stürmer und Dränger* considered themselves universal thinkers competent to write on anything. The age of rapidly expanding information furthered by the Enlightenment had not yet reached such proportions that writers thought they could not encompass everything in their purview. A broadening albeit still small reading public and the rapid growth of journals, such as the supportive *Frankfurter Gelehrte Anzeigen,* offered young critics a forum to express their views.

German literature has historically had close ties to criticism, that is, to philosophy and aesthetics, often as a preamble to a particular movement; one thinks here particularly of Romanticism, Young Germany, and Naturalism. The Storm and Stress can also be included in this group. In histories of literature one usually only finds detailed the lives and works of poets, dramatists, and novelists. So it is significant that in histories of German literature the only two "non-poetic" writers whose works are examined in detail both belong to the Storm and Stress: Hamann and Herder. They authored the most significant essayistic works of the period: Hamann the *Sokratische Denkwürdigkeiten* (1759), and Herder *Fragmente über die neuere deutsche Literatur* (*Fragments Concerning Recent German Literature* [1767/1768]), *Kritische Wälder* (*Critical Forests* [1769]), and the essays "Ossian" and "Shakespeare" (both 1771), collected in the manifesto *Von deutscher Art und Kunst* (1773).

The other important critical works (most of which will be discussed at length later) are Gerstenberg's *Briefe über Merkwürdigkeiten der Literatur* (1766/1767), Goethe's essays *Zum Shakespeares Tag* (*On Shakespeare's Anniversary* [1771]) and *Von deutscher Baukunst* (*On German Architecture* [1772]), Lenz's *Anmerkungen übers Theater* (*Observations on the Theater* [1774]), and Johann Kaspar Lavater's *Physiognomische Fragmente* (*Physiognomic Fragments* [1775-1778]). In these works a number of themes recur, varying from author to author, which express the salient features of the Storm and Stress.

During the Enlightenment established religion often came under attack, and many of the tenets of the church were questioned. During the Storm and Stress, the individualization of religion, begun by Protestant splinter groups, continued to a point of personalization by individual writers. Pietism emphasized the individual and the relationship to the world and God. Nearly all the Stürmer und Dränger had at some point, to varying degrees, contact with Pietism. Pantheism, heatedly discussed since Lessing's avowal (Reimarus/Goeze controversy), expressed the omnipresence of God, especially manifested in nature, and was defended by Herder and Goethe, both to a certain degree Pantheists. Herder struggled throughout his lifetime to synthesize his religious philosophy; Goethe exhibited a strong identification of nature with religious ecstasy appear in his early poetry.

As with most Storm and Stress theory, a strong element of subjectivism is evident in the belief that God can only be known through personal experience, an individualized experience. The danger of subjective internalization and introspection can be found in Moritz's *Anton Reiser*. For Hamann and Lavater this individualized experience evokes a fervent, mystical, and, in Hamann's case, sensual relationship with God. Hamann and Herder rejected the intellectualization of religion, the removal of religion beyond the realm of everyday activity and the common person. For them religion was an integral part of the personality that emphasized not God but humanity, revealing all human potential. In *Sokratische Denkwürdigkeiten* Hamann stresses belief, feeling, and self-recognition, and disdains reasoning as a means to religious insight. In *Kreuzzüge des Philologen (Crusades of the Philologist* [1762]) he ties together divine creation and human creation as being expressed in poetry. Within this work is the essay "Aesthetica in nuce," which can be termed the religious manifesto of the Storm and Stress. Here Hamann writes passionately of the internalization of religion, of feeling and intuiting God rather than "reasoning" Him.

Herder applies Hume's skepticism and Montesquieu's historical relativism to religion as he does in most of his writings of this period. Herder often agrees with his mentor Hamann, but does not indulge in the latter's mysticism and religious sensualism. Herder has great difficulty accepting the validity of any single religion and can be called eclectic in his beliefs. He believed in the intuitiveness of religion as a source of creativity and as essential to poetic endeavors. An atheistic poet would be inconceivable for Herder, as for the other *Stürmer und Dränger*, who rejected the materialist philosophy of the French *philosophes.*

The religious thought of the Storm and Stress can most often be found in essays such as those by Hamann and Herder or in collections such as Lavater's *Physiognomische Fragmente*, where the portraits of great men (including Goethe, Herder, and Lavater himself) are "analyzed" to reveal their inner powers as manifestation of the Divine. For the most part, however, religion remains detached from poetic production, and only a few lyrics reveal the concerns of the Stürmer und Dränger for religion, signalling a hiatus between the religious poems of the Baroque and the Enlightenment and those of Romanticism. Novels such as *Anton Reiser, Jung-Stillings Lebensgeschichte*, and *Siegwart* do, on the other hand, show the importance of religion in late eighteenth-century society and in the lives of the titular heroes.

The Storm and Stress is often labelled "*Geniezeit*," the "age of genius." For the *Stürmer und Dränger* the cult of genius represents at once a repudiation of conservatism in both society and poetics and a reaction against the depersonalization brought on by the rapid growth of cities. Many of the *Stürmer und Dränger* heeded Rousseau's call for a return to a simpler state where the individual lived unencumbered by an oppressive society. Drawing on models from England the writers formed a theory of genius to fit their own needs. In its extreme form it is unbridled subjectivism mixed with narcissism and egoism, a license to run rampant and condescendingly criticize those not included among the *Genies*. Goethe's *Werther*, Jacobi's novel *Woldemar* (1777), Lenz's *Der Hofmeister*, and several of Klinger's dramas (*Die Zwillinge* [*The Twins*] and *Simsone Grisaldo* — both 1776) show how early one tired of the surfeit of geniuses.

In *Sokratische Denkwürdigkeiten* Hamann recognizes as geniuses Homer and Shakespeare, who break all shackles to reach new poetic freedom. Hamann's concept of genius, like all his concepts, bears the imprint of his religious thought. The genius receives divine inspiration in order to create. In *Fünf Hirtenbriefe* (*Five Pastoral Letters* [1763]) Hamann compares a fig tree shaking off its fruit to the genius's discarding of all rules. For Hamann, genius is the antithesis of reasoning. As the poet rejects all rules, he becomes creative, draws on inner powers, becomes God-like, unfettered, with a limitless imagination.

Gerstenberg, like Hamann, releases the poet from all adherence to rules and also selects Homer and Shakespeare as his models. He rejects the school of imitative poetry and instead calls for originality. Significant for Gerstenberg's definition is his emphasis on the irrational as part of the creative world which must not be restricted.

Herder's idea of genius must be seen in conjunction with his definition of a unified personality and with his social criticism, the latter being particularly strong during the 1770s. There is no duality for Herder's "soul." Duality has arisen from the development of society. People have become "half-thinkers," "half-feelers"(*Übers Erkennen und Empfinden der menschlichen Seele* [*Concerning Cognition and Sensation in the Human Mind* — 1774]). Only the genius can unite all human powers and create. For Herder, as well as for Hamann, language, particularly one's native language, reveals the genius. In his *Fragmente*, Herder calls the language of reason "a curse for the poetic genius," and says that no genius "should be ashamed of his mother tongue." Only the mother tongue can express the inwardness of thoughts and feelings. Herder recognizes in Shakespeare the genius *par excellence*, for he created his own dramatic world independent of other dramatists. Herder, however, does not call for unbridled genius. In his essay *Ursachen des gesunkenen Geschmacks* (*Concerning the Cause of Decline in Taste* [1775]), he writes that genius without responsible education can lead astray.

Lavater imbued his idea of genius with religious feeling. Genius dwells within the poet, is not learned or acquired, but inspired by God. Inspired creativity is a key for Lavater's genius, God-like in human form, placed next to Christ as the embodiment of genius. Lavater's theories alienated him from orthodox Christians. At the same time, his transcendental emphasis drew the scorn of Enlightenment critics.

No matter how each writer varied the concept of genius, all envisaged a poet free from all ties, united in character, drawing on inner feelings to create what had not been created before. The young poets of the Storm and Stress viewed themselves as these geniuses and attempted to create a new poetic vision based on feelings rather than on reason. The plight of the misunderstood genius can be seen in Wagner's play *Prometheus, Deukalion und seine Rezensenten* (*Prometheus, Deucalion, and his Critics* [1775]).

In his essay on Shakespeare, Goethe writes: "And I cry out: Nature! Nature! Nothing is as much nature as Shakespeare's characters." Goethe employs nature here as meaning natural, unaffected, unadulterated, but also in a broader sense, which appears in his letters from this period, as a condition in which human capabilities and potential are fully realized. For all the Storm and Stress dramatists true art was an imitation of nature. Shakespeare's characters therefore embody the ideal unification of human powers, encompass all human attributes, are universal.

For the Storm and Stress in general nature had many shades of meaning. For Hamann nature had been ruined by the Enlightenment. It had been over-analyzed, classified, and reduced to fit into a rational system. Hamann wanted to free nature. For him it was living, pulsating, and reflected human existence and its ties to God. God was in nature as He was in all humans. "Nature affects us through our senses and passions," he writes, and not through our reflections on it.

Herder viewed nature as the organic realization of God's power. People gain spiritual sustenance from nature and see the workings of divine powers in it; humans live in a symbiotic relationship to nature. For Herder, nature also assumes the Rousseauian sense of primitive, harmonic. Although Herder did not hearken back to the same natural state that Rousseau did (or which Herder thought he did), he nevertheless viewed earlier times and uncorrupted civilizations as more natural, as embodying those characteristics of a unified human spirit before it was corrupted by modern civilization. (Goethe parodied this "natural" side of Herder in *Satyros* [1773].)

The *Stürmer und Dränger* revelled in nature. Goethe's early poetry is filled with nature imagery, not in the analytic sense of Enlightenment descriptive poetry, but for emotive reasons, and both Werther and Siegwart communed with nature and took solace in it. Since Klopstock, ice-skating had been popular, and now other outdoor activities such as hikes, picnics, walks, and boating became fashionable.

Poetry

What we now read in anthologies under the rubric Storm and Stress represents but a small percentage of the poetic output of the 1770s. If one glances through the journals for this period, for example Wieland's *Der Teutsche Merkur* or the sympathetic *Göttinger Musenalmanach* or *Iris*, one immediately notices the great mixture of good and mediocre poetry. The poet could not live from verse alone. Klopstock's laudatory gains in establishing himself as a *freier Schriftsteller* (independent writer) were not immediately shared by others; one need only think of the impoverished Hölty or Bürger. Of all the poets, only Bürger actually enjoyed popular, though not financial, success, and that primarily because of his ballad "Lenore."

The greatest influence on the poets of the Storm and Stress came from two main sources. Percy's *Reliques of Ancient English Poetry* (1765), as disseminated by Herder, opened up German poetry to the folk song and to the ballad. This vein affected primarily Goethe, Bürger, and the Göttingen poets. The greatest impetus to Storm and Stress lyrics came from Klopstock. His dynamic, neologistic use of language, powerful free rhythms, and the ability to arouse emotions influenced all the poets. Klopstock was revered by the Göttingen poets — who took their name (*Hainbund*) from one of his poems — and his poetry read by them under oak trees in the moonlight. Goethe describes in *Werther* the importance of Klopstock for this generation: "she [Lotte] looked toward the heavens and at me; I saw her eyes fill with tears; she laid her hand on mine and said: 'Klopstock.' I immediately recalled the magnificent ode she had in mind and became engulfed by the torrent of emotion which she poured over me with this password." The Storm and Stress poets transferred, however, Klopstock's ecstasy from the religious realm to the personal. The self in all its sufferings and joy, in all its trials and tribulations, became the overriding theme of their poetry. Never before had German poetry witnessed such a burst of feeling in such an expressive form.

Goethe's transition from an imitative poet in the light, Rococo style can be seen in the poetry he wrote before his university years in Strasbourg. While exhibiting the trappings of previous literary tradition, Goethe's early collections of love poetry, *Das Buch Annette*, *Oden an meinen Freund (Odes to my Friend)*, and *Neue Lieder (New Songs)*, nevertheless exude a freshness and vitality new to German poetry. In "Die Nacht" ("The Night" [1768]), the first of Goethe's night poems, one finds the customary references to Luna, zephyrs, and sensuality (*Wollust*), while the suspenseful, nightly atmosphere is reminiscent of Young's *Night Thoughts*. Yet the feelings of the speaker and the images are new and powerful, rivalled only by Klopstock.

While under Herder's tutelage in Strasbourg, Goethe entered the realm of Ossian and folk poetry and developed a sense of poetic mission. Combined with his love for Friederike Brion in neighboring Sesenheim, he produced his first Storm and Stress lyrics. The playful, contemporary theme of painted ribbons in "Kleine Blumen, kleine Blätter" ("Small Flowers, Small Leaves" [1771]) yields to a seriousness and sincerity out of step with similar poems. In his paean to spring, "Maifest" ("May Celebration" [1771]), Goethe uses short verses to depict the joy of nature and the speaker's oneness with it. The early version of "Willkommen und Abschied" ("Welcome and Farewell") shows clearly how Goethe has refined and expanded his use of language. The emotive verbs and visual adjectives create a scene of anxious anticipation, foreboding, and sympathy. Neologisms like *Nebelkleid* (dress of mist) and *Wolkenhügel* (hill of clouds) and the use of participles reveal Goethe's indebtedness to Klopstock and anticipate the language of the later hymns. The subjectivity of this poem surpasses that found in all previous eighteenth-century poetry, including Klopstock's.

The two hymns "Wanderers Sturmlied" ("Wanderer's Storm Song" [1772]), which Goethe later characterized as "half nonsense," and "Prometheus" (1773) show Goethe at the pinnacle of his Storm and Stress poetic production. Both poems reveal a self-reliant, rebellious spirit (both protagonists are "god-like"), and both extend the linguistic brilliance of "Willkommen und Abschied," particularly in the usage of neologisms and participles. In their use of motifs, both share the neo-classical vein that predominated throughout the century. The structured, rhymed verses of the love poetry gives way to free rhythms and short and long verses. The structure of the poems mirrors the inner turmoil of the lyrical self.

"Wanderers Sturmlied" rejects the playful Anacreon and the pastoral poet Theocritus as insufficient for the new poetic age and opts for the "inner glow" of Pindar. The god of revelry, Bacchus, cannot provide inspiration alone; the poet also requires the assistance of the sun god Apollo. Only then can the poet pass through all the trials and tribulations of life and arrive at his "hut," the symbol of refuge, solace, and a healthy, natural life, as it also is in "Prometheus." In mythology, Prometheus disdains Zeus and the concomitant privileges and powers of the gods in order to bring fire to humankind. Though Goethe transforms the myth somewhat, Prometheus still represents rebellion and creativity, the genius and strength to rely on one's own abilities to create what is good and necessary. As such, "Prometheus" can be said to stand for the entire Storm and Stress, to represent the struggles of the *Stürmer und Dränger* against literary tradition and against a rigid social and political order.

Representative of Goethe's interest in folk poetry are the poems "Heidenröslein" ("Little Rose on the Heath" [1771]) and "Der König von Thule" ("The King of Thule" [1774]). Along with Bürger, Goethe helped establish the ballad as a popular poetic form. "Neue Liebe, neues Leben" ("New Love, New Life" [1775]) signals, as the title indicates, a beginning. This poem belongs to those written for Lili Schönemann, Goethe's fiancée for a brief time. Gone is the rapture and linguistic boldness of the *Sesenheimer Lieder*. Only the theme echoes the Storm and Stress. For Goethe it was time to move on.

In poetry Goethe towered above his fellow *Stürmer und Dränger*. Nevertheless, there were a number of fine poets, chief among them Gottfried August Bürger. Today, unfortunately, Bürger's fame rests almost solely on his immensely popular ballad "Lenore" (1773) and on the unjust and devastating attack on him by Friedrich Schiller. For a short period Bürger had close ties to the Göttingen poets, and in 1774 he published "Lenore" in their *Göttinger Musenalmanach*.

Beneath the breathtaking narrative tempo, the chilling story of the return of Lenore's dead lover Wilhelm, and their ghostly nocturnal ride to a macabre wedding of death, lies a fascinating look at the social values of the late eighteenth century. Bürger's ballad shows the influence of Percy's *Reliques of Ancient English Poetry*, of Herder's essay *Ossian*, and of Goethe's play *Götz von Berlichingen*. The lengthy ballad (256 lines) combines elements of folk poetry, horror tales, and popular romance in a finely-crafted structure of alliterative, onomatopoeic verse. In his essays on poetry Bürger wrote that poets should not use "dead language," but should employ "living dialect." In "Lenore" Bürger turns theory into practice. Colloquialisms characterize the speech of Lenore and her mother. Indeed, the entire poem is rooted in the lives of the lower classes. The nearly contemporary setting of the Seven Years' War (1756-1763) also contributed to its popularity. Though Bürger never again equalled the popularity of "Lenore," he nevertheless wrote a number of other ballads which are still worth reading today, such as "Des Pfarrers Tochter von Taubenhain" ("The Minister's Daughter from Taubenhain") and "Der wilde Jäger" ("The Wild Hunter").

Bürger's "Der Bauer" ("The Peasant" [1773]) reveals the political side of Storm and Stress poetry. Such poems as this, Christian Friedrich Schubart's "Die Fürstengruft" ("The Princely Vault") and Leopold Friedrich Goeckingk's "Treibjagen" ("Battue" [to beat the underbrush to drive out game, thus ruining a farmer's crop]) decry the excesses of the nobility. But this outcry was futile and even led to incarceration in the case of Schubart. Much of Schiller's early poetry also echoes this theme of protest, one that resonates in his dramas *Die Räuber* and *Kabale und Liebe*.

Drama

The drama of the Storm and Stress best exemplifies the ideology of the movement, while at the same time revealing its strengths and weaknesses. More than poetry or the novel, the play was tailor-made for the explosive style and various themes of the *Stürmer und Dränger*. Nearly all the major writers of the Storm and Stress were dramatists first and poets second, and of the poets only Goethe can be called a great lyricist (Schiller's excellence in poetry comes later, during Classicism). All the dramatists concerned themselves not just with practice but also with theory, and their many theoretical essays reflect their efforts not only at establishing a "German" drama but also at revolutionizing a literary form and molding it to reflect their ideals.

The revolution in the theater came with the shifting of emphasis from the neo-classical French theater, imitated during the Enlightenment by Gottsched and his followers, to the "northern," (so called by Gerstenberg and Herder) theater of Shakespeare. Already during the latter stages of the Enlightenment Bodmer and Johann Elias Schlegel (1719-1749) had called attention to Shakespeare. In the "17. Literaturbrief" (1759) Lessing had pointed out the advantages for the German theater that Shakespeare's characters had over those of the neo-classical French theater. He reiterated this position in the *Hamburgische Dramaturgie* (1767/1769), but also warned of a too slavish imitation of Shakespeare. As mentioned earlier, Hamann had applied his definition of genius to Shakespeare and his works.

Gerstenberg first turned this admiration of Shakespeare into theory and practice, which set the tone for the entire Storm and Stress. The exuberant, explosive style of *Briefe über Merkwürdigkeiten der Literatur* (1766/1767), imitated by Herder and others, discounted the Enlightenment belief that Shakespeare had to be judged by classical standards, a theme Herder later defined more sharply. Gerstenberg stated that Shakespeare's tragedies could not be viewed from the "point of view of tragedy, but as copies of moral nature." Though Gerstenberg's views on the theater, like Lessing's, still yield in some ways to convention and do not represent a complete break from traditional dramatic theory, he nevertheless took the first step toward a new theater and encouraged others to follow. His excruciating tragedy *Ugolino* (1768), based on the story in Dante's *Divine Comedy* of the starvation of Count Ugolino and his sons, adheres to the classical unities of time, place, and action, but its hero, language, and atmosphere, all very Shakespearean, became a model for the *Stürmer und Dränger*.

In his essay on Shakespeare of 1771 Herder applied his theory of history to Shakespeare and his works. Herder sought to show how the classical unities evolved naturally as a part of Greek tragedy but that they did not belong to "modern" theater. Shakespeare, like the Greek tragedians, was a product of his times, and his theater represents that. As a "northern" writer, Shakespeare had much more in common with German culture than the (neo-)classical writers. The end of his essay praises Goethe, whose tragedy *Götz von Berlichingen* Herder knew about, as the herald of a new German theater. The importance of Herder's work can be seen directly in the essays by Goethe and Lenz, and indirectly in the Shakespearean plays of the Storm and Stress.

Other important theoretical works are Goethe's treatise *Zum Shakespeares Tag* (1771); Lenz's *Anmerkungen übers Theater* (1774), which stressed the importance of character over plot, extolled the genius of Shakespeare, and delineated tragedy and comedy; and Wagner's *Briefe die Seylersche Schauspielgesellschaft betreffend* (*Letters Concerning the Seyler Acting Troupe* [1777]) and *Neuer Versuch über die Schauspielkunst* (*New Attempt at Dramatic Art* [1776]), a translation of Sebastian Mercier's *Du Théâtre ou nouvel essai sur l'art dramatique* (1773). Mercier had praised Shakespeare, disdained classical rules and unities, called for the representation of all social classes on the stage, and demanded that the theater be socially involved.

The growth of the theater in Germany was a slow, belated process. Despite the efforts of Gottsched, Caroline Neuber (1697-1760), and Lessing, the German theater was still in an embryonic state by 1770, especially when compared to the theater in France and England. Its repertoire consisted largely of second-rate, often foreign, sentimental plays. Theatrical troupes were poorly paid, led a vagabond life, and were often looked upon condescendingly as the dregs of society. A glimpse of the miserable existence of these troupes can be gained from Moritz's *Anton Reiser* and Goethe's *Wilhelm Meisters theatralische Sendung* (*Wilhelm Meister's Theatrical Mission* [1776]). Only in the last twenty-five years of the century did German troupes begin to acquire a more respected status and enjoy prolonged patronage.

Propitiously for the Storm and Stress, a number of serious acting troupes emerged at this time across central and northern Germany. In 1774 Gotha (important in *Anton Reiser*) became the first court to establish a theater for German plays under the direction of a German, but it lasted only until 1777. Even with the increase of troupes and theaters it was not easy for the *Stürmer und Dränger* to gain access to the stage, and, indeed, plays often had to be toned down to be accepted, for instance Wagner's *Die Kindermörderin* (*The Infanticide* [1776]). Only after the success of Goethe's *Götz von Berlichingen* could Shakespeare's *Hamlet* be premiered in 1776, and then in a truncated version. The translations of Shakespeare undertaken by Wieland (1762-1766) and Johann Joachim Eschenburg (1775-1782) were well-intentioned but often inaccurate. Even in the last decades of the century, the sentimental dramas of August von Kotzebue (1761-1819) and August Wilhelm Iffland (1759-1814) dominated the theater over the plays of Goethe, Lenz, Klinger, and Schiller.

In his essay on Shakespeare Goethe pinpoints the central theme of Storm and Stress drama when he observes that the bard's plays "all revolve around the secret point — which no philosopher has seen or designated — in which what is particular to our self, the pretended freedom of our will, collides with the necessary course of totality."

Goethe's Götz is a man caught between times, between the Middle Ages and the new order of the Renaissance to which he will not yield. He thus symbolizes the struggle of the *Stürmer und Dränger* against a social and political order which they felt did not understand them. In dramatic fragments from this period, Goethe chose other figures — Caesar, Mohammed, and Prometheus — which like Götz were caught at that "secret point." Götz, "ein großer Kerl" (a grand fellow), like Macbeth and Hamlet, becomes a model for other dramatists, especially Klinger and Leisewitz.

The powerful language of *Götz von Berlichingen*, the characters (particularly Götz, Weislingen, and Adelheid), the secondary themes (family, brother-like conflict between Götz and Weislingen, the Middle Ages, the Shakespearean atmosphere, rapid and numerous place changes) all had a tremendous influence on Goethe's contemporaries. *Götz von Berlichingen* unleashed a flood of imitations (Klinger's *Otto* immediately followed as well as other regional, nationalistic knightly dramas). After Herder read the original version which Goethe had sent him, he commented: "Shakespeare has ruined you." Goethe then eliminated much of the political criticism and smoothed out the language, but it remained an offspring of Shakespeare and the best example of how strong Shakespeare's influence could be.

Goethe followed *Götz von Berlichingen* with several plays quite different from the tumultuousness and grandeur of his first dramatic work. *Clavigo* (1774) depicts another Storm and Stress theme: marriage and fidelity. Clavigo can be true to nothing and no one, and perishes because of his divided soul, a typical problem for Storm and Stress heroes torn between ideals and desires. *Stella* (1776), another "internal" rather than "external" play, examines the conflicts of lovers caught in a relationship society cannot condone. The wishful solution of a *ménage à trois* was later changed by Goethe into a double suicide.

The Storm and Stress excelled in farces and parodies. Here too Goethe was the master. *Jahrmarktsfest zu Plundersweilern (Annual Fair at Plundersweilern* [1773]) views the world as a fair and its participants as worthy of parody. Both *Fastnachtspiel vom Pater Brey (Carnival Play of Pater Brey* [1773]) and *Satyros oder der vergötterte Waldteufel (Satyros or the Deified Forest Devil* [1773]) ridicule contemporary excesses, the latter poking fun at Herder. *Götter, Helden und Wieland (Gods, Heroes, and Wieland* [1774]) ridicules the dispassionate characters and philosophy of virtue espoused in several works of Wieland. These farces reveal the lighter, comic-relief side of the period and show that not all was storm and stress.

All of Friedrich Maximilian Klinger's Storm and Stress plays throb with a fervent language and teeter on the verge of explosion. What Klinger lacks in original plots and ideas he makes up for in passionate language and characters. *Das leidende Weib* (1775) deals with the theme of adultery and is now most interesting, like its predecessor *Otto*, for its explicit and implied criticism of courtly society and contemporary morals. Ironically, the heroine is reproached for reading sentimental authors like Wieland, just as Countess LaRoche in Lenz's *Die Soldaten* (*The Soldiers* [1776]), in an interesting echo of Henry Fielding, blames, albeit falsely, Marie's downfall on Richardson's *Pamela*. Little did Klinger and Lenz (and Goethe in regard to *Werther*) realize the effect their plays would have on such receptive souls as Anton Reiser.

Klinger's best play, *Die Zwillinge*, concerns the common Storm and Stress theme of fratricide. The younger brother Guelfo is a variation of the "großer Kerl," bordering on the pathological, whose reasons for killing his brother, though superficially obvious — primogeniture, the "stealing" of Kamilla, whom he only wants in order to thwart his brother — are not well motivated except in the realm of abnormal psychology as a form of rebellion. Interesting is Guelfo's obsession for his deceased beloved Juliette; also of note is the criticism of Guelfo's friend Grimaldi as a Werther type, a criticism Klinger repeats in his next two plays *Simsone Grisaldo* (1776) and *Sturm und Drang* (1777).

Simsone Grisaldo represents already for Klinger a moving away from earlier sentiments. Storm and Stress rebelliousness has been tempered by Shaftesburian harmony. In *Sturm und Drang* one hears distinct echoes of *Romeo and Juliet* and *Richard II*. Of particular interest is Wild (!), a Byronic figure who finds a peaceful resolution of his problem in his love for Jenny. His "friends" Blasius and La Feu, caricatures of the Rococo sentimentalist and the Storm and Stress *Kraftkerl* (powerful fellow), want to retire to the Alps to lead, respectively, the life of a hermit and shepherd. *Sturm und Drang* represents for Klinger, as *Werther* does for Goethe, a recapitulation and an overcoming of earlier philosophies. Only four years later, in the novel *Plimplamplasko*, Klinger ridicules the *Genieapostel* Christoph Kaufmann.

Jacob Michael Reinhold Lenz, whose moral themes bring him close to the Enlightenment but whose language, structure, and characters anticipate Georg Büchner (1813-1837) and the Expressionists, led a wayward life similar to many dramatic figures of the Storm and Stress. In theoretical writings Lenz sought to define the distinctions between comedy and tragedy. In the manuscript of his first major play, *Der Hofmeister* (1774), Lenz designated the play a "comedy and tragedy." His second important play *Die Soldaten* (1776), was entitled "comedy," but Lenz later withdrew the classification. According to Lenz life was tragic and comic, and any depiction of life had to have elements of both, and was then deemed "comedy." Lenz the pedagogue viewed such a comedy as a means to raise the common viewer to real tragedy, the depiction of great characters, while comedy dealt with plot, the representation of everyday life.

More than any other Storm and Stress writer Lenz reveals the conflicts between the individual and society. All his major plays revolve around the confrontation between parents and children. In *Der Hofmeister*, Gustchen, the daughter of the Major, is seduced by Läuffer, the tutor, who has a symbolic father in the figure of Wenzeslaus, a schoolteacher. The play is not only a plea for public schools but an exposé of the miserable lot of university students who, after obtaining their degrees, often foundered in society before they could get a decent job. It is also a protest against a society whose rigidness precludes real love. The hero's castration and marriage with a simple woman, who does not want children but is satisfied with feeding her father's chickens and ducks, underscores the problem of bringing children into a corrupt society.

In *Die Soldaten* Marie rejects her social equal Stolzius, a linen merchant, for the charms of Desportes, a nobleman and officer. She is dishonored and eventually becomes a prostitute (along with death, seemingly the only possibilities for a young woman who had lost her "virtue"). Stolzius sacrifices all in order to poison Desportes and himself. At the end of the play Marie is reconciled with her father. In *Der Hofmeister* Gustchen eventually marries Fritz von Berg, a member of the upper class, while Läuffer is content with a farm girl. Here, Marie is punished for her aspirations to climb the societal ladder through marriage. While criticizing the rigidity of society, Lenz shows the difficulty in moving upward in that society. Lenz expanded the boundaries of the social drama and gave the theater a realistic view of life it had not seen before. *Der neue Menoza* (*The New Menoza* [1774]) is a parody of the Enlightenment and the play of mistaken identity. *Pandämonium Germanicum* (1775), in the tradition of Goethe's farces, pays homage to Goethe, Herder, Klopstock, and Lessing, while criticizing Enlightenment ideals.

Two minor playwrights, Johann Anton Leisewitz (1752-1806) and Heinrich Leopold Wagner (1747-1779), produced in the wake of the Storm and Stress a few works still worth reading today. Leisewitz's *Julius von Tarent* (1776), the runner-up to Klinger's *Die Zwillinge* in a drama competition by the Hamburg theater director Friedrich Schröder (1744-1816), depicts the theme of fratricide. Noteworthy in the play is the political thought, its anticipation of Friedrich Hebbel's *Agnes Bernauer* (1852), the Wertherian Julius, the social criticism, and the emancipated Cäcilia, a friend of the heroine. Two dramatic scenes by Leisewitz, *Die Pfandung* (*The Forfeit* [1775]) and *Der Besuch um Mitternacht* (*The Midnight Visit* [1775]), are interesting for their criticism of the nobility. In *Die Pfandung* a peasant and his wife discuss the impending seizure of their bed by the prince for their arrears. At the end the peasant consoles his wife with the thought that "they cannot take immortality away from me!" In *Der Besuch um Mitternacht* a prince is visited by the spirit of Varius the Cherusker who admonishes him to end his lascivious ways.

Wagner's two plays *Die Reue nach der Tat* (*Remorse after the Deed* [1775]) and *Die Kindermörderin* (*The Infanticide* [1777]) are remarkable, aside from their six acts and no scenes, for their realistic dialogue incorporating colloquialisms and dialect and for their social criticism. The former deals with a lawyer and the daughter of a coachman whose marriage is foiled by the mother of the lawyer because of the couple's social inequality. The latter play tells the story of the butcher's daughter Evchen who is seduced by the Lovelace-like rake Lieutenant von Gröningseck. Evchen's mother, in her desire to hobnob with the nobility (like Wesener in Lenz's *Die Soldaten*), unwittingly aids the seducer. Despite the unbelievable transformation of the protagonist, this variant of the Gretchen theme (Goethe accused Wagner of plagiarism) still rings true in its depiction of milieu. The father's exclamation at the end of the play, when he sees that his daughter has stabbed her baby: "The whole world is closing in on me," anticipates the famous line spoken by Master Anton at the end of Friedrich Hebbel's *Maria Magdalena* (1844): "I no longer understand the world."

Friedrich Schiller's early plays share with the Storm and Stress explosive language, powerful characters, and rebellion against convention, but like Lenz his moralizing tendency joins him with the Enlightenment. Schiller's first play *Die Räuber* (*The Robbers* [1781]) appears almost as a caricature of the Storm and Stress. It is no wonder that Goethe saw in it a return to a time he felt he had successfully escaped. Leftover themes from the Storm and Stress include the hostile brothers (which Schiller

Schiller in 1786, after a painting by Anton Graff

manages to imbue with new vigor), the Prodigal Son, the noble girlfriend, and Lear-like father. Schiller, however, possessed early a remarkable command of the theater, and only Goethe's *Götz von Berlichingen* competes with *Die Räuber* in theatrical effect.

Schiller's *bürgerliches Trauerspiel* (bourgeois tragedy) *Kabale und Liebe* can be seen as the recapitulation of the entire Storm and Stress drama. It is a play of social and political criticism whose first two acts contain in its delineation of character, plot development, and language some of the finest moments in German theater. Schiller turns the unequal love affair into a broad portrait of life and society in the late eighteenth century. As in *Die Räuber*, the destruction of the family (in itself a Storm and Stress theme) symbolizes the breakdown of the entire social order. As unforgettable as Walz in Wagner's *Die Reue nach der Tat* and Humbrecht in *Die Kindsmörderin* are, Schiller's music master Miller makes them pale in comparison, and the secretary, Wurm, the embodiment of the corrupt court, is evil incarnate and outdoes even Lessing's Marinelli in *Emilia Galotti*. What moves *Kabale und Liebe* beyond other Storm and Stress plays, besides its theatrical excellence, is the figure of Luise. In no other Storm and Stress drama, not even in *Faust*, does a heroine play such a convincing, tragic role. (The original title was *Luise Millerin*; the more sensationalist title was provided by August Wilhelm Iffland.)

The Novel

Unlike epic and lyric poetry, both of which enjoyed a long tradition and great prestige, and unlike the theater whose neo-classical productions played favorably at the courts in the first half of the century, the novel in Germany suffered from a poor reputation, to a large degree justified. More than any other genres, the German novel lagged far behind its British and French counterparts, due primarily to a smaller and less sophisticated reading public and to a lack of a cosmopolitan center such as London or Paris, which keep the German novel provincial. Prose fiction for the *Stürmer und Dränger* was not a primary medium. The drama and poem were much better suited for the explosive style of the Storm and Stress. Aside from Friedrich von Blanckenburg's 1774 essay on the novel (*Versuch über den Roman* [*Attempted Essay on the Novel*]), which only peripherally touched upon the Storm and Stress, no major theory on the novel was advanced during the 1770s.

Not until Christoph Martin Wieland's *Agathon* (1766-1767) did Germany offer a novel beyond the second-rate imitations of Richardson, Daniel Defoe (c. 1660-1731), Sterne, and Antoine-François Prévost (1697-1763). In Blanckenburg's opinion, however, even *Agathon* was too sophisticated for the German reading public. Johann Martin Miller, in the preface to *Siegwart*, laments about the "novel — a word which, unfortunately! has perhaps become despicable because of bad models..." And in *Aus Eduard Allwills Papieren* (*From Eduard Allwill's Papers* [1776]), Friedrich Heinrich Jacobi notes that a recent journal commented "that even a proper novel is accustomed only to being classified among the excrescences of literature..."

In spite of this prejudice, the novel continued to grow in popularity. More novels were published in the 1770s and 1780s (1,415) than in the previous seventy years. Translations of Richardson, Sterne, Fielding, and Rousseau proliferated along with imitations of *Don Quixote* and *Robinson Crusoe*. Finally, in the 1760s, German novelists began to write a "German" novel about German customs, and even though these novels did not rise above the *Trivialroman*, they cleared the way for the novel of the 1770s which revolutionized German prose. What sets the novel of the Storm and Stress apart is its introspection and internalization. All the major novels of the 1770s are autobiographical in nature; all deal with the problems of the individual and conflicts with society and self. Not until the 1770s did novelists concern themselves so deeply with the psychology of their characters. This psychological insight is the greatest legacy of the Storm and Stress, and it is nowhere more apparent than in the best novel of the period, Goethe's *Die Leiden des jungen Werther*.

Werther emerges out of a number of traditions that prevailed in the second half of the eighteenth century: a more vivid realism that turned its focus away from the aristocracy and the courts to the middle class; a sentimentality evidenced by copious tears and emotional outbursts, which was strongest in Germany primarily since it served as an outlet against restrictive political and social conditions; an introspection nurtured by Pietism and other religious sects; and the epistolary novel which had been in vogue since Richardson's *Pamela*.

Werther can boast of several firsts: in the traditional sentimental novel a woman was the main character. *Werther*, however, shows that effusiveness was also part of a male character; Werther depicts the problems of a young person in society; the theme of suicide was transferred from the stage to the novel; the playful eroticism of the Anacreontic poets and of Wieland took on a more serious quality as part of the troubled "psychology" of the hero; and it can be said that *Werther* is the first tragic novel in Europe.

As a contemporary novel, *Werther* vividly depicts a prototypical Storm and Stress figure, a would-be artist who struggles both with himself and his art and with the society he feels restricts him. It is easy to see in Werther different features of not just Goethe himself but also of his fellow poet Jakob Michael Reinhold Lenz. The reader sympathizes with Werther. He is good-looking, intelligent, and sensitive. He comments — at least initially — acutely on various subjects and struggles against a rigid society that looks down on nonconformists. But Werther is a dilettante who does not create but only makes excuses for his non-productivity. He does not look for love in a woman who can love him, views love as a game of conquest — at least in the past — and seeks a kind of motherly love to insulate him from the real world. Werther does not really try in life; he laments about "fate" and his half-hearted efforts at integration into society. Yet as we watch Werther disintegrate before our eyes, we are moved and disturbed and caught up in his turmoil to a degree unmatched by any previous character in a German novel.

With *Werther* Goethe closed a chapter of his life. His next significant prose work, the original version of *Wilhelm Meister*, begun in 1777, does not share the pathos-laden prose of *Werther*. In just a few years Goethe had moved far beyond his first novel, even to the point where he could parody it along with other sentimental novels in *Triumph der Empfindsamkeit* (*Triumph of Sentimentality* [1778]). Goethe saw the danger inherent in the introspection and sentimentality of the period and fought not to succumb to it. Although *Werther* represented the end of a period for Goethe, it marked the beginning of one for many of his contemporaries. *Werther* was imitated in verse and prose, depicted on tea cups and lamp shades. The novel had spoken to an entire generation of receptive souls who were caught up in Werther's sorrows but who misunderstood Goethe's message. The influence of the work throughout Europe was boundless as is evident by the imitative novels that followed in its wake.

In two novels, *Aus Eduard Allwills Papieren* (1775-1776) and *Woldemar* (1777), Friedrich Heinrich Jacobi dealt with the cult of the genius, which he saw embodied in Goethe, and its manifestations in a Werther-like figure. In the first novel, the hero is all will, a brooding, confused individual who cannot "find a place to rest his head" and who echoes passages from *Werther*. The obvious borrowings and the lack of focus limit the work's value, and its interest today rests mainly on it being an appendage to *Werther* and a prelude to the structurally and thematically more refined *Woldemar, which* continues the theme of *Eduard Allwill*. The father of the central female character, Henriette, tells her on his death bed she should not marry Woldemar because "he neither actually believes in God nor in man. He is by all means a desperate character: passionate, dissolute, reckless." The novel shows the attempts made by Woldemar's friends to integrate him into their society. Much of the novel reads like *Werther*, but lacks Goethe's psychological insight and character development, a failure most evident in Woldemar's unconvincing conversion and in an unsatisfying conclusion. *Woldemar* is for Jacobi what *Werther* was for Goethe: a reckoning with a troubled age.

Another novel in the *Werther* mold is Johann Martin Miller's *Siegwart: Eine Klostergeschichte (Siegwart, a Cloister Story)*, published in 1776. The extreme effusiveness of the novel, which made it a best-seller, makes the work nearly inaccessible today. Literary historians generally malign the novel, but it nevertheless offers an interesting view of German life in the 1770s. The portrayal of the young Siegwart as he moves through the educational system faintly recalls a *Bildungsroman*. The monastery atmosphere and

Göß von Berlichingen

mit der

eifernen Hand.

Ein

Schauspiel.

1 7 7 3.

Titlepage of Goethe's dramatic hit of 1773

longing for death anticipate Romanticism, and the conflict between city and country — also evident in *Werther* — will run throughout the nineteenth-century novel. Most interesting is Miller's depiction of a spectrum of society and its rigid class structure. Miller uses dialects and colloquialisms for characterization, and even though his figures lack the depth of Werther, they nevertheless represent an advance over the stock figures of the sentimental novel.

Jakob Michael Reinhold Lenz's *Der Waldbruder (The Hermit* [1776, first published in 1797]) even carries the subtitle "Pendant to Goethe's *Werther*." The hero Herz (heart) has many of the attributes of the *Stürmer und Dränger*. He has renounced society and withdrawn to a hut in the woods. Herz lives according to his inner convictions and criticizes his friend Rothe (read Goethe) for compromising his beliefs by accepting a position at court (as Goethe had in Weimar). *Der Waldbruder* represents Lenz's further estrangement from society.

Religious introspection, a renewed emphasis on the self, and a didacticism held over from the Enlightenment helped produce the autobiographical novel of the 1770s and 1780s. The two most prominent are Johann Heinrich Jung(-Stilling)'s *Heinrich Stillings Jugend* (*Heinrich Stilling's Youth* [1777, expanded over the next forty years]) and Karl Philipp Moritz's *Anton Reiser* (1785/1790). Both owe a great debt to Pietism, as do many of the novels of this period. Moritz's novel, however, shows the dark side of religious zealousness, while Jung-Stilling depicts a quiet ("still") life according to God's dictates. Noteworthy in Jung-Stilling's work is a detailed depiction of his boyhood and adolescence, various classes in society, including a positive portrait of peasant life, nature descriptions, and a fondness for the German past.

Anton Reiser foreshadows Charles Dickens's *Oliver Twist* and *David Copperfield* in its description of the tortured upbringing of its hero; only the optimism of Dickens is missing here. The vivid depiction of everyday life, of Reiser's strict education — like that of Fielding's Joseph Andrews — and of his aspirations for the theater allow one to enter Reiser's world. When combined with Goethe's *Wilhelm Meisters theatralische Sendung*, one also has a graphic account of the vicissitudes of theater life in the third quarter of the eighteenth century. Moritz has been called one of the founders of modern psychology — he edited a journal devoted to the study — and his novel is one of the earliest to probe systematically the sources of human behavior.

It must be remembered that at the same time the reading public was reveling in *Werther* and *Siegwart*, numerous novels of secondary quality were being read. In the 1780s robber and ghost tales abounded, of which Schiller's story *Der Verbrecher aus verlorener Ehre* (*The Criminal Out of Lost Honor* [1786]) and the promising novel fragment *Der Geisterseher* (*The Visionary* [1789]) are testament. Still, the few novels of the Storm and Stress had an immediate and lasting impact on German prose. More than anything else, the Storm and Stress novel deepened and enriched the study of character and milieu and prepared the way for the introspective novels of Romanticism.

Conclusion

The Storm and Stress never became a cohesive movement. As soon as it began there were signs of dissension and misunderstanding. Herder criticized what he saw as the excessive "Shakespeareiazation" of Goethe's *Götz von Berlichingen*, and he did not agree with Bürger's naturalistic call for the language of the people. At the high point of the period Goethe satirized Herder, Christoph Kaufmann (who was also ridiculed by Klinger), sentimentality, and, finally, his own work. Both Lenz and Klinger ridiculed aspects of the Storm and Stress in dramatic works, and

Klinger, like Goethe, turned his back on his youthful endeavors and sought a new poetic direction. Both Johann Heinrich Merck (1741-1791), who had close ties to Goethe and Herder, and Justus Möser (1720-1794), who contributed a historical essay to *Von deutscher Art und Kunst*, were often critical of their younger compatriots. Lenz and Klinger became an embarrassment to Goethe at the court in Weimar. The temperaments and backgrounds of the poets were too varied, their calling too unspecific to promote lasting cohesion. In this sense they lacked what would later bind together the Romantics. But the *Stürmer und Dränger* did have a sense of accomplishment, as Goethe notes in his autobiography. They gave new life to the theater, revitalized poetry, inaugurated the modern psychological novel, and drew attention to the importance of the self in a complex, changing world. The enormous influence of Goethe, Schiller, and Lenz, both inside and outside of Germany, is only a partial attestation of their success.

7 Classicism

Gabrielle Bersier

Beyond the National Myth: The Quest for Weimar Classicism

T he term German Classicism (*deutsche Klassik*) is a cultural construct of nineteenth-century German nationalism. It appeared for the first time as a concept in Georg Gottfried Gervinus's (1805-1871) *Geschichte der poetischen Nationalliteratur der Deutschen* (*History of the National Poetic Literature of the Germans* [1835-42]). In this politically motivated history of German literature, the age of Johann Wolfgang Goethe (1749-1832) and Friedrich Schiller (1759-1805), or "Die deutsche Klassik," is seen to represent the culmination of German intellectual culture ushering in the political formation of the German nation. It was in this context of surging patriotism that Heinrich Laube (1806-1884), who was the first to take up the term to designate the literary period, titled the fifth chapter of his 1839 literary history "Das Klassisch-Deutsche." Nineteenth-century German patriots in search of national cultural traditions turned Goethe and above all Schiller into literary pioneers and apostles of German unity. The most spectacular example of such political utilization was the 1859 Schiller centennial, the celebration of which across the German lands served to legitimize national cultural pride and to fuel patriotic fervor. The Goethe-Schiller cult reached a climax after the foundation of the German *Reich* in 1871. Elevated to mythical heights, cast and recast in bronze, the classical duo exhibited the triumph of German over French culture. The same era of chauvinistic elation produced its own consecration as a new "Augustan age" with the first systematic compilation of Goethe's works, the Sophien-Weimar edition in 143 volumes, a monumental and also often historically inaccurate shrine to the Apollo of the German Pantheon. The Goethe-Schiller cult stylized Weimar humanism into a timeless paradigm of the patriarchal order and exalted the aesthetic ideals of Neoclassicism to the heights of canonic art, while reducing all modern art forms to a lowly status of ephemerality. The "classical" became tantamount to the "immemorial," the "everlasting," the "consummate." While pious worship did little to facilitate the actual understanding of Goethe and Schiller's works, their nationalist appropriation did secure them a broad reception in schools and in public life. Finally, even the choice of Weimar as drafting ground of Germany's first democratic constitution in 1919 remained consistent with the utilization of "German Classicism" as a guidepost of national renewal.

Recent literary approaches, hermeneutic, socio-historical, and aesthetic, have stripped the monument of German Classicism of its mythical and chauvinistic varnish and sharpened our awareness of the intellectual context and the concrete preconditions of literary life in the late eighteenth century. The local attribute "Weimar Classicism" or "die Weimarer Klassik" that often replaces the national qualifier "German" in recent literary histories highlights an issue of prime concern for Weimar culture: its tension between narrow local confines and cosmopolitan aspirations. Seen in its actual context of production and reception, the literary culture of Weimar stands out as but one cultural option, albeit the most refined and revered, among the many intellectual trends animating late eighteenth-century German states. Historically confined to two decades, it evolved during Goethe's first Italian journey (1786-1788) to crystalize during the years of collaboration between Goethe and Schiller (1794-1805) in Weimar as a programmatic response to the French

Goethe and Fritz von Stein, son of Charlotte von Stein

Revolution. However, neither Goethe nor Schiller ever dared to ascribe to their own literary works, let alone to their own epoch, the attribute of "classical" or "classicism," aware as they were that only a truly national culture resting on a national state could support a literature worthy of the name "classical." They approached the notion of the "classical" or "classicality" as an evocative ideal attached to the model of ancient Greek culture, as an aesthetic means of transcending the limitations of their time and place.

Granted those restrictions, what was then the normative value attached to Classicism as a stylistic and artistic system that compelled Goethe and Schiller to take up their "classical" campaign? The word *classicus* originates in Roman antiquity where it was used since the sixth century B.C. to designate the free, tax-paying citizen class. Aulus Gellius, a Latin writer of the second century A.D., first placed the term in a literary context in his often-cited reference to the *classicus adsiduusque scriptor, non proletarius* (the first-class tax-paying writer, non proletarian). His phrase also affixed to the social status designation the notion of quality rating that it has since retained. Today the label "classic" and "classical," with its manifold commercial applications, from car to Coke and clothing, stands for good taste, goodness, and preeminence, and serves as a warranty for a higher price tag. Since the Late Middle Ages "classical" as a stylistic term has also become synonymous with "antique" to mark the high literary status and the model character conferred upon the artistic and literary works of the ancients. The canonization of Greek and Roman antiquity also bore nostalgic political and social connotations for the "classical ages" of antiquity; the age of Pericles (5th c. B.C.) and the age of Augustus (1st c. B.C.) were also ages of imperial power, domestic stability, and hierarchical social integration affirmed in highly disciplined artistic and poetic forms. The Renaissance of the mythological imagery and architectural structures of ancient Rome was fused with Baroque artifice to accompany the rise of absolutism in the Italian courts, in Spain, England, and France. Baroque Classicism based on Roman antiquity found its purified expression at the Versailles court of Louis XIV (1638-1715). Backed by the prestige of absolute monarchy, French Classicism exalted in allegorical verse, painting, and statuary the rulers' passions and heroic deeds. It also codified and established for over a century the rules and conventions of courtly culture in a Europe dominated by the power of the French crown.

Goethe and Schiller's defense of the cultural legacy of the antiquity, its poetological standards, highly disciplined literary forms, and "grand style" against the pressures of subjective tendencies and poetic experimentation swelled by the French Revolution places their classicism in direct continuation of the literary traditions that flourished in the European courts since the Renaissance. But if poetological criteria justify a taxonomy of periods contrasting Weimar Classicism with the parallel movement of Jena Romanticism, Goethe and Schiller can also be seen as Romanticists within the wider context of Western culture, insofar as they shared many of the intellectual prerequisites of the Romantic era: its connection, by no means uncritical, to the anthropocentrism of the European Enlightenment, its proud defense of artistic freedom from religious or political authority, and its belief in the formative and therapeutic mission of art as a means of transcending the alienation of modern life.

Toward a Morphology of Classical Art: Goethe in Italy

What stimulated Goethe's classical "revival" during his trip to Italy was probably not so much his experience of the glorious remains of ancient Rome or the colossal architecture of the Roman Baroque as his experience of Mediterranean nature in its colorful display of rocks, plants, animals, and people. From his careful observation of the natural environment of southern Italy, deepened by his study of selected Hellenistic and Renaissance masterpieces, evolved the symbiotic vision of art and nature that became Goethe's classicism. Rome, the artistic capital of eighteenth-century Europe, was then the center of the anti-Baroque, neoclassical revival led by the art historian Johann Joachim Winckelmann (1717-1768), whose aesthetic standards shaped Neoclassicism for several decades. The key factor in Winckelmann's break with Baroque art was a shift from Roman to Greek antiquity as a main source of inspiration and aesthetic doctrine. In his influential essay

Gedanken über die Nachahmung der griechischen Werke in der Malerei und Bildhauerkunst (Thoughts on the Imitation of Greek Works in Painting and Sculpture [1755]), Winckelmann celebrated the *edle Einfalt* (noble simplicity) and *stille Größe* (tranquil grandeur) of Greek statuary against the preciosity and the distortions of Baroque courtly taste. To imitate the Greeks meant, in line with the Enlightenment credo, a return to nature. Greek art, grown out of the natural beauty of the Greek landscape, expressed in beautiful forms the harmony between thought and feeling, body and soul, people and nature which he perceived to be the hallmark of

Johann Joachim Winckelmann (1717-68)

Greek society. In setting up simplicity against heroism as a new measure of greatness, Neoclassicism translated into aesthetics the Enlightenment's quest for a renewal of late feudal society. Winckelmann also echoed the Enlightenment with his keen interest in physiological health and the body. Greek statuary was stimulated by the cultivation of (especially male) physical beauty through nutrition, nakedness, and sports. In his equation of formal beauty with moral perfection, Winckelmann came close to the Neoplatonic aesthetics of the English Enlightenment. He idealized the *edle Einfalt* and *stille Größe* of Greek statues as a secular allegory of truth. Accordingly, the aesthetic enjoyment of art works was not a mere "amusement of the eye," but rather it took on a morally formative function. It is from the forceful impact of Winckelmann's theory of art, felt quite strongly in the artistically vital Roman environment, that Goethe's burgeoning classicism received decisive impulses.

The Goethe who arrived in Rome in October 1786 under the assumed name of Filippo Miller, *tedesco, pittore* (German, painter) had little in common with the Storm-and-Stress rebel and the successful author of his youth. He was a mature, tempered, 37-year-old court official and art amateur on leave. For over a decade following the invitation of the young Duke Karl August (1757-1828), Goethe had served in various administrative capacities as a member of the Duke's cabinet, and as a minister of the tiny state of Saxony-Weimar-Eisenach in central Germany. There, he had placed public and governmental service before his own literary endeavors and experienced the frustrations and limitations of civil service in a small feudal state. Moreover, his ten-year platonic affair with the older, married Weimar lady, Charlotte von Stein (1742-1827), had placed him in an increasingly awkward personal situation. Goethe's flight to Italy signified more than a touristic episode; it was, in his own emphatic terms, a new beginning, a rebirth to art and science and to a lifestyle more attuned to his creative personality. The Italian experience, however, hardly brought about new literary creations. The only piece directly inspired by the Sicilian landscape, the "Homeric" drama *Nausikaa* (1787), remained a loose sequence of evocative scenes. Rather, the manifold impulses gained from the journey made possible the accomplishment of the task that Goethe had set for himself, that is, the revision and completion of several plays — *Iphigenia, Torquato Tasso, Egmont* — and the elaboration of the *Faust* plan, all of which Goethe had been unable to work out in the busy Weimar years.

In Rome Goethe befriended the author of *Anton Reiser* (1785/1790), Karl Philipp Moritz (1756-1793). In spite of their divergent temperaments (the unstable and hypochondriac character of his "younger brother" was quite different from Goethe's more serene and healthy disposition), both shared a passionate interest in ancient art as well as in aesthetic theory. The main outcome of their intellectual exchange, Moritz's small book on aesthetics, *Über die bildende Nachahmung des Schönen* (*On the Imitation of the Beautiful in Art* [1788]), was valued so much by Goethe that he published it in condensed form in Christoph Martin Wieland's (1733-1813) *Teutsche Merkur* (*German Mercury*) of July 1789 along with his own Italian essay *Einfache Nachahmung der Natur, Manier, Stil* (*Simple Imitation of Nature, Manner, Style*). Written against Winckelmann's defense of allegory, Moritz's treatise lays the foundation for a symbolic theory of art. The "meaning" of beauty, Moritz contends, lies in itself and not outside of itself. Beauty is not the allegorical representation of an idea, it is the immanent manifestation of the perfection, beauty, and harmony found in nature. When Moritz speaks of the "intrinsic," "immanent" quality of beauty, he in effect provides the theoretical framework for Goethe's theory of the symbol. Two years before the publication of Kant's *Kritik der Urteilskraft* (*Critique of Judgement* [1790], Moritz established the idea of the autonomy of art.

Although pointing towards "art for art's sake" symbolism, Moritz's symbolic theory retains a rationalistic core which connects it to the Neoplatonism of the English Enlightenment (Shaftesbury [1671-1713] in particular) where art is perceived as a microcosm of the organic wholeness of nature, the coherence and perfection of the entire cosmos. Moritz echoes Shaftesbury in his repeated metaphor of art as a microcosmic "copy," a plastic "reflection" of the whole of nature. Although Moritz meets Goethe in his rejection of allegorical representation, his introvert bent moved his aesthetics in psychological and mystical directions, whereas Goethe's outgoing nature tended to the scientific and empirical. The aesthetic experience led the former to nature mysticism and the latter to natural science.

The essay *Einfache Nachahmung der Natur, Manier, Stil* presents a first and concise formulation of Goethe's new, "classical" aesthetics that parallels his efforts to derive a theory of science from empirical observation. The terms "simple imitation of nature," "manner," and "style" designate three methods of artistic creation. The first, the imitative approach, is limited in its scope to the reproduction of objects in the form of their superficial and specific appearance. The second one, which Goethe defines as "manner," gives more room to the artist's own individuality and is subjective in essence. The third mode, "style," is the greatest according to Goethe, for it is grounded on the deepest foundations of knowledge, on the "essence of things." The product of a grasp of morphological laws of nature acquired through empirical studies, "style," is achieved when art reaches such a grasp of natural forms that it is capable of selecting and creating symbolic, artistic forms.

A recurring preocupation of the Italian journey, which had grown out of the observation of the Mediterranean flora, was the search for the "secret of plant reproduction and organization," for what Goethe liked to call the *Urpflanze*

(primal plant). Accordingly, the botanical essay written after his return from Italy, *Über die Metamorphose der Pflanzen* (*Towards an Explanation of the Metamorphosis of Plants* [1790]), focuses on the underlying morphological identity between plants, and between the various parts of the plant, rather than on plant taxonomy. Looking at the vital energy animating plants, Goethe notes a regular pattern, an organic law guiding the growth, transformation, and reproduction of vegetative life. All plants follow the same cyclical pattern of growth and metamorphosis consisting, according to Goethe's observations, of six alternating stages of extension and concentration, or of anastomosis and metamorphosis. There is a single and unique purpose to this ceaseless mutation of the vegetative organ, and this purpose is procreation. The biological dynamism

Goethe in his Rome apartment.
Watercolor by Heinrich W. Tischbein

later generalized with the key terms of polarity and enhancement (*Steigerung*) is already outlined in this early scientific essay.

The connection between the morphological laws outlined in *Über die Metamorphose der Pflanzen* and aesthetic principles is not made explicit. Goethe established it in retrospect in his writings on morphology by pointing to the analogy between the creation of living forms and artistic creativity. His symbolic method of literary representation, similar to his morphological approach to science, searches for and reveals unity within diversity. It seeks in the specific occurrence the archetype, the type, the idea, or the symbol of the universal law. The essays on botany and osteology point towards a scheme of symbolic literary creations projected as polymorphic manifestations of a universal human archetype in constant mutation. Moving beyond Winckelmann's sentimental Graecophilia, Goethe's close encounter with the ancient world and Mediterranean flora during his Italian journey inspired a new aesthetic vision integrating science and art.

Goethe's First Classical Dramas

The theatrical prototype of Weimar Classicism, *Iphigenia auf Tauris* (*Iphigenia in Tauris* [1787]), adheres scrupulously to the classicist rules of composition. With its five-act-structure, its Aristotelian dramatic unity, and its stylized and symmetrical constellation of characters (Arkas-Thoas-Iphigenie-Orest-Pylades), it presents itself as a conventional, high-style drama written in the manner of the French *tragédie classique* for a courtly audience. The première of the original prose play, starring Goethe himself as Orestes and Corona Schröter (1751-1802) as Iphigenie, was performed on the Weimar amateur stage on April 6, 1779. Thematically, *Iphigenia* is a modern Enlightenment play dramatizing the clash, central to the epoch, of new humane and moral values anchored in individual conscience with divine authority, ancient ritual, and blood allegiance. The main character, Iphigenie, who frees the kingdom of Tauris from a barbaric practice and liberates her brother Orestes from the curse of an archaic fate, demonstrates the redeeming power of truth and humane feeling. In all likelihood, this *schöne Seele* (lofty soul) shrouded in Greek costume also embodied a slightly ironical tribute paid by the author to his sisterly lover, Charlotte von Stein. As to the play's optimistic message, its dramatic enactment of the power of reason against the use of brute force may have been inspired by the immediate context of the Austro-Prussian conflict, for at the time of its original composition in early 1779, Prussia was pressuring Duke Karl August to conscript Thuringian recruits for its war against Austria. Such functional use of an occasional work (*Gelegenheitswerk*) would have been consistent with the antimilitarist thrust of Goethe's practical work as director of the Duke's War Commission as well as with the literary strategies of the Age of Enlightenment with its staunch belief in the didactic role of art.

Charlotte von Stein at age 30. Engraving by G. Wolf

To recover the simplicity of expression and the musical qualities of his ancient Greek models, Goethe undertook the versification of *Iphigenia* in 1786 prior to and during his trip to Italy. When he wrote the original version of the play in rhythmic prose there still existed no German verse adaptation of Greek tragedies. Meanwhile the iambic blank verse of Elisabethan drama was making its entry in Germany, first with Wieland's *Lady Johanna Gray* (1758), then with Lessing's *Nathan der Weise* (*Nathan the Wise* [1779]) and Schiller's *Don Carlos* (1787). The rhymeless blank verse, which derives its melodic effect from rhythmical stress rather than from syllabic quantity, middle caesura, and verse rhyme, does not have the rigidity of the Alexandrine of French Classicism. At the time, Graecophilia was also at a height in Germany, as shown by the simultaneous translation of the *Iliad* by Friedrich Leopold von Stolberg (1750-1819) in 1778 and the *Odyssey* by Johann Heinrich Voß (1751-1826) in 1781, along with Georg Christoph Tobler's (1757-1812) verse adaptations of Sophocles (1781) and Aeschylus (unp. 1781-17-82) that familiarized Germans with the iambic trimeter of Greek tragedies. While opting for the more versatile blank verse, Goethe reclaimed the spirit of classical Greece by adapting to his poetic style many stylistical and lexical elements borrowed from Homer and the Attic drama.

Greek influence also comes through in the blending of nature metaphors with character, action, and feelings. The verse play expands, refines, and systematizes the natural imagery already prevalent in the original to create a web of symbolic correspondences between the main characters, Iphigenie and Orestes, and the surrounding natural world. Fog, darkness, and night becloud the unfortunate Orestes while the holy figure of Iphigenie is bathed in bright sunlight. The healing radiance of her love, reaching from the depths of the individual soul to the cosmic sphere, takes on universal dimensions. The play's symbolic language is rooted in the Enlightenment's belief in a universal system of living order, coherence, and beauty embracing the humane world. This ideal harmony and synchrony that Winckelmann revered in Greek landscape, in Greek society, and in Greek art is what Goethe sought to revive in the polished iambic verses of his *Iphigenia*.

Another prose play started in Weimar, *Torquato Tasso* (1790), was recast in blank verse after the return from Italy in the summer of 1789. The title figure, the Italian Renaissance poet (1544-1595), exerted great power of attraction on Goethe because of his giftedness, akin to his own, at modulating the intensity of his lyrical nature through the disciplined medium of classicist forms, and also because of the intensity of his conflicts as a creative artist with the courtly environment to which he owed his livelihood. The drama projects the author's own tension between creative and practical activity into a polarity of two character opposites, the ingenious Tasso and the pragmatic Antonio. Their conflict of personalities and their competition for their patron's favor weave the thin fabric of a play almost entirely void of dramatic action. Goethe later endorsed the characterization made of his *Tasso* by the French critic J. J. Ampère (1800-1864) as *ein gesteigerter Werther* (an intensified Werther). Indeed, the clash of Tasso's individualism with an environment perceived as constraining or even hostile reenacts in a courtly Renaissance setting an intensified Werther conflict.

The formal shift from letter novel to classical drama, however, creates new and multidimentional viewpoints on the subject: it turns Werther's monody into a polyphony. By presenting *Tasso* in constant verbal interaction with four other characters and by alternating his passionate soliloquies with their dispassionate discourse, the author focuses on that which is problematical, ill-balanced, and even pathological in the hero's psychological makeup. Tasso's emotional excesses not only challenge the rules of courtly etiquette, they also run against the norms of human interaction. The same unbounded nature that makes him blind and deaf to his friends and isolates him from his surroundings finally drives him to the brink of self-destruction. The potential for tragedy inherent in his lonely voyage is visualized in the shipwreck metaphor of the final lines.

Compared with the smooth conversion of free rhythms into iambic stichs in *Iphigenia*, the versification of *Torquato Tasso* is rigorous and technically impeccable, closer in style and tone to the rhetorical norms of the *tragédie classique*. At the same time that the courtly environment supplies the social standards by which the artist has to abide, it also sets his aesthetic guidelines. The same formal rules fixing the tectonic structure of the drama also permeate the metric lines with rhetorical figures, sententious style, and monotonous rhythm. The five-beat rhythm of the blank verse with its iambic alternance of stressed and unstressed syllables is closely observed throughout the play. Where irregularities occur, they are enunciated by the character whose nonconformism also transgresses the established norms. They therefore seem to reinforce the play's message that the artist must tune his instrument to the pitch of the orchestra, a prescript that competes with the artist's longing for autonomy, but also holds out promise of rescue, as suggested in the final metaphor where the shipwrecked sailor grasps for the firm, solid rock on the shore.

The revision during July and August 1787 of the historical drama *Egmont* (1788) also reflects a decisive shift of conception away from the Storm-and-Stress phase. What must have originally been a political tragedy in the manner of *Götz von Berlichingen* (1773) was sharpened psychologically and recast into a character drama. Count Egmont (1522-1568) was a popular military leader during the Spanish occupation, a native of the Netherlands condemned to death in 1568 by the tyrannical Spanish Duke of Alba (1508-1582). In his hero's charismatic personality Goethe embodied what he much later labeled the "daemonic" in the final chapter of his autobiography *Dichtung und Wahrheit* (*Poetry and Truth* [1811/1833]), i.e., an inner force manifesting itself in humans as an exceptional power of attraction (*attrativa*). The self-reliance inherent in a character endowed with such natural attributes, idealized in Storm-and-Stress dramas, becomes the tragic core of the classical psychodrama. Egmont's lack of tactical intelligence, his sole reliance on his personal courage and on his charismatic appeal, make him the easy prey of his political enemy Alba.

To polish the Shakespearian naturalism of the original manuscript with its rich polyphony of characters, environments, and language into a classicist form could not have happened without doing violence to the subject matter. Dramatic unity is achieved through the centripetal organization of plot and characters around the main figure. The scenes composed in Rome (end of Act IV and Act V) display this concentric, inward structure, as does the increasingly rythmical, inner-animated speech cadence of the final scenes. The inward development of the tragedy culminates just before Egmont's execution when he dreams of his beloved Klärchen, who has died in despair, transfigured as a freedom allegory to crown him with a laureal wreath. Empowered by this vision, Egmont faces his death in ecstasy, a hero in the liberation struggle of the Netherlands. This supernatural transformation of the tragic ending into an optimistic utopian vision was realized technically through the insertion of music, a formal device much criticized by Schiller as a "*salto mortale* into the realm of opera." While it is questionable whether the final neutralization of the political tragedy was historically and dramatically consistent, such a *saltus mortalis* was needed to coalesce the *Egmont* drama with the belief in the ultimate rationality of human life and in human progress on which the author founded his own brand of classicism. Goethe later repeated a similar leap into the supernatural in *Faust* and in *Die Wahlver-wandtschaften* (*Elective Affinities* [1809]).

Italian Elegies and Epigrams

One of the most sophisticated lyrical products of Goethe's Italian revival is the cycle of erotic poems titled first *Erotica Romana*, written after his return from Rome and published in 1795 under the name of *Römische Elegien* (*Roman Elegies*). Modeled after the erotic elegy of the Latin poets Ovid (43 B.C.-17/18 A.D.), Tibullus (50-19 B.C.), and Propertius (47-15 B.C.), the elegant distichs create an entirely new genre of erotic poetry, one that is non-courtly and non-aristocratic, housed in an atmosphere of middle-class domesticity. There, Amor, the winged god of erotic pleasure, exercises his functions in a thoroughly unthreatening fashion as a hospitable household deity. The erotic leitmotiv, adorned with an array of colorful mythological variations, blends with themes of hospitality, domesticity, loyalty, and fertility to form an unusual composition whose tone is erotic as well as idyllic, overtly sexual as well as comfortably domestic. For that reason Schiller himself did not hesitate to challenge Weimar polite society by publishing an expurgated version of the *Elegien* in *Die Horen* (*The Horae* or *Hours* [1795]), which prompted the sanctimonious pun attributed to Johann Gottfried Herder (1749-1803): "Now the *Horen* should be printed with the letter 'U'" (meaning "whores" in German). In a letter to his patron, the Duke of Augustenburg (1765-1814), Schiller retaliated by affirming that the subject of the *Elegien* could only hurt a "conventional," not a "true" and "natural" sense of "modesty."

The biographical source of the lyrical cycle is still disputed, for the poet's skill entwined in an intricate fashion recollections of a mysterious, perhaps fictive Roman Faustina with the present and powerful experience of his domestic felicity with Christiane Vulpius (1765-1816), the young worker with whom he set up house in Weimar in the summer of 1789 and lived for 18 years without the blessing of the church. (They finally married in 1806.) Thus the mythological, classical costume could also serve to legitimize a lifestyle much decried by Weimarian a r i s t o c r a t i c   a n d middle-class circles alike.

Italy was not to remain forever "classical ground" in Goethe's memory. An official trip to Venice in the spring of 1790 brought forth the *Venezianische Epigramme* (*Venetian Epigrams*), a set of 103 satirical distichs of uneven length and literary quality. Because of the fear of possible legal action, the work was printed without

Goethe in 1828
Watercolor and chalk by Joseph Stieler

the author's name in Schiller's *Musenalmanch* in 1796. If the happy cherub Amor had inspired the *Römische Elegien*, the *Epigramme* owe their composition to "boredom, mother of the Muses," the author avows. He drafted the acid verses during a rainy April while waiting alone in frustration for the return of Duchess Anna Amalia from southern Italy. The cacophony of contemporary life overrides the dream of Greek harmony conjured up and actualized in Rome and Sicily. Although less skillfully executed than in the *Römische Elegien*, Goethe distills his subjective mood into a classical form. With the help of Martial (c. 40-c. 104), the Latin master of the epigram, he transforms his own acerbity into aphoristic wit. The closest target of satire is the immediate physical environment, muddy Venice with its crowds of credulous pilgrims, its omnipresent clergy, its hustling populace and its "lizards," the prostitutes gliding into dark alleys and dives. Political actuality is just as immediate and irritating. "The French Revolution was also a revolution for me," Goethe confided on March 3, 1790 to Friedrich Heinrich Jacobi (1743-1819). The same stroke of pen that hurls darts at the religious superstition around him, scores also the political "madness" unleashed in France. Exploiters and exploited, betrayers and betrayed, despotic rulers and misguided masses merge into one unified, gloomy picture of a present time submersed in deceit and irrationalism. Eventually, personal irritations and menacing background blend into the Venitian fog. "Amor's torch" flickers dimly in the longer distichs of elegiac tone dedicated to creativity, nature, and love. This subdued light theme gradually dispels the foggy background to transform the end of the cycle into a cosmic love ode to Christiane and their new-born son August (1789-1830).

Cataclysm or Rejuvenation:
Goethe, Herder, and the French Revolution

Goethe's works of the first Weimar decade, scientific and poetic, all bear the imprint of the universalist mind of Johann Gottfried Herder. In 1776 Goethe succeeded in having his Strasbourg friend and Storm-and-Stress associate, the folk-song expert Herder, appointed as superintendent of churches in Weimar, where he remained until his death in 1803. Together with Herder and Charlotte von Stein, Goethe studied Spinoza's (1632-1677) *Ethics* intensively from 1784 to 1785. He was fascinated by the Dutch philosopher's demonstration of the immanence of God in nature. Spinoza was also a crucial formative experience for Herder, who incorporated his pantheism into his own concept of *Humanität* (humanism), one which was to become the ethical cornerstone of Weimar Classicism. Herder's anthropological history, *Ideen zur Philosophie der Geschichte der Menschheit* (*Outline of a Philosophy of the History of Mankind* [1784-1791]), presents a panoramic survey of human development founded on the premise of a genetic relationship between the vegetal, animal, and human species which paves the way to evolutionary theory. Free of the hierarchical thinking of theological historians, Herder affirms the distinctness and plurality of human cultures deriving from their organic relation to their natural and material environment. He combines his pioneering anthropological analysis with the postulation of a teleological convergence of human cultures towards the state of "practical reason" or enlightened humanism. Herder is the first to outline the idea of progress, fundamental for the age, in dialectical rather than linear terms. His evolutionary scheme also integrates the idea of revolution as a necessary element of rejuvenation, a ferment of progress in the history of humanity.

It was at this important juncture that Goethe and Herder were to separate and move gradually away from each other in the decade following the French Revolution. Whereas Herder immediately affirmed the historical importance of the French Revolution within a framework of humane advancement as the practical realization of the Enlightenment, and, later on, during the tense Jacobine years, remained faithful to a republican ideal of government in his *Briefe zur Beförderung der Humanität* (*Letters for the Advancement of Humanity* [1793-1797]), Goethe opposed the French Revolution very early. In his own evolutionist thinking based on geological observations, revolution was a natural and inevitable, but catastrophic event in human history, akin to seismic phenomena, a chaotic disruption of the morphological evolutionary process. Of the two contemporary schools of geological thought, the "vulcanists," who saw seismic explosions as a life-generating process and the "neptunists," for whom organic life originated from the slow and steady influence of water, Goethe favored Neptunism, as he favored evolutionary over revolutionary processes in politics. The satirical allegory *Reise der Söhne Megaprazons* (*Voyage of the Sons of Megaprazon* [1792]), a sequence of narrative fragments depicting the French Revolution in symbolic terms as a vulcanic eruption, is the most concrete illustration of the author's immediate reaction to the events in France. The revolutionary explosion in the Megaprazon fragments appears linked to the calcification of the *ancien régime* in a caste system. Yet, by its violent nature, it produce the disintegration of the formerly hierarchically interconnected social whole.

Like most of his contemporaries, Goethe had only a limited grasp of the social and political roots of the French Revolution. But his dislike of violent political changes did not make him a partisan of aristocratic reaction either. A moderate conservative in his political views, he remained a liberal in social issues and an advocate of friendly cooperation between middle class and aristocracy. When accompanying Duke Karl August in the autumn of 1792 during the Austro-Prussian war of intervention against Mainz and revolutionary France, Goethe's calculated posture was that of the unengaged bystander engrossed in his own biological and optical research. Immersion in the quiet order of nature counterbalanced the chaos of politics. Thus Goethe met the basic challenge of the Revolution by devoting himself primarily to science, at least until 1794, when, under the banner of a depoliticized aesthetic ideal his intellectual coalition with Schiller revived and energized the creative impulses gained on the Italian journey.

Schiller's Quest for the Classical Norm

Political differences, exacerbated by Herder's misanthropy, ended the alliance between Goethe and Herder. A similar commitment to an art that would transcend politics drew together Goethe and Schiller, two men diametrically opposed in temperament, mode of thinking, and life style: the lyrical and the oratorical poet, the empiricist and the conceptual thinker, the comfortable court official and the struggling intellectual. It took seven years, following Schiller's move to Weimar and Jena in mid 1787, to overcome their initial mutual antipathy. During those years, Schiller gradually distanced himself from the spontaneous and naturalistic manner of his Storm-and-Stress plays as he acquired a more distanced grasp of reality through the study of history and Kant's aesthetics. His thorough historical study of the liberation of the Netherlands (*Geschichte des Abfalls der vereinigten Niederlande* [1788]) and Goethe's recommendation gained him an appointment as professor of history at the University of Jena where he lectured on history, philosophy, and aesthetics until his health broke down through overwork in 1791.

Like many of his contemporaries, Schiller also underwent a Greek awakening inspired by Winckelmann. His *Brief eines reisenden Dänen (Letter of a Travelling Dane* [1785]), based on his visit to the antique collection in Mannheim, discovers in Greek art a new ideal of human wholeness much like Winckelmann's "edle Einfalt und stille Größe." There began for Schiller a period of enthusiastic reception of Greek culture, culminating at the end of 1788 with the translation of Euripides's *Iphigenia in Aulis* and *The Phoenicians*, as well as with a detailed review of Goethe's *Iphigenia auf Tauris*. In a letter of August 20, 1788 to

Christian Gottfried Körner (1756-1831), Schiller wrote that he hoped to learn classicism or classicality (*Klassizität*) from the model of simplicity found in ancient literature. That important record of his Greek experience deserves to be cited in its entirety: "I read almost nothing other than Homer. I've had Voß's translation of the *Odyssey* sent to me. [...] I'm reading the *Iliad* in a prose translation [by Stolberg]. I have decided that during the next two years I won't read any more modern authors. [...] None seem suited to me; each leads me astray from my own self, and the ancients give me true pleasure. At the same time I am in great need of them for the purification of my own taste, which was starting to get quite far away from true simplicity because of subtlety, artifice, and witticism. You will find that intimate association with the ancients will be quite good for me, will perhaps afford me classicism."

Schiller's poetic evocation of the Greek ideal, "Die Götter Griechenlands" ("The Gods of Greece" [1788]), occupies a special place in the genesis of Weimar Classicism. It is a philosophical elegy celebrating pagan Greece in Rousseauian anthropological terms as a lost stage of youthful innocence, a state of higher sensual perception, and greater harmony with nature, a world happier, more beautiful, and more humane than the alienated Christian present. Written one year later in the same philosophical vein, the 500-verse hymn "Die Künstler" ("The Artists" [1789]) makes a dialectical leap into the present and future. It highlights the mission of art and beauty in humanity's progression towards enlightenment as an immanent and syncretic form of knowledge and truth. In the teleological scheme of the poem, aesthetics becomes tantamount to a secular religion. In thus pursuing his own special philosophical and historical path, Schiller arrived in these years at an appraisal of the role of aesthetics in the contemporary world that converged with the direction set by Moritz and Goethe in Rome.

The two reviews, *Über Bürgers Gedichte* (*On Bürger's Poems* [1791]) and *Über Matthisons Gedichte* (*On Matthisson's Poems* [1794]) are less significant as expert assessments of the poets' respective accomplishments than as elaborations of Schiller's own concept of "classicality." The Bürger review, concerning which Goethe stated publicly that he wished he had authored it himself, establishes a theoretical bridge spanning over to Goethe's "classical" conception of art. In both reviews Schiller outlines a new concept of poetic "individuality." He demands that the poet transcend his own subjectivity, that he rise above the arbitrary, the private and personal to reach the generic, the general, and the universal. Only that which is common to the human species can be called truly human. Generalization, idealization, and moral "refinement" are the prerequisites of true poetry. The anthropological essence called on by Schiller has a Rousseauian core. It is the lost simplicity and innocence of mankind, "the lost state of nature" that the poet should evoke and revive. To reach up to that level of pure humanity, detachment of self and "estrangement" are required of the artist. In dealing with poetic representation, the Matthisson review sets off "true," or "ideal" nature against "real" nature, or the "essential" against the "accidental," in order to differentiate what Schiller calls "the grand style" (*der große Stil*) from Storm-and-Stress naturalism. Schiller's "grand style" stands in close proximity to the concept of "style" versus "manner" developed in Goethe's *Einfache Nachahmung der Natur, Manier, Stil.*

Schiller's Aesthetic Campaign

A "lucky event," is how Goethe refers to his casual encounter with Schiller after a meeting of the Jena Research Society on July 14, 1794. According to his retrospective narrative, their discussion about the empirical or speculative nature of the *Urpflanze*, Goethe's vegetal prototype, was the event that sealed a ten-year friendship and literary alliance. Poetic truth notwithstanding, Schiller's business letter of June 13, 1794 soliciting Goethe's contribution to his new literary periodical *Die Horen*, to which Goethe immediately answered positively, probably played a more decisive role in bringing together the two men. Indeed, Goethe was soon to become a main contributor to the journal, along with its main editor Schiller. One of the most talented contributors to the magazine was Friedrich Hölderlin (1770-1843), who contributed two poems, "Der Wanderer" ("The Wanderer") and "Die Eichen" ("The Oaks"), in 1787.

Die Horen was to be more than one other addition to the 250 journals that competed for the attention of the German reading public. What distinguished Schiller's publishing venture was its uncompromisingly high literary standards along with its emphatic exclusion of religion and politics, matters considered divisive and distracting. By focusing on matters "purely human" and "transcending the influence of the times" as its prospectus proclaimed, it hoped to "reunite the politically divided world under the flag of truth and beauty." Schiller's aesthetic campaign of conciliation under the aegis of the three Horae, the goddesses of legal order (Eumonia), justice (Dike), and peace (Irene), seems less high-flown and eccentric in the face of the horrendous spectacle of divisiveness and factionalism displayed by the French revolutionaries in the violent year of 1794 that brought about the successive fall of Georges Danton (1759-1794) and Maximilien de Robespierre (1758-1794) and the complete disintegration of the Jacobine Committee of Public Safety after its military victory over the Austro-Prussian coalition. With its lofty aesthetic goals, its self-proclaimed political abstinence, and its commitment to social harmony, *Die Horen* set the parameters of "classical" literary discourse in Weimar for the next decade.

The aesthetic intransigence of Schiller's publication, its political aloofness in a time of great political anxiety, combined with his refusal to compromise with the prevailing tastes of the German readership, sealed the fate of *Die Horen* before its first issue. The aspiring journal had to cease publication in 1797. But the crisis caused by the indifference or the outright hostility of the public also had productive effects. It forced Schiller and Goethe to a closer collaboration, a clearer elaboration of their goals, and even to a joint counterattack in the form of epigrammatic strokes at the literary world, the ill-humored *Xenien* (*Xenia* [1796]).

How art was to function as an alternative to political engagement Schiller would fully elaborate in his treatise on aesthetic education. His literary program of neutrality was timely. Its political counterpart, the treaty of Basel of April 5, 1795, ended the Austro-Prussian war against revolutionary France and committed Prussia to a policy of non-intervention, thus inaugurating a ten-year period of peace and neutrality for northern Germany. This short interlude of political neutrality and relative security — which left the north German states, and Karl August's dukedom in particular, untouched by either revolutionary transformations or counterrevolutionary repression — was undoubtedly a prerequisite for the blossoming of a classical aesthetic culture in Weimar.

The first issues of *Die Horen* (1, 2, and 6 [1795]) featured Schiller's treatise on aesthetics, titled *Über die ästhetische Erziehung des Menschen in einer Reihe von Briefen* (*Letters on the Aesthetic Education of Man*) because of its epistolary form based on seven letters to his sponsor, Prince Friedrich Christian von Augustenburg. *Über die ästhetische Erziehung des Menschen* sets forth what forms the theoretical credo of Weimar Classicism. In spite of its insistence on not being political, it is an eminently political text, written with the rhetorical urgency characteristic of the author.

Disillusioned with the violence and factionalism unleashed by the French Revolution, Schiller develops a psychological and cultural alternative to the revolutionary transfer of power, a "constitution for the aesthetic world." His essay is structured on a triadic dialectical model of human cultural history. It begins with an evocation of Greek culture, the ideal state of human "wholeness" manifested in the harmony of the social whole. There follows a critical assessment of contemporary culture, the state of disharmony, disconnection, and one-sided specialization. It then postulates the restoration of the lost harmony and totality of human nature through a "higher" aesthetic culture. Aesthetic education, that is, the aesthetic regeneration of the individual, Schiller argues, is the prerequisite for political change. "It is only through Beauty that man can make his way to Freedom." With his aesthetic path of human regeneration he proposes a non-violent substitute for the cult of reason and civil freedom which led to the spread of political violence in the French Revolution.

Kant's *Critiques* lent Schiller the theoretical foundation on which he grounded his triadic cultural model and his teleological projection of a utopian "aesthetic state." Kantian dualism was also the starting point for his detailed conceptual analysis of the transcendental category of "Beauty" in its interplay with other psychological forces. There are two fundamental potentialities in the human character in permanent conflict with each other: the *Stofftrieb* (sensuous drive) and the *Formtrieb* (form drive). That antagonism of inner forces which Kant resolves through the stern "categorical imperative," Schiller proposes to reconcile through the intermediacy of the joyous *Spieltrieb* (play drive). The object of the *Spieltrieb*, Schiller contends, is the "living form," or "Beauty." Located at the junction of the sensory and the rational, beauty alone has the power of restoring harmony between the conflicting human impulses. As a cultural phenomenon, it is the capacity for creative play, for make-believe, for what Schiller calls "aesthetic semblance,'' which differentiates humans from animals. The emergence of play marks the beginning of anthropological evolution and the dawn of culture.

What was to be the crowning part of the essay, the "constitution" of the "aesthetic state," was left incomplete. The utopian scheme sketched out in the last letter is at best tentative. It consists merely of a symbolic analogy between the love bond that resolves the war of the sexes and the social bond that reconciles the conflicts of the "moral world." Beauty, the same transcendental force bringing harmony into personal relationships, is called upon to mediate social relations. Schiller's substitution of a social bond for a social contract draws his scheme close to the Romantic utopias of the 1790s that also substitute the power of emotional bonds for the coercive enforcement of contractual bonds by the Revolution. Yet Schiller's vision does not bend towards a conservative, Romantic idealization of monarchy à la Novalis (1772-1801) either. As its unique "basic law" — "to give freedom through freedom" — intimates, the "aesthetic state" bends towards a libertarian alternative to both the *ancien régime* and the French Republic, one based on individual human integrity and on the cultivation of humane and civilized forms of social interaction.

The ideals of integral humanism, civility, and sociability advocated in *Über die ästhetische Erziehung des Menschen* met the aims of *Die Horen* to organize an educated circle of like-minded equals that would function as a model of human harmony and political neutrality in a time of political extremism. As fragile as it was, the synthesis reached in Schiller's treatise between the middle-class ideals of moral enlightenment and the aristocratic ideals of refinement and sociability constituted the social core of Weimar "classical" culture. Schiller and Goethe's cultural consensus rested on their common faith in the political viability of the German system of small, independent states, a system similar to the Greek *polis*, that both believed to be most suited for shared leadership by the best among the aristocracy and the middle-class.

Schiller's second treatise, *Über naive und sentimentalische Dichtung* (*On the Naive and Sentimental in Literature*), published in *Die Horen* (11 and 12 [1795] and 1 [1796]), is of equally high theoretical and rhetorical caliber and has been immensely influential in European aesthetics. Thematically linked to the debate which marked the transition from Classicism to the Age of the Enlightenment, the battle of the Ancients and the Moderns, its object also consists of assessing the respective value of ancient and modern poetry to chart a theory of poetry relevant to the modern age. At the dawn of the eighteenth century the debate was resolved by asserting the precedence of individual genius over the poetic norms of classical antiquity. At the twilight of the century Schiller uses his dialectic historical schema (nature-culture-nature) to devise a poetic theory that would be both modern in its cognitive model and classicist in its formal orientation.

Schiller's poetics have a Kantian epistemological basis. Proceeding from the poet's relationship to nature, he identifies two contrasting modes of perception: the first one defined as "naive" if the poet still has an instinctive, unbroken sense of unity with nature, the second one as "sentimental" if the poet's feeling for nature, born out of a sense of disconnection, is reflective, introspective, and nostalgic. In his own terms, the "naive" poet "is nature," whereas the "sentimental" poet "seeks lost nature." The sentimental poet represents nature as a lost ideal to be gradually retrieved, according to Schiller's teleology of history, through the means of "reason" and "freedom." The sense of naive communion with nature was greater in ancient times, hence the normative function of ancient Greek poetry, Homer in particular, as the ultimate expression of "naturalness." Although introspective perception is intrinsically modern, poets of the sentimental kind already existed in ancient times, just as poets of the "naive" kind, such as Shakespeare or Goethe, still exist in modern times.

With his new category of the "sentimental," Schiller emancipated modern poetry from the authority of traditional poetological norms. In so doing, he unwittingly laid the groundwork for the romantic poetic theory elaborated a few years later in the periodical *Das Athenäum.* Three genres are derived from his typology of the sentimental: the satire, the elegy, and the idyll. Whereas the satire concentrates on the clash between reality and ideal nature, and the elegy on ideal nature in its contrast with reality, the idyll shows the ideal of nature as a concrete poetic reality. With his celebration of the idyll, Schiller reaches the high point of his treatise. Unlike the pastoral idyll that looks back to an archaic state of nature, the "highest poetical work" on his new poetological scale would be an idyll of utopian character, one that would point towards the ultimate convergence of culture with a higher state of nature ("which [...] guides the human beings, who can never again get back to Arcadia, towards Elysium").

Schiller's treatise is as rigorous in its definition of "ideal realism" as it is reserved in its prescription of formal poetological rules. Poetry must adhere to the "laws of nature," he asserts laconically. By definition, prose narration, when strictly a by-product of artificial civilization, lies outside of the confines of poetry. Schiller's concept of "ideal" realism or "pure" naturalism, already introduced in the Bürger review, excludes both the "crude" naturalism of the Storm and Stress and its antipode, supernaturalism or surrealism, the romantic escape into immaterial fantasy. The label "classical" awarded by Schiller to the works combining "high purity of ideal" with "materiality of content," marks out an attribute of quality rather than a typological classification of his own school of literary style. The "ideal realism" prescribed by Schiller is one that would unite the two contrasting modes of perception, the "sentimental" and the "naive," to bring into poetic existence the total potentiality of human nature, the ideal of human wholeness already conjured up in *Über die ästhetische Erziehung des Menschen* and in his first Kantian treatise *Über Anmut und Würde* (*On Grace and Dignity* [1793]).

A Decade of Collaborative Literary Creation:
Classical, Epical, and Lyrical Works

The major product of Goethe's intellectual friendship with Schiller was the transformation of the unfinished manuscript of *Wilhelm Meisters theatralische Sendung* (*Wilhelm Meister's Theatrical Mission*), started twenty years previously (1777), into a three-volume novel, *Wilhelm Meisters Lehrjahre* (*Wilhelm Meister's Apprenticeship*). It was a two-year-long (1795-1796), intensive project accompanied at each stage by Schiller's critical suggestions. Several motives may have guided Goethe's work of renovation. By purging his theatrical narrative of its raw realism to reshape it into a sophisticated work of art, he could legitimate himself as a prose author against his friend's aesthetic reservations towards "the poet's half-brother," as Schiller called the novelist, and his inferior genre. By converting a modern, "impure medium" into a naive, "classical" form, he could also probe his own concrete approach vis-à-vis Schiller's reflective and deductive manner. And finally, how could he better counter the irritating correlation of classical antiquity with revolutionary France, and of classical prose with republican consciousness, against which he had argued in his polemical essay *Literarischer Sansculottismus* (*Literary Sansculottism* [*Die Horen* 5 — 1795]), than by offering his contemporaries a certified prototype of "classical prose" that was politically neutral, "void of any sansculottism," as Schiller puts it in his letter of July 5, 1786. In his efforts to rehabilitate narrative prose, Goethe found a French model, Mme de Staël (1766-1817), whose apology of the novel of character in her *Essai sur les fictions* (1795) he translated in German (*Die Horen* [2] — 1796). Against the flood of naturalistic or supernatural fiction, allegorical or historical narratives, that had greatly devaluated the genre, Mme de Staël commended those novels whose focus was "private life" or the "treatment of characters and emotions." Her model of form was the psychological, didactical novel of the Enlightenment.

With Christoph Martin Wieland's *Agathon* (1766-1767), already hailed by Gotthold Ephraim Lessing (1729-1781) as a novel of "classical taste," as the German forerunner, Goethe's *Wilhelm Meister* continues and transforms the narrative tradition of the enlightened novel of education. To implement the objectifying aims of his new style, the classical narrator hides behind his colorful canvas of characters. The didactical scheme of the work disappears behind the empirical demonstration of a personality gradually unfolding and maturing in close interaction with his environment. A novel of formation, a morphological *Bildungsroman* ensues, but one in which Nature, life itself, is to be the teacher. A very complex narrative, whose full range the Romantic theoretician Friedrich Schlegel (1772-1829) was able to embrace in one formula, "Lehrjahre der Lebenskunst" ("apprenticeship in the art of living"), *Wilhelm Meisters Lehrjahre* is no more and no less than "an apprenticeship in the art of living," a classical anti-*Werther*.

Guided by Schiller's conceptual approach, the poetry of the decade of "high classicism" (1795-1805) is highly reflective and didactic. The lyrical mode in the modern sense of a poetic overflow of intimate feelings was not congenial to Schiller.

For him poetic language was a rhetorical act, the verbal articulation of philosophical ideas rather than the modulation of private emotions. The label *Gedankenlyrik* (thought poetry, poetry of ideas), often assigned to Schiller's poetry, is accurate: his is genuinely a "poetry of ideas." To transform thought process into musical motion, concepts into concrete images, and moral ideas into dramatic parables, in short, to achieve the "aesthetic synthesis" he struggled for in his classical program, was also his greatest creative challenge. In the best poems, "Der Spaziergang" ("The Walk"), "Nänie" ("Nanie"), "Der Tanz" ("The Dance"), the didactic design almost disappears behind concrete poetic motion. Yet the same parabolic concreteness which made some of Schiller's verses so popular could also easily fall into platitude and cliché when it became schoolbook truth, as happened with "Das Lied von der Glocke" ("The Song of the Bell"), Schiller's hymn on family and social harmony.

What Schiller as a poet of the sentimental type gained in musicality during the classical decade, the Greek, the naive poet Goethe gained in object-centered concreteness, *Gegenständlichkeit*, as he liked to call his style. But scientific distance could also inhibit poetic spontaneity. Compared to earlier decades, Goethe's lyrical output is thin. Short, strictly lyrical forms such as the rhymed folk songs characteristic of the Storm-and-Stress phase are scarce. The lyrics "Meeresstille" ("Sea Calm"), "Glückliche Fahrt" ("Happy Voyage"), "Nähe des Geliebten" ("Nearness of the Beloved") stand out as isolated examples. The hexameter dominates in the satirical verses *Venezianische Epigramme, Xenien, Römische Elegien, Alexis und Dora, Euphrosyne*, and the didactic scientific poems such as "Metamorphose der Pflanzen" ("Metamorphosis of Plants"). Its rythmical balance was well suited to exemplary situations and normative statements. In 1797 Schiller and Goethe also experimented together with the non-classical form of the ballad. In the ballad, an archaic quintessence of the three poetic genres, one finds "the elements as yet not separated, but rather together, as in a living primal egg," as Goethe later commented. It can be epic, dramatic, and lyrical at the same time. Compared to the flood of polemic distichs poured out in 1796, the output of ballads the following year was modest. But it is impressive in literary quality. In a simultaneous effort, both Schiller with "Der Ring des Polykrates" ("The Ring of Polycrates"), "Der Handschuh" ("The Glove"), "Der Taucher" ("The Diver"), and "Die Kraniche des Ibykus" ("The Cranes of Ibycus"), and Goethe with "Der Schatzgräber" ("The Treasure Seeker"), "Die Braut von Korinth" ("The Bride of Corinth"), "Der Gott und die Bajadere" ("The God and the Bayadere"), and "Der Zauberlehrling" ("The Sorcerer's Apprentice") combine sensual appeal with moral and literary sophistication. In so uniting the disjointed features of contemporary German letters against which they had aggressively polemicized, they managed to popularize the literary objectives of their classical campaign.

To Schiller's call for a modern idyll Goethe responded in October 1797 with an epic poem in 2000 hexameters in the Homeric mode titled *Hermann und Dorothea*. Published in a popular, small-size edition, it became an immediate bestseller and was reissued thirty times in Goethe's lifetime. The author had not experienced such a popular success since *Werther*. The gratification felt at that warm reception radiates from his ironic note to Schiller on January 3, 1798: "In *Hermann and Dorothea* I did for once what the Germans wanted, at least in respect to subject matter, and they are extremely satisfied now." Schiller was ecstatic, calling the poem "the high point of the whole of his and our modern art." Notwithstanding a predilection for prose fiction, demonstrated by the recent completion of *Wilhelm Meisters Lehrjahre*, his friend Goethe had finally put forth a poetic epic worthy of Schiller's own aesthetic pronouncements, a "pure" narrative combining antique naiveté of style with modernity of consciousness. In order to maintain the concrete totality of character, action, and setting present in Homer, the author had to reduce the breadth of action of the ancient epic to idyllic, that is, private and domestic proportions. In thus transforming the epic into an idyll, Goethe took up a genre that had enjoyed widespread appeal since the middle of the century. With regard to the form of *Hermann und Dorothea*, the philosopher Georg Friedrich Hegel (1770-1831) noted in his *Ästhetik* (1835-1838) that in modern times, where the public sphere of action tended to become increasingly depersonalized, bureaucratic, and prosaic, the human totality depicted in heroic times by the epic could only be concretely shown in the reduced scope of the idyll. In these years, Goethe attempted twice to produce a truly Homeric epic. A planned sequence to Homer's *Iliad* called *Achilles* was abandoned after the completion of the first canto, and a projected "Iliad of modern life," titled *Die Jagd* (*The Hunt*), was recast much later into the private frame of a prose short story, the *Novelle* (1828).

Goethe's choice of literary medium also corresponded to his stance towards the subject matter of *Hermann und Dorothea*, the human impact of the French Revolution in neighboring Germany. A small town in the Rhineland is the idyllic mirror in which he projects the epic turmoils of the French Revolution. A friendly, peaceful, stable microcosm of bourgeois propriety, productivity, and sociability resting at the edge of a stormy ocean of social unrest and human disarray, his idyll has the exemplary quality of a utopian island. The realm of "pure, human existence" (Goethe to Hans Heinrich Meyer [1760-1832]), depicted here with an unusual concreteness of locale, lies beyond the bureaucratic maze of the old feudal order and the coersive centralism of the new French Republic in a small, self-sufficient environment that resembles Justus Möser's (1720-1794) ideal, also shared by Goethe, of the small patriarchal state. The classical features of the poem (hexameter, symmetrical plot division in nine cantos, each of them allegorically headlined by one of the Muses, typification of characters through Homeric epithets) envelop the peaceful sphere of bourgeois domesticity in an aura of timeless universality.

Canonized in the nineteenth century next to Schiller's "Das Lied von der Glocke" as Goethe's anti-French, anti-revolutionary manifesto, the small epic is all but one-dimensional. Its plot, borrowed from a 1734 chronicle, outlines a subtle model of integration of new social values, born out of the revolutionary upheavals, into the traditional patriarchal order. During the passage of a group of refugees driven out of their homes on the left bank of the Rhine by the revolutionary wars, Hermann, the son of the local innkeeper and well-to-do farmer, falls in love with the young refugee Dorothea and brings her home to his parents. Tall and proud, fearless and compassionate, a figure of epic stature, Dorothea comes forth in her tricolored dress like an allegory of the Revolution. Her passage from the epic into the idyllic sphere — her integration into the patriarchal realm of Hermann's family — traces also a symbolic conversion, a transformation of the subversive political ideals of the French Revolution, into a non-threatening, peaceful, humane ethos. Not surprisingly, the author reached back to a popular theme of the Enlightenment, the issue of free partner choice, to make it the thematic focus of his work. To its great satisfaction indeed, the German public, bewildered as it was by the social chaos of the revolutionary years, found in the simple and concrete outlines of Goethe's "bourgeois epic" a showcase of peaceful, organic rejuvenation that bypassed the thorny dilemma of revolutionary change.

The Weimar Stage: Schiller's Classical Dramas

Schiller also attempted to write an epic poem in Greek style. From the mass of material gathered in the early nineties during his historical investigation of the Thirty Years' War, there emerged the outline of an heroic epic. Then, in the summer of 1797, came the turning point of his study, along with Goethe, of Aristotle's *Poetics*. Two years previously Schiller's literary engagement had converted the scientist Goethe back to poetry. This time it was Goethe's influence that brought Schiller back to his home ground, the stage. In Greek classical drama Schiller found the ideal theatrical antidote to the pathos of his early plays, and in the Weimar theater, headed by Goethe from 1791 to 1817, Schiller found ready access to an optimal forum of aesthetic and rhetorical influence.

Since Goethe's return from Rome, culture had become, at his own wish, his sole area of administrative responsibility in the dukedom. As director of the Weimar theater, Goethe had complete control over repertoire, actors, and performances. The old stage was rebuilt in classicist style under his supervision in 1798. Under his strict aegis the Weimar theater became a key vehicle for the promotion of the new classical culture. Although many concessions had to be made to commercial solvency and public taste, a purpose well served by the serialized comedies and melodramas of the local playwright August von Kotzebue (1761-1819), the court theater was also used without restraint as an experimental stage, as the testing ground of the new anti-naturalist style. To the actors, used to the conversational tone and the spontaneity of Enlightenment plays, Goethe painfully taught declamation and scansion along with a more controlled performing style. The text, rather than the personality of the actor, was holy. Yet during the decade of "high classicism" his own contributions as a playwright were limited. One single new tragedy of classical design was completed and premiered in Weimar, *Die natürliche Tochter* (*The Natural Daughter* [1803]). It is Goethe's most substantial symbolic treatment of the fall of the French *ancien régime*. His *magnum opus, Faust,* started in 1772 only to be completed shortly before his death in 1832, partakes of a theatrical tradition that has little in common with the Aristotelian drama, and was not performed in its entirety (Part I and II) in Weimar until 1875.

The chief contribution to the Weimar repertoire came from Schiller. With the same resoluteness he had applied in the early nineties to the study of history and

Kant's philosophy, and later on to the promotion of his aesthetic revolution, in his last eight years of struggle against severe illness Schiller channelled all the creative energies he had left in one direction and achieved prodigious results. Five blank-verse dramas were completed: the *Wallenstein* trilogy (1798-1799), *Maria Stuart* (1800), *Die Jungfrau von Orleans* (*The Maid of Orleans* [1801]), *Die Braut von Messina* (*The Bride of Messina* [1803]), and *Wilhelm Tell* (1804); all except *Die Jungfrau von Orleans* premiered in Weimar. There was also a whole series of dramatic sketches and fragments, and the four acts of the tragedy *Demetrius*, completion of which was halted by his death in 1805.

History lent Schiller the "materiality of content" he asked for in his treatise *Über naive und sentimentalische Dichtung*, a realistic frame on which to probe the exercise of freedom. The critical junctures in the formation of nation-states between feudalism and absolutism offered an abundance of dramatic material and powerful characters from which to construct tragedies of Sophoclean depth. As carefully researched and concretely laid out as the historical canvas of each play is, the dramatic effect rests entirely on the stylization of history into poetic fiction and on the skillful structuring of character and plot along Aristotelian rules of composition. In complete accordance with Aristotle, the Schillerian tragedy is geared chiefly at emotional effect, at the arousal of *Furcht und Mitleid* (fear and pity). Reinstating *phobos* as the affective essence of tragedy, Schiller is a master at the calculated dosage and gradation of tragic fear through dialogue and plot development, as well as acoustical and optical manipulation. But with his Kantian theory of the Sublime, he moves beyond the Aristotelian concept of catharsis, the purifying effect of the emotional release provoked by drama, towards a rational definition of aesthetic pleasure in tragedy. Located in the hero himself, the Sublime, a rational response to pain connected with the human potential for freedom and moral autonomy, appeals to the spectator's idealism. Thus, didactic effect is the ultimate aesthetic goal pursued by Schiller in his dramatization of history.

Reclaiming the legacy of Greek classical tragedy meant a departure from the Enlightenment tragedy of the private sphere in order to put the political sphere back on stage. In Schiller's hands the theater becomes again a forum for state action, for tragedies of ample political and historical scope where strictly private conflicts (family, friendship, love) are reduced to a subordinate role. Diametrically opposed to the dichotomy of the private and the public in the modern bureaucratic state, from which Lessing derived his dramaturgy, the Schillerian stage creates an aesthetic public sphere where the unity of the private and political, lost in the abstract modern world, is restored. "The poet must re-open the palaces, he must once again bring the judges forth beneath the open skies, he must establish the gods anew, he must restore everything that is direct and which has been abolished by the artificial arrangements of actual life, he must cast off all artificial contrivances in man and around man which hinder the manifestation of his inner nature and his original character, just as sculptors cast away modern garments and accept nothing of all external surroundings except what renders visible the highest of forms — human form."

Immediacy, simplicity, totality of the human and social whole: Schiller's dramatic prescriptions are consistent with the cultural goals set in *Über die ästhetische*

Erziehung des Menschen. To recreate the unity of private and public lost in modern life the dramatist uncovers the arcanum of politics, exposing the interconnection of political with private motivations. Schiller chooses his historical agents in past pages of history, where political initiative and moral responsibility were still clearly located in the person of the potentate, rather than distributed and hidden in a bureaucratic state machine. Politics are made tangible, are personalized and simplified. Beneath the chaos of historical complexities and political entanglements lies "das rein Menschliche," the anthropological essence. To illuminate it is the task of the classical poet.

In need of a theatrical medium of publicity, Schiller brought the antique chorus back on stage. In ancient Greece the public elaboration of the action by the citizens' chorus formed an integral part of the drama, as democratic participation was an essential part of public life. In the essay *Über den Gebrauch des Chors in der Tragödie (On the Use of the Chorus in Tragedy* [1803]), Schiller calls the Greek chorus a "natural organ," by contrast to which his own chorus is an "artificial organ," a poetic means of externalizing and objectifying the action. The insertion of a chorus of knights commenting on the action of *Die Braut von Messina* adds a public dimension to a plot in other respects entirely domestic, modelled on the brotherly feuds of the *Sturm und Drang.* In the other plays, single figures or groups such as the army in *Wallensteins Lager (Wallenstein's Camp)*, or the country people in *Wilhelm Tell*, play a choric role. Chorus and public scenes restore the theatrical to its original Greek meaning of that which is "in sight, in view." Accordingly, the Schillerian plots are structurally integrated into important scenes of public life, receptions, court assemblies, banquets, tribunals, political ceremonies, and religious rituals. Strictly intimate, modern forms of human interaction are conspicuously absent from a dramaturgy designed to making concrete the intricate interplay of the personal and the political.

In the masterfully orchestrated *Wallenstein* trilogy, where historical realism prevails, the moral entanglement of the hero and the absence of any redeeming features in his catastrophic downfall appear to negate the idealistic goals of the Schillerian dramaturgy of the Sublime. Nevertheless, Wallenstein is generally regarded as Schiller's most accomplished dramatic creation. Based on the famous Bohemian general of the Thirty Years' War, who, after years of military success, brought about his own demise by plotting against the emperor, the trilogy takes place in the final days leading to Wallenstein's assassination by mercenaries under the orders of imperial officers. Since the playwright could not possibly condense the intricacy of his panoramic *Geschichte des Dreißigjährigen Krieges (History of the Thirty Years' War* [1791-1793]) into the formal confines of a classical drama, his ingenious technical solution was to separate the epic components of his subject matter, its historical and military background, from the dramatic action. A prologue, *Wallensteins Lager*, displays the soldiers' life of adventure and pillage and their devotion to their charismatic leader in a sequence of descriptive scenes anticipating Bertolt Brecht's (1898-1956) epic theater. Wallenstein's intended rebellion and his generals' conspiracy to overthrow him form the main frame of a vast tragedy, which Schiller divided into two five-act plays upon Goethe's suggestion, *Die Piccolomini (The Piccolomini)* and

Wallensteins Tod (*Wallenstein's Death*). It is in the dramatic exposition of his hero's character, a puzzling mix of grand design and self-delusion, staunch ambition and astrological credulity, political loyalty and cynicism, and in the interlocking of his complex psychological makeup with the intricate web of interests, intrigues, and circumstances leading to his tragic death, that Schiller was able to reveal the full measure of his dramatic genius. To this day his masterpiece, which may be a dramatic reply to Kant's famous tract *Zum ewigen Frieden* (*On Eternal Peace* [1805]), has lost none of its relevance as a powerful elucidation of the dialectics of politics and morality.

In his other plays, Schiller resolved the dichotomy of ethics and politics by increasingly emphasizing poetic over historical truth. Dramatic purpose, rather than historical accuracy, dictates the classical stylisation of character in *Maria Stuart*. Schiller added a layer of private motives to the political feud between Queen Elizabeth I of England (1533-1603) with Mary Queen of Scots (1542-1587) that casts a dark shadow on Elizabeth's character and on her decision to sign the execution warrant against her rival. By contrast, Mary's penance converts her death into a moral triumph. With its rigorously designed plot development and its perfect symmetry of characters, culminating in the fictive confrontation of the two queens in Act III, this most formally sophisticated of Schiller's plays has become a textbook model of classicist dramaturgy.

In the "romantic tragedy," *Die Jungfrau von Orleans*, the dramatist transposed history into the realm of legend. His Joan of Arc falls in love with an English commander. She does not die a witch and heretic at the stake, but a holy angel on the battlefield, winning a critical victory over both the English army and her own inclinations. In *Die Braut von Messina* history functions as a mere backdrop to a fictional family drama, whose plot of fratricide and incestuous love unfolds in conscious analogy to the progressive revelations in Sophocles's *Oedipus Rex*. Finally, in *Wilhelm Tell*, Schiller's play on the legendary Swiss archer, folklore merges with historical chronicle, and myth with revolutionary action, to make the archaic liberation drama a paradigm of the restitution of the state of nature claimed in *Über die ästhetische Erziehung des Menschen*. Only in the realm of a quasi- mythical Swiss past was Schiller able to reconcile political action with ethical goals. By virtue of its pastoral and national appeal, *Wilhelm Tell* had the widest popular success in the nineteeth century.

A Lone Hellenist: Johann Friedrich Hölderlin

Like two other cardinal authors of the age, Jean Paul Friedrich Richter (1763-1825) and Heinrich von Kleist (1777-1811), the Swabian poet Friedrich Hölderlin (1770-1843) oversteps the boundaries of strict literary classification. He was an outsider throughout his life, unable to associate either with the Weimar classical nucleus or with the Romantic circle in Jena. Only a few of his poems, the letter novel *Hyperion* (1797-1799), and his translations of Sophocles's *Oedipus* and *Antigone* were published in his lifetime. Hölderlin was a classicist in his fervent Hellenism and in his mastery of antique lyrical forms (distich, hexameter, Asclepiadic and Alcaic odes). But he was also a political radical in his enduring enthusiasm for the French Revolution and his hope that it could be imported to Germany. Finally, he was and became increasingly a Romanticist in his introverted poetic temperament and in his passionate longing for communion with nature, perceived as an all-encompassing, divine realm. Like Schiller and the philosophers Hegel and Friedrich Wilhelm Schelling (1775-1854), two of his fellow students at the theological seminary in Tübingen, Hölderlin was greatly influenced by both his Swabian pietistic background and by his thorough classical education. His early hymns leaned on Schiller's philosophical poems in their idealistic pathos and in their strophic structure. It was to Schiller, the hero and patron of his youth, that the young Hölderlin, who refused to settle down in a church office, owed his first appointment as a private tutor. To Schiller he also owed his belief in the visionary mission of the poet as an apostle of beauty and freedom. To him he also owed his idealized vision of ancient Greece as a stage of primeval freedom and pantheistic communion with nature, as well as his deep sense of deprivation and alienation in the present. But Hölderlin deviated from the conceptual classicism of his mentor in the nostalgic nature of his longing for a return to Greek "naturalness," an emotional yearning that strove to diffuse and neutralize modern rationality. His overwhelming sense of alienation from nature and a truly humane community, most pathetically expressed in the revolutionary novel fragment *Hyperion* and in the three versions of the unfinished tragedy *Der Tod des Empedokles* (*The Death of Empedocles* [1798-1800]), finally drove him into mental disorder. Hölderlin had to spend the last thirty-six years of his life, from 1807 to 1843, in the care of a local carpenter in Tübingen.

In the odes and elegies of his middle years (1797-1801), Hölderlin was able to strike the balance between sentimental and naive consciousness that Schiller had defined as a hallmark of the classical. That brief period of classicism coincided with the happiness found in his love for Susette Gontard (1769-1802), the Diotima of his poetry. A fragile happiness, always fraught with a sense of transience, brings into what Hölderlin calls his "mature song" a peculiar poignancy ("An die Parzen" ["To the Fates"] or "Die Kürze" ["Brevity"]). The awareness of humanity's tragic separation from the divine lingers painfully ("Hyperions Schicksalslied" ["Hyperion's Song of Fate"]). Love connects the poet with the all-encompassing, sacred realm, but it also isolates him from profane humanity ("Menschenbeifall" ["Human Applause"]). In the poetic celebration of his beloved native southern German landscape ("Heidelberg"), the feeling of alienation is silenced by the powerful magic bonds connecting him to the motherland. Viewed from the perspective of the free verse poetry of his later years ("Hälfte des Lebens" ["The Middle of Life"], "Andenken" ["Remembrance"]), Hölderlin's classical phase can be seen as a brief repose on a lonely romantic trajectory that produced verses of incomparable beauty but that also finally led him beyond the realms of human interaction and communicability.

Goethe and Classical Art

Together Goethe and Schiller were able to mark the Weimar theatrical sphere, which stood completely in their control, with the stamp of their aesthetic influence to the point that it eclipsed all the other German stages. By comparision, Goethe's efforts as a promoter of classicist art at a time of rapid transition towards Romanticism sparked little interest. For two years (1798-1800), his art journal *Die Propyläen* (*The Propylaea*), published in collaboration with the Swiss painter and art critic Hans Heinrich Meyer, attempted to rally contemporary artists under a now outmoded creed of academic Classicism. Never before had Goethe attempted to codify aesthetic principles with such forcefulness. The isolation of Weimar from the vital art centers of the time may explain the rigidity of his artistic pronouncements. In opposition to the revival of religious and patriotic painting, Greek plastic art, pagan and sensual, is posited as the timeless model of aesthetic objectivity. The artist must create "etwas Geistig-Organisches" (something mental and organic). To be aesthetically pleasing, the subject matter must obey the immanent laws of "order, lucidity, symmetry, contrast."

The topics proposed by the "friends of the arts" of Weimar for their artistic competitions and exhibits (1799-1805) were strictly mythological. The response was meager. Asmus Jacob Carstens (1754-1798), the last important representative of German Neoclassicism, a painter who came closest to Goethe's ideal without knowing him, had just died in Rome in 1800 without patrons or pupils. His Greek-oriented, anthropological classicism paralleled and counteracted the revolutionary Neoclassicism of the French painter Louis David (1748-1825) who had found inspiration in the heroic symbols of Roman antiquity. David became the leading official painter of the Napoleonic era. By contrast to the secularism of Neoclassicism, the younger generation of German Nazarene painters turned to medieval Christanity as a source of romantic inspiration and feeling.

The eulogy to Winckelmann which Goethe completed shortly before Schiller's death, and published along with letters and essays in *Winckelmann und sein Jahrhundert* (*Winckelmann and his Age* [1805]), keenly expresses his sense of an epoch drawing to a close. In paying tribute to Winckelmann's "antique," "pagan" character, Goethe also honored the secular humanism of a by-gone era against the growing religiosity of the new Romantic movement. It was a swan song of Neoclassicism, for in the following years the spell of the Romantic revival of national art and poetry would also draw Goethe further away from the plasticity of Greek art towards non-classical forms and themes.

Schiller's Death and the Napoleonic Wars

The death of Schiller on May 9, 1805 put an abrupt end to the cultural preeminence of Weimar in Germany. For a decade, Schiller's unbending, energetic, and combative spirit had sustained the classical campaign of cultural reform. With his death, Goethe lost "half of his existence," as he puts it to Carl Friedrich Zelter (1758-1832). Without his ally, the sense of a common aesthetic purpose and the will to assert and shape the vision into harmonious, classical literary forms against the growing tide of Romanticism were diminished. Slowly and painfully emerging from the grief of loss, the aging Goethe now sensed acutely his intellectual aloneness in the new era. The poetic "Epilog zu Schillers Glocke" ("Epilogue to Schiller's Bell"), written for the memorial performance of August 5, 1805, pays homage to an idealism, to a faith in "truth, good and beauty" that he could no longer maintain on his own.

Meanwhile the old courtly society, in which the aesthetic culture of Weimar had found its niche, was rapidly crumbling. From the seismic eruption of the French Revolution emerged a Romantic Caesar, Napoleon Bonaparte (1769-1821), crowned Emperor of the French on May 18, 1804, one who dreamed of rejuvenating the old European dynasties by armed force. Faced with the dynamism of the Napoleonic paradigm, Goethe reacted with a mixture of fascination and dismay. He later called "daemonic" that irresistible force of nature, amoral in essence, that was strong enough to upset the morphological organic order. Indeed, the upset was phenomenal. The Austrian army was defeated on December 2, 1805, the decayed Holy Roman Empire formally dissolved on August 6, 1806, and the last German stronghold, the Prussian army, disbanded in Jena and Auerstedt on October 14, 1806. The same day, French troops occupied and looted Weimar. Goethe escaped armed assault thanks to Christiane Vulpius's steadfast resistance. On October 19, 1806, Goethe thanked her by finally making the mother of his son his legitimate spouse after eighteen years of cohabitation. By mid 1807 most of the German lands had been turned into vassalages of France or occupied territories. The Weimar ducal dynasty on which Goethe's political and literary position rested barely escaped abolition by joining the satellite Rhine Confederation.

Turning Points: Goethe's *Faust*

Goethe's awareness of an era having run its course may have hastened the final revision of the manuscript of *Faust I* in the spring of 1806 after a pause of several years. That a work of such geniality of conception and such versatility of poetic talent, language, and style, one that engaged Goethe's imagination during his entire creative life, could finally come forth in the Napoleonic years may not be coincidental. Indeed, Faustian striving, with its simultaneously rejuvenating and destructive forces, participates in the phenomenon of the "daemonic" that Goethe sensed to be a hallmark of the new era and which he saw most strikingly impersonated in Bonaparte's overwhelming personality. In a psychograph of *Faust* (1827), the author diagnosed the entire psychological make-up of his hero, his sense of confinement, his restlessness, and his relentless longing for transgression as a syndrome of modern subjectivity. Furthermore, the medieval subject matter of the drama, drawing on the 1587 chapbook story of Dr. Johannes Faust's pact with the devil, and its unorthodox mixing of epic, lyrical, and dramatic elements, all at odds with the classicist doctrine of strict genre separation, came close to the aesthetic eclecticism professed by the Romanticists. In the words of the cultural agent of German Romanticism abroad, Mme de Staël's *De l'Allemagne* (*On Germany* [1813]), a poetic creation that so totally escaped traditional genre definitions, "neither a tragedy, nor a novel," could only be grasped with non-rational standards as the emanation of the northern, Germanic, romantic soul. And it is indeed as a prototype of German Romanticism that Goethe's *Faust* was welcomed in France and England.

Significantly, the two works most widely applauded by critics as Goethe's masterpieces, *Faust* and the novel *Die Wahlverwandtschaften*, both transcend the boundaries of Weimar Classicism. At various instances the author himself referred to his *Faust* as a "barbarian," "Nordic composition," and a "poetic monster." And to his friends, he presented *Die Wahlverwandtschaften*, a classically-constructed demonstration of the neutralization of secular humanism by fatal passion, as his "romantic message." In this work of unequalled symbolic depth and psychological sublimity opposing a rational and a romantic pair of characters (Charlotte and the Captain/Eduard and Ottilie), the narrator uses the scheme of a chemical experiment to scrutinize the moral tenets of his age.

The dramatic formula of *Faust* is for the most part non-courtly, non-Aristotelian, and non-illusionist. The grand scope of this stunning cosmo-drama, encompassing metaphysical, magic, and allegorical elements in a loosely related biographical scheme, is kindred to the "world theater" that prevailed in Europe from the late Middle Ages through the seventeenth century, and to Calderón's *gran theatro del mundo* (grand world theater) particularly, the Spanish Baroque dramatist much admired by the Romanticists and whom Goethe discovered with great interest in the early 1800s. Rather than focusing on human psychology, the "world" drama places the individual in the largest possible framework of his or her relationship to the totality of the human and cosmic order. Such panoramic pictures of human life orient the play towards typification and allegorical representation rather than psycho-dramatic impact. It draws the reader's, the spectator's attention to that which figures and scenes playfully enact. Whether seen as a typical representative of the Renaissance man, the Romantic hero, modern man, the nineteenth-century entrepreneur, or even of the corporate drive, the Faustian paradigm never ceases to provoke and fascinate. So does his subversive counterpart Mephistopheles, devil and clown in one, whose presence as an anti-illusionist stage agent highlights the theatricality of the play.

Balancing out the subjectivism of his hero with a Greek sense of totality, and the destructive impact of his relentless activity with the harmony of the classical world, in short, combining and reconciling the romantic and classical features of his work, must have been an early part of Goethe's poetic design, for the outline of 1800 already implies a two-part composition: "I. Lebensgenuß der Person nach außen gesucht: in der Dumpfheit Leidenschaft" (I. The person's joy in life sought in external things. Sultry passion); "II. Tatengenuß nach außen und Genuß mit Bewußtsein. Schönheit" (II. The person's joy in action asserted in external things and pleasure with awareness. Beauty.). The earliest document of Goethe's search for a classical synthesis, the Helena-fragment, was composed in September 1800, simultaneously and in contrast to the satanic scenes of the Walpurgisnight, the witches' sexual sabbath. It later became the dramatic nucleus of the third act of *Faust II*. Accordingly, the "classical Walpurgisnight" in the second act of *Faust II*, a 1483-line mythological retrospective, culminates in the festival of the Aegean Sea with a celebration of sensual pantheism that contraposes the demonization of sexuality in the Gothic Walpurgisnight of *Faust I*. Likewise, Faust's dreamlike union with Helena, the embodiment of Greek beauty and harmony, forms a contrast to his seduction of Gretchen and destruction of her small world.

The phantasmagoric, dreamlike illusiveness of Goethe's mythological imagery in Part II exemplifies a new, allegorical, rather than symbolic, mode of representation, moving radically from the dramatic poignancy of Part I towards the romantic art of mental evocation. Whereas Faust's short-lived immersion in the classical world calls forth the haunting dream of human harmony with nature, in the other acts the vast scope of his many ventures — gold supplier, fiscal reformer, army general, and, finally, land developer whose greed destroys the peaceful abodes of Philemon and Baucis — transcends the realm of individual action to point towards historical process, towards the dynamism unleashed in the ever-accelerating Western transformation of the world. In this allegorical mode of evocation, which is close to romantic poetry, the Faustian nameholder, ceasing to function as the hero of the play, appears as a mere figurative representative, an agent of violent change.

Such a highly self-reflective and syncretic poetic project could only be undertaken in the last part of Goethe's life, for, as also shown in his mutation of the *Bildungsroman Wilhelm Meisters Lehrjahre* into a social novel, *Wilhelm Meisters Wanderjahre (Wilhelm Meister's Journeyman Years* [1821-1829]), *Faust II* partakes of a changing sense of human activity in a Western world already actively engaged in the process of industrial transformation. Yet, unlike his counterpart Wilhelm Meister, Faust never manages to transcend the realm of self-centered action. Save for his perpetual yearning for love and beauty, and a more humane future, for which he is redeemed in the end, all of Faust's terrestrial ventures, from beginning to end, are fraught with the weight of his ominous alliance with the spirit of destruction, Mephistopheles. There lies the most compelling and enduring warning of this most genial of Goethe's works, which Alexander Pushkin (1799-1837) has rightfully called an "Iliad of modern life."

Organic and Poetic Metamorphoses: Goethe's Late Works

It is significant that Goethe's autobiographical reappropriation of his classical past in the *Italienische Reise* coincided with the end of the Napoleonic Wars, for one of the leitmotivs of his travelogue, peaceful organic renewal, a theme overshadowed in the works of the Napoleonic decade by chemical dynamism and subjective striving, seemed also to have reasserted its hold on the present. As for the autobiographical form, Goethe had already tested it successfully as a means of coming to terms with a decade of political and personal turmoil. In a similar fashion as his autobiography *Dichtung und Wahrheit* had served to stamp the imprint of his own literary genius on the Storm-and-Stress decade, the *Italienische Reise* was meant as a reconstruction of the genesis of Weimar Classicism around his Italian awakening. The impact of Goethe's autobiographical self-promotion was strong enough to lend canonic validity to his organic theory of classicism and thus to eclipse for a long time Schiller's reception-oriented classical aesthetics.

The *Italienische Reise* contain several instances of a purposeful use of the term "classical," most of which are embedded in the narrative of the April and May 1787 trip to Sicily, the closest Goethe ever came to Greece, the land of his dreams. There, on what he called "der überklassische Boden" (the transclassical ground), he had received renewed poetic inspiration. The ground, the soil itself, becomes the epitome of the "classical," for it is in the fertile valleys and fields of Sicily that he finds inscribed in a historical continuity reaching back to Greek antiquity a harmonious encounter between nature and human culture. It was the harmony of natural and human activity that produced the classical ground searched for by the artist rather than the "classical memory" of Hannibal's (247-c. 183 B.C.) battles zealously recalled by his travel guide. To the unholy remnants of past war wreckage, Goethe preferred such living deposits of the past as the rocks in the river, for he expected to get from the study of these remains a concept of "jenen ewig klassischen Höhen des Erdaltertums" (eternally classical heights of earth's antiquity). The eternally classical sights conjured up by Goethe are the mountains of Sicily, not her antique battlefields. Rooted in natural history, in the earth's antiquity and permanence, the notion of classicism evoked in this close encounter with the Mediterranean world took on geological connotations. The study of peaceful natural evolution, rather than the cultivation of the heroic past, was to supply and renew classical inspiration.

Goethe conjures up another time the term "classical," in connection with his description of Raphael's (1483-1520) fresco of the Sibyls in the church Santa Maria della Pace in Rome. The fresco, he states in most emphatic terms, had the magical effect of recreating for him "die Gegenwart des klassischen Bodens" (the presence of the classical ground). This revelation was attributed to a principle of Raphael's composition similar to his own principle of "style" sketched out three decades earlier in *Einfache Nachahmung der Natur, Manier, Stil*, a key chapter of which was inserted in the *Italienische Reise*: "There also comes to predominance here in the Sibyls, in the most ingenious fashion, the concealed symmetry upon which everything in composition depends; for, as in the organism of nature, so also in art the perfection of the expression of life reveals itself within the most precise limits." "Concealed symmetry," according to Goethe, was the principle of composition from which works of classical stature could evolve.

The formal standards of symmetry and closure in Goethe's dramatic, epical, and lyrical works of the two decades of Weimar Classicism no longer apply to his late writings. The radical opening of the closed form announced in *Faust I* becomes the poetological characteristic of all the works of the late period. It is as if the champion of *Gestaltung*, of formal coherence of composition as the essence of artistic creation, had recanted his classicist credo to embrace the eclecticism of romantic poetry. In the scientific notebooks of the 1820s Goethe's juxtaposition of a variety of essays in several scientific disciplines with philosophical poems, aphorisms, and reflections blurs the distinction between poetic and scientific discourse. Although *Faust II* is called a "tragedy in five acts," its scenic pattern, more circular than architectonic, is no longer focused around dramatic dialogue, plot, and character development. With its kaleidoscopic display of figures and scenes and its dream-like mode of allegorical evocation interspersed with scientific and philosophical reflections, Part II prefigures film techniques of self-reflective visualization. Likewise, one finds embedded in *Wilhelm Meisters Wanderjahre* a host of other literary forms: novellas, letters, poems and proverbs that complicate the narrative sequence and place Goethe's last novel on a par with the novels of early Romanticism as a pioneer in formal experimentation. There too the main protagonists' individual characteristics fade away for the sake of allegorical representation.

This shift from classicist closure towards romantic fluidity corresponds to a deepening preoccupation on the part of the older Goethe with motion, change, and transformation as the most important laws of organic and social life. Whereas it was the formative principle of living organisms that captivated Goethe's morphological interest in the first Weimar decades, an interest made concrete in the literary sphere in his passion for structural coherence, it is no longer the tangible immanence of concrete forms or their *Gegenständlichkeit* that engages his attention, but rather the elasticity of organisms, their expansive, mutative, transformative qualities.

With the law of metamorphosis a more fluid, verbal, and participial rather than nominal style coalesces, a linguistic feature of Goethe's later language. Since permanent mutation is seen as the main attribute of life, fluidity appears both as a poetological principle and as an essential component of Goethe's scientific thought. "The fluid (whether elastic or dripping like a liquid) is [...] the element of all organic evolution, or of all natural formation in general." It is a Neptunian view of natural evolution through the peaceful action of water that Goethe articulates throughout his late scientific and poetic works. Through his reaffirmation of the organic unity of nature, Goethe also reasserts his Spinozist belief in the immanence of God-Nature. A stronger call for renunciation, for selfless acts of love, now tempers the sensualism of the earlier decades. This ideal of self-denial for the sake of the community, thematic in the free associations of the League of Wanderers in *Wilhelm Meisters Wanderjahre*, also has its symbolic correspondence in the process of unending organic metamorphoses, in the permanent mutations of individual organisms, in interaction with the whole of nature.

8 Romanticism

Christopher R. Clason

Introduction: Social and Historical Background

A. The Term Romanticism

L iterary historians sometimes create more confusion than they put to rest through their attempts to categorize authors and works by movement or period. Romanticism has produced more than the usual number of problems in this area. Some critics of German literature have connected the Romantic rubric to a number of authors, while others have delimited the movement according to certain themes, ideas, and forms which readers encounter in works. Many have set the movement into a strictly temporally-bound historical period, while others have chosen to view the matter less restrictively as a category of styles and concepts which have appeared in many art forms throughout occidental cultural history.

Placed in an historical framework, German Romanticism has also been defined by several important critics in relation to literary-philosophical periods which precede or follow it. For example, H. A. Korff, in his famous literary history *Geist der Goethezeit* (1956, 1958) suggests a polar opposition between Romanticism and Enlightenment, while Fritz Strich emphasizes the distinctions between Classic and Romantic. Goethe himself contrasted "sick" Romanticism to his "healthy" Classicism. Several authors consciously applied the term "Romantic" to their own literature and ideas at this time, distinguishing their work especially from products of the Enlightenment.

B. Social and Historical Background

During the first part of the eighteenth century, politics, society, and intellectual life rested at a relative equilibrium in most of Europe. Strong monarchies and rationalistic philosophy held in check any large-scale deviance from the "God-ordained" order. But by the end of the century the order had begun to crumble in all areas of human experience. Revolutions in America and France had significantly changed the West's political map. Scientific advances had planted technological seeds that would germinate in the coming Industrial Revolution. In philosophy, the great thinkers had begun to doubt, not only concerning reality itself, but even regarding the human means of perceiving reality. The modern world was bursting forth from soil tilled with new technology and new ideas.

Of the major European nations, the linguistic and cultural entity known as Germany remained the weakest politically. The Holy Roman Empire, a northern vestige of the once-strong medieval kingdom, consisted of a loose conglomeration of German cities, states, duchies, monarchies, and principalities, each of which enjoyed a high degree of sovereignty, but none of which was powerful enough to dominate and unify the others into a single German nation. At various times the two largest states, Prussia and Austria, vied for primacy in the association, the former gaining the upper hand under the strong military leadership of Friedrich II (the Great [1712-1786]). But Napoleon's victories in the first decade of the 1800s placed most German land under French rule.

During a large part of the eighteenth century, France cast the long shadow of its culture over Germany in the form of neoclassicism, an aesthetic movement which looked to seventeenth-century French dramatists as models for imitation. The greatest problem besetting the German neoclassicists resulted from their inability to account adequately for the role irrational forces play in artistic creation. In the second half of the century, Enlightenment philosophy, based on reason alone, encountered difficulties in completely explaining experience, since it tended to reduce certain emotions to mechanistic cause and effect. In the literary world as well, critics raised their voices in protest more and more loudly. While Gotthold Ephraim Lessing (1729-1781) effectively assaulted that which essentially amounted to neoclassical "tyranny" with his "enlightened" criticism (which for Lessing included non-French elements), the Storm and Stress poets and dramatists lashed out in another direction, as they showed the powerful and spontaneous workings of the emotions in human endeavor, and of irrational forces in nature.

But as strong as these intellectual stirrings became, the Germans did not revolt politically, as other Europeans and the Americans had done. Friedrich Schlegel (1772-1829) designated the French Revolution as one of the three great "tendencies" of his time, but the German Romantics did not advocate the violent overthrow of any government. As on many other occasions in German history, the intellectuals, who might have wielded some power for a political revolt, turned inward and instead initiated a revolution of ideas. Some historians and critics have explained Storm and Stress, Romanticism, and other periods of German intellectual history, in which creativeness and imagination play central roles, as the result of redistributed revolutionary energy which can find no other outlet. That is, while some societies during certain eras experienced violent physical change, German society effected some of its most important changes on an intellectual and artistic level. Of course, such an observation can only be treated as a generalization, and there have been numerous exceptions to it, as the violent Revolution of 1848.

The social composition of the Romantic Movement strongly colors its political mood. Many Romantic authors come from noble lineage: Friedrich von Hardenberg (Novalis [1772-1801]), Ludwig Achim von Arnim (1781-1831), Heinrich von Kleist

(1777-1811), and Joseph Freiherr von Eichendorff (1788-1857) are notable examples of upper-class artists in this literary movement. Adelbert von Chamisso (1781-1838) stemmed from a landed French family which had escaped the bloody revolution during the 1790s; the family of Baron Friedrich de la Motte Fouqué (1777-1843) had emigrated a generation earlier. Others consorted with members of the nobility, and intellectual circles, especially in Berlin, were the salons of noblemen and noblewomen who invited their Romantic literary friends. Several Romantics, especially August Wilhelm Schlegel (1767-1845), enjoyed the companionship of Madame de Staël (1766-1817), perhaps the most important liaison between German Romanticism and the French during the first decades of the nineteenth century.

Furthermore, Catholic and feudal inclinations among some Romantic authors created a political atmosphere which supported the aristocracy and the old social order. Looking back on the Middle Ages the Romantics envisioned a unified culture on a unified continent, where harmony was built into a rigid social system. Of course, they concentrated on events in the lives of those highly-positioned individuals (lords, ladies, and knights) for whom chivalry could have real meaning, and paid little attention to the lower classes. Informing all levels of society, Roman Catholicism functioned as a kind of "world-spirit" and preserved the natural order and harmony. Some Romantics looked disdainfully upon the Reformation, which split the church and the society into two factions and which helped create the lamentable disunity in which they found their contemporary world. Some Romantics converted to or re-affirmed the Catholic faith, while many of their literary productions incorporated a medieval and piously Christian background.

Nationalism was fired by the coincidence of the philosophical climate and certain historical events. Johann Gottfried Herder (1744-1803) and poets of the Storm and Stress had engendered a fascination among intellectuals with the German *Volk*, especially regarding the naturalness and simplicity of expression in such art forms as the *Lied*. This fascination grew considerably during the Romantic era. Although the Germans experienced political disunity, they had a strong sense of their cultural, historical, and linguistic heritage. The word *Vaterland*, which could bring a tear to the eye or a song to the lips of many a Romantic literary figure, certainly transcended any narrowly political definition: it included all of what was considered *Deutschland*. By the end of the eighteenth century this concept was still an abstraction, but it was growing rapidly more concrete in the folk consciousness.

During the first decade of the nineteenth century Napoleon (1769-1821) conquered most of *Deutschland*. The Napoleonic Wars imposed great hardships upon many Germans, and several Romantic authors, including E. T. A. Hoffmann (1776-1822), approached the brink of personal disaster because of these conflicts. Many writers took to anti-French propaganda, while others penned essays extolling Germanic virtues. The largest political group of German Romantics, the "Christian-German Society," was formed in Berlin at this time. Its membership, which included Johann Gottlieb Fichte (1762-1814), Chamisso, Arnim, Kleist, Clemens Brentano (1778-1842), Eichendorff, and Fouqué, espoused nationalistic sentiment which at times bordered on chauvinism, particularly with respect to the group's anti-

Brentano (1778-1842), Eichendorff, and Fouqué, espoused nationalistic sentiment which at times bordered on chauvinism, particularly with respect to the group's anti-Semitism. While these feelings contributed to the campaign against the French occupation and helped to solidify a nationalistic tradition for the later unification of Germany (1871), they also continued a legacy of minority exclusion directed against Jews and those social elements considered to be "foreign."

C. Trends, Principles, Characteristics

German Romanticism was cultivated in a social environment. The deep friendship enjoyed by Ludwig Tieck (1773-1853) and Wilhelm Heinrich Wackenroder (1773-1798) became exemplary for relationships among the other Romantics. Almost all of the authors participating in the movement belonged at one time or another to a Romantic "circle" or society, and many of them lived in close proximity to one another. The "cult" of friendship which grew in their ranks was most beneficial for their work: the Romantics co-authored many volumes, edited each others' writings, and rendered complementary service to one another.

There were two distinct groups of German Romantics: the "Berlin-Jena" group of older Romantic authors, which included Tieck, Wackenroder (who, before he died, knew only Tieck among the major Romantics), the brothers August Wilhelm and Friedrich Schlegel, Caroline Schlegel (later Schelling [1763-1809]), Dorothea Veit (later Schlegel [1763-1839]), Friedrich E. D. Schleiermacher (1768-1834), Friedrich Wilhelm Schelling (1775-1854), and Novalis; the young Romantics counted among their number Clemens Brentano, his close friend and associate Arnim, and Hoffmann and Eichendorff. The latter group was less tightly-knit than the former, although close affiliations did exist, particularly in the later Berlin circle, which included Hoffmann, Chamisso, and Fouqué.

Novalis as an adolescent.
Courtesy the Museum Weissenfels

Although the Romantics reacted strongly against what they perceived to be the empty and sterile rationalism of the Enlightenment, they did not abandon logical processes, and in their writings they explored the major philosophical issues which had confronted thinkers for centuries. Almost all the early Romantic authors speculated in these areas; such inquiry was at the heart of the Romantic artistic program. However, they did not necessarily employ the methods and rigorous rationalism which the Enlightenment philosophers had developed, but chose instead to follow their own paths. While many of their philosophical utterances remain obscure and incomplete, much of what they produced has borne fruit, even into our present century. After all, Romantic thinkers were largely responsible for establishing the study of *Germanistik* (German studies) itself.

Romanticism is expansive: that is, Romantic authors seek complexity and multifariousness in their works. Philosophy and literature are primarily concerned with the "infinite" and the "universal." Thus, Novalis claims that the "Romanticizing" process is a "qualitative exponentialization," in which commonplace things, events, and ideas receive a mysterious, unusual, and eternal appearance, and thereby become uncommon and significant. According to this analogy, the "ordinary" is raised to a higher exponential power, and so gains another dimension. Simultaneously, Romanticism tries to reduce transcendental, mysterious, universal, and eternal realities to simpler and more easily understandable formulae. Novalis explains this phenomenon by analogy to another mathematical model, the logarithm, which reduces complexity to a lower order.

Romanticism is synthetic. Romantic authors attempt to combine and synthesize all areas of intellectual endeavor, including art, literature, religion, philosophy, criticism, and natural science. Thus, literary and philosophical metaphors can be drawn from new sources, such as the field of mathematics (as we see in Novalis's discussion of the exponential and logarithmic tendencies of Romanticism). Friedrich Schlegel calls Romantic literature "progressive" and "universal" in his "116th *Athenäum*-Fragment" (1798), and shows how its synthetic properties will "romanticize" all of society and even the entire world. Here we observe a key contrast between Enlightenment philosophy, which attempts to analyze, separate, and individuate, and Romantic methods, which intend to synthesize, combine, and universalize.

The poet achieves a primary position in the Romantic system, that is, stands between the world and society and romanticizes both of them, while providing the Romantic "lens" (which Brentano mentions in the novel *Godwi* [1801]) that colors reality romantically, expands it, synthesizes its disparate components, and lends it mysterious, unusual, and interesting aspects.

Because of its progressive and universal nature Romantic writing does not remain within temporal and spatial limits. Perfection and closure are not part of the Romantic aesthetic system, and Friedrich Schlegel asserts that the Romantic process is never finished, but eternally "becoming." Philosophical works often appear as fragments, without the thorough and painstakingly logical development that characterizes works from other periods. The fragmentary nature of Romantic writings partly accounts for their tendency to dwell in obscurity. Prose writers also incline to produce fragments, and many of the most famous German Romantic literary works are unfinished, such as Novalis's *Heinrich von Ofterdingen* (1802), or are "complete" as fragments, such as Hoffmann's *Kater Murr* (*Tomcat Murr*, [1820-1822]).

Another result of Romanticism's progressive and universal quality is its focus on the path to artistry. Much of the fiction of this time is devoted to the aesthetic education of a young man (*Heinrich von Ofterdingen*, Tieck's *Franz Sternbalds Wanderungen* [*Franz Sternbald's Travels* — 1798], etc.). Often, Romantic novels become novels of education (*Bildungsromane*), in which a naive hero attains poetic insight and vision, usually by travelling and searching for some indistinct goal, of which he has only a presentiment. Heroes feel compelled to journey ever onward on their quests by a vague longing, which is never fulfilled, but which ultimately forms the core of their artistic existences. Novalis summarizes Romantic longing in the *blaue Blume* (blue flower) which Heinrich von Ofterdingen perceives in a dream and which starts him on his journey to become a poet. Indeed, the blue flower becomes a symbol for Romanticism itself.

Dreams and other psychological events become important for most Romantic authors, particularly as part of the Romanticizing process. Objects and ideas that may appear to be finite, common, or even imperceptible when one is fully conscious and aware, can be experienced romantically as "eternal," "universal," or "mysterious," when one is dreaming them. Some Romantics investigate abnormal psychology, mesmerism, and somnambulism, since such states of mind also incorporate "magical thinking," paralleling the Romantic process. E. T. A. Hoffmann is well-known for such investigations in his tales, while the plots of many stories and dramas by Kleist depend upon the heroes' and heroines' semiconscious and unconscious states.

As we have already mentioned, many Romantics idealize the Middle Ages, looking back nostalgically upon a prettified epoch of knightly derring-do and cultural unity. Additionally, certain aspects of Catholic mysticism exert a strong attraction on Romantic philosophers. Many tales (by Novalis, Fouqué, and others) depict a medieval milieu, and interest in medieval German texts contributes to the founding of *Germanistik* as the study of such literary treasures. But the strong interest in medieval institutions and Roman Catholicism, combined with some Romantics' political conservatism, draws the sharpest of Heinrich Heine's cutting criticism of German Romanticism in *Die romantische Schule* (*The Romantic School* [1838]).

Many Romantics develop an interest in gathering folk literature. Jakob Grimm (1785-1863) and his brother Wilhelm (1786-1859) assembled their great collections of folktales (1812-1815) and sagas (1816-1818) as part of the Romantic impetus. Achim von Arnim and Clemens Brentano produced a treasury of folksongs, *Des Knaben Wunderhorn* (*The Boy's Magic Horn* [1806-1808]), the charm of which endured throughout the nineteenth century. Less well-known are *Die Teutschen Volksbücher* (*The German Folkbooks* [1807]) of Joseph Görres (1776-1848), which reflect a strong revival of German nationalistic feeling.

The Romantics structure many of their works on a triadic principle, which they derive from folk literature and religion. Romantic numerology designates "one" as the original unity which was destroyed by the dissention and division implied by "two," the number of polarity and disharmony, historically represented by the religious state of affairs in Europe after the Reformation. "Three" corresponds to the future "Golden Age," with its special unity, reflecting the perfection of the Divine Trinity. While the Romantics yearn for the third age, they realize that it cannot exist. Many novels incorporate triads, whether in the number of sub-genres they contain (as the three fairy tales in *Heinrich von Ofterdingen*) or as their structure. For this reason, several of the Romantics' novels have two parts but remain fragmentary or incomplete; the conclusion of such a novel represents a second stage, "in-between," at which the reader now finds him- or herself, longing to recapture the lost, primary unity of the past in a blissful and unrealizable future.

Because the idealized past and utopian future are unattainable, the Romantic remains necessarily frustrated. This frustration creates much of the tension inherent in Romanticism, and leads sometimes to nihilism, particularly and surprisingly early in an anonymously authored novel, most recently attributed to Ernst August Friedrich Klingemann (1777-1831), entitled *Nachtwachen von Bonaventura* (*Night Watches of Bonaventura* [1804]). One might speculate that the perception of contradiction and the feeling of futility could account for the large number of authors with Romantic tendencies (such as Jakob Michael Reinhold Lenz [1751-1792], Friedrich Hölderlin [1770-1843], Edgar Allan Poe [1809-1849], and others) who suffered from insanity, alcoholism, or other psychological disorders, or who (like Chamisso) embarked on voyages to distant lands, perhaps to escape their dull present by fleeing geographically toward the infinite horizon.

Romantic authors preferred prose and poetry to the drama. In the novel and the novella they were very much at home. In prose, a narrator mediates between subject matter and the reader, "coloring" perceived reality with the narrator's artistic sensibility. Friedrich Schlegel and Novalis established aesthetic guidelines in Romantic prose in their fragments on poetics and in their literary criticism. For both Romantic theoreticians Johann Wolfgang von Goethe's *Wilhelm Meisters Lehrjahre* (*Wilhelm Meister's Apprenticeship* [1795/1796]) became the point of departure for some of their most important utterances on the genre: Schlegel praised Goethe's novel as one of the great "tendencies" of the Romantic age (since in it Goethe represents universal ideas through specific characters and events, especially through the two Romantic figures Mignon and the Harpist), and Novalis condemns it as a *Candide* against poetry (since Goethe largely replaced poetic concerns with everyday, real existence). Romantic authors were fascinated with the poet's artistic evolution, and most novels follow the Wilhelm Meister example as *Bildungsroman*. Many authors create narrators to act as mediators in relating their stories, either under the guise of a fictitious editor (Hoffmann, for example) or as a character who actively enters into the story (as Maria in Brentano's *Godwi*). Some novelists interspersed Romantic lyrics, fairy tales, and even dramatic episodes with prose, as they attempted to synthesize all of the genres. Through the novel form the Romantics were able to realize much of their aesthetic program.

The Romantics were also adept at shorter prose fiction. The German novella reached its first high point in Romanticism; during the period there appeared such masterpieces as Tieck's *Der blonde Eckbert (Blond Eckbert* [1797]) Kleist's *Das*

Erdbeben in Chili (*The Earthquake in Chile* [1807]), Arnim's *Der tolle Invalide auf dem Fort Ratonneau* (*The Mad Invalid at Fort Ratonneau* [1818]), Chamisso's *Peter Schlemihls wundersame Geschichte* (*Peter Schlemihl's Marvelous Tale* [1814]), Eichendorff's *Aus dem Leben eines Taugenichts* (*From the Life of a Good-For-Nothing* [1826]), and Hoffmann's *Der goldene Topf* (The Golden Pot [1814]). In most Romantic novellas the realm of irrational, mysterious, and supernatural forces intrudes upon everyday reality and creates havoc which the authors do not always resolve. In this way the struggle between daily reality and the "other world" is externalized and universalized. The German Romantics, exploring the borders between reality and the imagination, had a strong international influence, especially on the American Romantics Nathaniel Hawthorne (1804-1864) and Edgar Allan Poe. Fairy tales, which the Romantics both collected (*Volksmärchen*) and wrote themselves (*Kunstmärchen*), were perhaps the most popular prose legacy of the German Romantic era. Elements from the fairy tale tradition (magic, numerology, etc.) emerge in many other genres as well, such as in Tieck's folktale drama *Der gestiefelte Kater* (*Puss-in-Boots* [1797]).

E.T.A. Hoffmann 1776-1822)
Drawing by Wilhelm Hensel,
Nationalgalerie Berlin

Poetry became the second important genre for the Romantics, and most artists produced verses copiously. Typically, poets composed in three forms: the lyric, the ballad, and the folksong, and during the period they write some of the finest examples of each.

In Romantic lyric poetry, the author presented an inner world such that the reader may participate directly in it. Thus, the poet became the facilitator for the aesthetic experience, fulfilling principles expounded by the influential Romantic philosopher Johann Gottlieb Fichte, which suggest that in society the poet is the central figure and that the free poetic imagination is the most important tool. Such poetry is especially striking because it can communicate a great range and depth of emotion immediately and effectively. In particular, Novalis's *Hymnen an die Nacht* (*Hymns to the Night* [1800]) capture a personal, emotional, and mystical experience of death as a spiritual union between the poet, Christ, and his deceased beloved. Other Romantic poets attempted to create verbal music in their lyrical verses by approximating musical tones and rhythms through the sounds of the words they employ. Eichendorff, who claims that a "song sleeps in all things" and that it is the poets task to awaken it, creates some of his most beautiful poems through this type of verbal composition.

Frontispiece to Werner's Romantic play
Die Templer auf Cypern

The ballad attracted other Romantics, especially because it enabled the poet to combine lyric and dramatic elements in a narrative form, thus synthesizing the three main genres. Poets strove to include magical, irrational, and supernatural subjects and themes in a gripping narrative, supporting it musically with recurring rhymes and unrelenting rhythms. Chamisso, Brentano, and Heine constructed many superb ballads in such a manner, and a large number of other Romantics tried their hand at this synthetic poetic form.

Recalling Herder's utterances regarding folk literature, many Romantics became keenly interested in the folksong, not only as an object of indigenous art worthy of collection (as, for example, those which Arnim and Brentano collected), but also as a poetic genre for original creation, in the same manner as the *Kunstmärchen* (as opposed to a folk tale, or *Volksmärchen*). Folk verses by Tieck, Brentano, and Eichendorff provide fine examples of poetry composed in the *Volkslied* tradition.

Of all literary genres, the drama afforded the least opportunity for the artist to employ Romantic techniques: this drawback resulted from the limitations on imagination which the immediacy and realism of the stage imposed on the audience. Furthermore, authorial mediation by means of a third person narrator in the drama is only seldom employed (Tieck's *Der gestiefelte Kater*). By far the most successful dramatic artist of the period is Kleist, who does not fit strictly into the Romantic mold. Among the other dramatists of this era, the most notorious is Zacharias Werner (1768-1823), in whose "fate tragedy" *Der vierundzwanzigste Februar* (*The Twenty-Fourth of February* [1809]) supernatural forces have disastrous effects upon everyday existence. In much of his work (which most modern critics do not highly regard), Werner relies heavily upon religious plots and themes and follows formulae from the German and Spanish Baroque periods. Arnim and other Romantics also attempted to work in dramatic forms, but they proved far more successful with their efforts in prose and in poetry.

Romantic Authors

A. Wilhelm Heinrich Wackenroder

Insatiable yearning, boundless emotional extremes, dissatisfaction with the prosaic present, and pious longing for eternal fulfillment informed the German Romantic spirit. Wackenroder's short life reflected these psychological aspects strongly. Having survived a difficult childhood filled with illness and unhappiness, he was forced to study law by his overbearing and unsympathetic father. Clearly, his interests lay elsewhere. For several years Wackenroder shared a friendship with Ludwig Tieck, whom he had met at the University of Erlangen in 1793. Later, during a year at the University of Göttingen, they became avid travel companions. The Catholic towns of southern Germany held a particular fascination for Wackenroder, and his experiences there marked much of his work. Unfortunately, he produced but a few prose pieces, mostly in collaboration with Tieck. These became the first literary documents of the German Romantic movement. His death in 1798 prematurely silenced one of the Romantics' most important early voices.

Wackenroder's most significant contribution to Romanticism is the prose work *Herzensergießungen eines kunstliebenden Klosterbruders* (*The Emotional Outpourings of an Art-Loving Friar* [1797]), which contains fourteen essays honoring the old masters — painters like Raphael and Dürer. The art-loving monk treats his subject as the tangible manifestation of divine power, and he contemplates paintings in a devoted fashion, as if his critical writings were acts of prayer. He endows the works which he discusses with religious meaning, connecting their symbols with Christian references, whether or not the religious significance is obvious. Thus, the interpretations became a projection of Wackenroder's own inspired, ecstatic feelings. He made no effort to mask his tendentiously theological program.

The final essay, "Das merkwürdige musikalische Leben des Tonkünstlers Joseph Berglinger" ("The Remarkable Musical Life of the Composer Joseph Berglinger"), portrays Wackenroder's own enthusiasm for music. Music becomes the "art of the arts," for it brings the listener directly into a state of pious devotion. At the same time, Berglinger's views introduce the quintessential existential problem of the Romantic artist, that the inwardly subjective way of life is impossible in the real world. After Wackenroder's death, Tieck published a continuation of the rapturous, mostly musical essays, the *Phantasien über die Kunst für Freunde der Kunst* (*Fantasies on Art for Friends of Art* [1799]). In this work, Tieck maintains that music is simultaneously divine and dangerous, for while it elevates the listener, it also renders her or him unfit for life in reality.

B. Ludwig Tieck

Tieck, Wackenroder's friend and editor, enjoyed a long life that spanned several literary movements. Tieck was more detached and objective than Wackenroder, and his thoughts were more firmly grounded in reality. If one might describe Wackenroder as the "soul" of German Romanticism, then Tieck certainly deserves to be known as the "pen." Not only was he solely responsible for the editing of Wackenroder's works, but, in collaboration with Friedrich Schlegel, he published Novalis's major poetry and prose, and, with August Wilhelm Schlegel, contributed to the supremely important Romantic translation of Shakespeare's works. Therefore, Tieck is primarily responsible for the appearance in print of many of Romanticism's most seminal writings.

Understandably, Tieck's aesthetic viewpoint changed over time. While at the beginning of the Romantic era he took a place at the forefront, his writings bear the marks of realism as well. He never lost his ability to combine fantastic elements with a realistic background. However, in his later works, realism and the hero's search for stability, portrayed against an authentic backdrop, begin to take precedence over the earlier, more Romantic traits.

Tieck was productive in all genres. *Franz Sternbalds Wanderungen* (1798), his most important novel, establishes the tradition of the Romantic *Bildungsroman* and glorifies the simple, pious art, particularly painting, of the Middle Ages (which for the early Romantics includes Dürer and other Renaissance artists). It also continues the tradition of the wandering Romantic artist, who, like Goethe's Werther, yearns for something indefinable and elusive, who feels more than he produces, and whose aesthetic experiences remain primarily within the mind.

Among Tieck's many fine works, two stand out as literary gems. *Der blonde Eckbert* (1797), one of the most popular tales (*Kunstmärchen*) from the period, masterfully incorporates irrational and realistic elements into a suspenseful and terrifying narrative. *Der gestiefelte Kater* transforms Charles Perrault's classic fairy tale into an amusing satirical comedy. Because Tieck set the fairy-tale action in a framework of characters from the audience, the play successfully synthesized dramatic and epic elements, yielding one of the few Romantic works for the stage which can still entertain a modern audience.

In his later years Tieck embraced political and aesthetic conservatism more and more fervently, and his works begin to warn about the dangers of extremism and revolution. Although he remained artistically involved with the tension between the real and ideal, his last few works bridge the gap between Romanticism and the Biedermeier period.

C. Novalis

Friedrich von Hardenberg, better known by his pseudonym Novalis, was most responsible for giving poetic expression to many of the young movement's most

telling characteristics: the inclination to mysticism, mythologizing, and philosophiz-
ing; the tendency to fragmentary utterances, which were often both obscure and
profound; the concern with the "dark side" of human experience, such as night
and death; the combination of scientific, philosophical, religious, and literary ideas
into a single, unified expression; the primacy of the poet in a Romanticized society;
and, finally, *die blaue Blume* (the blue flower), which became the literary symbol
for Romantic longing, for Romantic poetry, and ultimately for Romanticism itself.

Like other early Romantic poets, Novalis attempted a synthesis of philosophy
and poetry: thus, his philosophical fragments rely on intuition and analogous
thinking for their effects, while in his poetic works he often digresses at great
length on abstract philosophical subjects. In *Die Lehrlinge zu Sais (Apprentices of
Sais* [1802]), Novalis illustrates a basic Romantic episte-mological problem, the connec-tion between the knowledge of nature and the knowledge of self, with a fairy tale entitled "Hyazinth und Rosenblüt-chen" ("Hyacinth and Little Rose Blossom"). By contrast, Klingsohr's poetic message to his apprentice, Heinrich von Ofterdingen, becomes a philo-sophical digression couched in abstract and symbolic lan-guage.

*Novalis's engagement ring with miniature
portrait of Sophie von Kühn
(Courtesy Museum Weissenfels)*

Novalis's most political essay, *Die Christenheit oder Europa (Christianity or Europe* [1799]) presents the image of
the Middle Ages, which became very popular during the period. Novalis considers
pre-Reformation Europe to be a time of naive unity which Martin Luther (1483-
1546) tore asunder and which was pounded further into the dust by the rational,
analytical Enlightenment. Novalis calls for a second Reformation, which will create
a new future order for Europe and the world based upon a synthetic cultural unity.

The six-part *Hymnen an die Nacht,* which appeared in *Athenäum,* the
movement's literary journal, in 1800, arose from Novalis's deep grief at the death
of his beloved Sophie von Kühn, and from his resulting strongly religious feelings.
Novalis composed the hymns partly in lyric form and partly in a rhythmic prose
that approaches poetry. Sophie becomes the mediator for the poet and death, and
at the conclusion, the poet expresses a longing for a *unio mystica* in death for
himself, Sophie, and Christ. Few literary works in German achieve the emotive
power of the *Hymnen,* and they remain an outstanding example of evocative lyric
poetry in the German language.

Heinrich von Ofterdingen (1802) still proves to be a treasure chest for the student of the Romantic novel. The fragmentary work consists of two parts. The first and longest of these describes the poet's development from childhood to artistic maturity ("Die Erwartung" ["Expectation"]). The second part, entitled "Die Erfüllung" ("Fulfillment"), remains unfinished (!), but it promises to reveal a second stage of the poetic apprenticeship directing Heinrich toward an "apotheosis" of poetry, which diverges from ordinary reality, and which lifts such restrictions as time and space, or past and future. Novalis evokes moods and emotions via embedded lyrics and songs. Three fairy tales, including Klingsohr's narrative, convey philosophical and poetic lessons to young Heinrich. As a result of his dream of the blue flower, he sets out on journeys over the land and under the earth, longing for something of which he has only a vague idea. His yearning leads him ever homeward, implying that his development is the unfolding of the truth which is latent within him, and not something which he learns. Finally, Novalis shows the poet to be both savior and magician, who in the act of creation gains salvation for the world through a mystical union with divinity. Although the novel breaks off abruptly because of Novalis's death, Tieck reconstructed the author's final plans in a paralipomena that he published with the text.

D. August Wilhelm Schlegel

Romantic philosophy and aesthetics reflect simultaneously expansive and reductive, as well as universalizing and fragmenting tendencies in consciously literary texts. Clearly, such discourse does not lend itself easily to a logical systemization, for which the Romantic program had a definite need. For this great task the Romantics owed a considerable debt to August Wilhelm Schlegel. While the older of the Schlegel brothers lacked creative originality, he possessed organizing skills and a deep and productive knowledge of classical scholarship, history, and aesthetics. In several critical and historical essays Schlegel discusses many difficult Romantic concepts, imbedding them in the tradition of classical philosophy and literature, thereby providing them with an historical context and scholarly legitimacy.

During his sojourns in Berlin (1801-1804), and later in Vienna (1808), he delivered a series of lectures which clarified many Romantic theories and principles, at first for German intellectuals. Later the lectures were translated into many languages and distributed throughout Europe. They bore great influence on an international group of Romantic authors, including Samuel Taylor Coleridge (1772-1834), Victor Hugo (1802-1885), and Alexander Pushkin (1799-1837).

Another important contribution which Schlegel made to the Romantic movement came as a result of his efforts to further Shakespeare's popularity among the Germans. The English bard had already enjoyed a German audience, since Lessing and the Storm and Stress poets had claimed him as their own, and since Christoph Martin Wieland (1733-1813) had translated a number of his plays into German. Schlegel wrote two critical essays on Shakespeare and produced excellent German

A. W. Schlegel ca. 1820
Painting by H. C. Kolbe

translations of fourteen plays (Dorothea Tieck [1799-1841] completed the remaining works; many of their translations are still in use today). Schlegel's praise for Shakespeare differs from the impassioned laudation which the Storm and Stress heaped upon him. According to Schlegel, Shakespeare was not a naive and spontaneous genius but an adept artist who carefully fashioned his plays. Schlegel held that Shakespeare, like the Romantic poets, demonstrated in his works his disciplined talent and the arduous development of his craft. When Schlegel translated Shakespeare, he attempted to capture the Englishman's essence and meaning, advancing far beyond the earlier translators, who paid stricter attention to form.

E. Friedrich Schlegel

While August Wilhelm Schlegel distinguished himself through his talents for systems and organization, his younger brother Friedrich preferred other, more creative endeavors. The younger man's more volatile temperament sometimes made him a difficult leader for the new Romantic circle in Jena, although he most certainly provided the young movement's spark. He was restless, troubled by contradictory feelings, argumentative, and yet at the same time compulsively social, constantly proposing group projects, and testing his new theories in conversations with his colleagues. He moved rapidly from task to task, burning with an intellectual energy that he transferred to most of the other early Romantics.

Friedrich Schlegel's preferred vehicle for his philosophical writings was the prose fragment, which he produced in profusion and published in the periodicals *Lyceum* (1797) and *Athenäum* (1798-1800). The famous "116th *Athenäum* Fragment" has been critically recognized as the most succinct statement of the Romantic aesthetic program. In it, Schlegel emphasizes the progressive and universal character of Romantic literature: it is synthetic, expansive, and constantly in progress. In this area Schlegel's ideas sharply contrast with Goethean Classicism, which always seeks completion and perfection. Schlegel wishes to unite all intellectual fields into one great body of Romantic literature, thereby unifying and harmonizing the world through art. The poet accomplishes this task through intelligence and wit, and he or she combines unlimited abundance with infinite unity in the creative work. Schlegel expanded and elaborated these principles in a number of essays and lectures, the most important of which he collected in *Die Griechen und Römer* (*The Greeks and the Romans* [1797]) and *Geschichte der alten und neuen Literatur* (*The History of Ancient and Modern Literature* [1815]).

Schlegel's most important creative work in a poetic form is his novel *Lucinde* (1799), which he intended as a realization of his aesthetic theories. Unfortunately, it fails because it lacks unity: there is little continuity in the narrative, and the work as a whole strikes the reader as a somewhat contrived amalgamation of various prose forms (letters, conversations, etc.) which do not necessarily fit together. The novel treats the themes of love and marriage intellectually. Lucinde has often received critical notoriety as a sexually frank and shocking novel, but whether it deserves this reputation is questionable. Some critics have claimed that Schlegel presents a new view of the woman as an autonomous agent, as an equal partner with a man in a relationship, striving for harmony. The idea of love evolves substantially as well: *eros* and *caritas* become the same emotional force. Schlegel's resulting concept of love is intended to reflect infinity and to inform all Romantic literature.

Schlegel's many intellectual pursuits directed him more and more toward religion. His Sanskrit studies led him to the history of religion, and made Roman Catholicism more important in his world view. In his later writings religion becomes the great unifying principle, and to an ever increasing degree he considers the Roman Catholic Church to have preserved Romantic principles throughout history. The last ten years of his life Schlegel took a politically conservative standpoint, supporting the Church's position in society as he assumed a role as the chief German exponent of Catholic mysticism. While Schlegel's influence diminished considerably during the last years of the Romantic era, his place as the leader and spokesman for the early Romantics before 1810, as well as his role in igniting the infant movement with his literary and philosophical writings and his fiery personality, cannot be denied.

F. Clemens Brentano (1778-1842)

Few authors of the Romantic period were more subject to emotional extremes than Clemens Brentano. Feelings of religious ecstasy and guilt battled natural urges and insatiable sensual longing for possession of his soul, and they could strike no lasting balance. His moods swung from celestial and divine joy through heated passion to deep melancholy. Catholicism's traditional stability provided no shelter for his troubled heart, since Brentano's penchant for total involvement led him to various unhappy extremes.

German Romantic poetry reached a high point in Brentano's lyrics. In many poems of unusual beauty, Brentano writes as if he were precariously perched between sensuality and religion, tormented by the choices he must make. Especially before his return to the Catholic faith in 1816, the gifted poet exploited the musicality of language and the sonorous effects of human speech, qualities which can be most fully realized in lyric poetry. He used similar techniques in his ballads — "Lore Lay" (1800) and "Auf dem Rhein" ("On the Rhine"[1801]) are perhaps the most popular examples — and created a uniquely musical type of poem which narrates tales and legends from specific German regions.

Brentano's more mature poetry embraces religious themes and symbols. Later he sought salvation through works of mercy, by contributing to charity, and by documenting the ecstatic visions of a stigmatized nun, Anna Katharina Emmerick, at her bedside over a period of five years. Even in his late writings Brentano was able to capture musical qualities in religious verse, as "Nachklänge Beethovenscher Musik" ("Echoes of Beethoven's Music" [1814]) beautifully attests.

Brentano is no less a master in the prose genres. The tales which he composed mostly from Italian and Rhenish materials reflect a high degree of sophistication and wit. *Die Geschichte vom braven Kasperl und dem schönen Annerl* (*The Story of Honest Casper and Fair Annie* [1817]) is considered a thoroughly Romantic novella, particularly in view of the intrusion which marvelous and supernatural powers make on everyday reality in it. However, the narrator presents the story in such a matter-of-fact, realistic manner that the reader feels compelled to accept its veracity. Therefore, some critics have claimed Brentano's novella contains elements which look ahead to more realistic literature later in the nineteenth century.

One of the most interesting experiments of the Romantic period, Brentano's *Godwi*, appeared in 1801 in two parts. Brentano incorporates many of Friedrich Schlegel's ideas directly into the novel. He particularly emphasizes the autonomy of the author as creator of the novel's universe, and erects an apparently chaotic structure, which, in fact, is a carefully planned and crafted fiction. Subtitled *Ein verwilderter Roman* (A Novel Run Wild), the book seems to lead the reader on a hopelessly confused romp. Letters from and to Godwi comprise the first part, while in the second part the author (under the pseudonym Maria) and his characters initiate a discussion of Romantic principles and debate how the book should progress. The author, Maria, dies before finishing the novel, and Godwi himself takes over the narrative. However, even the new author leaves the novel uncompleted and fragmentary. The wild plot creates a special relationship between the reader and the author: Brentano takes great pains to point out the fictitiousness of his work, and the author and the reader share in an ironical perspective on it. With this "fiction of a fiction" — a type of Romantic irony — Brentano also fulfills Schlegel's dictum, to exponentialize poetry and prose and to create a "literature of literature." *Godwi* resembles many modern structural experiments in prose which treat texts in a similar manner, and where authors purposely invent discontinuous plots and relativize time and space for certain aesthetic effects.

G. Ludwig Achim von Arnim

Like Brentano, Arnim was plagued by inner feelings in conflict with external reality. To a greater extent than most other Romantics Arnim produced visions of terror and mystery that fill everyday existence. Many critics have been dissatisfied with the final products of Arnim's active imagination, and, until recently, have neglected or underestimated his prose fiction. There is need for a re-evaluation of his two major novels and his masterfully woven novellas before a fair, modern assessment of this Romantic artist can be drawn.

Arnim's association with Brentano began with their collaboration on *Des Knaben Wunderhorn* (1806 ff.), a popular collection of German patriotic folk songs, which has lost much of its effect since its publication more than 180 years ago. At that time, feelings of German nationalism, arising from the defeat of Prussia by Napoleon and the later occupation of German soil by French troops, formed the social-political impetus for the work, which was enormously successful in the nineteenth century. Since two world wars have curbed such nationalism in this century, *Des Knaben Wunderhorn* has become an interesting literary anachronism, yet the primary reason for Arnim's fame.

Arnim wrote two significant novels, *Armut, Reichtum, Schuld und Büße der Gräfin Dolores* (*Poverty, Wealth, Guilt, and Penance of Countess Dolores* [1810]) and *Die Kronenwächter* (*The Crown's Watchmen* [(vol. 1, 1817 and vol. 2, 1854]). The former takes the reader through the sin, sorrow, suffering, and ultimate salvation of a noblewoman, underscoring Arnim's message that the aristocracy must undergo an ethical and spiritual reform if it is to survive. The unfinished historical novel *Die Kronenwächter* (in the tradition of Sir Walter Scott [1771-1832]) presents a secret society of powerful landed aristocrats in conflict with the Emperor Maximilian at a time of transition from old traditions to new ones. Arnim constructed a large portion of both novels around the principle of the "arabesque" by inserting anecdotes, poems, short dramas, and other digressions which illuminate aspects of the main plot and central themes.

Perhaps his most significant literary contributions are the novellas, especially *Die Majoratsherren (The First-Born's Inheritance* [1819]) and *Der tolle Invalide auf dem Fort Ratonneau (The Mad Invalid at Fort Ratonneau* [1818]). Some critics consider the latter to be one of the major prose pieces of the Romantic era. *Der tolle Invalide* describes an incident where an insane soldier, Francoeur, commandeers a fort and its munitions and threatens the city of Marseilles. His wife, Rosalie, cures him, ostensibly through her piety, although there is significant psychological development in both characters as well. Mental phenomena are presented on several symbolic levels, especially through fire imagery.

H. Adelbert von Chamisso

After the outbreak of the French Revolution the members of the aristocratic Chamisso family fled their estate in France and made their way to Berlin. This event proved to be the most significant in Adelbert von Chamisso's life, for the Romantic poet with two nationalities felt estranged from both cultures. Ultimately, Chamisso found some measure of contentment as a world traveler and scientific observer, transcending nationalistic particularism through "tending the world's garden" in his botanical and biological investigations.

Although Chamisso's mother tongue was French, he rapidly gained facility with the German language after his arrival in Berlin. He wrote a good deal of German poetry: however, critics have objected to a lack of depth in much of his lyrical work. Nevertheless, when he enters the realm of the epic (as in his excellent ballads, or in the novella *Peter Schlemihls wundersame Geschichte* [1814]), his own "marvelous" literary talent becomes manifest.

The Schlemihl tale depicts the fate of an individual who, like Faust, deals with the devil and gives up something essential for earthly rewards. However, Schlemihl's bargaining chip is not his soul, but rather his shadow. The symbolic significance of the shadow has been the source of broad speculation among critics: since every human (and, in fact, every physical object) casts one, its loss immediately and finally places Schlemihl outside of the social (and natural) order. Some critics have equated the shadow with the soul, implying strong connections with the Faust figure. Others have related the loss of the shadow to the money Schlemihl received for it, emphasizing the bourgeois exchange of essential, human properties for profit. Others (such as Thomas Mann [1875-1955]) have suggested that Schlemihl represents the Romantic artist who lacks something essential and therefore cannot relate to normal, healthy and "whole" members of society. Certainly, one cannot mistake the autobiographical features which Chamisso wrote into his character: alienation from society, homelessness, and the strong longing for normalcy. The repentant, shadowless man ultimately comes into possession of the mythical seven-league boots, which enable him to seek release from his personal torments in all corners of the earth.

The novella proved to be prophetic for Chamisso's own life. For three years (1815-18) he participated in a scientific exploration which circumnavigated the world, upon which he made important biological discoveries. Only through travel could Chamisso learn to accept himself and his place within the natural order as a kind of "world citizen" who found the greatest satisfaction in studying biological minutiae far from society's torments. Chamisso's transition from a Romantic man of letters to a scientist and a Biedermeier recluse was not a complete one, since he still wrote Romantic poetry until his death. However, the total volume of his scientific output far outweighs his poetic writings. Even today, his *Peter Schlemihl* retains great importance as one of the most entertaining and enduring works to have emerged from the German Romantic period.

I. E. T. A. Hoffmann (1776-1822)

Hoffmann must be counted among the best and most creative Romantic prose writers. After Goethe and Schiller, he was the first German to achieve an international reputation, gaining a following in Russia and France and influencing such American Romantics as Poe and Hawthorne. Hoffmann preferred musical composition and performance to other professional endeavors, but the opportunity to pursue them in earnest eluded him, except during brief periods of his life. He found employment in the Prussian civil service and held a variety of judicial positions, including a key post as a chief justice in the legal bureaucracy of Berlin toward the end of his short life. His scathing wit, which he sometimes expressed in caricature and in satirical writing, often aroused the ire of the authorities, however, and at one point several injudicious drawings nearly brought about the end of his career.

Hoffmann first embarked on a literary career in 1808 with the fantastic story *Ritter Gluck*. In this bizarre tale he introduces the reading public to a theme which would become central for his *oeuvre*: the existence of a reality separate from everyday life, a transcendental realm to which one gains access via art (particularly music), and imagination and dreams, where magic, mythology, and fantasy inform the experience of those "childlike sensibilities" which are prepared to perceive it.

In the four-volume cycle of novellas *Die Serapionsbrüder* (*The Serapion-Brothers* [1819-21]), Hoffmann develops the Serapion principle, which connects the realistic quality of an artistic product in direct proportion to the imaginative intensity involved in its creation. A third important element in Hoffmann's aesthetics arises from the grotesque etchings by the caricaturist Jacques Callot (1592-1635) of figures from the *commedia dell'arte*. In these Callot masterfully combined fantastic and realistic elements. Hoffmann employs such grotesque techniques, in his writing as well as in his drawing, as a means of achieving a heightened psychological state by producing unusual, striking, and Romantic combinations.

Hoffmann's *oeuvre* consists primarily of fairy tales, novellas, essays, and two novels. Critics have argued that two works stand out as masterpieces of German Romantic prose. The tale *Der goldene Topf* (1814) contains *in nuce* the essence of Hoffmann's world-view, as it attempts to create a new Romantic mythology of creation and redemption. The novel *Lebensansichten des Katers Murr...* (*The Life and Times of the Tomcat Murr...* [1820-1822]) juxtaposes a fictional feline autobiography with fragments of a biography of Kapellmeister Johannes Kreisler (*nebst fragmentarischer Biographie des Kapellmeisters Johannes Kreisler*), Hoffmann's literary double. Its brilliantly crafted structure and textual reflexiveness forecast developments in the modern novel which would gain importance over a century later.

J. Joseph von Eichendorff

For many years critics have associated Joseph von Eichendorff's lyrics and prose with the essence of German Romanticism. The great number of his poems, which some of the most illustrious nineteenth-century composers set to music, attests only partly to his reputation, especially in Germany. Even during his lifetime he enjoyed popular renown as the "Last Romantic" and the "Last Knight."

Eichendorff's greatest contribution to German Romantic literature lies in the realm of lyric poetry. Few other Romantic poets could capture the essential, elementary Romantic qualities in simple commonplaces with such musicality and power. The naiveté, with which Eichendorff's poetic voice speaks, masks an artistic depth which captures profound thoughts in uncomplicated folksong verses. The catalog of Romantic clichés, including panoramas from mountain peaks, solitary ventures into deep woods, avian songs at daybreak in the springtime, and bucolic scenes of simple country folk, forms the backbone of numerous poems, which nevertheless transcend formulaic blandness through Eichendorff's mastery of lyrical acoustics.

His two novels are qualitatively lesser achievements. *Ahnung und Gegenwart* (*Presentiment and Present* [1815]) criticizes Romantic aesthetics, which in Eichendorff's view do not adequately represent the world. Both nature and art must find redemption through religious virtue: the main character Friedrich ultimately seeks the path to true poetry in a monastery. Similarly, Eichendorff traces the poet's journey through life in *Dichter und ihre Gesellen* (*Poets and their Companions* [1834]), and again juxtaposes "decadent" Romantic aesthetics with the "true way" to sublime artistry through a virtuous Christian existence.

Thematically, Eichendorff often concerned himself with the duality between good and evil inherent in the world. Having been born and raised in the Catholic Silesian nobility, he clung to conservative political views and devout Catholic faith throughout his life. Therefore, Eichendorff defined the good as the path which leads directly to God, and the evil as the many false roads which lead one astray. A pitfall his heroes sometimes confront is the seductive lure of eroticism, at times symbolized by the pagan goddess Venus. Although many voluptuous but uni-dimensional female figures exert a strong attraction on the heroes (who invariably possess a childlike innocence and curiosity), the devout young men usually return to the "proper" course through their pious belief and trust in Providence.

This duality (sensuality vs. piety) forms a central issue in two of Eichendorff's most important short pieces, *Das Marmorbild* (*The Marble Image* [1819]) and *Aus dem Leben eines Taugenichts* (*From the Life of a Good-for-Nothing* [1826]). Young Florio, the hero of the former work and a poet, is saved from Venus's entrapments by his friend Fortunato, who sings a pious song of Christian virtue and thereby miraculously destroys the seductress's mansion. Similarly, the *Taugenichts*, an innocent, care-free miller's son who leaves the philistine constraints of his father's home, encounters wild adventures and seductive traps on his journeys, which he relates uncomprehendingly in a first-person narrative. According to the critic Oskar

Seidlin, Eichendorff expresses the essence of the erotic/religious duality, particularly in the Good-for-Nothing's description of Rome from a perspective before the gates of the eternal city: at first, Rome is a "holy card" image, in which church steeples and Baroque angelic figures welcome the weary pilgrim to the heart of Catholicism; but soon the image changes to the worldly grave of seduction and corruption where Frau Venus lies in wait for the unsuspecting vagabond. Of course, Eichendorff's devout Good-for-Nothing hastens onward to his final utopian destiny, a marriage with a faithfully Christian maiden and a life of spirituality, virtue, and innocence. Critics have maintained that the narrator comprehends the world through a series of hieroglyphs (such as the lonely heath, ruins, lush gardens, fresh mornings, etc.) which symbolically support the thematic complex. This feature is one of the most telling characteristics of Eichendorff's poetry and prose, in which nature becomes a series of hieroglyphs, awaiting the poet to decipher them. Eichendorff summarizes the concept in one of his most famous poems: a latent song resides in all natural objects, and one only needs the "magical wand" (i.e., the correct poetic disposition) to release its wonderful music.

K. Heinrich von Kleist

While most secondary works on German Romanticism do not treat Kleist strictly within the boundaries of the movement, he nonetheless explores many Romantic themes in his dramas and stories, which are arguably among the most entertaining and at the same time the most terrifying in the German language. Kleist's life was erratic and extreme: his military commissions brought him into danger, while his familiarity with certain aspects of Kantian philosophy produced in him a sense of intellectual futility and desperation. After much restless wandering and a nervous collapse, he committed a double suicide with a woman (Henriette Vogel) near Wannsee in Berlin.

Throughout his literary career, Kleist sustained a very high level of quality in both his dramas and his novellas. Some of his essays are German prose masterpieces, especially his treatment of the puppet theater *Über das Marionettentheater* (*On the Marionette Theater* [1810]). Here he concisely investigates the polarity between natural, instinctive behavior and human self-consciousness, implying the negative effect which mental reflection bears upon human action.

Many of the stories and plays develop themes concerning human knowledge and legal systems. Some critics have asserted that Kleist's acquaintance with Kant's philosophical principles forced him to doubt the possibility of absolute knowledge, and thereby to question the philosophical foundations of justice, since he felt that nothing perceived via the senses is absolutely certain. His plots revolve around actions which occur when characters sleep (for example, in *Die Marquise von O...* [*The Marquise of O...*] — 1808), daydream (as in the drama *Prinz Friedrich von Homburg* [*Prince Friedrich of Homburg*] — 1821), or in some other manner find themselves in a less-than-conscious state. Circumstances, fate, and other irrational, universal powers force characters into untenable situations which often cost them their lives (as in the novellas *Michael Kohlhaas* [1808] and *Das Erdbeben in Chili* [*The Earthquake in Chili*] — 1807). Because of the great concentration of action and the detached, objective style, some critics have maintained that Kleist's writing reflects classicistic principles, which place him in a special category between German Classicism and Romanticism. In any case, most agree that his dramas far outstrip other attempts by mainstream Romantics in quality, tension, and stageability. Even today many of Kleist's plays make good theater for modern audiences.

L. Jean Paul (Friedrich Richter)

Scholars of the Romantic period usually situate Jean Paul Friedrich Richter (1763-1825) between German Classicism and Romanticism. Thus, like Kleist and Hölderlin, he remains an outsider to the mainstream movements of his time. Richter nevertheless exerted an important influence on much of contemporary literature, particularly on the prose of E.T.A. Hoffmann, and his writing remains an interesting and challenging study.

Richter employed the pen name Jean Paul in his first novel, *Die unsichtbare Loge* (*The Invisible Lodge* [1793]). From that moment the pseudonym became synonymous with both the living author and a fictitious one. The artist's dual existence in both the real world and the world of fiction became the focus of public interest and amusement, such that Jean Paul enjoyed the devotion of his followers who, in their daily lives, even imitated the characters and events about which they read.

Jean Paul's greatest literary contributions were his novels and essays, but his shorter prose works also merit attention. Possibly the most popular among these is the novella *Das Leben des vergnügten Schulmeisterlein Maria Wuz in Auenthal* (*Life of the Cheerful Schoolmaster Maria Wuz in Auenthal* [1793]). In this amusing tale an impoverished but eternally optimistic village schoolmaster is unable to purchase the books he loves, and so he writes his own. Selecting titles of classical works, he composes for them what he considers to be fitting texts. Such a remarkable character from a humble and provincial background became a type to which Jean Paul repeatedly returned in subsequent works.

The critical edition of Jean Paul's works encompasses thirty-three volumes, the greatest part of which consists of novels. Most of these are satirical, witty, and amusing, and they require the reader's detailed familiarity with the culture and politics of the author's times. Their titles tend to echo strains of Baroque complexity and mannerism, for example the three-volume work from 1796-1797 *Blumen-, Frucht- und Dornenstücke oder Ehestand, Tod und Hochzeit des Armenadvokaten F. St. Siebenkäs im Reichsmarktflecken Kuhschnappel* (*Flower, Fruit, and Thorn-Pieces: or, The Married Life, Death and Wedding of the Advocate of the Poor, F[irmian] St[anislaus] Siebenkäs*). For the most part the novels take the form of fictional biographies which relate the life and circumstances of remarkable persons from small German courts or from villages in the provinces. Notable are the previously mentioned *Die unsichtbare Loge* and *Siebenkäs*, as well as *Hesperus oder 45 Hundsposttage* (*Hesperus: or, Forty-Five Dog-Post Days* [1795]), *Quintus Fixlein* (1796), and *Flegeljahre* (*Adolescence* [1804/1805]). The last three novels carry the subtitle "A Biography." In each work Richter cuts through the barriers separating art from reality: Jean Paul constructs the text and appears in it as a character who interacts with his creations. Thus, Richter anticipates the complex narrative play that typifies such Romantic novels as Brentano's *Godwi* or Hoffmann's *Kater Murr*. As his narrator creates a path into the work as a participant in the fiction, he invites the reader to enter as well and to engage the characters as if communicating with flesh-and-blood people. The technique anticipates and parallels twentieth-century narrative strategies and underscores Richter's literary modernity.

In the treatise *Vorschule der Ästhetik* (*Pre-School of Aesthetics*) from 1804 Richter discusses some of his complex narrative concepts. Drawing on many of Herder's ideas he examines the varieties of "genius" in art. He strongly defends the Romantic literary program and claims that Romantic humor achieves a high level of aesthetic merit.

The traditional difficulty in categorizing Richter may arise from the relentless humor in his best works. Perhaps it is most helpful to view Richter as a phenomenon in the tradition of humorists such as Cervantes, Rabelais, Swift, and Sterne. Doubtlessly he owes much to Sterne's narrator, such as in *Tristram Shandy*, and to Sterne's satirical narrative voice.

Philosophy, Religion, Science

A. Philosophy

The central figure in philosophy during the last half of the eighteenth century was Immanuel Kant, who exerted an immeasurable influence upon the discipline for the next fifty years. Philosophical discourse became a discussion of principles based on what Kant had outlined in his *Kritik der reinen Vernunft* (*Critique of Pure Reason* [1781]). Although the great Romantic philosophers carried Kantian ideas farther, Kant's work formed the basis and the point of departure for the digressions of almost all who came after him.

Kant's most basic and valuable contribution to contemporary philosophy was his re-evaluation of the relationship between the self and objective reality. Philosophers had previously granted primacy in the world order to the objects themselves. But Kant insisted that one cannot set the focus upon things; one's understanding of things becomes primarily important. Human understanding operates from sense perception, or how one sees, smells, tastes, hears, and touches the universe. Other factors further determine how humans perceive the objective world, specifically: the temporal and spatial qualities which the object possesses, and the categories of understanding to which it belongs, which provide a contrast to other objects based upon pre-established thought patterns. For example, a chair exists in time and space, and an observer uses the senses to perceive the phenomenon. In the "understanding," a category "chair" also exists, into which the observer fits the sense data, and by which the chair can be contrasted with other objects, identified, and "understood" as a chair. One possible conclusion which may be drawn from this argument asserts that the chair obtains very little importance, while the subject performing the cognitive act matters greatly, in defining the relationship between human subjects and the objective world.

Following Kant's methods, Romantic philosophers attempted to separate not only appearance from reality, but also philosophical inquiry from objective law and pure reason. These findings exerted a great, liberating influence on artistic creativity because they bestowed philosophical legitimacy upon imagination and fantasy. After Kant, philosophers followed paths and entered into regions which previously had been either forbidden by "good taste" or found intellectually impenetrable, since reason alone had been an inadequate tool for this exploration.

For Johann Gottlieb Fichte, the objective world became dependent upon the "subject," the "self," or the "ego," as the perceiving and thinking entity was variously termed. The powerful self perceives that it is limited, and, confronted with this limitation, it simply posits the existence of the non-self, or objective reality. The relationship between the self and the non-self is a dialectical process which maintains the world of objects.

Clearly, this relationship stems from a creative act. On the aesthetic level, the artistic process mirrors the essential, elementary, and constant creation which the self performs. For this reason, the artist becomes a central figure, and imagination becomes the central tool in Fichte's subjective philosophy. As the free artistic imagination reaches out farther and farther, it creates more and more. Thus it serves as a key concept in the expansive tendencies which the early Romantics (such as Friedrich Schlegel) value highly. Of course, in such a system freedom is a central ethical value, for an unbound, autonomous self achieves the highest creative levels though its ever-responding imagination and its strong will.

The other great Romantic philosopher, Friedrich Wilhelm Schelling, retreated a large step from Fichte's extreme subjectivity. As early as 1795 he began to develop his *Naturphilosophie*, which gives nature and self equal importance. Schelling focuses entirely upon consciousness; he sees an unconscious intelligence at work in nature, becoming conscious intelligence in the human mind. Following Herder's and Goethe's ideas on organic nature, Schelling creates an organic model of the objective world, in which there is no separation between subject and object. Employing Spinoza's language, he describes the essential duality of nature: the organizing force, *natura naturans*, and the end-product, *natura naturata*. Although nature organizes, it is unconscious. A "world-spirit" inhabits it, and functions through dualistic natural forces, such as polar attraction and repulsion, magnetism, electricity, etc. At the heart of this dynamic natural system, Schelling posits an

"Absolute," a homogenous entity in which all polar opposition is canceled and which achieves final unity.

In Schelling's system the artist takes a central position once again. The "world-spirit," which creates in nature without consciousness, creates consciously through the artist's mind in the artistic process. During the creative act the artist's mind becomes the object to its subjective self, fusing subject and object in the same entity. Art fulfills the most important principle in Schelling's system, for it sets as its primary goal the representation of the ultimate harmony and unity which exists in the "Absolute," and the solution to the problems of polarity and dichotomy which nature presents to mankind.

German Romantic literary works variously incorporate this primordial harmony, usually as a vision of the Golden Age which had once existed and which, the Romantics expect, will one day return. In *Die Christenheit oder Europa* Novalis equates the Golden Age with the European Middle Ages, when the Catholic Church mystically unified the continent. Some critics assert that he mythologizes the quest for unity and harmony in *Heinrich von Ofterdingen*, where Klingsohr narrates an allegorical account of the struggle between Romantic characters and the evil forces of division and empty rationalism. Other authors create their own visions of the Golden Age: for Wackenroder, it is the bygone era of Medieval and Renaissance art; for Tieck, the sixteenth-century Italian landscape; for Arnim, Fouqué, and others, the age of chivalry and knighthood; for Brentano, a world of Catholic piety free of sensual torment; and for E. T. A. Hoffmann, an "other world," where magic, music, mythology, and madness dominate. Of course, this catalogue is far from complete; each author envisions an ideal existence, in which disharmony and dissention give way to peace and unity.

B. Religion

For many of the Romantics, one of the most important areas for their philosophical speculations was religion, since it clearly provided a direct path to universal and eternal truth. Among the most influential of the religious philosophers was Friedrich Schleiermacher, whose essay *Über die Religion* (*On Religion* [1799]) describes religion as the most important means by which an individual develops a "sense and taste for the eternal." As such, religion is prerequisite for artistic endeavor. Thus it is not mere morality and metaphysics, but rather it is the active search for eternity within the finite. Religion became one of the three essential areas of Romantic philosophy next to speculation (the natural sciences) and application (art).

C. Natural Sciences

The Romantic synthesis of the disciplines led philosophers and poets to the natural sciences. Contemporary experiments in electricity and magnetism, and advances in other areas of human scientific knowledge, seemed to corroborate Romantic philosophical speculation, particularly in relation to the polar nature of objective reality. The vital principle informing all things, which Schelling describes as a world-spirit, coincidentally reflects some chemical properties of the element oxygen, which scientists observed for the first time in laboratory experiments.

Philosophical foundations for Romantic studies in the natural sciences came primarily from Gotthilf Heinrich Schubert's (1780-1860) influential work *Ansichten von der Nachtseite der Naturwissenschaft* (*Views of the Night-Side of Natural Science* [1808]). While Schubert acknowledged his debt to Enlightenment scientific discoveries, he claimed that rational science cannot present the full range of phenomena. He suggested that a complete view of the phenomenal world — and particularly of a person's relationship to nature — looks back to the distant past, in which humankind and nature were unified in human consciousness through myth, saga, nature, and cults. At this time people did not attempt to tame nature, but nature instructed people. Since nature includes not only that which can be brought into a rational system, but also irrational forces and dark drives (exemplified by such phenomena as abnormal psychology and human sacrifice), Schubert proposed that the latter also deserved study. These ideas exerted a profound influence, especially on Kleist and Hoffmann, in whose works irrational elements collide with daily reality and create immense, often unresolvable conflicts. Hoffmann develops a particular interest in bizarre psychological events, such as somnambulism, animal magnetism, vampirism, doubles (*Doppelgänger*), automata, and various types of insanity.

Decline

By the time Eichendorff achieved prominence (after 1826), the movement had entered its decline. Thereafter, its adherents became largely imitators and epigones. Signs of the degenerating status of Romanticism in Germany were reflected in the critical works by the very talented poets Eichendorff and Heine. Each produced magnificent lyrics in the Romantic tradition from almost diametrical points-of-view; yet, each of them also rejected his inheritance in his own history of Romanticism, in which each took sharp aim at his forebears.

How did Romanticism influence subsequent literary production? Critics sometimes refer to Romanticism as one polar extreme of human artistic experience (in contrast to Classicism or Realism) which is ever-present in all ages. However, this most general definition of Romanticism has little practical use for the student who seeks delimitation and clarity. Still, one can find many instances where a later author discovered specific ideas among the Romantics which formed the basis for

Heinrich Heine in 1827.
Engraving by Ludwig Emil Grimm

more modern ideas. Although the legitimacy and importance of influence seeking is an open question, there exists much evidence that Romantic writings have been extremely influential, and this phenomenon deserves some mention.

Specifically, German Romanticism exerted a lasting influence on literary art inside and outside of Germany, long after the movement's glowing embers died out. Throughout the nineteenth and into the twentieth centuries various authors revived aspects of the Romantic aesthetic in important ways. Some poets of German Poetic Realism (the most outstanding example is Theodor Storm [1817-1888]) began their literary careers in the late Romantic style, composing especially musical verses. Among the best known later Romantic or Neo-Romantic literary exponents are Stefan George (1868-1933), Hermann Hesse (1877-1962), the younger Hugo von Hofmannsthal (1874-1929), and Thomas Mann (1875-1955), all of whom were strongly influenced by Romantic emphasis on irrational powers. These writers also adapted aspects of the cultural pessimism of Friedrich Nietzsche (1844-1900) and the drive for artistic mythification of Richard Wagner (1813-1883), themselves both heirs of nineteenth-century German Romanticism and also its final representatives.

Many critics have maintained that for Thomas Mann, perhaps the greatest representative of German letters and culture in our century and in many ways a thoroughly Romantic author, love, death, and art were tightly bound in a Romantic thematic complex throughout much of his *oeuvre*. An early Mann short story, *Tristan* (1903), reveals a character who, while she is a patient in a sanatorium, performs on a piano the love and death themes from Wagner's *Tristan und Isolde*; the excitement of the performance aggravates her condition and causes her death. In one of Mann's last works, the novel *Doktor Faustus*, the protagonist contracts a sexually-transmitted disease which ultimately kills him, but not before bringing him to the heightened creative state in which he invents a new form of music. The union of the erotic, the artistic, and the theme of death, as well as a great number of other elements in Mann's prose, connects him directly with his artistic predecessors from the Romantic era.

The term Neo-Romantic, used to describe a number of authors in Germany and Austria at the turn of the century, could be applied with equal validity to many, more contemporary writers. The quest for transcendental and spiritual states through art, the artist's inability to integrate oneself into a so-called "normal" life, the exploration of complex psychological phenomena in literature, the exploitation of fantasy and emotion in the quest for ultimate but elusive truth, all have roots in the Romantic movement. Much of our intellectual heritage owes a debt to German artists of the early nineteenth century, whose uninhibited dreaming, questioning, and striving stretched the limits of our consciousness and enriched almost every aspect of our intellectual traditions.

9 Young Germany

Robert C. Holub

Defining the Movement

The first half of the nineteenth century has presented students of German literature with enormous dilemmas with regard to defining literary periods. Although there is general agreement that the end of Classicism and almost the entirety of Romanticism belong in the initial decades of the century, various opinions exist about what occurred after the demise of these movements. Many scholars consider the entire period from 1815 to 1848 to be the era of Prince Klemens Metternich's (1773-1859) restoration or the Biedermeier period. A few opt for the label *Vormärz* (Pre-March) to indicate the gathering of oppositional spirit and radicalism that led to the 1848 revolution. Still others see the first half of the nineteenth century sharply bifurcated: on the one side a conservative group of writers, usually identified with the label Biedermeier, and, on the other, a more progressive group placed variously under the rubric of *Junges Deutschland* (Young Germany) or *Vormärz*. A history of German literature such as this one, which includes separate chapters on Biedermeier and Junges Deutschland, obviously belongs to the last group. A further distinction is necessary, however, inside the progressive camp itself. Because only one writer, Heinrich Heine (1797-1856), participated prominently in the progressive movement of the 1830s and the 1840s, the following discussion will deal first with the Young German opposition from roughly 1830 to 1835 and then with the pre-revolutionary literary movement of the *Vormärz* from 1840 to 1848.

Young Germany

Following the Napoleonic Wars of Liberation and the Congress of Vienna (1815), Germany entered into a quiet period marked by conservatism and the partial restoration of political power to aristocratic rule. For a number of reasons, however, changes in the cultural climate occurred rather abruptly in the early 1830s. Perhaps the most important political development contributing to this change was the July Revolution of 1830 in France. The conservative Bourbon rulers, who had been placed on the throne after Napoleon's defeat and exile, were deposed by Louis Philippe (1773-1850), known as the Citizen King and identified with sectors of the middle class. This was a signal for other European uprisings, and even in some German states there were disturbances and protests. These political changes, however, were only the manifestations of deeper structural alterations in Europe brought on by the onset and continuation of the industrial revolution.

Although Germany lagged behind its Western European neighbors, the industrial revolution was not without impact there. In many parts of the country a shift in the constellation of classes took place, and along with it arose a consciousness of the need for changes in the political, social, and economic spheres. In addition, the climate for change was fueled in Germany by the coincidence of the death of a number of luminaries among older intellectuals. The noted novelist Jean Paul (Friedrich Richter) died in 1825 (b. 1763); the greatest philosopher of the age, Georg Wilhelm Friedrich Hegel (b. 1770), and the greatest writer, Johann Wolfgang Goethe (b. 1749), died in 1831 and 1832 respectively. Even the cholera epidemic that swept through Europe in the late twenties and thirties (claiming Hegel as one of its victims) seemed to be an omen from the heavens that the *ancien régime* had run its course and that something new must take its place.

These changes in the economic, political, and cultural spheres form the background for the opposition movement known as *Junges Deutschland*. A group of five writers has been identified as its members: Theodor Mundt (1808-1861), Ludolf Wienbarg (1802-1872), Karl Gutzkow (1811-1878), Heinrich Laube (1806-1884), and Heinrich Heine. Occasionally the group has been expanded to include Gustav Kühne (1806-1888), Ludwig Börne (1786-1837), Georg Büchner (1813-1837), Anastasius Grün (1806-1876), or Hermann Fürst von Pückler-Muskau (1785-1871). The name *Junges Deutschland* itself is of uncertain origin. It may have come from the dedication Wienbarg included in his *Ästhetische Feldzüge* (*Aesthetic Campaigns* [1834]), or it may have been applied to these writers by analogy with other European groups such as Young Italy.

In contrast to most literary movements in England or France and even to the Classicists and Romantics in Germany, the Young Germans did not form a cohesive movement. In fact, for the most part they carried out their activities in virtual isolation from each other. Heine, for example, the most prominent writer in the group, lived in self-imposed exile in Paris during the years of the most extensive production of the Young Germans (1831-1835), and he was on good terms with only Laube. What unified these writers, other than the paranoia of the German government that considered them conspiratorial and subversive, were three factors. Almost all the Young Germans were born after 1800 — the exception is Heine, who, however, liked to claim he came in with the new century — and they were therefore identified as part of a young generation, embarking on writing careers around 1830. Furthermore, they all evidenced a propensity for liberal values in contrast to the more conservative Biedermeier authors who wrote during the same period. And finally, they tended to prefer the larger cities of Germany and Europe to the isolation of the country, a characteristic of the Biedermeier writers. The Young Germans, in short, can be seen as the first representatives of a progressive literary modernity to appear in Germany, and in this regard they are the predecessors of the Naturalists at the end of the century and the Expressionists during the 1910s and 1920s.

Perhaps the most consistent belief the Young Germans articulated was the feeling that they were living and writing in an age of transition. It is easy to understand why they felt this way. In the political sphere Europe was still shaken by the memory of the French Revolution and of Napoleon. The changes that events in France had brought to Germany were enormous. As a result of the Napoleonic conquest, the Holy Roman Empire, which had existed for over 1,000 years, had been abolished, and several hundred German principalities had been reduced to about three dozen states. Although the restoration following the Congress of Vienna had turned back the clock slightly, the July Revolution was widely interpreted as a signal for the continuation of a restructuring of European society. In the cultural sphere the demise of Classicism and "high" Romanticism and the apparent exhaustion of German idealism, seemed to indicate a transition to a new state of affairs. Among the Young Germans the dominant sentiment, therefore, was that they were somehow no longer part of the old world of their fathers, and that they were heading toward a more fruitful, albeit vaguely defined, period of cultural renaissance.

This notion of a transitional period was quite possibly influenced by Saint Simonism, a philosophical and utopian socialist movement that stirred up considerable controversy in Germany, particularly since large sectors of the liberal opposition, including the Young Germans, were identified with it. Founded on the writings of Claude-Henri de Rouvroy, Comte de Saint-Simon (1760-1825), the movement was propagated by faithful disciples and managed to attract quite a few adherents in the late twenties and early thirties before it degenerated rapidly into an eccentric cult. The historical scheme presented in Saint Simonian writings was attractive to the Young Germans and provided them to a large degree with a confirmation of views already familiar to them from historical sketches in the German tradition (Gotthold Ephraim Lessing [1729-1781], Friedrich Schiller [1759-1805], Hegel). The Saint Simonians viewed contemporary society as a critical period, that is, a period in human development when all communal values and organizations cease, and society becomes a conglomeration of isolated individuals struggling against each other. This discordant period is always preceded and followed by an "organic state" in which there exists a general ordering of activities under an encompassing theory and in which the goal of social action is clearly defined. Thus, the critical period in which contemporary society found itself around 1830 was viewed as a transitional stage between a harmonious and unified era of the past, variously identified with Christianity or German Classicism/Idealism, and a new period just over the horizon.

The Young German belief in the critical and transitional nature of contemporary society determined to a large extent their attitude toward the literary heritage. They were particularly attracted to writers they identified with a democratic, oppositional tradition, those who had achieved some popular acclaim and who had remained uncontaminated by the pretense of the German court. For these reasons Jean Paul (Friedrich Richter), one of the most prolific novelists of the early nineteenth century, was a primary model. Friedrich Schiller, because of his championing of individual rights, was also heralded by the Young Germans, even though he had a close connection with Goethe and the Weimar court theater during the last decade of his life. From a different part of the tradition, Young Germany was also influenced by writers like Wilhelm Heinse (1746-1803) and the young Friedrich Schlegel (1772-1829) because of their advocacy of sensualism and the emancipation of the senses. Goethe, on the other hand, was not a favorite of many of the Young Germans. In contrast to other detractors, who disliked Goethe's irreverence and irreligiosity or his lack of patriotism, the Young Germans reviled his general indifference to political affairs, and his lack of engagement for emancipatory causes. He was frequently accused of egotism and ridiculed for his long-time association with the Weimar court. Goethe's writing was seen as belonging to an era of stability and harmony; his genius could not be ignored, but his works were deemed untimely and irrelevant for the turbulence that characterized the transition period.

The aesthetic and critical predilections of the Young Germans also are a reflection of their belief in the transitional nature of the age in which they lived. Abandoning the demand for harmonious forms and objective, sovereign style, they affirmed the subjective, the contingent, and the marginal in their writings. Often their narrators assumed the pose of insanity, mental abnormality, or simple confusion to emphasize their subjective response to social and cultural norms. Mundt's *Moderne Lebenswirren* (*Modern Vicissitudes of Life* [1834]) and Gutzkow's *Briefe eines Narren an eine Närrin* (*Letters from a Foolish Man to a Foolish Woman* [1832]) are two excellent illustrations of works that use this technique. In part, these devices were employed to circumvent censorship; social criticism that could not possibly be uttered in a straight-forward manner was somewhat more palatable to the authorities if it was placed in the mouth of a deranged person or a fool. In part, the feigned insanity underscored the discord of the times. But no matter what the intention, the result is a body of work that valorizes openness, expressiveness, and individuality over closure, literary etiquette, and the classical tradition.

The affirmation of alternative, critical models in an age of dissonance also had a noticeable influence on other facets of Young Germany, affecting both the forms in which the Young Germans wrote and the activities in which they engaged. In contrast to both the Classicists and the Romantics, who had preferred traditional literary genres, the Young Germans leaned toward more popular and journalistic works. Unlike Biedermeier authors who drew on these older traditions, they sought direct communication with the public in journalistically influenced prose, essays, and travel literature. To insure that their works would reach a broader readership, they did not shy away from direct involvement in the publishing world. Almost all the Young Germans became involved with journals: Gutzkow edited *Phönix* and co-edited with Wienbarg the *Deutsche Revue*, which was banned by the authorities before it could appear; Kühne was involved with *Wissenschaftliche Jahrbücher* (*Scientific Almanach*); Mundt was editor of *Blätter für literarische Unterhaltung* (*Journal for Literary Entertainment*) and *Literarischer Zodiakus*; Laube worked for the influential *Zeitung für die elegante Welt* (*Newspaper for the Elegant World*); and although Heine was not involved with editing during this period, almost all his works during the thirties appeared first in one journal or another. The Young Germans thus sought more direct intervention in their world and adapted themselves in their choice of genre and literary activity to the exigencies of nineteenth-century German society.

The message the Young Germans wanted to communicate to the reading public was one that could best be captured by the word "liberalism." With regard to religion this meant taking the Enlightenment critique of orthodoxy and dogmatism a step further. Although most did not reject religion or some form of spirituality entirely, they viewed the practice of Christianity in the West as world-negating and one-sided. More favorably inclined toward Protestantism than Catholicism, they advocated a synthesis of spirit and body, a new unity of mind and matter that would restore a harmony to the human being and overcome the age of dissonance. Their attitudes toward morality were similarly oppositional for their time. Like the Saint Simonists, they spoke of a restoration of the flesh to overcome the dominant spirituality. While the Saint Simonists, however, developed a program that included divorce reforms, open marriages, and the emancipation of women, Young German thoughts on morality remained mostly confined to their literary realm. In their novels and essays they situated themselves as more open and liberal than the establishment, but they lacked any platform or program for change. In fact, the political positions of the Young Germans have to be inferred from their remarks on religion, morality, and culture. Since Germany lacked a public sphere in which political issues could be debated, their politics remain vague, defined by their opposition to the *status quo* more than by the alternatives they posited.

The vagueness of the Young German political stance, however, did not deter the hegemonic powers in Germany from taking swift and repressive measures against the group. In fact, the *Bundestag* (Federal Diet), a body consisting of representatives of the various principalities, actually constituted what has become known as Young Germany out of a group of authors with similar, but by no means, identical, social and political views. The reasons consistently cited for official government intervention were the dangerous moral, religious, and social views of the group. Such novels as Laube's *Das junge Europa* (*Young Europe* [1833-1837]), which depicts in part the uprising in Poland in the early thirties, and Mundt's *Madonna* (1835), a book promulgating sensuality and criticizing religion, were exemplary for the kinds of works the government classified as objectionable. Gutzkow's *Wally, die Zweiflerin* (*Wally the Skeptic* [1835]), however, is most often cited as the work that served as the immediate pretext for repressive action. The novel portrays the trials and tribulations of a young woman who becomes passionately involved with one man, only to marry another. Her brother-in-law, who also falls in love with her, commits suicide in front of her; eventually she and her lover are reunited. Offensive in this book, besides the steamy eroticism, were the frequent and unflattering discussions of Christianity. Wally's lover Caesar is an indefatigable critic of religion, and ultimately his treatise on this topic leads to Wally's demise: she cannot live without religion, and since she finds his arguments persuasive, she takes her own life in despair.

The government was evidently convinced that such arguments could be persuasive to others as well. In fact, official action to censor the Young Germans had been prepared to some extent by various polemics against the group from conservative and jingoist writers and critics. The most vociferous and damaging of these tirades came from the pen of Wolfgang Menzel (1798-1873), the editor of the Stuttgart *Literaturblatt* (*Literary Journal*), who railed against the Young Germans for their frivolity, their Francophile attitudes, their immorality, and their Jewishness (although only Heine was of Jewish origins). Such attacks evidently did not instigate government reaction, but they did establish a climate in which repressive measures were palatable, perhaps even inevitable. A ban on Young German writings was promulgated by the Prussian government on 14 November 1835, and, at the request of the Austrian representative to the *Bundestag*, the representatives of the German governments agreed to take similar action. On 10 December 1835 they passed a resolution that prohibited the publishing, printing, and distribution of all past, present, and future writings of Heine, Gutzkow, Laube, Wienbarg, and Mundt. The reasons given for such harsh measures had to do with a putative undermining of law and order, particularly through the propagation of immorality and the defamation of Christianity. Significantly, the *Bundestag* also noted that the Young Germans had put their criticism into belletristic form and made it accessible to all classes of society. Unfortunately, the Young Germans' strategy for enlightening society through their writings was more successful in the minds of the ruling powers than it actually was in reality.

In a sense the decree of the *Bundestag* both created and destroyed the Young German movement. Before this time, none of the writers involved had considered himself to be part of a subversive literary coterie, although all of them shared a similar oppositional attitude. But after the decree almost everyone directly affected by the ban went out of his way to deny that he had anything to do with Young Germany. Several of the Young Germans wrote responses either to the *Bundestag*, to Menzel, or to both. But none of them actually stopped writing, nor did any publisher stop publishing, because of government actions. In this sense the decree was a failure. It created a phantom against which it took severe measures, but nobody felt particularly affected. Prussia was even forced to rescind its ban on future writings when it was discovered that such a prohibition violated its own censorship regulations.

Although the decree did not succeed in preventing the Young Germans from writing and publishing, it did establish an atmosphere of repression that affected each of the alleged members of this group. Gutzkow spent two months in jail for writing *Wally, die Zweiflerin*, and Laube was incarcerated for interrogation for nine months in 1834-1835 and later sentenced to house arrest for a year and a half in

1837-1838, but it was probably not physical punishment as much as the threat of such punishment that destroyed the collective will of Young Germany. With the exception of Heine, the only Young German writer not residing in Germany, there is no continuity between the opposition of the thirties and the forties. Eventually many of them ended up as members of the establishment against which they seemed to protest. Laube became a noted theater director; Mundt managed to obtain a position at the university in Berlin and then in Breslau; Gutzkow continued to be very active as a journalist and author. Only Wienbarg, the most unfortunate of the group, never integrated himself into bourgeois society, sinking into alcoholism and eventually mental illness. Gutzkow and Heine were the only ones who composed any notable literary works after 1835.

Vormärz

The years 1835-1840 were relatively quiet in Germany. The radical nationalists from the Napoleonic Wars had either left Germany or become less active. The Young German opposition had been effectively silenced by a combination of fear and oppression. And genuinely radical groups such as the one organized in Hesse by Ludwig Weidig (1791-1837), an associate of Georg Büchner, had been betrayed or disbanded. Cultural production during this five-year period reflected this quiescence. Few works of importance written by an author associated with Young Germany appeared. When Heine collected a few miscellaneous pieces for a volume which appeared in 1837, he suggested "das stille Buch" (the quiet book) or "Märchen" (fairy-tales) as the title; either would have been unfortunately appropriate.

Three things contributed to a change around 1840. The first was the reappearance of nationalist consciousness stemming mostly from the so-called *Rheinkrise* (crisis along the Rhine). Prussia, which had received territories along the river as a result of the settlement of the Congress of Vienna, found itself opposed to France in an international crisis. When it was mentioned in the French Parliament that the border of the Rhine could be disputed, an alarm was set off in Germany. The result was a reawakening of anti-French sentiment that had been lying dormant since the Napoleonic Wars. The nationalist fervor was also stoked by the recent ascension to the Danish throne of Christian VIII (1786-1848), who apparently harbored thoughts of integrating the duchies of Schleswig and Holstein, both of which had predominantly German inhabitants, into Denmark. The perception of threats to German sovereignty over German territory acted like a spark in the cultural sphere. Numerous patriotic poems appeared in the early 1840s concerning the Rhine and Schleswig-Holstein. The most famous of these, Nikolaus Becker's (1809-1845) "Rheinlied" ("The German Rhine"), is typical in its belligerent attitude toward the non-German world and its adamant insistence on the inviolability of German soil. More important than any specific poem, however, was the notion of German unity once again becoming a theme for public consumption.

Perhaps more significant for the liberal and nationalist cause was the death of Friedrich Wilhelm III of Prussia on 7 June 1840 and the succession of his son Friedrich Wilhelm IV (1795-1861). Friedrich Wilhelm III had been viewed as a ruler loyal to Metternich's restoration policies; he was considered a conservative monarch, more interested in the army than in political rights. His son, however, had the reputation of being a liberal reformer and German nationalist, and the first years of his reign suggested to many that he might very well confirm this image. On 10 August 1840 he declared a general amnesty for all political prisoners. This was particularly important for various nationalist intellectuals who had been discriminated against following the suppression of the *Burschenschaften* (nationalist student fraternities) in 1819. Ernst Moritz Arndt (1769-1860), for example, widely known for his nationalist sentiments, was reinstated as a professor at the University of Bonn after nearly two decades, and many other like-minded intellectuals followed him into the German civil service. Friedrich Wilhelm IV also reformed censorship laws, making political writing and publication during the early forties possible. Furthermore, his interest in German literature and his support for the "Society to Complete the Cologne Cathedral"(satirized in Heine's *Deutschland. Ein Wintermärchen* [*Germany, A Winter's Tale* — 1844]) indicated to the general public that his regime was interested in furthering the goals of German unity. Although the hopes of reform from above were soon dashed by various repressive measures starting in 1842, Friedrich Wilhelm IV had contributed to a change in attitude essential for the German *Vormärz*.

A third aspect that makes 1840 a turning point was the appearance of the Young or Left Hegelians. Since Hegel's death in 1831 the legacy of his works had been disputed on the one hand by a group that interpreted him as a conservative supporter of the Prussian state and on the other by a radical group of disciples who believed that his thought provided the basis for a progressive philosophy of action. The Left Hegelians felt that Hegel's identification of reason with reality was a plea to make reality conform to reason, a call to introduce freedom into the world. Most of their early writings, however, concerned themselves less with government than with issues of religion. David Friedrich Strauß's (1808-1874) *Das Leben Jesu* (*The Life of Jesus* [1835]) and Ludwig Feuerbach's (1804-1872) *Das Wesen des Christentums* (*The Essence of Christianity* [1841]) both argued against orthodox Christian positions. The former considered Jesus as a man, rather than the son of God, while the latter work represented religion as the result of human projection. Both were viewed as attacks on Christianity and invitations to atheism. The most celebrated Young Hegelians were Karl Marx (1818-1883) and Friedrich Engels (1820-1895), whose early writings at least reflect the typical themes of their contemporaries. But in the early 1840s Marx and Engels were only two members of a younger generation that included such writers as Bruno Bauer (1809-1882), Moses Hess (1812-1875), Robert Prutz (1816-1872), and Arnold Ruge (1802-1880), who shared similar attitudes toward religious, social, and political issues. In various journals — *Hallische Jahrbücher* (*Halle Almanach*), *Deutsche Jahrbücher* (*German Almanach*), *Vorwärts* (*Onward*), and *Die Deutsch-Französischen Jahrbücher* (*The*

German-French Almanach) — the Left Hegelians mercilessly critiqued contemporary society and agitated for fundamental change.

The *Vormärz* thus designates the spirit of revived political interest that appears after 1840 and continues through the revolution that began in March of 1848. The literary forms most preferred by the writers of this period were accordingly those that afforded them the greatest possibilities for agitation: the political essay and the *Lied* (song). The young Hegelians were the foremost practitioners of the former genre, while poets such as Ferdinand Freiligrath (1810-1876), Georg Herwegh (1817-1875), Georg Weerth (1822-1856), and Heinrich Heine are known for the latter. While the political essayists published almost exclusively in the journals mentioned above, political verses appeared in a variety of publications, from magazines and newspapers to almanacs and pamphlets. Among the most noted volumes of political lyric poetry were August Heinrich Hoffmann von Fallersleben's *Unpolitische Lieder* (*Unpolitical Songs* [1840/1841]), Herwegh's *Gedichte eines Lebendigen* (*Poems of Someone Alive* [1841-1843]), Franz Dingelstedt's (1814-1881) *Lieder eines kosmopolitischen Nachtwächters* (*Songs of a Cosmopolitan Nightwatchman* [1841]), and Freiligrath's *Ein Glaubensbekenntnis* (*A Confession of Faith* [1844]) and *Ça ira* (1846). These collections provide a panorama of the progressive political sentiments of the times, from Hoffmann von Fallersleben's petty-bourgeois political pathos to Freiligrath's revolutionary commitment to a proletarian upheaval.

Thematically the works of these writers touched upon a limited number of issues. Besides the critique of religion, one finds a great concern for social questions. Poor harvests in Germany and throughout Europe, coupled with workers' uprisings, such as the celebrated revolt of the weavers in Silesia, contributed to a concern for the miserable plight of the lower classes. Weerth's "Hungerlied" ("Song of Hunger") and Heine's "Die schlesischen Weber" ("The Silesian Weavers") are exemplary in dealing directly with these topics in verse. Engel's *Die Lage der arbeitenden Klassen in England* (*The Situation of the Working Classes in England* [1845]), Wilhelm Wolf's (1809-1864) descriptions of the working conditions of the weavers, or Bettina von Arnim's reportage on the working class in Hamburg in *Dies Buch gehört dem König* (*This Book Belongs to the King* [1843]) are illustrations of how these matters were treated in journalistic prose. Another thematic concern already touched upon above was German patriotism. All too often patriotic feelings assumed the form of chauvinistically informed verse such as Becker's "Rheinlied," but at other times writers made a simple plea for a united Germany, such as in Hoffmann von Fallersleben's controversial "Deutschlandlied" ("Song of Germany") or for a democratic form of government, illustrated by the many poems evoking the "republic" as the political goal of the movement. Patriotic verse gained a popularity it had not enjoyed since the Napoleonic Wars, although there were some voices, notably writers like Heine, who perceived retrograde movements in this new-born nationalism.

A third prominent issue in the writings of *Vormärz* was the role of partisanship. When Freiligrath asserted in a poem that the poet stands above partisanship, he was criticized by a variety of writers who asserted the contrary. Ultimately Freiligrath himself changed his views on this matter and recanted his former indifference. Another aspect of partisanship that was more difficult to resolve, however, concerned tendentiousness in literary works. The question was usually framed in terms of how much of the writer's subjectivity should be injected into the work, and how much should be objective depiction. In "Die Tendenz" ("Tendentiousness") Heine, one of the most subjective of poets himself, mocks his colleagues for their bombastic and ultimately empty demands for freedom and equality. This issue, which was never settled during the forties, continued to be a topic for politically engaged writers well into the present century. Finally, one finds a significant thematic preoccupation with satires of middle-class life. Heine's satire of church, state, and nationalism in *Deutschland. Ein Wintermärchen*, and Weerth's persiflage of the conservative aristocracy in *Leben und Taten des berühmten Ritters Schnapphahnski* (*The Life and Deeds of the Famous Knight Schnapphahnski* [1848/1849]) are two primary examples of this genre, but they were by no means the only writers to employ this ironic mode. An entire genre of *Michellieder* appeared during the *Vormärz*, in which "der deutsche Michel," the sleepy indifferent German citizen, is subjected to ridicule. Although these works are generally humorous on the surface, they make a serious point about the deficient political consciousness of the German populace.

Like Young Germany, the *Vormärz* came to an abrupt end because of political developments. Even during the height of revolutionary fervor, the views represented by most *Vormärz* authors were not accepted by the majority of Germans. The progressive wing of the 1848 revolution, which supported a form of republican government, was outnumbered by more conservative factions which favored a constitutional monarchy. But even this more moderate position was destined to fail. When the revolutionary tide turned in the years 1848-1849, reactionary forces were able to regain power, disband the parliament, and restore the old ruling houses to their thrones.

The response to the failure of the revolution from those writers and intellectuals most active in the *Vormärz* assumed a variety of forms. Some regrouped and continued the struggle. Marx and Engels, for example, persevered with both their journalistic and their theoretical activities while in English exile. A large number of lesser known progressives emigrated to the United States. Some, like Herwegh, after a period of exile, returned to Germany and again agitated the ruling classes. A second group moved away from their progressive political position. Freiligrath, for example, eventually made his peace with the prevailing powers and wound up supporting the Prussian unification of Germany from above in 1870/1871. Weerth is exemplary for a third alternative. After serving a few months in prison, he resumed his life as a businessman; but from later letters it is obvious that he had become cynical toward the possibilities for revolutionary action and uninterested in lending his support to political goals. In general, then, the literary *Vormärz* does not survive the disappointment of 1848/1849, and the spirit that informed this movement is almost totally absent in German culture for the next few decades following the revolution.

A. Heinrich Heine

Any treatment of Young Germany and the *Vormärz* has to devote special attention to Heinrich Heine. The best known German author from the nineteenth century, Heine is the only major oppositional figure whose works span the period from the 1820s to the 1850s. He is remembered today primarily for his early lyrics, which have been set to music more than those of any other poet. His most celebrated poems appeared in *Buch der Lieder* (*Book of Songs* [1827]) and deal with the theme of unrequited love. Although they appear to be simply constructed from familiar romantic motifs, closer inspection reveals meticulous poetic craft and insight. Their outstanding feature is undoubtedly the turn or ironic twist that frequently concludes a poem. Readers are lulled into a false sense of security when they encounter the familiar imagery of lyrics from the Age of Goethe. But in the final lines Heine calls this imagery — and the ideology behind it — into question with a note of discord or ironic distancing.

During most of his life, however, Heine was renowned for his witty prose, his political journalism, and his caustic satires rather than for his lyric poetry. These were the writings which earned him a controversial reputation among his contemporaries and after his death. Frequently censored for his liberal views and his attacks on religion, he was despised by narrow-minded German nationalists for his cosmopolitan feelings and discriminated against by a bigoted German society for his Jewish origins. While his writings became very popular among enlightened sectors of the European intelligentsia, in his native land he was often subjected to scorn or ridicule. This prejudice against Heine culminated during the period of National Socialism, when he was stripped of his German background; during the Third Reich the author of the "Loreley," Heine's most celebrated poem, was listed as "an unknown poet."

Heine was not only identified as a leader of the Young Germans; his *Reisebilder* (*Travel Pictures*) also served as the chief model for their works. The first volume of this serial work appeared in 1826, and it was followed by a second, third, and fourth volume in 1827, 1829, and 1831. Although the sales were unimpressive at first, by the time Heine left Germany in 1831 *Die Reisebilder* had made him a famous writer, especially in the circles of young, liberal intellectuals. The success of this series can be attributed largely to its controversial content and innovative form. Heine takes up matters of current concern and comments upon them in a witty and critical fashion. Because of censorship he had to be very cautious. Rarely does one find a sustained or direct treatment of an issue or personality. Most often Heine operates with an apparently free-floating technique of associating ideas. Something he witnesses or experiences will remind him of a politically more sensitive topic which he then discusses with humor, allusions, and innuendoes. Heine had developed this technique earlier in the 1820s in a set of correspondence articles he wrote entitled *Briefe aus Berlin* (*Letters from Berlin* [1822]) and in a short travel description *Über Polen* (*On Poland* [1823]). By the end of the decade he had perfected his art, and it was this style of writing with its apparently free subjectivity that the Young Germans found so conducive to their own oppositional prose during the early thirties.

Heine with his wife Mathilde Mirat. Painting by Ernst B. Kietz 1851.

Heine himself turned to a slightly different task during the years 1830-1835. By the end of 1830 it was clear to him that he had no future in Germany. His various attempts to secure a position were all unsuccessful, and in May of 1831 he left for France. He took up residence in Paris, and aside from vacations and two trips to Hamburg, he remained there until his death in 1856. One of Heine's principal activities in the French capital was to mediate French cultural and political events to the German public. During the first decade and a half of what began as a self-imposed exile, he was an on-the-scene correspondent for some of the more popular German newspapers and journals. His first project was a series of reports on an art exhibit in 1831, later published as *Französische Maler* (*French Painters* [1834]). In the second half of the 1830s Heine carried out a similar task for French theater with *Über die französische Bühne* (*Concerning the French Stage* [1840]). Heine's most successful writings about France, however, were collections of correspondence articles he wrote during the thirties and forties. *Französische Zustände* (*Conditions in France* [1833]) consists of reports published originally in early 1832 for the Augsburg *Allgemeine Zeitung*, while *Lutezia* (1854), Heine's longest published work, is a collection of articles composed for the same newspaper in the early 1840s. In both, Heine shows himself to be an acute observer of the political and cultural scene. Using more intuition than investigative procedures, and writing in the witty, sometimes associative style that was his trademark, Heine analyzes various aspects of cultural and political progress in the most revolutionary European city of the early nineteenth century.

But Heine also endeavored to mediate German culture to the French. His two most important essays of the early thirties, *Die romantische Schule* (*The Romantic*

School [1833, rev. 1836]) and *Zur Geschichte der Religion und Philosophie in Deutschland* (*On the History of Religion and Philosophy in Germany* [1835]) attempt to correct the view of German intellectual life found in Madame de Staël's influential book *De l'Allemagne* (*On Germany* [1813]). It was especially important for Heine to combat de Staël's favorable portrayal of German Romanticism, and his first essay contains a sustained discussion of and attack upon this current in German letters. What emerges from this literary history — which was one of the first of its kind to be written in German — is a view of two antagonistic tendencies in German culture. The first is identified with the Enlightenment, sensualism, Protestantism, and progressive politics; Gotthold Ephraim Lessing (1729-1781), Johann Gottfried Herder (1744-1803), Schiller, Johann Heinrich Voß (1751-1826), and the Young Germans are placed in this tradition. Opposing it is a mystical, spiritualist, Catholic, and politically regressive turn to the Middle Ages that Heine associates with the Romantic movement. By introducing this typology to deal with German literary history, Heine is attempting to discourage French intellectuals from their admiration of the German Romantics, while simultaneously showing them that Germany, too, had a critical and forward-looking literature.

The identical set of dichotomies, influenced to a degree by Saint Simonism, structures Heine's essay on German religious and philosophical thought. Heine sets up an historical narrative according to which the spiritualism of the Catholic Middle Ages is gradually eroded by advances in the domain of German intellectual life. The major stages in this erosion process — Luther's clash with the Roman Catholic Church, Spinoza's doctrine of pantheism, and Kant's *Kritik der reinen Vernunft* (*Critic of Pure Reason* [1781]) — are the focal points for the three sections. Heine's general strategy was thus to describe a culture in which reason and progress struggled with superstition and obscurantism.

After a quiet and unproductive period following the decree of the *Bundestag* in 1835, Heine resumed political writing with a book on Ludwig Börne, a radical Jewish author who, like Heine, had resided in Paris for many years. Heine's book, *Ludwig Börne. Eine Denkschrift* (*Ludwig Börne: A Memorial* [1840]), was ostensibly a memorial for Börne, who had died in 1837, but his real goal was to sketch the difference between his and Börne's oppositional stance. This marks a turning point in his works, a radicalization that was to continue through the midforties. During this period Heine moved closer to Young Hegelian positions. There is evidence that he was acquainted with the writings of many members of this diverse group, and he befriended for a time the most celebrated Young Hegelian, Karl Marx, while the latter was in his Parisian exile from 1843 to 1844. In fact, some of Heine's most rousing political verse was written for the radical newspaper *Vorwärts*, to which Marx was also a frequent contributor. The culmination of Heine's political poetry came in 1844 with the mock-epic *Deutschland. Ein Wintermärchen*. In twenty-seven brief chapters containing clever rhymes and witty barbs the poem describes a fictitious coach trip from the French border to Hamburg. Heine's biting satire has three major objectives. First, he attacks the German government, especially Prussian bureaucracy and the limitations placed on individual freedom. Second, he criticizes a rabid nationalism which advocated a political revolution without a liberation from religious and ethical bondage. And finally Heine takes to task the German people themselves for their Romantic quietism and political acquiescence to authority.

Even while he was most allied with the political poetry of the *Vormärz*, however, Heine was occupied with works that cast doubt upon the possibilities for political change. His verse epic *Atta Troll* (1847) targets the German political opposition for its politically limited, religiously tainted, and ethically backward notion of revolution. Although one can conceive of this work as an endeavor to separate his notions of political poetry from the crudities of the poetasters during the *Vormärz*, its defense of poetic imagination against partisanship distinguishes it from the mainstream valorization of politics over poetry.

With the failure of the revolution of 1848 and the onset of a long and crippling illness, Heine's oppositional writings once again change their tenor. From the revolution until his death in 1856, Heine created some of his most beautiful poetry, but he appears to have changed his attitude considerably during this period of his life. Although he had earlier been one of the harshest critics of religion, during his final years he expresses a strong belief in a Supreme Being. Perhaps more significant for his writing was the abandonment of the sensualist position which had characterized his thought from the early twenties. Thematically his late verse most often deals with the futility of existence and the ultimate victory of evil over good. Despite this pessimism in his later years, however, Heine did not completely relinquish his progressive political stance; his later lyrics still evidence a sense of moral outrage at social injustice, and quite a few treat contemporary topics with the satirical wit for which he had become so famous. But a sense of melancholy pervades even those poems, and like the soldier in the war for human liberation in his poem "Enfant Perdu" ("Lost Child"), Heine knows that he must count on others who are younger and stronger to fight future battles.

B. Georg Büchner

The other author from this period who deserves individual treatment because of his significance in German letters and for world literature is Georg Büchner. Like Heine, Büchner shares some aspects with the Young Germans, most notably his advocacy of sensualism, but in contrast to the writers of the thirties, his political views were much more radical. Nothing in his childhood and education would have suggested the activism that characterized Büchner's position. Born to a middle-class family — his father was a surgeon in Darmstadt, his mother came from a family of high Hessian officials — Büchner seems to have enjoyed a rather uneventful childhood and conventional education for a youth of his social status. After attending the *Gymnasium*, he went to Strasbourg in 1831 to study medicine and there became acquainted with a variety of political views. He was especially close to the republican opposition, and when he returned to Germany in 1833 to continue his studies in Giessen, he began to apply the political lessons he had learned in France to the German situation.

Büchner soon became involved with the opposition in Hesse, which was led by Ludwig Weidig, and was given the assignment of writing an polemical pamphlet for the peasants of the region. The result was *Der Hessische Landbote* (*The Hessian Courier* [1834]), a seething condemnation of the upper classes and the wealthy. Although some scholars have argued that Weidig toned down the original text by altering key words and supplying Biblical quotations, it was nevertheless still an explosive document when it was secretly printed and distributed in 1834. The underground network of agitation was betrayed, however, and the results were rather disastrous. Weidig eventually died under suspicious circumstances in prison in 1837, and other conspirators were either captured or left the country.

After the betrayal, Büchner returned to his parents' home, but he was not safe there. A few months later, on 1 March 1835, he barely escaped arrest by fleeing to Strasbourg. Here he studied philosophy and worked on his doctoral dissertation, a biological investigation of the nervous system of the barbel, a large European fresh-water fish. A warrant for his arrest followed him to France, however, and he was forced to leave for Zurich in October of 1836. His dissertation was accepted by the university there, and an invitation was extended to him to join the faculty. His inaugural lecture on the cranial nerves in fish was well received, and it seemed that a promising career lay ahead. At this point in his life — Büchner was barely twenty-three years old — he had already achieved some fame as a scientist. His literary work, which had attracted no notice at this point, was something he did on the side. His brilliant career as a scientist and author was cut short, however, by typhoid fever. He fell ill at the beginning of February 1837 and lived only until the nineteenth of that month.

Büchner's literary work is characterized by a concern for social issues. His first play, *Dantons Tod* (*Danton's Death* [1835]), was written at his parents' home in 1834/1835, and it was the only literary work that was published — albeit in a severely censored version — during his lifetime. The drama is set in revolutionary France in March and April of 1794, shortly before the demise of Georges Danton's (1759-1794) more moderate faction at the hands of the group around Maximilien Robespierre (1758-1794). Through the use of extensive documentary material, including several speeches quoted directly from historical sources, Büchner stages a conflict between Danton and Robespierre that problematizes central issues of revolutionary action. This work can be likened to some of Heine's writings during the thirties in that it questions a political revolution that excludes a more encompassing emancipation of the human being. Robespierre, like Börne or Atta Troll, represents a limited, ascetic, and almost spiritualist perspective, while Danton is fashioned into a cynical, sensual fatalist. Although Büchner's own sympathies appear to be with his title figure, the play does not unequivocally advocate one stance over the other. Rather, Büchner points to the strengths and weaknesses of both positions, and in this way produces a more profound and realistic portrayal of conflict and contradiction in revolutionary situations.

Büchner's next two works, the comedy *Leonce und Lena* (1836) and the novella *Lenz* (1839), give evidence of the diversity of style and mood in the precocious writer. The play borrows from both Shakespearean drama and the *commedia dell'arte* tradition, presenting a farce in which the petty mentality of German court life is ridiculed. Prince Leone, from the kingdom of Po, is trying to avoid the arranged marriage to Princess Lena, from the kingdom of Pee, but on his travels away from his native land he meets and falls in love with her, without either person knowing the other's true identity. While in Leonce the qualities of boredom and frivolity are satirized, in the person of his father, King Peter, and his entourage, Büchner derides the pretentiousness and servility of life at a small German court.

In *Lenz* Büchner describes the mental anguish of the German writer Jakob Michael Reinhold Lenz (1751-1792) during his stay with Pastor Johann Friedrich Oberlin (1740-1826) in January of 1778. Like *Dantons Tod*, the novella relies heavily on documentary accounts; much of the work is taken directly or adapted from Oberlin's own account in his diaries. In Lenz, the noted Storm and Stress playwright, Büchner found an archetypical outsider. The narrative technique, which is third person, yet often interior to Lenz's consciousness, affords the reader a unique perspective on the pathology of insanity.

Büchner's last work, the fragmentary drama *Woyzeck* (1836/1837, published 1877), takes up the plight of a lower-class victim of society. Based on documents from medical case studies, the play again makes a social outsider its focus, but in contrast to Lenz, the actions of the title figure are more consistently bound to social conditions. Woyzeck is driven to murder his girlfriend Marie, not only by the jealousy he feels when he witnesses Marie's infidelity with a drum major, but also by mental derangement induced by his being the subject of medical experiments. Büchner's brilliant sketches of the captain and the doctor clearly indict the more privileged classes for Woyzeck's crime. But perhaps more significant is that for the first time in German drama we find a member of the lowest stratum of society assuming the role of hero in a serious drama. Büchner had already displayed in *Dantons Tod* his keen sense for depiction of the lower classes, but in *Woyzeck* he captured more perspicaciously how society denies its victims all freedom and dignity.

Although German literature has to wait until the advent of Naturalism in the 1880s before seeing anything comparable, thematically there exists some relationship between Büchner's play and some of the dominant social concerns of the *Vormärz*. Büchner's partisanship for the oppressed, however, is combined with cynicism toward change, and this combination often brings his works into the orbit of a fatalistic world view, distinguishing him from the authors of the thirties and forties. It is perhaps not entirely fortuitous that his works had to wait until the twentieth century before they were fully appreciated.

10 Biedermeier

Lee B. Jennings

Background

Biedermeier is a term now widely used to designate the conservative mainstream of post-Classical and post-Romantic German literature in the period known in European history as the Restoration (1815-1848), that is, the period between the final defeat of Napoleon (1769-1821) and the Revolution of 1848, during which the Bourbon monarchy was restored to power in France. Though the term Biedermeier was already in use in the realm of interior design, it began to be applied to German literature in the 1920s by scholars who felt that the writing of this period belonged to a distinct cultural and intellectual epoch, as opposed to the similar realistic writing of the latter part of the century, known as "Poetic Realism" or "Bourgeois Realism."

There have of course been disputes about the time limits of the period and about authors, such as Jean Paul (Friedrich Richter [1763-1825]), Theodor Storm (1817-1888), Gottfried Keller (1819-1890), or even Johann Wolfgang Goethe (1749-1832), who fall outside the time limits or are usually placed in other categories, but who seem to show a kinship with the movement at least in some of their works. There are problems, too, with the basis of classification. Are we really dealing with questions of literary style and technique, or perhaps rather with attitudes, life-styles, personalities, and ideologies of the individual authors? By far the most nagging problem, however, is the existence of different styles and ideological orientations within the same period. Ideology, in fact, becomes increasingly important as the inevitable politicizing of culture and art proceeds, a process encouraged by some authors and resisted by others. Thus, apart from the traditionalist literature of Biedermeier, regarded by most authorities as the dominant trend, there exists within this period a second group of avowedly political authors devoted to more liberal, cosmopolitan, and emancipated goals, the group known as Young Germany (*Junges Deutschland*). Biedermeier and Young Germany are opposite sides of the same coin, each forming a type of reaction to the tumultuous conflict of values and ideologies in the post-Napoleonic Years.

This plurality of styles within the same period, though, has led some authorities to question whether the term Biedermeier ought to be applied to the entire period, which might better be called simply Restoration Literature, or, as some prefer *Vormärz*, the time before the March Revolution of 1848. It is indeed rather confusing to have to refer to "true" or "proper" Biedermeier writing within the period which bears its name. It has been questioned, too, whether the more conservative and realistic literature before 1848 is indeed different from that which followed this date, and whether, in fact, Biedermeier is not merely an early phase of the larger movement called Poetic Realism. This is a question that, in the end, the informed reader must decide, always bearing in mind that literary periods are not closed compartments but rather part of an arbitrary contextual framework designed to help us understand the uninterrupted flow of changing culture. The question is not into which period the work of a certain author should be put, but how that work reflects certain contemporary complexes of ideas, and how this affects our reading of it.

Certain characteristics of the Biedermeier era have been mentioned in the earlier attempts to establish it as a separate body of literature. To be sure, they tend to refer more to a way of life or to an attitude than to writing techniques as such. One of these is *Andacht zum Kleinen* (reverence for small things), a tendency to find significance in phenomena, whether in nature or in human life, that are, on the surface, unimposing. Another is *Sammeln und Hegen*, a proclivity to "collect and cherish," that may range from the desire to preserve traditional ways in the face of radical change to a superficial collector's mania. The peculiar virtue of the Biedermeier citizen, however, is that of *Entsagung* (resignation), a stoical attitude in the face of unfulfilled desires that implies a distrust of all exertions of strong will, all egoism and heroics. A veritable Biedermeier manifesto is provided by Adalbert Stifter (1805-1868) in his foreword to *Bunte Steine* (literally: *Colorful Stones* [1853]), written in his own defense against a satirical verse by the dramatist Friedrich Hebbel (1813-1863) accusing him of writing about June bugs and other trivia of nature instead of the heights of human greatness. Stifter retorts that he does not necessarily regard outbursts of emotion and tumultuous egocentricity as "great," but that this appellation should be reserved rather for an exercise of self-control, a just and reasonable life, and efficacy within one's own limited sphere of action. The natural laws that govern volcanic eruptions, he points out, are the same ones that cause a housewife's cooking pot to boil over, and it is the mysterious, long-term working of these laws for which we should reserve our admiration. Likewise, he maintains, there is a law at work in human affairs, a "gentle law" (*sanftes Gesetz*) of justice and altruism, that subtly informs all of our actions and leads humankind slowly but surely toward its goal of harmony. The first sign of a declining civilization, he comments, is the loss of moderation and a preference for the bizarre.

Biedermeier, like Victorian literature in England, is the product of an expanding bourgeoisie aspiring toward gentility but fascinated by idyllicized conceptions of the simple and well-ordered life of rustic folk. It seeks to promulgate the bourgeois values of good name, respectability, productive activity (if not actual labor), and the sanctity of marriage, home, and the family, values which it tends to perceive as eternal and universal. Eroticism, outside of this framework, is feared and scorned, and, with some notable exceptions, the prevailing tone is idyllic rather than tragic or demonic. Though a certain community of spirit in the German-speaking lands is taken for granted, regionalism abounds, partly as an attempt to recapture the simple life, which is necessarily indigenous, and partly, no doubt, as a colorful curiosity for the jaded city-dweller.

It will be seen that Biedermeier owes much to preceding literary eras. Though art can no longer claim the cultural primacy and philosophical validation it had enjoyed in the Age of Goethe, the restrained elegance of Goethean style lives on, and the idea persists that literature must instruct and edify and must be aesthetically well-constructed according to accepted standards. The Romantic heritage can be observed in the near-magical status that "Nature" still enjoys; "Fate" lingers as a metaphysical residue, and one cannot help thinking that the new use of symbol owes something to Romantic explorations of the unconscious. Considerable strides are made toward realism, at least in terms of specific setting and concrete description. Yet the idea persists that literature, however regionally and socially anchored, is not of the workaday world and has to remain universally comprehensible throughout all time. A growing interest in individual psychology can be traced, but the free play of fantasy is avoided, except in accepted vehicles such as the fairy tale (*Märchen*), that is, in the sophisticated literary adaptation of this folk genre, generally referred to as *Kunstmärchen*. Though some emotionalism is cultivated, it resembles late eighteenth-century sentimentality more than Romantic exuberance.

A final problem encountered by advocates of the term Biedermeier, though one not so frequently discussed, is the sense of triviality that unjustly adheres to it. Biedermeier inevitably calls to mind the stubbornly old-fashioned ways and the provincial narrow-mindedness of the emerging bourgeoisie, especially as expressed in the popular art and literature of the time. (The term goes back to a contemporary satire consisting of verses purportedly written by a schoolmaster Biedermeier, a naively pretentious and pedantic figure. The name suggests *bieder*, "staunch, righteous," the suffix *meyer* indicating one who behaves in a stereotyped way.) But even the major literature of the time often seemed escapist to more liberal writers and must still seem so to those who see political involvement as the touchstone of literary significance.

The anti-heroic stance of Biedermeier, to be sure, goes against some of our general expectations of the literary masterpiece. Here one might draw upon the findings of Existentialist philosophy and depth psychology. As Stifter claimed, a life of self-control and regular activity may indeed be "great," in that it represents a maintenance of the self in the face of futility, chaos, and nothingness. Many great works of literature portray this inner struggle. Indeed, the boundary between Biedermeier and Young Germany tends to blur when it comes to *Weltschmerz*, a variety of pessimism endemic to the period, characterized by a paralysis of the will, a flagging of vital energy, a sense of futility and *ennui*, and feelings of unreality. Favorite themes are: the world as a stage and life as play-acting, the individual as a puppet manipulated by unknown forces, the fragmented world, and the notion that the present age is but a pale imitation of bygone greatness — one is a latecomer or *epigone* on the stage of history. In Young Germany, this dismal state of mind is seen as a malaise of the times and may be channeled into social protest, while in Biedermeier it is generally suppressed but serves as a foil for the modestly mystical enhancement of the existing order that this movement inclines toward. In the former case, we sometimes feel that criticism of the social system extends to life in general, while in the latter case the dark undercurrent may appear more significant than the overt utopian projection.

Probably the most significant single feature of Biedermeier literature is its opposition to the concept of *Zeitgeist*, the spirit of changing times and ephemeral fashions, the sense of partaking in a continuous process of change, of being "modern." Most authors of the period would be considered moderate liberals by present standards. While favoring evolution toward a less repressive society, they abhorred violent change and sought to preserve the values that they felt to be essential to the very survival of European civilization.

The literary genres show no radical innovations in Biedermeier. Historical verse tragedy, a traditionally aristocratic form, remains the emulated high style of writing though outside of the conservative mainstream iconoclastic forms of drama do arise. Lyric poetry, in terms of its outward forms, adheres to Classical and Romantic patterns (Greek strophes and folk-song forms). Poems written to commemorate special occasions are still extraordinarily popular. Notable in the realm of prose is the popularity of the *Novelle* (novella), the traditional short-story form following Renaissance models and introduced into German literature mainly through the efforts of Christoph Martin Wieland (1733-1813) and Goethe. It continued to be the most practicable prose form (apart from trivial literature) throughout the century, becoming more theoretically regimented in the process. As regards the novel, one has to wonder at its failure to achieve the ascendancy that it had in England, France, and Russia. There are a number of significant novels, but they give the impression of being isolated phenomena. It has been suggested that the lack of a unified nation inhibited the development of the epic scope that the novel requires. While this view rests upon a rather naive understanding of the novel, there is a certain truth in it. More probably, though, shorter prose works drove longer ones out of the market, because of the extreme popularity of journals among the increasingly educated middle class. Then, too, lingering notions of high artistic mission did little to encourage a fresh appraisal of the passing scene.

Biedermeier clearly reflects the general transition from a more idealistic to a more empirical way of thinking. The very concept of history was changing, and many of the values that had imparted a sense of worth to individual existence were being questioned. The crisis of confidence in a benevolent cosmic order was perceived clearly by Heinrich von Kleist (1777-1811); recognizing that the philosophy of Immanuel Kant (1724-1804) tended to shift the impact of reality to the individual perception of it, he struggled toward some experiential means of dealing with the effective dismissal of a benign deity and the non-assurance of a perpetual continuation of the individual ego. Others saw no such crisis and sought to intensify their beliefs, either in an all-caring God or in the primacy of reason, or, where possible, in both.

The most significant philosophical development of the nineteenth century was undoubtedly Georg Wilhelm Friedrich Hegel's (1770-1831) inspired transmogrification of idealistic thought to conform to the tenor of an empirical age. For Hegel, universal mind is supreme, but rather than informing an otherwise static nature it is the force behind change, manifesting itself progressively in dialectic surges, as history. Though Hegel's universal mind (*Geist*) moves as mysteriously as God is thought to do, and though skeptics such as Georg Büchner (1813-1837) began to doubt that there was any helpful pattern to history at all, there was a certain comfort in participating, in however small a way, in the millennial evolution of the universe. Hegel, the last proponent of a philosophical system, aptly demonstrates his own theory by fashioning a system so exhaustive that it cancels its own usefulness.

While Hegel's influence grows steadily within our period, it is Arthur Schopenhauer (1788-1860) who is its true child. His philosophy is a reservoir of the subdued turmoil underlying the calm face of the age. The unknown ground of reality that Kant called the *Ding an sich* (thing in itself) is identified by Schopenhauer as Will, that is, the vital force of nature, and he sees most of life as a self-defeating struggle to assuage its insatiable demands. His Will is thus quite similar to Eros, a thing-in-itself of a more earthy sort that, at least to the Biedermeier mind, can neither be fully known nor assimilated into an ordered and benign system. Within our time-span, Schopenhauer was not so much a seminal thinker (his impact was much delayed) as the spokesman of a residual discontent. One continually finds seeming references to his ideas where no direct influence can be demonstrated.

In a body of literature still dedicated to emphasizing "lasting values," favoring the allegedly timeless aspects of human behavior over mundane affairs or suggestions of environmental conditioning, correlation with historical events necessarily proves difficult and has to be measured mostly in terms of its absence. Thus, the turbulence of the French Revolution of 1789 and the terror of the 1790s cause scarcely a ripple in the determined classicism and the romantic flights of fancy found in German literature of the time, unless these forms of writing in themselves are regarded as the signs of an upheaval so overwhelming that its impact could not be immediately grasped. The Wars of Liberation from Napoleonic occupation called forth much popular patriotic writing advocating a vaguely-articulated ideal of "freedom," but literary fairy tales and neo-Aristotelian drama may be in the larger view a more accurate reflection of the tenor of the time.

The period after Napoleon's final defeat in 1815 represented a "restoration" only for France; for the German states it was rather a restructuring, based more on territorial treaties and compensations for lost land than on any idea of political order or form of government. Still, the net effect had been to create more plausible state-like entities under somewhat more enlightened rulers than had been the case before the Revolution. The aristocracy was deprived of much of its feudal justification and its allegiance regionally centralized. Somewhat more liberal constitutions were framed, especially in the new states that had been formed. The main concern of the Congress of Vienna, called in 1815, was to settle the territorial disputes of major European powers. One might think that the time was ripe for the establishment of a German nation or empire, and indeed there was some excitement at this prospect. A confederation of the thirty-nine new German states was formed under Austrian leadership, but hopes that it might give rise to some central government soon faded, and its main function, that of military protection of the component states, was never tested.

The power behind the Confederation, and the de facto ruler of the German states, until his flight before the unrest of 1848, was the Austrian chancellor, Prince Metternich (1773-1859). His goal was simple: preservation of the existing order and suppression of any revolutionary activity, an aim shared by the powerful state of Prussia, where such democratic reforms as had been planned in the heat of popular resentment at the French occupation were gradually forgotten. In the states whose rulers supported Napoleon there had been little direct intervention by the French, whose occupation even had a certain liberalizing influence. These states developed relatively liberal constitutions soon after the Congress of Vienna, which, though they fell far short of direct popular representation, were viewed with some alarm by Prussia.

Because of Metternich's machinations, a climate of political repression, of censorship and police intervention, gradually came to dominate public life, waning only in the years just before 1848, when republican sentiment could no longer be contained. On the other hand, the French July Revolution of 1830, seen by liberal intellectuals as a beacon of hope, had otherwise passed by with little impact on the populace at large.

The "restoration" in the German states was thus a time of recovery from a turbulent period of wars, foreign domination, shifting boundaries, and a reshuffling of the entire political structure. Yet, in a sense, little had changed. The liberation from foreign rule had been accomplished by the great powers for their own purposes and had rather accidentally resulted in a slight increase in political freedom in some areas. Aristocrats had lost some of their power and status, but what was "restored" was not much different for the average citizen than what had prevailed in the interim or what had gone before. There was still no national government, whether of a liberal or reactionary nature, but that there was even a nominal confederation of states must have raised hopes; nor had the lesson been lost that governments can be overthrown. Monarchs were slowly becoming administrators, and absolutism was giving way, not to republicanism but to bureaucracy. The period was relatively uneventful and prosperous. The new bourgeoisie was politically naive and used to thinking in feudal terms. Most citizens had little interest in fomenting rebellion; they had seen the horrors that can result from political abstractions. One wonders, in fact, whether Metternich's fear of revolution and the repressive measures that grew out of it did not actually bring forth a degree of discontent that might not otherwise have arisen.

While Biedermeier authors, even when cultivating regional realism, aim at a
timeless quality, this quality was hardly difficult to attain in view of the slow
progress of the industrial revolution. In works set in rural areas, it is often unclear
whether the setting is contemporary or several decades in arrears. In both art and
music, the terms "classical" and "romantic" have tended to dominate criticism.
Yet the peculiar persistence of the neoclassical manner, often in the depiction of
quite ordinary scenes, seems to reflect the Biedermeier attempt to lend a timeless
context to bourgeois concerns, to make eternal the matter of everyday life, always
with decorous restraint. One suspects, too, that much of what passes for "Romantic" art could as well be labeled Biedermeier. Though the figures in Caspar David
Friedrich's (1774-1840) paintings stare out with apparent longing into infinite
landscapes, they do so impeccably attired and from within sparsely but neatly
furnished rooms. Similarly, Moritz von Schwind's (1804-1871) fairy tale
illustrations call up a mythical past, but they do so in a curiously down-to-earth,
concrete, domesticated way. The literature of the period sometimes reminds us, too,
of Ludwig van Beethoven's (1770-1827) almost parodistic bravado and the playful
embellishment of folk material by Franz Schubert (1797-1828) and Felix
Mendelssohn-Bartholdy (1809-1847). Dignity is the key word of the age; if there
is humor, it is peripheral and clearly identified, quite in contrast to Romanticism's
refusal to take anything seriously except this refusal, which, to be sure, it
sometimes took too seriously. Likewise, if there is despair, it is muted, not raging.
Biedermeier tends to find the very meaning of life in observation of the proper
forms. Decorum is, for this movement, an existential "given."

The Writers

A. Franz Grillparzer

Franz Grillparzer (1791-1872), Austria's most beloved dramatist, is probably
the main exponent and practitioner of classical drama in the nineteenth century,
though in the rather muted form we have come to expect of this less ebullient
epoch. He was born in Vienna and lived and worked there, apart from a few trips,
until his death. For more than forty years he worked however unenthusiastically,
as a civil servant and at the time of his retirement in 1856 had become a director
of archives. Vienna of the Metternich era, favorable as it was to music and the
popular theater, was often the scene of bureaucratic vexations for the more creative
authors, and Grillparzer, loyal Habsburgian though he was, was not spared.

Many of Grillparzer's works express to perfection the Biedermeier attitude,
with its distrust of historical greatness and strong will, its glorification of the
modest and humble life, and its virtual elevation of renunciation to the status of a
virtue. Some element of renunciation, to be sure, is inherent in all tragedy, and
while Friedrich Schiller (1759-1805), too, had stressed the victory of inner moral
conviction over egoistic volition, it is a question of emphasis. In Grillparzer's

plays, the outcome seems more predetermined, and the advantages of a strong resolve tend to be discounted from the outset. At times, a basic skepticism about the absoluteness of moral precepts and about the very nature of reality can be glimpsed beneath Grillparzer's general traditionalism, and it may well be this very undercurrent of unresolved doubt that lends his works their continuing appeal, along with his unerring instinct for theatrical effect and dramatic structure, his gracious, yet homely wit, and his genius for subtle psychological motivation that sometimes borders on a pre-Freudian recognition of the role of the unconscious in human behavior. It is probably just as much Grillparzer's personality as his writing that invites the label Biedermeier. He was of a retiring nature, easily embarrassed and distracted. Upon meeting Goethe he could think of nothing to say. His failure to marry his "perpetual fiancée" is usually attributed more to his own irresoluteness than to any pressure of circumstances. The concentration and peace of mind that he found necessary for his literary production was easily disrupted, his sensitivity such that the theatrical failure of his comedy *Weh dem, der lügt* (*Thou Shalt Not Lie*) in 1837 (published 1840) caused him to withhold his remaining plays from the public.

At least after the early play *Die Ahnfrau* (*The Ancestress* [1817]), an homage to the fatalistic horror drama of the Romantic period, Grillparzer's dramatic works begin to show a uniform thematic pattern. Though this cannot be reduced to a simple formula, there is very often a conflict between the inner realm of absolute values and the pragmatic external world of action, will, and material progress.

Thus, in *Sappho* (1817) the ancient Greek poetess, tiring of the barrenness of her divinely inspired poetic mission, seeks the love of a young athlete and, eventually recognizing her mistake, and unused to the vagaries of love, rededicates herself to the gods and plunges to her death.

The trilogy *Das goldene Vließ* (*The Golden Fleece* [1822]), consisting of *Der Gastfreund* (*The Guest Friend*), *Die Argonauten* (*The Argonauts*), and *Medea*, is a remarkable attempt to impart thematic unity and plausible motivation to the ancient legend while preserving its mythic power. This is done mainly by making the magical fleece the embodiment of material greed and the vain quest for fame and glory. Work on the trilogy was interrupted by Grillparzer's despondency at the suicide of his mentally unstable mother.

König Ottokars Glück und Ende (*King Ottokar, His Rise and Fall* [1825]), a play showing Grillparzer's indebtedness to the Baroque age, with its persistent theme of the fall of the mighty, records the beginnings of the Habsburg empire. The power-hungry King Ottokar of Bohemia is on the verge of becoming emperor when his fortunes mysteriously reverse, and he must yield to Rudolf of Habsburg, who humbly regards himself as the agent of God's will. Despite the patently patriotic intent of the play, its performance was long delayed because the censors, perhaps wise beyond their apparent competence, glimpsed in Ottokar an allusion to Napoleon, and this was considered by some oblique political reasoning to represent a threat to the state.

Ein treuer Diener seines Herrn (*A Faithful Servant of His Master* [1828]),
composed as a festival drama to honor the Emperor's Hungarian connections,
details the nearly disastrous efforts of an aging and punctilious viceroy, Bancban,
to maintain the order of the realm against rebellion and the machinations of his
devil-may-care rival, Otto, during the King's absence. As often happens, Otto's
ostensibly reprehensible egoism and his lust for life tend to captivate the audience
more than the characters representing the author's professed values.

Des Meeres und der Liebe Wellen (*Hero and Leander* [performed 1831,
published 1840]) is Grillparzer's treatment of the Hero and Leander legend. Hero
is a priestess, and, like Sappho, half-consciously betrays her high calling for a taste
of life, encouraging Leander to swim the Hellespont for a fateful tryst. The overt
emphasis upon spiritual devotion is intriguingly undermined by the heroine's
evident lack of whole-hearted devotion to the abstract concept which she purports
to serve.

Der Traum ein Leben (*A Dream Is Life* [1834]) is based on a story by Voltaire
(1694-1778) and has little to do with the similarly titled play by the Spanish
Baroque author Calderón (1600-1681), though Grillparzer much admired Calderón
and his compatriot Lope de Vega (1562-1635), and the theme and general
atmosphere of the play are reminiscent of that earlier period. A further influence
was that of the popular Viennese stage, where plays of magic and mystery were
popular. Set in a vaguely Persian bucolic background, the play frames the dream
of a young peasant, Rustan, who has been urged by a diabolical black servant,
Zanga, to seek fame and glory. In the dream, his projected life is realized and ends
badly, as he is drawn ever farther into unscrupulous deeds that are eventually
uncovered, and he is only too glad to awake to his insignificant but familiar
surroundings. The play is a veritable Biedermeier manifesto, glorifying inner peace
and the simple life as against all striving for corrupting "greatness." Yet, the point
is made somewhat equivocally. The renunciation of fame, glory, and the active life
means also withdrawing from external reality in favor of an inner realm whose
claim to timeless verity is less than convincing; and if a dream may prefigure life,
then life itself may be an illusion.

Weh dem, der lügt represents Grillparzer's excursion into the realm of comedy;
despite its initial failure, the play has since enjoyed some success. Leon, a young
and naive cook, agrees to rescue a medieval bishop's nephew from captivity, on the
condition that he tell no lie nor distort the truth in anyway. Since no one believes
that he is so naive as to tell the truth at all times, he is, in effect, lying, and
therefore succeeds. This leads the severe bishop to modify his views, and the
audience tore-examine, perhaps, its views about the concept of truth in human
discourse.

Libussa (written 1844 published 1872), the first of the plays that Grillparzer
withheld from publication, is based on legendary accounts of the founding of
Prague. The visionary princess Libussa bows to the political necessity of accepting
the enterprising commoner Primislaus as husband and co-regent. He founds Prague,
while she, deploring the implications of material progress, relapses into the

visionary mode and welcomes death. The play is noted for its highly formalized poetic style, which has elicited comparisons to Goethe's *Iphigenie*.

Ein Bruderzwist in Habsburg (*Family Strife in Habsburg* [published 1873]) depicts Rudolf II futilely attempting to hold the Empire together on the eve of the Thirty Years' War (1618-1648), in the face of modern ideas of pragmatism and rule by the masses.

Die Jüdin von Toledo (*The Jewess of Toledo* [published 1873]), inspired by a work of Lope de Vega, details the half-hearted efforts of a young and naive king to avoid betraying his queen with the beautiful Rahel, who emanates an animalistic charm. Meanwhile, he neglects his battles against the Moors, and a cabal indirectly brings about Rahel's death. The King, awakened to his responsibilities, abdicates in favor of his son. The needs of the state prevail — but at what cost? The question is unresolved.

Though drama was Grillparzer's forte, his considerable body of lyric poetry deserves attention, at least for its elaboration of some of the themes of his dramas. He is noted also for two short stories. *Das Kloster bei Sendomir* (*The Cloister at Sendomir* [1828]) is a wild tale in which a count confesses killing his wife because she had agreed to his demand that she kill the child of her adulterous union, thus revealing her lack of humaneness. The count enters the cloister and repents. Much more modern-seeming is *Der arme Spielmann* (*The Poor Fiddler* [1848]), in which the author-narrator, pleading insatiable psychological curiosity, pursues an inept street musician to find out the story of his life. The result is an almost Naturalistic study of the effects of environment on character, or, indeed, a pre-Freudian case history of an Oedipus complex. (The musician is a slow learner whose father was demanding and severe.) However, since the father-dominated wretch, in his idiosyncratic fiddling, claims some mystical insight, we suspect not only a certain self-irony on the author's part but also a questioning of the idealistic/Romantic view of the artist's supernal calling. By Grillparzer's time, revelations that cannot be readily communicated to others had become suspect.

In most of his work, Grillparzer seeks to rescue some canon of absolute values in the face of moral relativism and pragmatic mass culture. Often he places this effort in the service of the waning Habsburg Empire as the bastion of enduring values. What is fascinating is that he does this so equivocally, as if surreptitiously admiring the very forces of will, eros, and experiential self-realization that he seems to be condemning. Though this ambiguity is symptomatic of the age, it reaches a level in his work that transcends historical limitation and reaches a broad audience even today.

B. Jeremias Gotthelf (Albert Bitzius)

Albert Bitzius (1797-1854) began to write fiction under the name of Jeremias Gotthelf at the age of thirty-nine. He then wrote prolifically; the standard edition of his works comprises twenty-four volumes of short stories, novels, and the popular *Kalendergeschichten* (calendar stories). He is known for his colorful, often crassly realistic yet mythically tinged portrayals of Swiss peasant life, told in a compelling epic style and in a rough-hewn language unable or unwilling to free itself from regional dialect.

Gotthelf (as we shall now refer to him) was a Protestant clergyman, as his father had been. He studied theology at the Bern Academy (now University) and was for a time vicar to his father in the semi-rural community of Utzenstorf, leaving for a time to further his studies in Göttingen. Prevented by church rules from taking over his father's ministry, he served as vicar in Herzogenbuchsee and Bern, finally obtaining his own ministry in Lützelflüh in 1832, where he married the granddaughter of his senile predecessor. It would be a mistake to think that Gotthelf led the life of a self-absorbed rustic pastor. He was passionately interested in educational reform and, especially in the Bern period, had acquired a formidable reputation as a liberal journalist and presence on the political scene. Such activity, in fact, probably interfered with his more rapid advancement in the clerical hierarchy. Gotthelf was decidedly liberal in his championing of popular representation, his opposition to aristocratic privilege, and his insistence upon a well-educated citizenry. Especially in the Bern period, however, he began to feel that he was occupying a losing position between the reactionary advocates of the *status quo* and the radical exponents of an antireligious materialism. At the same time, he was repelled by the growing signs of deterioration of the traditional bases of society: the work ethic, family tradition, and an inherent sense of uprightness and fair dealing. Ironically, a new law promoted by the liberal faction prohibited clergymen from participating in political organizations, and this is what propelled Gotthelf into literary activity — perhaps fortunately so, since he says that his need to create fiction had taken on the nature of a dammed-up stream.

Gotthelf, in fiction and non-fiction, was always didactic and often polemic. He remains an educator, but one able to draw upon phenomenal creative powers to carry out his overt intent, which was to prepare the Swiss rural population for the increasing participation in self-government that was becoming available to it. Central to his philosophy was a closeness to God that would serve as a guide to those faced with difficult decisions in their social environment. Even politicizing, insofar as it strayed from these ideals and became an all-consuming preoccupation, came under his severe scrutiny.

Gotthelf's best-known novel, *Uli der Knecht* (*Uli the Farmhand* [1846]) delineates the hero's progress from simple farmhand to leaseholder and manager of a large farm. Along the way he learns through painful experience, and with the help of a kindly mentor manages to avoid such pitfalls as financial speculation, dubious romantic liaisons, and the wiles of marriageable women, and he suffers all the tribulations of an overseer who must deal with family prerogatives, recalcitrant workers, and mismanagement; he must also deal with his own temptation to advance his career by means of an unwise marriage. In the sequel, *Uli der Pächter* (*Uli the Tenant Farmer* [1849]), Uli must achieve, as the author puts it, an "emancipation of the soul." Beset by financial hardships, he begins to resort to questionable business practices, to listen to the advice of exploiters, and to neglect his new wife. When a hailstorm destroys his crops, it is seen as divine intervention. Uli falls ill and undergoes a spiritual renewal. The farm is saved by a kindly relative. In Gotthelf's most widely-read short story, *Die schwarze Spinne (The Black Spider* [1842]), an idyllic rural baptismal celebration is the scene of the grandfather's tale of the past hardships that beset the now-flourishing estate, toward the purpose of reminding the celebrants of the constant vigilance against evil and chaos that an orderly society presupposes. Gotthelf draws upon regional folk tales of the plague years to create the mythic image of the supernaturally evil Black Spider that once ravaged the countryside and is even now imprisoned in a doorpost of the peaceful homestead. The spider plague was originally visited upon medieval peasants who sought to outwit the Devil, whom they had promised a first-born child in return for his help. The Spider and its minions are overcome by the self-sacrificing acts of a clergyman and by the mother of a new-born child. A second escape of the Spider, centuries later, results from affluence, irresponsibility, and the frivolity of some unruly and poorly-managed servants, again requiring the self-sacrifice of a pious individual. In the story *Elsi, die seltsame Magd (Elsi, the Strange Peasant Girl* [1843]) the vagabond heroine's self-sacrifice on the battlefields of the Napoleonic wars is at least as much inspired by a new-found devotion to the Gotthelfian ideals as it is by love and patriotism.

Much has been written about Gotthelf's membership in the Biedermeier movement. In his advocacy of traditional values in the face of *Zeitgeist*, he certainly belongs squarely in this category. Yet, his direct confrontation of controversial issues, as opposed to a passive-aggressive toleration or escape from them, is atypical and may be attributed to the greater degree of democratization achieved since 1830 in Switzerland, and hence to the absence of the repressive atmosphere that discouraged any sort of pronounced political standpoint among the "establishment" authors of the other German-speaking areas. Traditional scholarship has tended to think in terms of left and right, revolutionary fervor or reactionary escapism, making no allowance for a spirited defense of the conservative or moderate-liberal position in intensely realistic terms, such as Gotthelf has provided.

C. Adalbert Stifter

Adalbert Stifter is an undisputed master of prose narrative in the Biedermeier tradition. However, he is one of those authors who tend to arouse highly positive or negative reactions on the part of the more casual reader. This can be explained partly by ideology, in his own time as well as in ours. His belief in the subtle depiction of eternal verities, at the expense of any great concern with current social developments, usually in a timeless-seeming rural setting, with painstaking descriptions of the natural surroundings and with a minimum of overt action, have caused many to charge him with escapism. Some may be frustrated initially by the relative absence of action and epic scope in most of his work. To appreciate Stifter, one has to be aware of his belief in a millennial evolution of humankind toward spiritual purity, a process manifesting itself only in minuscule fashion at any point in history. (Friedrich Nietzsche [1844-1900] was among his admirers.)

Stifter was born in Oberplan, Bohemia, then a part of the Austro-Hungarian Empire, the son of a weaver and textile merchant. After the sudden death of his father, the twelve-year-old Adalbert took up the life of a peasant with his paternal grandfather, until his maternal grandfather made it possible for him to receive academic training for a professional career. He eventually studied law at the University of Vienna; however, he seems to have suffered a curious flagging of enthusiasm at the time of his final examinations and never received a degree. He had meanwhile begun writing, adopting the extremely subjective style, the artist-outsider role, and the touch of cosmic anxiety favored by late Romantic authors and especially by his particular model, Jean Paul, a highly original figure standing somewhat apart from the main literary currents of the early 1800s. Stifter matured late, and his entrance into adult life seems to have been overshadowed by his perception of his artistic mission. He came perilously close to proposing marriage to two women at the same time — the popular, highly placed Fanny Greipl (1808-1839), his ideal, whose parents probably would not have permitted the marriage in any case, and to the seamstress Amalie Mohaupt (1811-1883), whose relatives seem to have insisted on the marriage which Stifter entered into in 1837. For a time he supported himself with meager author's royalties, editorial work, and private tutoring.

Contrary to what the reader of his works might think, Stifter was hardly a political arch-conservative. He welcomed at first the revolutionary developments of 1848 as an end to repressive government. As the agitation grew, however, he was repulsed by the demagoguery, disunity, and self-seeking intrigue of the revolutionary movement and foresaw renewed repression. He came to favor gradual improvement of society through influence upon its individual members. Repeated efforts on Stifter's part to gain a responsible position and source income were finally rewarded in 1850, when he was appointed inspector of the Upper Austrian elementary school system, a position he held, despite his frustrated attempts at school reform, until his retirement in 1865.

Stifter's marriage seems to have embodied that stoic resignation in the face of unalterable circumstances so often advocated in his works. Chief among his tribulations was the recalcitrance of his unruly foster-daughter and niece Juliane, who, at the age of eighteen, disappeared and was found drowned in the Danube. Stifter's last decade represented a losing battle of productivity against ill health. Afflicted with cancer of the liver, he committed suicide by cutting his throat with a razor, something that was long suppressed.

Stifter's early works, as noted, show a subjectivity skirting nihilism. These were short stories, published in popular journals. In his collection *Studien* (*Studies* [1844-1850]) he republished these stories with thorough revisions, thereby providing literary scholars with a valuable tool for tracing his stylistic development. In general, the more subjective, pessimistic, and fatalistic elements of the early versions, along with the stress on limitless self-development, are eliminated in favor of adaptation to society, perhaps as a result of the new political climate, and characters that earlier appeared as positive outsider figures come to be presented as immature narcissists. Resignation is the key word; a satisfying life has to be forged within existing limitations. Yet, the brief, almost casual references to turbulent passion, often with regard to long-past events, are compelling in their terseness and offer fleeting glimpses of what has been repressed.

The story in the *Studien* that has most attracted the attention of scholars is *Die Mappe meines Urgroßvaters* (*My Great-Grandfather's Diary* [1841-42]). The narrator's great-grandfather, as a young doctor, was close to suicide because of a disappointment in love, but, on the advice of an older man, came to terms with life and society by keeping a diary, which then makes up the narrative. *Brigitta* (1844) takes up the interesting theme of a physically unattractive woman whose husband has strayed but is reunited with her years later when both are managing neighboring estates on the Hungarian steppes. The husband has gained maturity and has learned to appreciate her inner beauty. The story unfolds gradually through the account of an observant traveler. The story that is perhaps least illustrative of Stifter's usual didactic optimism and most illustrative of the range of his imagination is *Abdias* (1843), the story of a north African Jew who gains wealth, loses it, and migrates to a remote Bohemian village with his daughter Ditha, in whom he now seeks to inculcate the spiritual values that he himself had formerly neglected. Born blind, but with a strange affinity for electricity, Ditha has her sight restored by lightning but is later killed by it, and Abdias ends his days in madness.

Stifter's next collection of stories, *Bunte Steine* (1853), was originally intended as a work for children, but, as finally completed, it rather reflects the Biedermeier fascination with the childlike mentality. The titles of the stories all represent specific minerals, though the connection between story and title is often less than clear. The preface, as mentioned, sets forth the author's conception of a subtle cosmic regularity, and most of the stories can be understood as bearing out this viewpoint in some way. The best known of them, *Bergkristall* (*Rock Crystal*), is quite simple as regards its story line. Two children, a boy and a girl, on their way back from a visit to their grandmother in a neighboring village, are surprised by a snowstorm and stray onto a glacier. They manage to survive by intuitive resourcefulness, and their rescue brings about a slightly more harmonious relationship between their parents and greater tolerance within the miniature society of the village. The plot, however, is almost incidental; what holds the attuned reader in suspense is the breathtaking account of natural phenomena. In another of the better known stories, *Granit*, an old man tells his young grandson a tale about the adventures of another village boy during the plague years; he thereby wisely implants a sense of cultural continuity (symbolized by a well-worn rock) while relieving the boy's distress at a thrashing he has gotten.

Stifter's novel *Der Nachsommer* (*Indian Summer* [1857]) represents a culmination of the Biedermeier standpoint. There is little action. A rather effete youth with aspirations to become a natural scientist happens onto the estate of the Baron von Riesach, an avowed conservationist in every sense, and he eventually learns of the older man's past life and his disappointments in love. In a curiously static tableau-like scene, he espouses the daughter of the woman who is the Baron's lost and regained love and is now his frequent visitor. Again, the true emphasis is on matters other than the story line, primarily the many practical means — gardening, furniture restoration, a study of meteorology and geology — whereby the old gentleman farmer seeks to create a sanctuary for the things he values in an uncertain world. The novel *Witiko* (1867) is set in the twelfth century and embodies Stifter's vision of the ideal state, ostensibly medieval Bohemia, founded upon a principle of justice. In his own time Stifter was regarded as a regional, "realistic" author, i.e., one who devotes a good deal of space to describing things. A revaluation of his work occurred with the application of the concepts of Existentialist philosophy to his work. The image of the poetic chronicler of minutiae then gave way to the heroic image of the stoic forging a meaningful existence in the face of nihilism and despair. Indeed, Stifter was well aware of the bestial and demonic side of human nature, and his work is to a great extent an attempt to come to terms with it. Thomas Mann (1875-1955) once remarked that one always has the feeling of impending catastrophe when reading Stifter, even when none develops. The struggle succeeds so well that the casual reader may be unaware of it. His quest is ultimately metaphysical; yet he scorns outright metaphysics. The peculiar fascination of his nature description lies not in the creation of a mood, but in its very scientific accuracy. He views God in the creation, but always along rigorously empirical lines. Stifter was an accomplished amateur painter, whose concern with the nuances of landscape suggests the Impressionism of a later age.

Stifter's style becomes almost childlike in its simplicity as he refines it throughout his career, seeking to emulate the classical style of Goethe, and his admiration for the majestic spareness of the Luther Bible is also increasingly evident. Here, too, his effort may have succeeded too well, concealing the chaotic origins that attest to creativity.

D. Annette von Droste-Hülshoff

Annette von Droste-Hülshoff (1797-1848) had the fortune, or misfortune, to have been born into the landed aristocracy of Westphalia. The misfortune was that her family, though of modest means, was subject to all of the restrictions and conventionalities of her caste, which looked askance upon intellectual or professional independence or public utterances by its female members. Her early life moved within a limited circle of relatives and peers. It was only gradually that her innate poetic talent became clear even to herself and was able to find resonance among persons with influence in the literary world. Thus, though she helped to gather folk material for the Grimm brothers (Jacob [1785-1863] and Wilhelm

[1786-1859]), she seems to have taken little notice of the entire Romantic movement.

She was musically talented, a quality favored, within limits, by her relatives, but she is also said to have been possessed of "second sight," a clairvoyant capacity that took the form of oppressive prophetic dreams. In any case, like many poets, she had the dubious gift of heightened and perhaps distorted perceptions. She was by all accounts a highly complex personality, sometimes facetious, mocking, and convivial, at other times withdrawn and introverted. Like many women of her class, she spent a good deal of her time making lengthy, obligatory visits to the estates of relatives. She never married: in her youth, she seems to have been equally enamored of two aristocratic young students who visited the family estate of Hülshoff, but, having found out about this, they both renounced her.

In later years, she made the acquaintance of the budding author and literary critic Levin Schücking (seventeen years her junior [1814-1883]), with whom she developed what must at least be termed an intimate friendship. Schücking, a prolific author of rather modest talents, possessed enough critical sense to appreciate Annette's poetic genius and enough prestige to be of help in getting her works published. The two were together in Rüschhaus, a small family estate where Annette had lived since the death of her father, and at Meersburg on Lake Constance, the estate of the elderly medievalist Baron Joseph von Lassberg, Annette's brother-in-law, where Schücking had taken the position of librarian. The relationship had its problems, one of which was that Schücking insisted on "correcting" Annette's manuscripts, and he eventually married a younger woman author, whereupon the friendship cooled. The liaison had been not only tactically beneficial to Annette's career, however, but had effected a remarkable thawing of the creative block that was undoubtedly aggravated, if not caused, by her upbringing. Though deeply affected, she took the parting in her stride but produced no more major works. Her death was the result either of tuberculosis or a psychosomatically induced asthmatic condition.

Though religiously tolerant and sympathetic toward such emancipated causes as were espoused by Levin Schücking, Annette von Droste-Hülshoff was inclined to think that the patriarchal feudal system was divinely ordained. She was deeply committed to, even obsessed by, the Catholic faith, even as she questioned it. The possible loss of faith and attendant guilt form the substance of most of her lyric poetry, though her continuous self-examination for signs of guilt suggest an existential anxiety going beyond the bounds of orthodox belief. Her poetic language is highly individual, complex, somber, even lugubrious, but, even when pathetic in tone, it is never sentimental. The vocabulary tends toward the abstruse; it is regionally tinged and adapted to contemporary terminology, but not "elevated." Her epic poetry, which occupies a large part of her production, lends a new depth to the traditional genres of epic verse and ballad, since there is neither a clear moral intent behind them nor a linear development of events.

In view of Droste-Hülshoff's introspective and idiosyncratic lyrics, it is surprising to find that she is one of the innovators of regional realism in prose, both in her unfinished novel *Bei uns zu Lande auf dem Lande* (*Country Life in Our Land*) and in the story *Die Judenbuche* (*The Jews' Beech Tree* [1842]). The latter begins with a description, anticipating the Naturalistic movement in its sociological objectivity, of the environment in which the young protagonist grows up, an enclave of rugged lumbermen who collectively defy new forestry laws. The young hero, uncertain in his values, disappears after the murder of a Jewish money-lender (it never becomes clear whether he actually committed the crime). Later he reappears (if it is really he, and not his double), having survived Turkish slavery, in an addled condition and is finally found hanged from a beech tree bearing a Hebrew inscription suggesting divine or supernatural retribution. Thus an astonishingly modern-seeming account of environmental determination of character is combined with an eery sense of fate suggestive of lingering Romanticism.

E. Lenau (Nikolaus Niembsch)

Nikolaus Niembsch (Lenau [1802-1850]) was born in a part of the Austro-Hungarian Empire that is now Rumanian. After the family had moved to the Hungarian area, his grandfather was granted the title "Edler (Noble) von Strehlenau," and our author, taking the pen-name Lenau, was accustomed to refer to himself as a Hungarian nobleman. He studied various subjects at several universities but received no degree. Having come into an inheritance, he traveled to Germany and continued, for a time, his medical studies. At the same time, he cultivated relations with various authors, especially in the Swabian region, becoming something of a social lion and ostensible poetic genius. While probably already showing signs of the syphilitic infection that caused his ultimate madness, Lenau embarked on a voyage to America, apparently out of a desire to renew his creative powers by an encounter with raw nature. After a desultory attempt to manage a farm in Ohio, where he was known to neighbors as "the crazy German," he decided that America was a prosaic, decadent land where poetry could not flourish, so he returned to Germany in 1833, having spent less than a year in the New World. The following decade saw the publication of his verse epics *Faust, Savonarola,* and *Die Albigenser* (*The Albigenses*) and a second collection of his poems, but a series of broken engagements gave evidence of increasingly erratic behavior. In 1844 he became recognizably psychotic and was institutionalized.

Lenau's lyric poetry and verse dramas occupy a position somewhere on the border of major literature, but, as is so often the case, they are especially representative of the period. The view that he dealt in a fashionable *Weltschmerz* and used the traditional trappings of melancholy merely as a literary device is somewhat unjust, in view of the psychic torments that he increasingly suffered; but his pose of Byronic pessimism fulfilled a definite need of the Biedermeier period. His earlier epics largely support the conservative, late-Romantic, patriotic camp of religious sentiment, as opposed to the rationalistic, materialistic skepticism of Young Germany and the left-wing Hegelians. When, in *Die Albigenser*, while suffering from a depressive crisis of faith, he began to adopt some of Hegel's ideas himself, seeing, for instance, suffering and bloodshed as necessary concomitants of the impersonal historical process, his traditionally-minded Swabian friends were horrified, and it is clear that he had begun to escape the confines of Biedermeier.

F. Eduard Mörike

Eduard Mörike (1804-1875) is undoubtedly one of the most significant lyric poets of the nineteenth century. In its outward form, his poetry is not ostensibly innovative; he slips with equal ease into the Romantic and Classical modes, writing now in the manner of the folk song, now in ancient Greek strophes. But since his poetry is usually neither the vehicle for philosophical statements nor a direct expression of significant personal experience, its craftsmanship and creativity may escape the casual reader.

Mörike was born in Ludwigsburg, in the Swabian region, the seventh child of a prominent physician. An earthy strain of indigenous culture and folklore is often to be noted amidst the classical refinement that he sometimes aspires to. After the customary schooling, Mörike entered the theological seminary at Urach and later the renowned seminary at Tübingen, where the philosophers Hegel and Friedrich Wilhelm Schelling (1775-1854) and the poet Friedrich Hölderlin (1770-1843) had also studied. Hölderlin, in fact, having become schizophrenic (though some are skeptical of this) was being cared for in Tübingen while Mörike was a student there, and we may assume that the sight of the addled poet exacerbated the young Mörike's uncertainties about his own mental stability and his occasionally somber reflections about the artistic temperament. With a poetically-minded fellow student, Mörike lavished much attention on the systematic invention of a fantasy land, Orplid, a theme that recurs in some of his writing. What may have been the most formative experience in Mörike's career also took place during the Tübingen years: his passion for Maria Meyer (1802-1865), a young woman of uncertain origins and dubious reputation, whom he refers to in a cycle of poems as Peregrina (the Wanderer). Mörike eventually came to the conclusion that he had to break off the affair, and he makes no mention of it in later years. No doubt, though, it aroused the fear and distrust of strong emotion that was to characterize his later personality — another case in which individual traits of prominent persons tend to mirror those of the age.

After graduating from the seminary, Mörike embarked on a theological career, serving as vicar in a succession of Protestant churches in small towns in his native region. It was not until 1834 that he was granted the modest parsonage in Cleversulzbach, a post that he held for nine years, until his voluntary early retirement. A curious sidelight of this period is his painstaking account of paranormal phenomena in the old parsonage, which he was convinced was haunted. Toward the end of his eighteen-year apprenticeship to the ministry, Mörike broke off a five-year engagement to Luise Rau (1806-1891). His love letters to her have been published, and they testify to the intensity of the relationship; it is not clear why it turned sour, though the complexity of Mörike's personality, his less-than-resolute pursuit of his ostensible career, and perhaps a basic lack of commitment on his part are probable reasons.

After Cleversulzbach, Mörike taught literature for several years at a women's school in Stuttgart, the Catharinenstift. In 1851 he married Margarete Speeth (1818-1903), an event that caused raised eyebrows because the bride was Catholic. The union lasted twenty-one years (there were two daughters) but seems to have been marred by Mörike's closeness to his sister. Apart from his lecturing, Mörike subsisted

Mörike as a young man.
Pencil drawing by Schreiner.
Courtesy Schiller Nationalmuseum Marbach

mostly on pensions and stipends in later years and spent much of his time visiting friends, taking cures at spas, and travelling to nearby places. As an author, he was never widely popular in his lifetime but did enjoy a modest critical acclaim.

Mörike was frequently ailing. He has often been accused of hypochondria and indolence, both during his lifetime and since. Some have seen in his very indolence a basic character trait of the lyric poet. Yet an examination of his day-to-day activities gives evidence of a relatively busy life, and it is quite possible that he suffered from some debilitating ailment that could not then be diagnosed. His literary output, at least, is quite respectable.

Mörike, in his lyrics, is the master of the fleeting impression, captured in uncannily precise language. Anything short of a detailed analysis cannot do justice to his verse, though then the spontaneous effect may be lost. A few comments on individual poems may give some idea of their ambience. "Verborgenbeit" ("Seclusion") is one of Mörike's more forthright "message" poems, a plea to the world to be spared its excesses of both pleasure and pain, to be given over rather to the ineffable sensations of his inner being. "Auf eine Lampe" ("On a Lamp"), written in classical hexameters, begins by describing a decorative lamp, dating from the Rococo period, now stored in an abandoned room. It is suggested that the lamp represents art itself, which contains its own blessedness or meaning. Or does it only seem so? The poem is generally thought to represent a somber reflection on the passing of an age in which art reigned supreme or was at least an integral part of the society — yet another testimonial to the Biedermeier latecomer-syndrome. "Der Feuerreiter" ("The Fire Messenger") — reputedly inspired by the mad Hölderlin pacing in his tower room — is written in the Romantic ballad form, but it shows an ability to forge new myth that makes it more than an imitation of past tradition. The central figure exists on various levels: as a simple mounted announcer of fires, as a clairvoyant who can sense distant fires, as a pseudo-priestly conjurer or shaman who can put fires out, and as a spirit of fire himself. The effect is as compelling as it is mysterious. "Um Mitternacht" ("At Midnight") is a curiously muted exercise in personification and metaphor. Night, a mother figure, pauses in her approach at a null-point in time, to hearken to the voices of the wellsprings, her children, singing of the bygone day. The ethereal blue of eternity beckons, but the drag of temporality and earth is irresistible, and perhaps in the end preferable. "Erinna an Sappho" ("Erinna to Sappho"), in Grecian cadences, renders the thoughts of a young pupil of the Greek poetess Sappho. The young girl relates her experience of a realization of death, visualized as a black-feathered arrow, while gazing in a mirror.

Mörike was not only a lyric poet. His story *Mozart auf der Reise nach Prag* (*Mozart on the Way to Prague* [1855]), while somewhat prolix for those not versed in Mozart lore, offers both a credible portrayal of the composer as he experiences a minor triumph at a remote ducal estate toward the end of his life, and a somber comment on artistic creativity, its semi-conscious, playful origins, and the momentary conquest of mortality that is its essence. His novel *Maler Nolten* (1832) is important mainly as an attempt to continue the tradition of this genre. It is hardly a *Bildungsroman* (a novel of self-realization through experience), since the hero is more defeated than triumphant at the end and in fact seems to wander off, in Romantic fashion, into the other world. There is considerable cynicism, too, about the constancy of human dependencies amidst all lingering idealism. It is a strangely poignant work, but one that falls out of the traditional categories.

Several of Mörike's other prose works and verse epics embody fairy-tale themes, sometimes as mere folkloristic re-creations, sometimes as a vehicle for myth, fantasy, and symbol. His more progressive literary friends objected to this apparent retreat from contemporary issues. Though their criticism was undoubtedly short-sighted, there is some justification in their complaint that Mörike seems to seek out innocuous themes. In his personal life, he lavished a great deal of attention on bizarrely humorous messages to his friends; but even his humor contains a dark element that lends substance to it.

Mörike's lifestyle is distinctly Biedermeier. The case for his literary work is somewhat less compelling, since we expect some such traits in any author who specializes in lyric poetry. The decisive features are his regional bonds, his general obeisance to prevailing mores and abhorrence of strong passion, and his persistent avoidance of the contemporary. The somber aspects of his work, the grotesquery and melancholy, are as much in the Biedermeier spirit as are his idylls.

Conclusions

We have considered a group of authors who, for various reasons, fall into a historical-literary grouping known as Biedermeier, a term intended to denote some common trend in the literature of the Restoration period. Literature within this period seems to divide itself into that expressing overt opposition to a repressive establishment and that expressing some degree of affirmation of it as the guardian of tradition. The latter, more affirmative trend, is the Biedermeier proper. Membership in the category is necessarily vague. Its characteristics — advocacy of bourgeois and traditional values, resistance to rapid historical change, rejection of "greatness," a drawing in of horizons, a celebration of propriety, and the belief that the arts stand above real life — are exemplified to varying degrees by the authors discussed.

Mörike demonstrates the Biedermeier personality. His works show a preoccupation with past literary traditions and a general feeling of epigonic inferiority to the great past, a tendency to dwell upon regional, ahistorical minutiae, and a vehement avoidance of passion and tragedy. No doubt, however, his Biedermeier persona has tended to obscure his genius as a lyricist. Grillparzer seeks to recreate classical dramatic forms, but with a basic affirmation of the sociopolitical *status quo* and, for that matter, a distrust of greatness that interfere with true tragic spirit. To be sure, the equivocation of his affirmation lends it its modernity. In his proto-Naturalistic story of the shabby musician, he transcends the prevailing literary tradition and anticipates new trends. Stifter seeks a mysterious inner harmony of all things that will justify stoic resignation and form a bulwark against disruptive change. His attitude perfectly illustrates the Biedermeier tendency to universalize the current social system. Gotthelf bears out the Biedermeier quest for preservation of the old values against the deterioration of the social core that he fears; but he does so in an unusually pugnacious way and without the usual resignatory withdrawal. Droste-Hülshoff seems to exemplify also Biedermeier non-commitment, but her gender, class, and religious beliefs obscure the issue. Like Grillparzer, she conveys the resignatory aura of her time, but she combines what appears to be *Weltschmerz* with doubts and questions of a quite individual nature. At the same time she is able to forge powerfully realistic passages presaging a new age. Lenau had the misfortune of being overtaken by his own melancholic pose. Biedermeier *Weltschmerz* was a mourning of lost or absent harmony, to be assuaged by faith, tradition, social bonding, or constructive activity — not, however, to be put into the service of renewal, social change, or the questioning of accepted values.

Hegel was the key figure in our period. His philosophy was ambiguous enough to provide conflict in itself, upholding as it did the moribund social system while providing a theoretical basis for the advocates of violent change. His very name served as an ideological touchstone, separating all progressives from the orthodoxy whose vehicle Biedermeier is. There was a profusion of political, religious, and philosophical allegiances in this period, and on any particular occasion they could enter into endless combinations of alliances. The most significant such occasion was the publication of David Friedrich Strauß's *Das Leben Jesus* (*The Life of Jesus* [1835-1836]), an attempt to arrive at the historical basis of the New Testament, avowedly without questioning its actual doctrines. The vehemence of the resulting controversy bears out both the continuing power of the orthodox view and the fear with which it viewed the threat from the progressive side. None of this would have been possible without Hegel's fruitful contamination of idealistic metaphysics with the erosive dross of empiricism.

The Biedermeier age is one in which abstract theory waned in importance while the whole thinking of the time shifted toward empiricism, even in the manner in which professed anti-empiricists went about their work. Thus, we naturally expect an increase of realism and a rejection of the metaphysical in literature. This indeed took place, but the question is what sort of "realism" was to ensue. Most literature of the time shows an abandonment of the supernatural and to some extent a blurring of clear conflicts of good and evil, of spiritual and physical. There is a gain in plausibility of events and motivations, even with some depth-psychological probing, and the practice is to locate things in a definite time and place. The ideological cleft occurs in connection with social realism.

The authors grouped under the rubric Young Germany describe contemporary conditions that they want to change, often in a pejorative manner, and the view of the world presented may approach nihilism as the target of criticism expands. Biedermeier authors tend to describe conditions that they wish to remain unchanged, often in an idyllic way and with the aura of cosmic approval — though their fear of change, on the other hand, is likely to call up images of apocalyptic doom. It is a misfortune of nineteenth-century German literature that, although there are grey areas of overlapping ideology, there appears to be no solid middle ground where the forces of change and conservation might have united to paint a panorama of the whole society, an appraisal that might have savored the existing reality rather than look to the past or to the future.

11 Realism

Nancy Kaiser

Introduction

As a literary epoch Realism designates the period in German literature between the unsuccessful revolutionary struggles of 1848 and the end of the century. Since the failed revolution of 1848 is a clear historical and cultural boundary, it is easier to specify the beginning of German Realism than to establish a terminal date. The political spirit of pre-revolutionary lyric poetry by authors such as Ferdinand Freiligrath (1810-1876) and Georg Weerth (1821-1856) or the oppositional *élan* of the Young Germans is clearly missing from poetry and prose after 1848. Literary discussions in the 1850s reject the subjective stance and fantasy of the Romantics, the Biedermeier obsession with descriptive detail, and the political commitment of the *Vormärz* authors. Fanny Lewald (1811-1889), Louise Aston (1814-1871), Ida Hahn-Hahn (1805-1880), Louise Mühlbach (1814-1873), all authors of emancipatory novels of the 1840s protesting the lack of social and sexual freedom for women, either quit writing novels or drastically switch the tone and content of their literary work at mid-century. There is no denying the significance of 1848 in literary history. The end of the nineteenth century, on the other hand, offers no such decisive event as closure for the epoch of German Realism. The final decades bring instead a diversity of cultural and literary phenomena. The ironically skeptical novels of the Berlin Realist Theodor Fontane (1819-1898) or the social-ethical narratives of the Austrian Realist Marie von Ebner-Eschenbach (1830-1916) are contemporaneous with the more harshly realistic and socially critical dramas and manifestoes of the Naturalists in the 1880s and 1890s or *Jugendstil* and the other cultural movements of the *fin-de-siècle*. The socio-economic transformation of Wilhelmine Germany (1888-1918) in the wake of industrial-technological modernization and the break with aesthetic traditions in cultural and literary modernism mark the final years of German Realism.

Literary realism, with a thematic emphasis on everyday social existence against the background of historical change and a narrative style that emphasizes objectivity and verisimilitude, is characteristic of European literatures in the second half of the nineteenth century. It is generally recognized as a literary mode of the middle classes, and the contours of realistic narrative in the nineteenth century are formed by the divergent developments of the middle classes within each national culture. Within this context, German Realism is often characterized as aberrant, as not achieving the criterion established by the critic Erich Auerbach for the European form of literary realism: "a serious representation of contemporary everyday social reality against the background of a constant historical movement." In assessing the various aspects and stages of German Realism, it is important to consider the historical development in German lands from the unsuccessful liberal and democratic attempts at a revolution in 1848 through the unification in the German Empire under Prussian hegemony with the exclusion of Austria in 1871 to the modernized, industrialized Germany and the multinational Hapsburg empire at the century's close. It is impossible to speak of a homogeneous "German" Realism, one that could fit the Swiss authors Gottfried Keller (1819-1890) and Conrad Ferdinand Meyer (1825-1898), the North German writer Theodor Storm (1817-1888), the Swabian Berthold Auerbach (1812-1882), Berlin's Theodor Fontane, Austria's Marie von Ebner-Eschenbach and others. The confident middle-class ideology of Gustav Freytag's novel *Soll und Haben* (*Debit and Credit* [1855]) cannot be equated with the failed protagonist in the first version of Keller's Bildungsroman (traditional German novel of individual development) *Der grüne Heinrich* (*Green Henry* [1856]), nor can the progressive political stance of Keller's novella *Das Fähnlein der sieben Aufrechten* (*The Banner of the Upright Seven* [1861]) be assimilated to the melancholy tone of his late novel *Martin Salander* (1886). As an additional complication, the literary works that have received the most scholarly attention were not necessarily the books popular with the reading public in the second half of the nineteenth century. The literary market and new forms of cultural commodities such as serialized novels must also be included in an account of the period.

Contexts: Social-Historical, Literary, Philosophical

The political and social conflicts that generated revolution and emancipatory strivings across Europe in the mid-nineteenth century and the restricted development of bourgeois liberalism in German lands in the second half of the century are the reality against which the literary epoch of German Realism must be read. The dual goals of the 1840s, political self-determination for the middle classes and the establishment of German national unity, came uncoupled after the unsuccessful attempts in 1848/1849 to realize the liberal program. The middle classes surrendered their hopes for political autonomy and adjusted their sights toward economic gain. Instead of "freedom and unification," the slogan of the middle classes from the 1850s on was closer to "unification and economic success." Otto von Bismarck's (1815-1898) *Realpolitik* of the 1860s, the pragmatic politics of military strategy, compromise, and power, corresponds to the loss of the political idealism of the pre-1848 period. The decisive opposition to democratization from the autocratic state, exemplified in 1848 by such monarchs as King Friedrich Wilhelm IV of Prussia (1795-1861), continued in the German Empire. In addition, the German middle classes were made increasingly insecure by the position of the working classes. The delayed industrialization in German lands in the early portion of the century and the rapid development after mid-century, especially after the unification in 1871, created a proletariat rarely portrayed in the standard texts of German Realism but implicitly present as a threat in the insistence on the values and life-style of the middle classes. When Julian Schmidt (1818-1886), editor of the influential journal *Die Grenzboten* (*The Border Messengers*) in the 1850s, calls for the portrayal of the "German *Volk* at work" in the contemporary novel, he is propounding a middle-class ethic and not advocating representation of the lower classes. The same rapid expansion of the economy that afforded the middle classes prosperity and a compensatory sphere of activity after the political losses of 1848 generated destabilizing factors. With the founding by Ferdinand Lassalle (1825-1864) of the *Allgemeiner Deutscher Arbeiterverein* (General Association of German Workers) in 1863 and the organization of the *Sozialdemokratische Arbeiterpartei* (Social Democratic Workers' Party) by August Bebel (1840-1913) and Wilhelm Liebknecht (1826-1900) in 1869, a political basis was established for the working classes. Both organizations joined at a congress in Gotha in 1875 to form the *Sozialistische Arbeiterpartei Deutschlands* (Socialist Workers' Party of Germany), and Bismarck's dogged persecution of the socialists through anti-socialist legislation from 1878 to 1890 attests to their oppositional force.

Without having achieved political autonomy, the middle classes therefore found themselves beleaguered from below. It was, after all, the workers in the factories of middle-class industrialists who were organizing. With the upper echelons of governmental, diplomatic, and military bureaucracies in the new Empire following the traditional Prussian patterns acceding the primary role to the upper classes, access to power involved upward assimilation. The entrepreneurs and financiers wielding economic power in the so-called *Gründerzeit* (promoters' boom) after 1871 assumed the attitudes and emulated the life-style of the nobility. This segment formed a bourgeoisie (*Großbürgertum*) distinguishable from the remaining segments of the middle classes, composed of such vocational groups as independent shopkeepers, tradespeople, academics, mid-level bureaucrats and office workers. Despite the rapid economic expansion of the initial *Gründerzeit*, a series of economic crises beginning in 1873 shook confidence at all levels of society. The popularity of Arthur Schopenhauer's (1788-1860) pessimistic philosophy throughout the second half of the century is a sign of the shaky status of what appears on the one hand to be a firm belief in economic and technological progress. The contradictions and conflicts inherent to the period between 1848 and the century's close form the complex reality for the literature of German Realism. A brief consideration of three literary works spanning this period provides paradigmatic insight into the tangled ideological implications of middle-class reality and literary realism in the second half of the century. Friedrich Hebbel's (1813-1863) drama *Maria Magdalena* (1844), Gustav Freytag's novel *Soll und Haben*, and

Theodor Fontane's novel *Frau Jenny Treibel* (1892) span the literary epoch of German Realism and allow an introductory characterization of its varied aspects.

Hebbel's dramas form an exception in the literary history of Realism, which relied mainly on the genre of prose fiction. Doubly exceptional is his drama *Maria Magdalena*, written before the watershed year of 1848. However, the work is a prescient new stage in the development of bourgeois tragedy, representing the development of the middle classes after mid-century. Set in the artisans' milieu of the master carpenter Anton, the drama portrays the decline of his traditional world and values in the face of expanding capitalism. At the same time, the rigid inhumanity of Meister Anton's traditional values is emphasized. His daughter Klara becomes the victim of double jeopardy. Pregnant by the scheming, upwardly mobile Leonhard, she cannot turn to her father for help. His rigid middle-class morality could not tolerate her situation. A former suitor, the only possible rescuer of both Klara and the positive, humanistic side of middle-class values, cannot overcome the dictates of the masculine social code to marry a woman pregnant by another man. Suicide disguised as an accident remains Klara's only option. Even then she fails at the disguise, bringing disgrace upon her father. Meister Anton's closing words presage the historical rupture of his milieu: "I no longer understand the world." The world no longer comprehensible to Meister Anton's value system is the world of the second half of the nineteenth century. Leonhard's treatment of Klara places commercial advancement ahead of humanistic values.

Hebbel's dramas consistently used female protagonists to embody the vicissitudes of his historical moment. For Klara, the patriarchal values which deform her life are not altered by historical change. The nineteenth century is also marked by the struggle of women against the gender system which defined their femininity and limited their public position and opportunities. The liberal public sphere of the 1840s afforded women for the first time in appreciable numbers the opportunity to earn their living by writing. The novels written in the 1840s by Louise Aston (1814-1871), Louise Mühlbach (pseudonym for Clara Mundt [1814-1873]), Ida Hahn-Hahn (1805-1880), or Fanny Lewald (1811-1889) diverge from their post-1848 production in parallel fashion to the diminished emancipatory demands of the male liberal middle-class writers after mid-century. Aston, who had been on the barricades in 1848, quit writing novels; Hahn-Hahn's conversion to Catholicism colors all her later works; Lewald continues to work for women's rights but models her novels on those of Goethe; and Mühlbach writes numerous historical novels in the fashion of the latter part of the century but without sharply emancipatory content. Women's participation in public affairs was sharply curtailed by a Prussian law in 1850 that denied women the right to participate in political organizations. The law was directed at women such as Louise Otto (1819-1895), who used the motto "I am scouting for female citizens for the realm of freedom" for her *Frauen-Zeitung* (*Women's Journal*), founded in 1849. Nevertheless, German women continued to struggle in the realm of practical politics. The first German Women's Confederation (*Allgemeiner Deutscher Frauenverein*) was founded in 1865, and women continued to struggle for the right for education and a professional life in the second half of the century. The existence of a middle-class and a proletarian women's movement by the end of the century is a further testimonial to the socio-economic developments after 1848. Hebbel's *Maria Magdalena* depicts the continuing oppression of women by traditional middle-class morality and by the coming orientation toward economic success; in this regard the drama is somewhat ahead of its time. The middle-class ideology of the immediate post-1848 period is perhaps best reflected in a popular novel of the 1850s which was central to literary debates of that decade concerning realism. Julian Schmidt's words calling for the portrayal of the "German *Volk* at work" became the motto for Gustav Freytag's novel *Soll und Haben*. The redirected priorities of the liberal middle classes after the failures of 1848 are clearly evident in this work, which remained a bestseller well into the next century. Told in a straightforward manner with the sympathy of the narrative voice distinctly on the side of the protagonist, *Soll und Haben* traces the development of Anton Wohlfart. Beginning as an apprentice in the firm of T.O. Schröter, Wohlfart is ultimately rewarded for his prosaic diligence, honesty, and national fervor with partnership in the firm and marriage to Schröter's sister. Wohlfart's adventures on the Polish border in the novel serve to emphasize the superiority of the Germans, while the dependence of the von Rothsattel family on his ingenuity and efforts demonstrates the superiority of middle-class virtues as opposed to the literal and spiritual bankruptcy of the nobility. The von Rothsattel family nevertheless exerts a fascination for the young Anton as he matures. The parallel story of the moral decline of the Jewish figure Veitel Itzig provides a scapegoat for the economic setbacks of the middle classes. Even a brief plot summary reveals nationalistic posturing, anti-Semitism, and a complex relationship between the middle and upper classes. The book's bestseller status and the praise of many contemporaneous critics for its "realism" attest to the functionality of the ideology imparted. In this version of the *Bildungsroman, Soll und Haben* provides for the seamless integration of personal maturation and the social codes of the profit-minded, nationalistically oriented middle classes. A telling comparison can be made with the protagonists of two contemporaneous novels of development, less popular in the 1850s, but central to scholarly accounts of German Realism a century later. Gottfried Keller's Heinrich Lee (*Der grüne Heinrich*) and Adalbert Stifter's Heinrich Drendorf (*Der Nachsommer*) develop out of step with or in utopian distance to the prosaic reality of their age. These two novels, in different ways, maintain an allegiance to humanistic values and a critical detachment from contemporary developments. Such an allegiance coupled with detachment has come to be viewed as characteristic of German Realism. However, it was Freytag's *Soll und Haben* that was at the center of literary debates about realism in literature in the aftermath of 1848. Freytag himself went on to join the National-Liberal party, one of the driving forces in the formation of the German Empire.

Despite the popularity of Freytag's novel and its key position in discussions of literary realism in the 1850s, there is a certain anachronism to the world he portrays. The warehouse manufacturing of T.O. Schröter's firm was already obsolete in 1855, and some of Anton Wohlfart's more innocent and admirable qualities were less characteristic of the success formula for the middle classes than the portrayal in Hebbel's drama. The realism of Freytag's novel pales in comparison with the depiction of commerce and the social costs of capitalism in French novels such as Honoré de Balzac's (1799-1850) *Père Goriot* or in Charles Dickens's (1812-1870) works. While still avoiding representation of the proletariat or the more sordid sides of industrialization, Theodor Fontane's novels of the 1880s and 1890s come closest to the French and English models of literary realism. Fontane, like Hebbel, often concentrates on female characters. His novel *Frau Jenny Treibel* characterizes the social conditions in Wilhelmine Germany and highlights the limited opportunities for women. The title figure began as a shopkeeper's daughter and married an industrialist, a member of the upper middle classes who aspired to titles and the life-style of the nobility in the German Empire. Fontane depicts in Jenny the "purse-strings mentality" behind hypocritical bourgeois lip-service to humanistic ideals in the German Empire. Concerned that her son might marry Corinna, the independently minded daughter of the suitor she once spurned for the status of a better match with *Kommerzienrat* (Commercial Councilor) Treibel, Jenny's machinations reveal the hollowness of her professed sentimental idealism. Corinna, daughter of an academic, is attracted by the power she would have as Leopold's wife but ultimately chooses her cousin Marcel. Marcel is Fontane's positive figure, modelled on Heinrich Schliemann (1822-1890), the merchant turned archaeologist who combined business sense and culture. The future at the novel's end is bright for Marcel, while Corinna will have to be content with the role of companion and spouse, tending the home while he is off on scholarly excavations.

Hebbel's play from the 1840s, Freytag's novel from the mid-1850s, and Fontane's novel from the Wilhelmine period of the German Empire illustrate the complexity of German Realism. Juxtaposing Freytag's *Soll und Haben* with Stifter's *Nachsommer* and Keller's *Grüner Heinrich* raises questions regarding the reading public, the literary market, and nineteenth-century critical discussions in literary and cultural journals. Records show one lending library in Berlin acquiring 2,316 copies of Freytag's novel for its patrons between 1865 and 1898. During the same time period, acquisitions of Keller's novel numbered 630. The nineteenth century saw the development of a mass readership because of advances in transportation and the postal service, increasing urbanization, rising levels of income and literacy, and technological advances such as the introduction of rotary presses. Concomitant developments central to a discussion of Realism are the institution of popular weeklies and family journals, the custom of prepublication of literary works in periodicals, serialized novels, and the position, especially in the early stages, of literary and cultural journals in the discussion of literary realism.

Popular taste in the second half of the century favored adventure stories, family novels, and historical narratives. In many ways, Gustav Freytag's *Soll und Haben* fit the popular pattern. As the century advanced, the turn to historical novels such as Felix Dahn's (1834-1912) *Ein Kampf um Rom* (*A Struggle for Rome* [1876-1878]) corresponded to the conservative nationalism and the interest in the Empire in monumental actions, figures, and events. Serialized novels in family journals and popular weeklies brought fame to authors such as Eugenie Marlitt (a.k.a. Eugenie John [1825-1887]). Marlitt's works, such as *Goldelse* (*Gold Elsie* [1866]), *Das Geheimnis der alten Mamsell* (*The Old Mam'selle's Secret* [1867]), *Im Hause des Kommerzienrats* (*At the Councillor's* [1877]), *Reichsgräfin Gisela* (*Countess Gisela* [1869]), appeared first in the journal *Die Gartenlaube* and then in book form. The journal with the sentimental title *Die Gartenlaube — Illustriertes Familienblatt* (*The Garden Arbor — an Illustrated Family Journal*) was the prime medium for popular literature during its years of publication from 1853 to 1890. The editor Ernst Keil (1816-1878) promulgated the policy "good German *Gemütlichkeit* . . . which speaks to the heart," and circulation reached 382,000 in the weekly editions of 1875. Comparable figures for regional newspapers were about 3,000; Die *Grenzboten*, the leading literary journal in the 1850s, reached about 1,000. *Die Gartenlaube* found competition in the decidedly Christian conservative *Daheim — Ein deutsches Familienblatt mit Illustrationen* (*At Home — A German Family Journal with Illustrations* [1864-1944]) and in *Westermanns illustrirte deutsche Monats-Hefte — Zeitschrift für das gesamte geistige Leben der Gegenwart* (*Westermanns Illustrated German Monthly — a Journal for the Comprehensive Intellectual Life of the Present* [1857-1944; again after 1953]). These journals were not only a forum for popular literature; the Realists Fontane, Wilhelm Raabe (1831-1910), Theodor Storm, Friedrich Spielhagen (1829-1911) wrote for *Westermanns Monatshefte*, and Fontane, Keller, Storm and Ebner-Eschenbach published sporadically in the Stuttgart journal *Über Land und Meer — Allgemeine Zeitung* (*Across Land and Sea — General Journal* [1858-1913]). Particularly influential for the career of the Austrian Marie von Ebner-Eschenbach was the journal *Deutsche Rundschau* (*German Survey*). Although many of these writers led professional lives aside from their novel and story writing, Wilhelm Raabe was able to earn a living over a long period of time by publishing in the periodicals.

A separate phenomenon were the literary journals, which were influential in the first decade and a half of German Realism. Die *Grenzboten*, already mentioned in connection with the novel *Soll und Haben*, was published between 1841 and 1922. With the full title *Die Grenzboten — Zeitschrift für Politik und Literatur* (*The Border Messengers — Journal for Politics and Literatur*), the journal was a central forum for the definition of "realism" in art and literature under the editorship of Gustav Freytag and Julian Schmidt in the immediate post-1848 period. Carried out in essays and reviews, the discussions about realism emphasized the positive, plausible presentation of everyday occurrences in a coherently structured, descriptively detailed narrative. There is a firm rejection of the partisan literature of the political writers who worked for social change in the pre-1848 period. Such authors are charged with a lack of stylistic clarity and with confusing literature with political agitation. Criticism was also handed out to the Romantics for their lack of contact with experiential reality. Models for the *Grenzboten* critics were Dickens and William Makepeace Thackeray (1811-1863), especially in the use of detail and humor. Yet detail for its own sake was deemed insufficient, as outlined in the essays on village literature such as Berthold Auerbach's (1812-1882) *Schwarz-wälder Dorfgeschichten* (*Black Forest Tales* [1843ff.]). Auerbach's stories, which achieved fame throughout Europe and contributed to the development of realistic prose narrative, were criticized for a provincialism which achieves only a partial portrayal of contemporary reality. The aim of the *Grenzboten* version of realism was to provide a version of reality which aimed at the truth of a totality behind individual social phenomena. This program makes sense in the 1850s. The reorientation of the middle classes toward economic success after the political defeat of 1848 was conducive in the 1850s to a dual perspective concerning external, historical reality. Despite the insufficiencies of existing conditions, the potential direction of historical development was viewed optimistically by many segments of the middle classes. It was the positive foundation which was to be presented and reinforced by the literature hailed in *Die Grenzboten* as realistic. The initial theorizing about German literary realism thus retained a basis of idealism, evident as well in another journal published in Leipzig: *Das deutsche Museum — Zeitschrift für Literatur, Kunst und öffentliches Leben* (*The German Museum — a Journal for Literature, Art and Public Life*). Founded by the liberal writer Robert Prutz (1816-1872), *Das deutsche Museum* appeared between 1851 and 1867, suspending publication as Bismarck's strategies began to have the impetus toward national unity which the liberals could support.

The discussions in the 1850s about literary realism, particularly in *Die Grenzboten*, are as close to a cohesive "movement" as German Realism ever came. There is no elaborate aesthetic theory; most of the positions are detailed in practical literary criticism, either reviews or reflective essays. One such essay from the 1850s which has a paradigmatic quality is Fontane's *Unsere lyrische und epische Poesie seit 1848* (*Our Lyric and Epic Literature since 1848*). Written in 1853, the essay proclaims realism to be the characteristic trend of the times. Similar to the positions taken by Freytag and Schmidt, the essay renounces the literary modes of the first half of the century in favor of the "springtime" of realism. The imagery used by Fontane in his essay is instructive. The realist author is seen as a sculptor awakening prestructured forms in a marble quarry. The image corresponds to the *Grenzboten* brand of realism as providing a version of reality which aimed at the truth of a totality behind individual social phenomena. The underlying idealism of this conception of realism is seen in the rejection of an unadorned reproduction of reality in a work of art as being the equivalent of rough ore instead of refined metal. The refinement (*Läuterung*) demanded of German Realism is a distinction attributable partly to the continued influence of the philosophical tradition of idealism and partly to the historical situation after 1848 which retained the realistic ideal of national unity. Both are evident in Fontane's essay of 1853 and in his high praise two years later for Freytag's *Soll und Haben*.

Fontane did not publish his first novel until 1878, well after the founding of the Empire and the initial economic crises of modern Germany. The critical realism of Fontane's narrative works such as *Frau Jenny Treibel* is very different from his affirmative essays of the 1850s. Yet the "refinement," the remnant idealism, remains a central trait of German Realism throughout the century. The concept of *Verklärung* (transfiguration) is used by the writers to designate this notion of "refinement." Friedrich Theodor Vischer (1807-1887), the author of the last systematic aesthetics of the nineteenth century (*Ästhetik oder Wissenschaft des Schönen* [*Aesthetics or the Science of the Beautiful*] — 1846-1857), used the term "Ideal-Realism"; the author Otto Ludwig (1813-1865) and critics since have used the designation "Poetic Realism" to specify the German form of Realism. Surprising in a century where the influence of various materialist philosophies was increasing, literary Realism in German lands retains an idealist tone. The materialist philosophies which presented a critique of metaphysical systems such as that of Georg Wilhelm Friedrich Hegel (1770-1831) were logical in an era when scientific and technological advances were rapid and central to historical developments. The theories of the French philosopher Auguste Comte (1798-1857) formed the foundation for Positivism, which emphasized immediate "positive" facts based on experiential observation as the basis of all knowledge. The materialist methodology of the natural sciences was popularized in German in Ludwig Büchner's (1824-1899) *Kraft und Stoff* (*Force and Material* [1855]), and the ideas of Charles Darwin (1809-1882 [The Origin of the Species — 1859]) were applied to human nature and history in Ernst Haeckel's (1834-1919) *Die natürliche Schöpfungsgeschichte* (*The Natural Story of Creation* [1868]). The antimetaphysical trend in theology had been initiated by David Friedrich Strauß's (1808-1874) *Das Leben Jesu — Kritisch bearbeitet* (*The Life of Jesus in a Critical Rendition* [1835]) and continued in the work of Ludwig Feuerbach (1804-1872 [*Das Wesen des Christentums — The Essence of Christianity*; 1841]; [*Grundsätze einer Philosophie der Zukunft — Principles of a Future Philosophy*; 1843]).

Feuerbach had a lasting influence upon the literary works of Keller, who first met the philosopher during the controversy over his university appointment in Heidelberg. The influence is evident in Keller's emphasis on earthly life and his rejection of Christian doctrines of life after death. Poems such as "Ich hab in kalten Wintertagen" from the cycle "Aus dem Leben" ("Taken from Life") in his 1851 collection *Neuere Gedichte* (*Recent Poems* [1851]) expressly renounce the "deceptive illusion of immortality" and rejoice in nature and temporal existence. Keller is, however, the exception among the German Realists, most of whom were not influenced by the materialist philosophies of the second half of the nineteenth century except in a general emphasis on experiential, everyday reality and a rejection of abstract theorizing. There is little interaction, for example, with the materialist analyses of Karl Marx (1818-1883) and Friedrich Engels (1820-1895) in the literary works of German Realism. The standpoint of Marx and Engels concerning Lassalle's presentation of German history in his drama *Franz von Sickingen:. Eine historische Tragödie* (1858), central to Marxist discussions of literary realism, was without influence upon the contemporaneous development of German Realism.

The idealist tinge remained with German Realism, coloring as well the works of the Realists who did not share the optimism of the discussions and programmatic calls for literary realism in the 1850s. Conditioned by the German philosophical tradition of idealism from Immanuel Kant (1724-1804) to Hegel and shaped by the historical developments after 1848, German Realism diverged in thematic emphases and formal aspects from the other European literatures. The main achievements of all European Realist writers were in the genre of narrative prose, and the German writers whose works have been canonized as the primary texts of German Realism were no exception. The novels and novellas by Gottfried Keller, Theodor Storm, Wilhelm Raabe, Marie von Ebner-Eschenbach, Conrad Ferdinand Meyer, and Theodor Fontane share certain characteristics. At the same time, the wide diversity among them attests to the disparate character of the literary epoch known as German Realism.

Genres

Although narrative prose was the main genre of European Realism, several of the leading German authors wrote lyric poetry as well, and developments in drama and the theater deserve mention. The essential role held by political poetry in the pre-1848 period was of course lost in the second half of the century, but numerous anthologies of poetry were published. A popular school of minor poets gathered in Munich included Paul Heyse (1830-1914) and Emanuel Geibel (1815-1884). Their works do not really belong to the category of Realism but were prevalent on the market in this period. Of the Realist authors considered in this chapter, Keller, Storm, and Meyer made major contributions in the lyric genre. Keller and Storm preferred relatively simple forms and poetic subjects taken from individual experience. Meyer is the primary German contribution to the development of modern poetry in the nineteenth century. His highly symbolical imagery and aestheticized forms make him a precursor of the symbolist poetry of Rainer Maria Rilke (1875-1926) or Stefan George (1868-1933). Fontane also wrote poems, particularly ballads, which are worthy of note. Among other poets of the period, Ada Christen (Christiana von Breden [1844-1901]) deserves mention for her volume *Lieder einer Verlorenen* (*Songs of a Lost Woman* [1868]). This collection displays an unrelenting realism in its portrayal of social misery. Her work was of influence on the Naturalists later in the century.

It is generally said that there was little significant literary drama between Friedrich Hebbel (1813-1863) and the Naturalists. Hebbel's *Maria Magdalena* is his most streamlined drama, as his others convey the complex philosophical system which he developed. The cosmic tragedy which Hebbel perceived in the world and the process of history are generally portrayed at a historical turning point which pits the individual against the emerging world order. The individual plays include realistic psychological motivation for the characters' actions. His post-1848 dramas include *Herodes und Mariamne* (1849) set at the dawn of the Christian era, the political drama *Agnes Bernauer* (1852), and the "German Tragedy" *Die Nibelungen* (1855).

Hebbel's plays were not particularly successful, and drama was not a central genre for German Realism. The publication of Gustav Freytag's *Technik des Dramas* (1863) as a "handbook" for writing dramas only attests to the paucity of qualified dramatists in the age of Realist prose. Similarly, the development of Richard Wagner's (1813-1883) *Gesamtkunstwerk* as a unity of music and language has been aptly designated by Andreas Huyssen as a symptom of the plight of literary drama in this period. Narrative prose was the prime genre of the German Realists, and it is necessary to consider specific forms of German narrative in the nineteenth century.

A striking characteristic of German Realist literature is the predominance of novellas. Longer than a short story but lacking both the length and the epic scope of a novel, novellas were the preferred genre of the German Realists. The dictates of the literary market with its journals and weeklies favored relatively short, self-contained narratives, and the authors complied. The journal *Daheim* once received 300 such manuscripts for consideration in a period of nine months. The advantages and limitations of the novella were also consistent with other cultural and historical variables in the second half of the nineteenth century. Realist theories of narrative emphasized objectivity, yet at the same time the idealist heritage resulted in the retention of a subjective dimension. In aesthetic terms, this tended to reinforce a tightly structured narrative which could present a limited totality. By way of contrast, the European social novels such as Balzac's cycle *La Comédie humaine* or Emile Zola's (1840-1902) *Rougon Macquart* or the works of George Eliot (Ps. for Mary Ann Evans [1819-1880]) were more panoramic, presenting a broad vista of human behavior and social institutions and situations. The German novella typically concentrated on a single event or on the psychological development of a main character. The subjectivity of the event in the eyes of the characters was balanced by an objective narrative voice. Especially Keller wrote cycles of novellas (*Die Leute von Seldwyla* [*The People of Seldwyla* — 1856, vol. 2 1874]; *Das Sinngedicht* (*The Epigram* [1881]); *Züricher Novellen* [1876/1878]). A prescriptive theory of the novella was formulated by Paul Heyse, the first German author to win a Nobel prize (1910) and the editor of the popular anthology *Deutscher Novellenschatz* (*A Treasury of German Novellas* [1871-1876]). The dramatic structure of the novella is often emphasized, as there is often one central conflict. It is significant, however, that the dramatic presentation of conflict is in a restricted narrative form, while drama itself with the public performance of social conflicts is a neglected genre until Naturalism. The primary role of the novella therefore has a social-historical dimension as well, appropriate for the withdrawal of the middle classes from the public political arena after 1848.

Keller's *Romeo und Julia auf dem Dorfe* (*A Village Romeo and Julia*) is deservedly one of the best known novellas of German Realism. A brief analysis of the work, published in 1856 in the first volume of *Die Leute von Seldwyla*, illustrates many traits of the Realist novella. Occasioned by a Swiss newspaper report, Keller's narrative version of Shakespeare's dramatic conflict announces its limited scope in the title. His star-crossed lovers are the children of feuding families disputing ownership of a fallow field between their own two prosperous plots. The title to the untilled field should go to a social outcast, who cannot produce acceptable identity papers. The constellation invokes central issues of economics and social identity. The opening scene of the novella presents the issues in symbolic fashion. The children meet and play in the untilled field, its untamed growth the equivalent of the natural affection between them. Their fathers, each finished with his own field, wordlessly begin to till the fallow ground, flinging the rocks they clear onto a heap. The heap ultimately forms a wall, dividing the two families and representing the injustice done to the owner of the third field. Involved for years in costly litigation against each other, the once prosperous farmers deteriorate. Meeting by chance years later on a bridge, one father nearly kills the other. The same symbolic moment brings the two children together again and ignites their passion and love. The rest of the novella concerns their attempts to realize their love, hampered by economics, social restrictions, and their own internalized social identity and mores. Creating a fantasy for their love, they manage one day of togetherness and a mock wedding presided over by the outcast before committing suicide.

Romeo und Julia auf dem Dorfe engages critical issues in a provincial milieu. With a formalized structure culminating in dramatic symbolic scenes such as the opening section or the struggle of paternal enmity accompanied by the awakening of the children's love on the bridge, the novella is hardly a mimetic portrayal of everyday life in nineteenth-century Switzerland. Yet its "poeticized" realism combines the lofty, supposedly timeless themes of the human spirit with concrete, detailed depiction of circumstance. Indirectly, Keller deals with the reality of his time: the encroachment of social constraints upon individual self-realization, the inescapable force of economic considerations, the definition of community by the exclusion of outsiders. The two-volume cycle of novellas with which *Romeo und Julia* was published contains texts treating similar themes, often in a humorous manner. The materialist philosophies of Keller's time, for example, receive a light-handed treatment in *Spiegel, das Kätzchen* (*Spiegel, the Kitten* [1856]). The cat of the title, gifted with the power of speech, adjusts his ideas in proportion to his diet. Having originally contracted to sell his flesh to a sorcerer in exchange for food, he changes his mind and rebels after he makes a comeback from near starvation. An internal story delineates the incompatibility of love and wealth. The pious identity of a Beguine nun turns out to conceal a witch, and in general the animals in the story are more humane than the human figures. The novella is a mixture of fairy tale and realistic description, the humor an example of an attempt to reconcile idealism and realism or subjective and objective tendencies. Similarly, the village Seldwyla which lends the framework to the two collections of novellas is both a distillation of the contemporaneous Swiss character, existing as an ideal composite rather than as a geographically extant entity, and a village depicted with detailed realistic description, in the tradition of Auerbach's village tales presenting his hometown of Nordstetten. German Realist novellas were limited in scope, often symbolic in presentation, and indirect in their presentation of the issues of their times.

The novels of German Realism also exhibited the mixture of idealism and realism and, in many cases, the humor of the novellas. Despite attempts at a panoramic social novel similar to that of other European literatures, the typical German Realist novel turned inward. Several of the most notable ones followed in the pattern of what literary historians often term the *Bildungsroman*, the novel of individual education and acculturation patterned on Goethe's *Wilhelm Meisters Lehrjahre* (*Wilhelm Meister's Apprenticeship* [1795]). Karl Gutzkow's (1811-1878) *Die Ritter vom Geiste* (*The Knights of the Spirit* [1850-1851]) and the novels of Friedrich Spielhagen (1829-1911) tried to provide an all-encompassing portrait of the social forces of their times, but they did not achieve the lasting reputation of the works by Stifter, Keller, Raabe, Ebner-Eschenbach, Meyer, and Fontane. Fontane's novels of the 1880s and 1890s come the closest to the European tradition of the social novel but without granting a major position to the working class and with the refinement (*Verklärung*) characteristic of German Realism. German novels did not carry subtitles such as "les moeurs de province" (Gustave Flaubert [1821-1880]: *Madame Bovary* [1857]) or "chronique du 19$^{\grave{e}}$ siècle" (Balzac: *La Comédie humaine* [1842-1848]) or "a novel without a hero" (Thackeray: *Vanity Fair* [1848]). Instead, the problematic integration of self and world becomes an emphatically German theme.

Freytag's *Soll und Haben* is an affirmative *Bildungsroman*, tracing the development of Anton Wohlfart from his parents' home through an apprenticeship in the solid middle-class world of commerce. His final stage of maturation is the assumption of the position of partner in the firm of T. O. Schröter and marriage to Sabina Schröter. The personal development coincides with the dictates of social role, and both are presented as compatible with the historical developments of the nineteenth century. Other examples of such Realist novels of individual education and acculturation do not share Freytag's optimism and did not share his bestseller status. However, they have become the more highly acclaimed texts of the period. An example which demonstrates the critical potential of German Realism and once again emphasizes German deviance from European Realism is Adalbert Stifter's *Der Nachsommer*. Published two years after Freytag's text, this Austrian *Bildungsroman* begins with the sentence "My father was a merchant." However, the path of Heinrich Drendorf is not the pattern for middle-class economic success. Set in the late 1820s, the novel scrupulously avoids historical references and bourgeois everyday existence. The education of the main character takes place mainly in the milieu of Baron Risach and Gräfin (Countess) Mathilde, two cultured members of the aristocracy who live on neighboring country estates. Drendorf's repeated visits and his wanderings through nature form the external world of his maturation. His lessons include the regularity of nature, the beneficial harmony of great works of art, and the blessings of human restraint and bridled passions. His harmonious development leads to a marriage with Mathilde's daughter Natalie, and the order and harmony of Stifter's depicted world find a correlate in the sedate prose and the patterned repetition of the very lengthy novel.

The optimism of the ideal development of the protagonist in *Der Nachsommer* is not the affirmative belief of Gustav Freytag's novel. Stifter's utopia is a counterbalance to his age and its conflicts, a measured resistance to the recent social upheavals and the world of commerce, urbanization, and quantified human experience of his times. History and a broader societal realm of activity are banned from the novel. Baron Risach spends much time at the collection and restoration of past works of art; similarly, Stifter's vision is a restorative one, with an implied censure of the social-historical developments of his own century. The realism of his critique lies in the idealism of his vision.

Most of the well known nineteenth-century Realists tried their hand at historical narratives as well. Among them are Stifter's *Witiko* (1865/1867), Keller's novella-collection *Züricher Novellen*, Fontane's *Vor dem Sturm* (*Before the Storm* [1878]), Storm's "chronicles" such as *Aquis submersus* (*Beneath the Flood* [1876]) or *Renate* (1878), Raabe's *Das Odfeld* (*The Odin Field* [1888]) or *Hastenbeck* (1899), and Meyer's novellas plus his only novel *Jürg Jenatsch* (1876). In addition, there were many popular historical narratives in the second half of the century, and the trend is indicative both of historical developments and of German historiography after 1848. With the well known historians Leopold von Ranke (1795-1886), Gustav Droysen (1808-1884), and Heinrich von Treitschke (1834-1896), historicism came to be the dominant school of history writing. Instead of tracing the continuous pattern of unfolding historical progress, attention was paid to the individuality of each historical epoch. Gustav Freytag's *Bilder aus der deutschen Vergangenheit* (*Pictures from the German Past* [1859-66]) offered a series of cultural historical vignettes from Roman times to 1848. His stated purpose was to characterize stages of the German character (*deutsches Gemüt*) with the goal of raising national consciousness. As the century advanced, both historiography and the popularized historical narratives became legitimation for German unification under Prussian hegemony with the exclusion of Austria. After 1871 the fictionalized historical accounts favor portrayal of grandiose historical actions and figures, again serving a legitimating function. With the revival of the legend of Friedrich Barbarossa and the emphasis on medieval emperors or Germanic tribes, the representation of history endorsed the authenticity of the German Empire. Perhaps the most exaggerated example is Wilhelm Jordan's (1819-1904) verse-narrative *Die Nibelunge* (1867-74). And the publication history of Joseph Viktor von Scheffel's (1826-1886) *Ekkehard. Eine Geschichte aus dem zehnten Jahrhundert* (*Ekkehard. A Story from the Tenth Century*) attests to the popularity of the genre; originally published in 1855, the novel was only in its third printing by 1865 but had seen ninety printings by the author's death in 1886. It would seem that German history, like the culture and *Bildung* of Jenny Treibel, had become a commodity in the Empire.

The Writers

A. Adalbert Stifter

Within the broad framework sketched for the novella and novel, each of the main authors of German Realism developed a particular style and individual themes. Adalbert Stifter is considered here briefly as a transitional figure. His Austrian heritage and the adherence to traditional values are evident in the conservative tone of his works. His historical novel *Witiko* sanctions a harmonious conception of historical development, a political parallel to the pattern of individual maturation in *Der Nachsommer*. Tracing the history of Stifter's homeland Bohemia in the twelfth century, *Witiko* was his decided statement countering the revolutionary events of 1848-9. Similar sentiments are found in the preface to his collection of stories entitled *Bunte Steine* (lit. *Colorful Stones* [1853]). Here the emphasis is on the universal regularity present both in nature and in human life and history. Partly because of this "gentle law" (*sanftes Gesetz*; in the preface), Stifter may also be designated as a "Biedermeier" author, and many of his works were published before mid-century. The critic Walter Silz has stated of Stifter: "Optimism about life may be Stifter's wish, but pessimism is his conviction." The apparent naiveté or nostalgia of Stifter's two novels which fall into the period of Realism accompanies a critique of the infirmity of his era. Though the cure is hampered by adherence to a traditional ethos, the diagnosis is astute. Stifter was a favorite author of the later cultural critic and philosopher Friedrich Nietzsche (1844-1900), and Thomas Mann (1875-1955) returned repeatedly to the narratives of the author whom he termed "one of the strangest and wiliest, secretly one of the boldest and most fascinating story-tellers in world literature."

Both of Stifter's novels leave the reader with the impression that a providential force is directing the flow of events. Heinrich Drendorf's steady progress in *Der Nachsommer* is a development of qualities inherent to his character. He learns to respect the intrinsic value of the natural world and of the cultural artifacts he encounters at the Aspernhof of Freiherr von Risach and at the neighboring Rosenhaus. There are no dangerous clashes between protagonist and environment, and he does not suffer negative experiences which deform his character.

B. Gottfried Keller

A contemporaneous novel by Gottfried Keller forms a decided contrast to this pattern. Keller's Heinrich Lee, in *Der grüne Heinrich*, must bear the consequences of his active imagination and his interactions with the varying social realms in which he finds himself. A harmonious reconciliation of the individual and external social reality is not achievable in *Der grüne Heinrich*. The first version of the novel (1855) ends with the protagonist's return to his home town coinciding with his mother's funeral procession, soon followed by his own death. The second version

(1878/1880) has a more unified narrative stance in a first-person narrator and does not end with death. However, the artist Heinrich Lee returns to settle for a bureaucratic job and a friendship with the woman he had once hoped to marry. Despite an undeniable difference in degree, the two endings carry a similar message.

Gottfried Keller
Painting by Karl Stauffer-Bern

The insistence upon everyday social reality and the discrepancy between individual imaginative sensibility and the constraints of prosaic bourgeois existence are recurring themes in the work of the Swiss author Keller. Like the protagonist of his *Bildungsroman*, Keller lost his father early in life, aspired to a career as a painter, and studied at an art academy in Munich. In the 1840s he wrote political poetry, and from 1848 to 1850 he studied at the university of Heidelberg. These years brought the influential exposure to the materialist-atheist philosophy of Ludwig Feuerbach. The first-hand experience of the revolts and violent repression in the Grand Duchy of Baden in 1848-1849 was a formative event in his life. A letter from this period states his intention to abandon the subjective literary form of poetry for genres closer to the conflicts of real life. After further study in Berlin, Keller returned to Zurich in 1855 and lived for a time from his earnings as a writer. From 1861 to 1876 he held the position of chief executive (*Staatsschreiber*) in Zurich. His works include the two novels *Der grüne Heinrich* and *Martin Salander*, the collections of novellas *Die Leute von Seldwyla, Züricher Novellen, Das Sinngedicht*, poetry, and *Sieben Legenden* (*Seven Legends* [1872]), a light-spirited, ironic collection of revised lives of saints with the emphasis on earthly pleasure.

Keller's Swiss heritage is evident in the emphasis on community in his works and in his optimistic didacticism. The democratic liberalism characteristic of Switzerland's historical development is especially evident in the community festivals which play a role in many of Keller's works. In *Der grüne Heinrich*, the Wilhelm Tell celebration is an example of a significant public event which also carries private significance. The same healthy weave of public and private spheres is at the center of the novella *Das Fähnlein der sieben Aufrechten* as well. Written in 1860, this novella mirrors an underlying faith in progressive liberalism. Keller was certainly capable of poking fun at the foibles of his middle-class citizens, but it was an ironic humor based on a confidence in conceivable communal amelioration and personal self-improvement. Throughout Keller's works, humor functions as mediation between the ideal, imaginative realm and the prosaic sphere of everyday social reality. It is a reflection of the function of critical literature in the second half of the nineteenth century. For Keller, the microcosm of the human community was marriage, and the entire cycle of novellas entitled *Das Sinngedicht* revolves around the choice of a suitable partner. Keller's later years, however, were marked by a fading of his optimism. Even the figures in the frame story for *Das Sinngedicht* seem exceptional rather than average, as though Keller had begun to doubt the resilience of the average Swiss citizen. The late novel *Martin Salander* exposes the negative side of the economic success of modernization; the critique here is parallel to the Realists writing in Imperial Germany.

C. Theodor Storm

Keller carried on an extensive correspondence with Theodor Storm, although the two writers never met. Their letters comprise a thoughtful exchange on the craft of writing prose; that their acquaintance remained epistolary reveals the isolated lives of many authors in the absence of a central cultural site in nineteenth-century Germany. The regional character of the Austrian Stifter or the Swiss Keller is even more pronounced in Theodor Storm. His poetry and prose are inextricably tied to the North Sea region near his hometown of Husum. Although provincial, his life was nevertheless touched by history. In 1850 he was forced into exile because of his opposition to the Danish occupation of Schleswig. When Denmark relinquished the duchies of Schleswig and Holstein in hostilities with Prussia in 1864, Storm returned home. Trained as a lawyer, he held several official judiciary positions before retiring from public life in 1880.

Theodor Storm was a lyric poet and the author of over 50 novellas. His poems are melancholy in tone and regional in character, with a special focus on the seascapes around his hometown of Husum. In his poetry, the potency of memory is often played out against the transitory character of existence. A similar mood and related themes characterize his prose fiction as well. Particularly in his early novellas and stories there is a sentimental nostalgia and a somber awareness of the erosion of love and youthful hope with the passing of time. *Immensee* (1850) is the best known example of the early lyrical novellas. G. Wallis Field has termed the next period of Storm's prose that of his "problem-novellas." In works such as *Auf dem Staatshof* (*At the State Court* [1856/1858]), *Späte Rosen* (*Late Roses* [1859]), *Im Schloß* (*In the Castle* [1862]), or *Veronika* (1861), a psychological and social realism predominates over the Romantic-lyrical character of the early stories. The father-son conflict evident in such novellas as *Carsten Curator* (1878) or *Hans und Heinz Kirch* (1882) is often said to reverberate with personal themes from Storm's own life. At the same time, these works emphasize the failure of human lives to interconnect in a broader sense. A persistent theme in *Hans und Heinz Kirch* is arriving "too-late," the belated nature of insight and concern for others as well as self-understanding. There is a pessimistic critique of his age as well as biographical undertones in Storm's works.

Theodor Storm ca. 1879.
Painting by Marie von Wartenberg

Such texts as *Auf dem Staatshof* or *Im Schloß* are historical in the manner in which the historical process is presented through family chronicle. Both convey the progressive aspects of middle-class liberalism. Storm's more specifically historical narratives include *Aquis submersus, Renate* (1878), and *Eekenhof* (1879). All three of these use a frame-story (*Rahmenerzählung*) and relate an incident from the seventeenth century in the internal, historical narrative. In *Aquis submersus*, the framework is partially provided by a personal memoir, itself susceptible to deterioration with time. Even the portraits preserved from the internal story are preyed upon by worms. The result for the reader is a sense of the historical vulnerability of all stories, a sense of history as the inexorable passage of time.

Storm's rightfully most famous work is his last novella *Der Schimmelreiter* (*The Rider on the White Horse* [1888]). Here the complex narrative structure involves a triple frame and an internal story. The author-narrator recalls a story once extant in his grandmother's house, but since lost. That story was narrated by a traveller who took refuge from a storm in the 1830s and was told the internal story by a schoolteacher. The schoolteacher's rational perspective interrupts the story at several points, but even the vantage point of the schoolteacher is exposed to the elemental force of nature as the storm continues to pound the sea outside. The internal narrative relates the rise of Hauke Haien to the powerful position of *Deichgraf* (dike reeve in the North Sea milieu). His insistence on mastery, both of the humans in his environment and the forces of nature, ultimately brings his downfall. The title of the story comes from his ghost, still seen riding the dikes in stormy weather on a white horse (*Schimmel*). In many ways, the novella is typical of the literature of the *Gründerzeit* in its portrayal of exceptional figures and monumental forces. Yet, as Jost Hermand has convincingly analyzed in his delineation of literature of the *Gründerzeit*, an implicit critique is also evident in the work. Hauke Haien ultimately fails, and his neglect of his wife and marriage may be read as a reminder of the dangers of self-importance and a rapid rise to power. Even in the regional restriction of his narrative prose, Theodor Storm confronted the issues of his times.

D. Wilhelm Raabe

The work of Wilhelm Raabe experienced a scholarly re-evaluation beginning in the 1970s, and his earlier reputation as a writer of humorous idylls and gently provincial ethics has been sharply revised. As with Storm, even his more limited narratives often engage crucial aspects of the second half of the nineteenth century. Renewed scholarly interest in the over 65 novels, novellas, and stories written by Raabe has especially concentrated upon the modern traits of his narrative style. Particular attention has been paid to the techniques of multiple narrative perspectives and temporal manipulation. His astoundingly complex first novel *Die Chronik der Sperlingsgasse* (*The Chronicle of Sparrow Alley* [1856]) and his late novels from the Braunschweig period have received much scholarly acclaim and careful investigation. The revised evaluation stands in sharp contrast to the most dismal period of Raabe's reception as a German author: the enthusiastic complicity of the Raabe Society with fascist ideology during the Third Reich. Founded in 1910 as "The Society of the Friends of Wilhelm Raabe," the organization became the second largest of all German literary societies, surpassed only by the Goethe Society. With anti-democratic and anti-Semitic essays appearing in the *Mitteilungen für die Gesellschaft der Freunde Wilhelm Raabes* (*Communications for the Society of Friends of Wilhelm Raabe*) as early as 1921, the naming of a Nazi schoolteacher as the president in 1932 marked the complete assimilation of the journal to Nazi policies and politics. The Nazi co-option of Raabe encumbered his post-war reputation abroad and provides a sobering example of the scope of the destructive developments in twentieth-century German history.

Wilhelm Raabe himself was an informed participant in his own historical moment. He was a stalwart nationalist and proponent of the pragmatic liberal goal after 1848 of German unification under Prussian leadership. In 1860, Raabe became a member of the *Nationalverein,* the precursor of the National-Liberal party. Joining a year after its establishment, he attended the conventions in 1860 and 1861 and had harsh criticism for proponents of any form of regional patriotic particularism. The founding of the German Empire in 1871 was a momentous event for the author. At the same time, he was disrespectfully critical of trends to momumentalize German culture. In his novella *Der Dräumling* (*The Dräumling Swamp* [1872]), Raabe recalls the ardent celebration of the Schiller centenary in 1859. This event combined political aspirations for reform with celebration of the cultural heritage. In his satirical portraits of the townspeople of Paddenau and the visiting Hamburg businessman whose materialist orientation holds no truck with ideals, Raabe well captures the contradictions of German historical development. From the vantage point of the 1870s, he provides the necessary critique of a trend which became cultural chauvinism while still recognizing the enlightened ideals of humanity inherent to the tradition of German Classicism. Similar attention to the disturbing developments accompanying historical "progress" is found in such works as *Pfisters Mühle* (*Pfisters Mill* [1884]), which treats industrial pollution in the *Gründerzeit.*

Wilhelm Raabe's biography and literary *oeuvre* are marked by two major relocations in his life: the move to Stuttgart in 1862 and then to Braunschweig in 1870. He himself designated three periods in his writing: his early narratives written in Berlin and Wolfenbüttel, the Stuttgart works, and the Braunschweig novels, novellas, and stories. He was a prolific writer, perhaps partly because he made his living solely by writing. Raabe's *oeuvre* is variable and requires a differentiated evaluation. The popularity of specific works is not a reliable guide to the author's talents or to the quality of the individual texts. One of his most widely read works, for example, was *Der Hungerpastor* (*The Hunger Pastor* [1863-4]). The novel is a lumbering *Bildungsroman* with parallel Gentile and Jewish figures reminiscent of *Soll und Haben* and an overstated metaphorical structure driven by the motif of "hunger." The heavy-handed technique stands in decided contrast to the subtle narrative complexity of novels such as *Die Akten des Vogelsangs* (*The Documents of the Birdsong* [1896]). Here the constellation of staid bourgeois narrator and aberrant figure prefigures Thomas Mann's *Dr. Faustus* (1947).

Much has been made of Raabe's affinity for the pessimistic philosophy of Schopenhauer, whom he began to read in the late 1860s. Characteristic of all of Raabe's narratives is a fundamentally somber tone. There is a persistent awareness of the fragility of human lives and ethical values. The acquiescent tranquillity of the narrator of his first novel is the gentle attitude of dignity which is present in many of Raabe's works. Yet this first novel, *Die Chronik der Sperlingsgasse*, begins: "It is truly an evil age! Laughter has become dear in the world, furrowing one's brow, and sighing cheap indeed." The endangerment of individual existence finds expression throughout Raabe's works in two main forms. The Braunschweig novel *Unruhige Gäste* (*Restless Guests* [1885]) refers in its subtitle to the "saeculum," and the juxtaposition of imperiled individual humanity and the inexorable influence of the "saeculum" is a theme throughout Raabe's works. His most recent biographer Jeffrey L. Sammons has perceptively defined the "saeculum" as "the inescapable environment of human life and society," referring to "the polarity of secular worldliness and spiritual value." A second main form which the pessimistic insights take is the figure of the outsider, often united with a few others against the overly materialistic values of their environment. In the late novels of the Braunschweig period, this constellation receives increasingly skeptical treatment. The humor characteristic of much of Raabe's *oeuvre* results from rueful insight into the discrepancy between the hopes and potential of men and women and the circumstances beyond their control.

E. Marie von Ebner-Eschenbach

Marie von Ebner-Eschenbach occupies an unusual position within the middle-class orientation of German Realism. Her father was a baron who became a count through another marriage, and she later married a baron. Her background and lifestyle were that of the nobility, making her an exception among the authors being considered in this chapter. Nevertheless, Ebner-Eschenbach's thematic concerns and narrative style place her firmly within the tradition of German Realism. Her prose works are characterized by a social-ethical liberalism. Keenly observant of the social ills of her age, she responded with an empathetic sense of responsibility. Marie von Ebner-Eschenbach was able to place faith in the basic good in human nature, which she attempted to awaken with her stories and novels. The narratives provide sharply realistic depictions of the misery of a rural proletariat which she knew from first-hand experience. The village tales are a contrast to the idealized, often sentimental stories by Berthold Auerbach, as Ebner-Eschenbach shared the sense of determinism, heredity, and milieu characteristic of writers at the end of the century. Yet her humanistic optimism distinguished her from the contemporaneous writers of Naturalism. Within the traditional confines of Austrian culture she addressed members of her own class, urging them to assume a social-ethical responsibility for progressive change. Two of her well known aphorisms describe the import of Marie von Ebner-Eschenbach's work:

Not to participate in the intellectual progress of one's time is to be morally behind the times.

There would be no social plight if the rich had always been humane to others.

The author's early years were spent on the prosperous Catholic Moravian family estate Zdislawice in what is today Czechoslovakia. Her initial languages were Czech and French, and her family (Dubsky) was loyal to the Hapsburgs. Her autobiography *Meine Kinderjahre* (*My Childhood Years* [1905]) gives a detailed account of the life of the landed nobility in the Austrian Empire. It was hardly customary for women of her class to become professional writers, and Ebner-Eschenbach braved the prejudice, advice, and critique of her family and associates as she began to write. In 1848 she married her cousin Baron Moritz von Ebner-Eschenbach (1815-1898), and they lived in the provinces for a decade before moving to Vienna. Early support for her literary efforts came from the Austrian playwright Franz Grillparzer (1791-1872), and after initial attempts at lyric poetry in French and German, she began to write dramas. Her plays from the 1860s and 1870s include historical dramas in the style of Grillparzer and Schiller. In several of them, a female figure is the main focus. The best known of her dramatic efforts was the historical tragedy *Maria Stuart in Schottland*, which was performed in 1861 under the direction of Eduard Devrient (1801-1877) in Karlsruhe. Her last completed historical tragedy, in classical blank verse, was *Marie Roland*, based on the memoirs of the Girondist figure from the French Revolution. None of the dramas, including her society plays and comedies, were well received. It was with the turn to prose fiction in the 1870s that she began to establish her reputation as a writer. One of her later stories, *Ohne Liebe* (*Without Love* [1888]), eventually reached the stage in dramatic form. It was performed in 1897 under the direction of Paul Schlenther in the *Freie Bühne*, the forum of the Naturalists in Berlin.

Although Marie von Ebner-Eschenbach was not politically active in the German women's movement in the latter nineteenth century, she maintained a network of contacts with other women writers and thinkers. Prominent among them were Luise von François (1817-1893), Betty Paoli (Barbara Elisabeth Glück [1814-1894]), Enrica von Handel-Mazzetti (1871-1955), and Ida von Fleischl-Marxow (1824-1899). Her advocacy of women's issues is characterized by several of her aphorisms, including the following:

A smart woman has millions of born enemies: all the dumb men.

When a woman first learned to read, the "woman question" began.

Journals associated with the German and Austrian women's movements such as the *Centralblatt des Bundes deutscher Frauenvereine* (later *Die Frauenfrage*; *Central Journal of the Union of German Women's Associations* — later *The Woman Question*), *Die Frau* (*The Woman*), and *Dokumente der Frauen* (*Documents of Women*) acknowledged the contributions of Ebner-Eschenbach as a role model. She was an active member of the *Verein der Schriftstellerinnen und Künstlerinnen in Wien* (*Association of Women Writers and Artists in Vienna*) and left the largest bequest of any to this organization in her will. Toward the end of her life Ebner-Eschenbach received many honors and distinctions, becoming the first woman ever to receive an honorary doctorate from the University of Vienna. This was in 1900, only three years after the first women were admitted with full rights to study in the philosophical faculty. In the first decade of the twentieth century, she was made an honorary member of the Schiller Foundation and the Goethe Society, and the annual Marie von Ebner-Eschenbach Prize was established.

The honors and recognition were based on her prose writings: stories, novels, and aphorisms. Her initial volume of stories (1875) and the longer narrative of the life of a household maid Božena (1876) met with only modest success. Her original publisher Cotta abandoned her, and it was the wisdom of Julius Rodenberg (Ps. for Lulius Levy [1831-1914], editor of the journal *Deutsche Rundschau*, which guaranteed her access to the reading public. The best known of her works are the tales in the two volumes *Dorf- und Schloßgeschichten* (*Village and Manor Tales* [1883]) and *Neue Dorf- und Schloßgeschichten* (*New Village and Manor Tales* [1886]), and the longer narratives *Das Gemeindekind* (*The Child of the Parish* [1887]) and *Unsühnbar* (*Beyond Atonement* [1889]). The title "village and manor tales" characterizes the world of many of Ebner-Eschenbach's narratives. It is the complex interdependence of the peasantry and the landed nobility in the Habsburg empire which she addresses. The Peasant Revolt in Galicia of 1846 plays a direct role in the stories *Der Kreisphysikus* (*The District Doctor*) and *Jakob Szela*. Her narratives convey the reality of life among the peasant and rural working class and sharply criticize the oppressive practices of the nobility. One of the best examples of her themes and narrative style is the novella *Er laβt die Hand küssen* (*He Sends Obedient Greetings*). The frame story has a relatively liberal count telling his conservative neighbor, who is also a countess, a story from the time of his grandmother. The purpose of his tale is to convert his listener to more modern, tolerant views. The inner tale condemns the "good old days" of serfdom and inhumane control by the estate owners over the lives of their peasants. It also provides a realistic depiction of rural life in the story of Mischka and his love for the mother of his child. The loyal love of Mischka contrasts with the servile attitude of the manor servant Fritz. The positive voices in the novella represent reason, progress, and humanity. The deaths of Mischka and his lover were unnecessary and should stand as a lesson to a "modern" aristocracy. By telling the story, which also reflects upon the conventions of realistic narrative, the count atones for the harsh regime of his grandmother and provides a model of historical progress. The tale is typical of Ebner-Eschenbach's social-ethical liberalism and confidence in personal responsibility and insight.

Related emphases are evident in two other of the best known stories. *Das Gemeindekind* presents in the main character Pavel a representative of the most disastrous influence of heredity and milieu who nevertheless develops into a productive human being. And the story *Krambambuli*, with the title figure of a dog caught between two masters, depicts both the increasing human isolation in the nineteenth century and the necessity of humane treatment of animals. For her animal stories such as *Krambambuli* or *Die Spitzin*, Marie von Ebner-Eschenbach received a medal from the *Weltbund für Tierschutz* (*World League for the Protection of Animals*) in 1912. Her concerns were therefore those of her century and of the Austrian empire in transition to modern times.

F. Conrad Ferdinand Meyer

Conrad Ferdinand Meyer, like Gottfried Keller, was Swiss. Meyer himself characterized one of the major differences between the two writers as being Keller's penchant for humble topics and ordinary people as opposed to his own insistence upon "History" with the grand figures of kings, generals, and heroes. Meyer's ten novellas and one longer narrative were all written after 1873 and are representative of the interest in the German Empire in fictional portrayals of grandiose historical actions and monumental figures. The cathartic moment of tragedy is important in his work. At the same time, the ethical questions typical of Marie von Ebner-Eschenbach form an important dimension of Meyer's prose writings. In addition to the narratives, Conrad Ferdinand Meyer's poems may be considered an inaugural moment in German contributions to the modern tradition in European poetry.

Meyer's biography reveals crises and extended depressive periods. Born into a wealthy family in Zurich, he lost his father at the age of fourteen. Precariously introverted as a young man, he relied upon his mother until her suicide in 1856 and then upon his sister Betsy until finding a caretaker in his wife Luise Ziegler Meyer (1837-1915) in 1875. Two lengthy stays in asylums in 1852-1853 and 1892-1893 attest to the extent of his psychological distress. Clearly destined for a literary life, Meyer did not publish his first book until 1864. This was a volume of 20 ballads published anonymously and republished under his own name in 1867. His first narrative was *Huttens letzte Tage (Hutten's Last Days)*, published in 1871. This epic verse narrative established his reputation in the newly founded German Empire, and the Swiss author became an admirer of Bismarck and increasingly oriented toward a reading public in the Empire. The sixteenth-century figure of Ulrich von Hutten (1488-1523) was an appropriate choice for the nationalism of the German reading public.

Meyer's first prose novella was *Das Amulett*, published in 1873. The historical period in this initial prose work was the Counter-Reformation, and several of Meyer's subsequent stories are set in the Renaissance and Baroque eras. A novella set in twelfth-century England which earned high praise from Realist writers and critics such as Theodor Storm, Gottfried Keller, and Julian Schmidt was *Der Heilige (The Saint)*. Published in three installments in the journal *Deutsche Rundschau* in 1879-1880, it tells the story of Thomas Becket (c. 1120-1170). Becket was Chancellor of England to the tyrannical King Henry II (1154-89), whom he, as the Archbishop of Canterbury, later opposed. When his one-time aide becomes an advocate of a higher authority and no longer supports him in his struggle with the Church, Henry has Becket murdered in the Canterbury Cathedral. Thomas Becket, later raised to sainthood, triumphs historically. Henry is forced to do penance at his grave in 1174, four years after his martyrdom. The figures represent the major medieval forces of the Crown and the Church, and the novella is a prime example of Meyer's historical narratives. The tragic shaping of the ethical dimension by death is typical for the conception of history in Meyer. An additional element in the ethical and psychological motivation of the story is Henry's seduction of Becket's daughter by the sister of a Moorish caliph. The daughter had been raised in hiding, and Henry's discovery leads to her death. Complex personal loyalties and emotions are thus added to the historical plot. Meyer distances the intensity of the material through his narrative frame, as the story is told by the simple figure of Hans on the day of Becket's elevation to sainthood.

The narrative technique in *Der Heilige* and the focus on historical personages and events of great import are characteristic of Meyer's most mature work. One of the most complex narrative frames is to be found in *Die Hochzeit des Mönchs (The Monk's Wedding* [1883/1884]). Dante narrates the story of a renitent (defrocked) monk and his moral degeneration. Many of the characters resemble members of his audience, and various figures take over the narration at various points in the story. Meyer's one novel-length narrative, *Jürg Jenatsch*, draws upon the history of the Swiss canton of Graubünden in the seventeenth century and reflects an ambivalence on the issue of political expedience versus ethical accountability. The theme has a clear relevance to contemporary questions in Bismarck's German Empire.

The poetry of Conrad Ferdinand Meyer is his other main contribution to the literary history of the second half of the nineteenth century. The initial volume of ballads from 1864/1867 was followed in 1871 by the volume *Romanzen und Bilder* (*Ballads and Images*) and then by his first major volume of poems *Gedichte* (*Poems*) in 1882. Meyer's poetry forms the transition from the German lyric tradition emphasizing experience and spontaneous subjective emotion (*Erlebnislyrik*) to symbolist poetry in the European mode of the turn of the century. His innovative themes and techniques make use of symbolic images. Often repeated motifs include water, sails, boats, clouds, and the evening star. Although Meyer's poems do not transform individual lived experience into lyric form, his most famous poems often convey human situations such as calm resignation — "Im Spätboot" ("Nocturnal Boat"), "Eingelegte Ruder" ("Oars at Rest") — or a moment of harmony — "Zwei Segel" ("Two Sails"). Meyer's most famous poem, "Der römische Brunnen" ("The Roman Fountain"), underwent many revisions, and the final version stands itself as a total image of balanced movement. Meyer's lyric heritage was picked up by Rainer Maria Rilke and Stefan George in forms of Symbolism which far transcend German Realism.

G. Theodor Fontane

Theodor Fontane was also a lyric poet who broke with the tradition of *Erlebnislyrik*, but in a very different fashion from Conrad Ferdinand Meyer. Fontane's most memorable contributions in poetry were in ballad form. Influenced by the English and Scottish traditions, Fontane's best ballads have a conversational tone, often with a humorous or ironic twist. His Prussian ballads portraying famous figures achieve in this manner a distanced patriotism, characteristic of the author's suspicion of all fanaticism. However, it is not as a lyric poet that Theodor Fontane established his place among the German Realists. His career as a novelist began very late in his life, but his social novels depicting life in Berlin and the province of Brandenburg earned him a lasting reputation among the European realists. Fontane's narratives depart from the strong German traditions of the novella and the *Bildungsroman*. His works most closely approach the conventions of the realist social novels in France, England, and Russia. Although a contemporary of the older generation of German Realist writers, Theodor Fontane produced novels of his society and times which found their successor in twentieth-century novelists such as Thomas Mann. It is perhaps not coincidence that Fontane's last completed novel *Der Stechlin* appeared in 1897, the same year in which Thomas Mann began the story which eventually became *Buddenbrooks* (1901). The title of Mann's novel itself contains a Fontane reference, as the family name is that of a minor figure in Fontane's *Effi Briest* (1894/1895). Theodor Fontane is therefore an appropriate figure for concluding a survey of the literary epoch of Realism. Firmly rooted in the nineteenth century, his works nevertheless reveal a cosmopolitanism and narrative style which surpass the limitations of much of German Realist prose.

Born a contemporary of the earliest Realist writers, Fontane participated at the end of his life in the diversity of cultural phenomena characterizing the end of the nineteenth century. His review of Gerhart Hauptmann's (1862-1946) incendiary play *Die Weber* (*The Weavers* [1892]), for example, was crucial for the reception of Naturalist drama.

Theodor Fontane's long life was a rich and varied one. Born into the Huguenot community in Berlin, he was trained as an apothecary and worked in that profession until 1849. His early political sympathies were liberal-democratic, although a formative literary influence was his association with the Berlin literary circle *Tunnel über der Spree* (The Tunnel Above the Spree). This group of writers tended to be more conservative and also championed a separate aesthetic realm. Throughout his life, Fontane advocated the power of the literary to "refine" reality (*Verklärung*). He is often said to assume the position of the detached observer, and irony is a much discussed element of his narrative style. However, it is important to emphasize the socially critical import of his novels and ballads. His was a paradoxically intimate detachment, as he portrayed with exactitude and critical familiarity the foibles of his age.

Besides the novels and poetry, Fontane also authored travelogues and journalistic reportage, including war correspondence. Extended visits to England were immensely formative, and his non-fictional writings include many essays and articles on English culture. His attachment to his home region is clear in the multi-volume *Wanderungen durch die Mark Brandenburg* (*Excursions through the Mark Brandenburg* [1862-1882]), a sensitive depiction and history of Brandenburg. The complexity of Fontane's politics is evident in his journalistic affiliations; in 1870 he switched from the conservative *Kreuzzeitung* to writing theater reviews for the liberal *Vossische Zeitung*. Fontane's assessment of Bismarck is similarly complex, according to Walter Müller-Seidel a mixture of admiration and incisive critique. Thomas Mann once characterized Fontane as regarding everything from at least two sides, and the statement does not so much suggest ambiguity as a perceptive sense of the complexity of politics and society at the end of the nineteenth century.

At the age of sixty Theodor Fontane published his first novel, and the remaining twenty years of his life brought the writing on which his lasting literary reputation was based. While some of his novels have a historical setting, the most acclaimed are narratives of his contemporary social milieu in imperial Germany, most often set in Berlin. *Vor dem Sturm* and *Schach von Wuthenow* (*A Man of Honor: Schach von Wuthenow* [1883]) are set in the Napoleonic era, and Fontane also contributed to the genre of *Kriminalromane* (detective/criminal novels) with *Unterm Birnbaum* (*Under the Pear Tree* [1885]) and *Quitt* (1891). But his best known works are the social novels written after 1888, including *Irrungen Wirrungen* (*Delusions, Confusions* [1888]), *Frau Jenny Treibel*, *Effi Briest*, and his last completed novel *Der Stechlin*. One of the main characters in *Effi Briest* makes a statement which well characterizes the subject material of Fontane's social novels: "One is not simply an individual, one belongs to a totality, and we constantly have to take that social totality into account; we are altogether dependent upon it." The focus of Fontane's novels of imperial Germany and Berlin society is the realm of human activity and interaction bounded by social conventions, values, and norms. His novels do not have extravagant plots, as the emphasis is on language in conversation and social ritual. Witty, apparently informal dialogue forms the substance of a Fontane novel, and yet it is this casual conversation which provides insight into the social rituals which shape the "social totality" and the individuals dependent upon it. The corresponding narrative technique is one of multiple perspectives, as all issues are reflected in conversation and dialogue and refracted in a network of positions belonging to the individual characters.

Several of Fontane's novels deal with marriage and treat sympathetically the restricted sphere of female experience in the late nineteenth century. In *Effi Briest*, the title figure is married off at a young age to a successful provincial nobleman, once the suitor of her mother. Isolated and stifled, she drifts into a brief affair which she does not want. Years later, her husband finds incriminating letters from that past period and regards himself as bound by social custom to a specific course of action. Without really desiring to do so, he kills the former lover in a duel, exiles Effi from his house, and thoroughly stifles their daughter's affection for her mother with an exaggeratedly strict, socially proper upbringing. The conversations and discussions among the characters in the novel emphasize the manner in which all are defined and restricted by a rigid social structure of convention. The connections to contemporary German society are abundantly clear, as the rise of the husband's career and his neglect or manipulation of the emotional needs of his younger bride are related to the shadowy presence of Bismarck in several references throughout the novel. Effi's fate is more severe than the restricted marriage of Corinna at the end of *Frau Jenny Treibel*; she dies soon after her parents finally relent and allow her to return to their estate. Fontane's is not an angry novel, but rather a somber portrayal of his society in the late nineteenth century.

The Naturalists, writing social dramas contemporary with Fontane's novels, are angry. Theirs is a literature of outspoken social protest, a protest which Fontane recognizes in his theater reviews. Yet Fontane's novels carry the social critique with humor, tolerance, and the more temperate *Verklärung* of German Realism. Perhaps the words of Melusine, one of Fontane's most extraordinary women characters, are an appropriate summary for the position of the German Realists. In *Der Stechlin* she states: "To the extent that it may deserve it, we should love the old; but we should truly live for the new." Her words best represent the dilemma, the limitations, and the legacy of German Realism between 1848 and the end of the century.

12 Naturalism

Siegfried Mews

Historical Background

When Gerhart Hauptmann's (1862-1946) "social drama" *Vor Sonnenaufgang (Before Daybreak)* opened at the Berlin *Freie Bühne* (Free Stage) on 20 October 1889, it was generally perceived to signify a departure from traditional theatrical fare. In retrospect, the performance of Hauptmann's play marks the breakthrough of a new theatrical style and the establishment of Hauptmann, until then virtually unknown, as the foremost dramatist of a movement that came to be known as Naturalism. Hauptmann himself called the opening night a "battle" that pitted traditionalists against the *Jüngstdeutschen* (Youngest Germans) or *Das jüngste Deutschland* (The Youngest Germany), as the modernists referred to themselves in pointed reference to the group of liberal, progressive writers during the 1830s such as Heinrich Heine (1797-1856) and Karl Gutzkow (1811-1878) known as *Junges Deutschland* (Young Germany). Critics, who had witnessed the event, went so far as to compare it with a similarly significant opening night that had taken place some fifty years earlier in Paris, that is, the premiere of Victor Hugo's verse drama *Hernani* (1830) that resulted in the demise of French Classicism and the triumph of the new Romanticism, a movement, to be sure, quite different from German Romanticism.

Although both the Paris and Berlin audiences seemed to know what they were cheering or booing, the literary terms Classicism, Romanticism, and Naturalism are more easily used than defined. In fact, as Gerhard Schulz has noted, German Naturalism has been characterized as a movement that is not "unequivocal" since it represents an "interlacing of different tendencies and trends which have as common denominator solely the intention of turning away from the conventional literature of the 'seventies and representing accurately and veraciously what is seen as a new reality." This new socio-economic reality evolved in part because of changes brought about in the political realm, notably the defeat of France in the Franco-Prussian War and, in 1871, the subsequent unification of German states that formed the new German Empire. The *Reichsgründung* (founding of the Empire) was essentially the work of the dominant political figure of the 1870s and 1880s, the royal Prussian and then imperial Chancellor Otto von Bismarck (1815-1898). It resulted in a widespread mood of national euphoria that induced the former liberal bourgeoisie to abandon the idea of a unified, democratic Germany — the goal of the bourgeois revolutions of 1848. For the new Bismarckian Reich afforded the bourgeoisie the opportunity for economic expansion and the chance to engage in profitable laissez-faire capitalism that was supported by tax laws favorable to the bourgeoisie and laws designed to keep organized labor in check. Speculation and reckless capitalism were the hallmarks of the *Gründerzeit* (founding era), a period in which large fortunes were amassed (and lost), and the wealthy enjoyed a grandiose life style that was marked by the ostentation of the parvenu. The bourgeoisie's gain in economic opportunity was counterbalanced by its insignificant role in politics; in the Prussian-German Empire, political influence was exerted by the staunchly conservative groups of the aristocracy, the landed gentry, and the military.

Because of rapid industrialization, a proletariat formed; the proletarian masses lived in poverty and in the squalor of large tenements in the big cities. Notably Berlin, the capital of the Empire, attracted migrants from the countryside on a massive scale. Whereas Karl Marx (1818-1883) and Friedrich Engels (1820-1895) propagated socialist ideas from abroad, indigenous efforts to address the "social question" that in the eighties began to concern the Naturalists contributed to the formation of Ferdinand Lassalle's (1825-1864) *Allgemeiner Deutscher Arbeiterverein* (General German Workers' Association) in 1863 and, in 1869, the Marxist *Sozialdemokratische Partei* (Social Democratic Party), founded by August Bebel (1840-1913) and Wilhelm Liebknecht (1826-1900). Despite Bismarck's *Sozialistengesetze* (anti-socialist laws), in effect from 1878 to 1890, that proscribed socialist publications and meetings, the Social Democrats continued to gather strength and to elect their members to parliament, the *Reichstag*. In 1890, the year of Bismarck's dismissal as Chancellor, they gained thirty-five seats.

International socialism was one of the intellectual currents and social theories that influenced the views of Naturalistic writers, and the advances made by science induced skepticism toward a religiously or metaphysically grounded world view. Such a skeptical-critical attitude towards religion was also promulgated by Friedrich Nietzsche (1844-1900) who, despite his quasi-aristocratic and individualistic stance, shows affinities with the Naturalists in his pronounced anti-bourgeois sentiments and his psychologizing tendencies. But especially Charles Darwin's *The Origin of Species by Means of Natural Selection* (1859) and *The Descent of Man* (1871), which postulated evolution instead of creation and posited the animalistic-instinctual elements of human nature, exerted influence on Naturalism. Popularized in Germany by Ernst Haeckel (1834-1919), Darwin's works implicitly and explicitly minimized the individual's spiritual essence and fostered a scientific orientation. A telling example of the endeavors among Naturalists to base their new literary aesthetic on science is provided by Wilhelm Bölsche (1861-1939) in his programmatic manifesto, *Die naturwissenschaftlichen Grundlagen der Poesie* (*The Scientific Foundations of Poetry* [1887]), in which he summarily stated, "Science forms the basis of our entire modern thinking." Bölsche's manifesto concluded that only scientific observation and the application of the laws of science would further the development of modern literature. It is, of course, no coincidence that Bölsche's statements recall pronouncements made by Emile Zola (1840-1902), the influential leader of the French Naturalistic school.

Literary Predecessors

The influence that Zola began to exert in Germany during the seventies points towards a curious paradox: whereas France had been militarily defeated, Germany's newly gained political prominence and economic prosperity did not result in a comparable rejuvenation of the arts and a flowering of literature — a state of affairs much lamented by critics. In fact, the older masters of Realism from the German-speaking countries such as Gottfried Keller (1819-1890), Conrad Ferdinand Meyer (1825-1898), Wilhelm Raabe (1831-1910), and Theodor Storm (1817-188) remained geographically remote from Berlin, the political center of the Empire, and rather reserved with regard to the social changes wrought by the *Gründerzeit*. In general, they were not enamored of the newly acquired wealth of the rising bourgeoisie that might have provided the material basis for a vigorous intellectual and artistic life. The day belonged to lesser and more flexible talents like Paul Heyse (1830-1914), Emanuel Geibel (1815-1884), Friedrich von Bodenstedt (1819-1892), and Viktor von Scheffel (1826-1886). Even they were surpassed in the public's favor by the producers of trivial literature who enjoyed immense popularity among the great mass of readers who subscribed to family magazines — by far the most important disseminators of instruction and entertainment in an era before radio, the cinema, and television and thus an invaluable source for the study of the cultural atmosphere of the time. The family magazines that both reinforced and reflected their readers' family-oriented ethical conservatism, patriotism, and general belief in progress, are indicative of the intellectual climate that inhibited new, significant, literary developments. Moreover, it has been argued that the creative energies of Germans were spent in the political and social realm — hence the erstwhile people of *Dichter und Denker* (poets and thinkers) were following pursuits that did not promote literary activities. The weakness of German literature in the seventies, which tended to be dominated by effete epigones who preferred to dwell on the aesthetically non-offensive rather than on the harsh social reality of the *Gründerzeit*, afforded works by foreign creative writers such as Alphonse Daudet (1840-1897) and Charles Dickens (1812-1870) the opportunity to gain a sizable share of the German book market. The traditionally sympathetic attitude towards *Weltliteratur* (world literature), a term coined by Johann Wolfgang von Goethe (1749-1832), was but little affected by the national euphoria that accompanied the *Reichsgründung* and facilitated an indiscriminate importation of works by contemporary foreign poets, prose writers, and dramatists — among them the heralds and much imitated models of a new literary movement, Zola and Henrik Ibsen (1828-1906).

Zola provided the term "Naturalism"; in the preface to the new, 1882 edition of his novel *Thérèse Raquin* (1867), he referred to "le groupe d'écrivains naturalistes"("the group of Naturalist writers") to which he belonged. Although the works of Ibsen, Zola, the brothers Goncourt (Edmond [1822-1896] and Jules [1830-1870]), Bjørnstjerne Bjørnson (1832-1910), Feodor Dostoyevsky (1821-1881), and Leo Tolstoy (1828-1910) — both Russian authors were then considered Naturalists — were being read, performed on the stage, and heatedly discussed by critics, one cannot speak of the favorable reception of Naturalism by larger segments of the reading public or even a majority of critics until approximately 1890.

The general acceptance of Naturalism was preceded by an intense debate about its artistic merits and social relevance; notably Zola's theory and practice were subject to close scrutiny inasmuch as Naturalism owed to Zola its scientific, mechanistic, and deterministic theory. Apart from such theoretical writings as *Le Roman expérimental* (*The Experimental Novel* [1880]) and *Les Romanciers naturalistes* (*The Naturalistic Novelists* [1881]), Zola was the author of the crowning achievement of the Naturalistic novel, the twenty-volume cycle *Les Rougon-Macquart* (1871-1893), in which he attempted to trace the effects of race, moment, and milieu — concepts derived from the literary and art historian Hippolyte Taine (1828-1893) — on five successive generations of a fictional family during the French Second Empire.

Social Criticism

The main contribution of Ibsen is generally considered to be the social criticism implicit in the dramas of his middle period that dealt with contemporary bourgeois society. Although both Ibsen, some of whose plays were translated into German as early as 1872, and Zola, about whom comparatively few German essays were written before 1879, were known in the 1870s, their impact was not felt in full until around 1880. At that time, the young literary revolutionaries — most of the early German Naturalists, among them Hauptmann, were born in the decade between 1855 and 1864 — attempted to change radically the literary *status quo*. The adherents of *Das jüngste Deutschland* or modernists — who later came to be known as Naturalists — set out to relate literature more closely to contemporary life, to make literature a mirror of the social, economic, and moral problems that beset the *Gründerzeit*. Less gifted as prose writers, dramatists, or poets than as critics, they lacked a significant literary production of their own during the eighties. Therefore, the modernists expounded what they conceived to be the theory of Naturalism to a small, hardy band of dedicated followers; in the absence of major works by German authors these followers' attention was constantly directed to exemplary Naturalistic writings from abroad.

Periodicals

Periodicals served as a major forum for the dissemination of new ideas. Especially the literary dioscuri, the brothers Heinrich (1855-1906) and Julius (1859-1930) Hart, were actively engaged in the promotion of Naturalism. Between 1877 and 1890 they founded five journals — all of which were rather short-lived and did not appeal to a mass audience. Yet these journals cannot be entirely disregarded since they represent a continuous and determined effort to change the course of literature and, hence, the reading public's taste. Even if the Harts cannot be credited with the transformation of the literary scene, they were among the first to give utterance to profound discontent with a literature that lacked candor and enthusiasm. As the title of *Deutsche Dichtung* (*German Poetry*), a journal of which only three issues appeared in 1877, suggests, the Harts' chief concern was the rejuvenation of German literature. In their second venture, *Deutsche Monatsblätter* (*German Monthly*), which appeared from 1878-1879, the Harts drew attention to such foreign authors as Bjørnson and Ibsen, Taine and Zola — without, however, characterizing them as role models. The catholic rather than partisan literary taste of the Harts is evident, for example, in their inclusion of such contemporary authors as Ivan Turgenev (1818-1883) and Bret Harte (1836-1902).

Deutsche Monatsblätter soon disappeared from the literary scene; the journal was replaced by *Kritische Waffengänge* (*Critical Jousts*), the Harts' only periodical written entirely by themselves. Published from 1882 to 1884, the journal became the Harts' best known and most influential publication. As the belligerent title implies, the intent of the editors and sole contributors was primarily to discuss critically contemporary literary figures. In accordance with their emphatically stated program for the renewal of German literature, the Harts focused their attention on German authors. The invocation of the *germanische Volksseele* (soul of the Germanic people), the rejection of the Greek and Oriental traditions in German literature, and the frequent employment of the terms "national" and "modern" in the six issues of *Kritische Waffengänge* display the Harts' reformatory zeal: the creation of a both national and modern German literature that did not slavishly imitate foreign models. The Harts presented a balanced view of Zola's prose fiction and aesthetic theories. They steered clear of the hero worship in which some of Zola's German followers engaged; in contrast to the critics of the literary establishment, who tended to employ moral philistinism as a criterion of literary value, they avoided censure. Zola's novels from the Rougon-Macquart cycle, *L'Assommoir* (1877) and *Nana* (1880), were "true" in their mimetic representation of shocking conditions and achieved an ethical effect by catharsis, the Harts opined. The former novel showed the debilitating effect of alcohol and established Zola's reputation as the head of the Naturalistic school, and the latter explored the *demi-monde* and prostitution. Zola's obsession with scientific observation resulted in the accumulation of nonessential details and sordid subject matter that detracted from the "poetic" quality of his work. In the Harts' view, both truth and poetry (*poesie-getränkte Wahrheit*) were not to be found in contemporary letters — not even in

Zola — but in the young Goethe, an indigenous, albeit not contemporary, national model.

Berliner Monatshefte für Literatur, Kritik und Theater (*Berlin Monthly for Literature, Criticism, and Theater* [April-September, 1885]), the fourth major journalistic venture of the Harts — specifically, Heinrich Hart — signifies a shift from ultimately destructive literary criticism to literary creativity and productivity in that large sections of the journal were devoted to prose narratives and poetry. One may reasonably doubt, however, that the creative efforts of younger writers could match the vehemence of their attacks on older and established authors. In fact, there were hardly any contributors of more than ephemeral significance — the new German literature remained somewhat of a desideratum in the middle of the eighties. Moreover, the Harts' fervor for a new literature seemed to be conducive to a certain vagueness of direction and errors of judgment. Whereas both Zola and Ibsen were received cautiously by the Harts, they accorded the minor lyrical poet, dramatist, and prose writer Count Adolf Friedrich von Schack (1815-1894) considerable recognition. But lapses in judgment notwithstanding, *Berliner Monatshefte* was named after the city that was to become one of the foremost centers of Naturalism on account of its rapid expansion and attendant social problems that were suitable subject matter for Naturalistic writers. Moreover, the intellectual climate of the big city fostered the exchange of ideas among young writers; *Berliner Monatshefte* followed particularly closely the theatrical fare that was offered in Berlin and other major cities. The contributors decried the baleful dominance of plays by French authors and their German imitators that presented titillating amusement instead of intellectual challenge and spiritual edification and prevented the improvement of the theater audience's literary taste. And it was in the theater, of course, where the fiercest battle of German Naturalism was eventually to take place.

Kritisches Jahrbuch (*Critical Yearbook* [1889-1890]), the last periodical published by the Harts in the seventies and eighties, was devoted to literary criticism and to the discussion of aesthetic problems. Like its predecessors, the two issues of the periodical reveal the Harts' intense desire to break with the effete and mediocre German belles-lettres of the day without resorting to the adulation of foreign models. To be sure, Zola, Ibsen, and Tolstoy were declared to be harbingers of a new art — but not its creators.

Prose

In contrast to the Berlin-based Harts' cautious approach to Zola, the Munich writer Michael Georg Conrad (1846-1927), founder of the periodical *Die Gesellschaft* (*Society* [1885-1902]), displayed unabashed admiration for the French writer's "documents of social processes" — an admiration that was not initially shared but then surpassed by Karl Bleibtreu (1859-1928), who in 1888 became co-editor of *Die Gesellschaft*. Although the periodical continued to be Zola's chief

German champion, the adulatory tone in the assessments of the French novelist was less evident as time went on; furthermore, there was a noticeable decline in the number of articles devoted to Zola after 1885 — with the possible exception of 1888. The circumspect distancing from Zola is, in the final analysis, attributable to Conrad's aggressive stance towards all manifestations of the bourgeois literary establishment that, in his view, lacked candor and vigor and was in dire need of renewal. In essence, *Die Gesellschaft* shared the Harts' condemnation of the literary *status quo* and their efforts to achieve a flowering of German literature, but the two basic impulses governing Conrad's revolutionary zeal, hero-worship of Zola on the one hand and the desire to bring about a transformation of German literature on the other, had to conflict sooner or later. By 1889, Conrad's position resembled that of the Harts; he boisterously — and with ill-founded nationalistic pride — claimed that the potential productive energy of German Naturalists would make the example of foreign literary works superfluous. Conrad's own major literary effort, the Munich novel *Was die Isar rauscht* (*The Murmurings of the [River] Isar* — 1888) was intended as the beginning of a cycle — never completed — in the manner of the *Rougon-Macquart*. Today it merits only an occasional mention in literary histories.

Although one of the most important programmatic Naturalistic tracts, *Die Revolution der Literatur* (*The Revolution of Literature* [1886]), was penned by Bleibtreu, Conrad's collaborator, Munich could not maintain its position as a center of the new movement and eventually lost out to its rival, Berlin. In part, the reasons for Berlin's literary ascendance are to be sought in the Munich Naturalists' low esteem of the drama. Somewhat curiously, around 1885 lyric poetry seemed the preferred genre of the young writers as evidenced, for example, by the anthology *Moderne Dichter-Charaktere* (*Portraits of Modern Poets* [1885]), edited by Wilhelm Arent. However, Bleibtreu, who himself had contributed to Arent's anthology, called lyric poetry — the most subjective of genres and remote from scientific objectivity — outdated and declared the "social novel" to be the genre most appropriate for the aspirations of the new movement. There was a veritable slew of Naturalistic novels; however, apart from such exceptions as *Meister Timpe* (*Master Timpe* [1888]) by the prolific Berlin writer Max Kretzer (1854-1941), they have largely been forgotten. Kretzer's proletarian origins were a rarity among the Naturalists, who generally came from lower-middle-class environments. Similarly underrepresented among the Naturalists were women writers. Clara Viebig (1860-1952), whose prose fiction began appearing in the 1890s, published almost twenty novels through the beginning of the 1920s; several of them were bestsellers. Influenced by Zola, Viebig dealt openly with sensuality and female sexual desires in her collection of novellas, *Kinder der Eifel* (*Children of the Eifel* [1897]).

Theater

Conrad's and Bleibtreu's emphasis on prose fiction proved ultimately to be a dead end; the true achievement of German Naturalism is the drama influenced by Ibsen, August Strindberg (1849-1912), and Tolstoy that was usually staged in Berlin. Actually, *Die Gesellschaft* refused to publish Hauptmann's seminal drama *Vor Sonnenaufgang* — although it printed his novella *Bahnwärter Thiel* (*Flagman Thiel* [1888]). Eventually, the different emphases with regard to genre and the foreign writers to be acknowledged as models led to tensions and publicly vented feuds between the Munich and Berlin camps.

In Berlin, the Harts provided the focal point for the young generation, but at the end of the 1880s the Harts, Bölsche, and Bruno Wille (1860-1928) left the big city — the quintessential locus and subject matter of Naturalism — and established the *Friedrichshagener Dichterkreis*, named after Friedrichshagen on Lake Müggel, then outside the city limits of Berlin. Most of the members of the quasi-Bohemian artists' colony began turning away from the social commitment of Naturalism and opted for individualism in the manner of Nietzsche. The *Friedrichshagener Dichterkreis* was preceded by a literary association with the aggressive name *Durch* (Through!), founded in 1886, that postulated a literature that was "modern." *Durch* eventually attracted some of the rising stars of German Naturalism, especially Arno Holz (1863-1929), his sometime collaborator Johannes Schlaf (1862-1941), and Hauptmann. Hauptmann participated in the proceedings by delivering a lecture on Georg Büchner (1813-1837), a virtually forgotten forerunner of the moderns, to whose discovery he contributed.

Perhaps more consequential than the literary activities of *Durch* was the 1887 Berlin visit of André Antoine's (1858-1943) Paris-based *Théâtre-Libre*, a group of amateur players who stressed greater realism in subject matter, naturalness in acting, and verisimilitude in staging. As an independent theater that was open only to season-ticket subscribers, *Théâtre-Libre* was free from censorship. Antoine's theater served as the model for the Berlin *Freie Bühne* that was founded in 1889 by the critic Theodor Wolff (1868-1943), the writer Maximilian Harden (1861-1927), and the literary historians Otto Brahm (1856-1912) and Paul Schlenther (1854-1916). Brahm, subsequently and successively director of the *Deutsches Theater* and *Lessingtheater*, became one of the most influential proponents of Hauptmann and developed a Naturalistic style of staging that de-emphasized theatrical effects, stressed teamwork among the actors, and strove for faithfulness in adapting the often extensive stage directions of Hauptmann.

The *Freie Bühne* differed from the *Théâtre-Libre* in that it employed professional actors at matinees that took place in various theaters. But the performances were for members only and hence escaped the censorship public theaters were subject to. *Freie Bühne* opened on 29 September 1889 with Ibsen's (in German translation) *Gespenster* (*Ghosts* [1890]), a production that was followed one month later by Hauptmann's *Vor Sonnenaufgang*. Although the repertory during the first years of the *Freie Bühne* was dominated by the plays of foreign and, to a lesser extent, German Naturalists, dramas by assumed forerunners of Naturalism were also staged. The most notable among these forerunners was the Austrian Ludwig Anzengruber (1839- 1889), creator of *Volksstücke* in the tradition of Ferdinand Raimund (1790-1836) and Johann Nestroy (1801-1862), albeit *Volksstücke* in a mostly serious vein and with a decidedly mimetic, social, and didactic intent. In contrast to the staunchly modernist or Naturalistic orientation of the *Freie Bühne*, both the *Freie Volksbühne* (People's Free Stage), founded in 1890, and the secessionist *Neue Freie Volksbühne* (People's New Free Stage), founded in 1892, followed a somewhat conservative course. In accordance with the cultural notions of the Social Democratic Party they endeavored to introduce members of the working class to the bourgeois cultural heritage and to foster its appreciation by offering a mixed fare of modern and classical plays.

When in 1890 *Freie Bühne für modernes Leben* (Free Stage for Modern Life), a periodical that voiced the aspirations of the founders of the theater society *Freie Bühne*, began appearing in Berlin, *Die Gesellschaft* lost its near monopoly as the chief — and consecutively published — organ of the German Naturalists. Although *Freie Bühne für modernes Leben* did not reach the height of its reputation until the beginning of the twentieth century, and although the periodical's initial history was plagued by frequent changes of editors and massive secessions of contributors, the determined efforts of the Naturalistic publisher par excellence, Samuel Fischer (1859-1934), succeeded in overcoming these calamities. A wide range of interests, the adaptability to changing conditions, notably the view that Naturalism was not necessarily the last word in literary matters, and, finally, its exile and return to (West) Germany after the Second World War secured the periodical an important place in the history of German letters. It is still being published today under the name of *Die Neue Rundschau* (*The New Review*).

The Writers

A. Arno Holz and Johannes Schlaf

Among the members of *Durch* Arno Holz (1863-1929) stands out as one of the foremost supporters of Naturalism. He started out as a journalist and in the early eighties began publishing conventional poetry that earned him some recognition. He achieved his first real success with a collection of poetry, *Buch der Zeit. Lieder eines Modernen* (*Book of Our Time. Songs of a Modern [Poet]* — 1884), which exhibits compassion with the socially downtrodden, speaks in the confessional voice of a social revolutionary, and features as its subject matter the big city. But Holz's revolutionary zeal is muted; the middle-class origins he shared with the overwhelming majority of his fellow Naturalists presumably prevented him from embracing the Marxist notion of class struggle. He offered moral commitment instead. Furthermore, Holz did not entirely reject traditional poetry; the modern poet's interest in machines, steam engines, and the poverty of the proletariat is couched in impeccable end rhymes and presented with wit and irony — characteristics that betray the influence of Heine.

In 1888 Holz's collaboration with Johannes Schlaf (1862-1941) began. In the following year they published their joint work *Papa Hamlet* (1889) under the pseudonym of Bjarne P. Holmsen because they were convinced that a Norwegian name would attract immediate attention. The identity of the true authors soon became known; but Hauptmann dedicated *Vor Sonnenaufgang* to Bjarne P. Holmsen, "dem konsequenten Realisten" (the uncompromising realist), as a sign of his appreciation of Holz and Schlaf's achievement — specifically in matters of style. Of the three prose sketches assembled in the small volume the

Arno Holz.
Etching by R. H. Isenstein

title story has attracted the lion's share of the critics' attention; "Papa Hamlet" presents a radical departure in prose fiction in that it dispenses with a clearly defined plot and disorients the actual reader, who is confronted with a beginning that may be an interior monologue by the protagonist, the Shakespearian actor Thienwiebel, the voice of the impersonal narrator, or even the anticipatory response of the implied reader whose expectations are shaped by the implied author's values and norms. Holz and Schlaf hoped to achieve the reproduction of total reality through the use of interior monologue, dialogue, and the device of *erlebte Rede* (free indirect discourse) that shifts the point of view from the narrator to the characters themselves and presents their nonarticulated sensations in an objective, impersonal manner. Holz and Schlaf's Naturalism in *Papa Hamlet* is, then, one of style and form rather than of subject matter. Thus Thienwiebel's poverty is hardly a consequence of capitalist exploitation; rather, he leads the life of a Bohemian, and his pretensions to playing tragic prince Hamlet are in ironic contrast to the squalor in which he and his family live. Indeed, the very title "Papa Hamlet" seems to be a contradiction in terms and to subvert the concept of *Künstlernovelle*, a type of novella featuring an artist's striving and his position in and versus society, in that it is far from such well-known, early twentieth-century *Künstlernovellen* as Thomas Mann's *Tonio Kröger* (1903) and *Der Tod in Venedig* (*Death in Venice* [1913]). At any rate, Thienwiebel's strangling of his baby boy in a fit of anger and his own death because of alcohol-induced exposure are not very convincing as indictments of the *Gründerzeit*, that is, its materialism and contempt of modern art.

In *Die Kunst. Ihr Wesen und ihre Gesetze (Art. Its Essence and Laws* [1891 f.]), Holz presented his theory of uncompromising Naturalism (*konsequenter Naturalismus*) in a nutshell, that is, by means of a mathematical equation: *Kunst = Natur - x* (art equals nature minus x). Art cannot completely reproduce nature or, in other words, the absolute mimetic intent cannot be realized on account of the "x," the subjective human aspect, the artist. However, by developing the *Sekundenstil* (second-by-second style), a literary technique that seeks to reproduce the actual duration of the minutest details such as sounds or silences — for example, the dripping of melting snow from the roof into the gutter in "Papa Hamlet" — Holz hoped to surpass Zola's mode of presentation which made allowances for the subjective factor, the artist's temperament. In his essay "Le Naturalisme au théâtre" ("Naturalism in the Theatre" [1881]) Zola wrote: "Il est certain qu'une oeuvre ne sera jamais qu'un coin de la nature vu à travers un tempérament," ("It is certain that a work of art will never be anything but a bit of nature seen through one's temperament"), a quotation often rendered as "Une oeuvre d'art est un coin de la nature vu à travers un tempérament" ("A work of art is a bit of nature seen through one's temperament"). The Harts criticized Holz's ultimately unpersuasive attempt to carry mimesis to its extreme — a view generally shared today.

On 7 April 1890 *Die Familie Selicke (The Selicke Family* [1890]), a further collaborative effort of Holz and Schlaf, who permanently parted ways in 1892, was staged by the *Freie Bühne* as only the second drama by a German author. A product of Holz's *konsequenter Naturalismus, Die Familie Selicke* strictly adheres to the three unities of time, place, and action. The misery of the Selicke family can be attributed to the father's alcoholism — a favorite subject of Naturalism — but the hopelessness of the situation is exacerbated by the psychologically motivated inability of the parents to overcome their estrangement. Even the death of their youngest child — the family cannot afford a doctor — does not lead to a reconciliation, and the sacrifice of their oldest daughter, who forgoes the prospect of marriage and escape from the intolerable family situation, is in vain. The play is not entirely free of sentimental features — ridiculed by contemporaries — in the manner of the *comédie larmoyante* (sentimental comedy); it depicts an utterly hopeless and presumably unchangeable state of affairs that has led the young theologian Wendt, who had hoped to marry the Selickes' oldest daughter, to lose his faith. But in keeping with his emphasis on aesthetic experiments, the theoretically inclined Holz did not consider external social reality of prime importance; rather, the concept of "nature" also included the internal states of minds that Holz and Schlaf sought to convey through nuances of language. The Naturalistic tendency of presenting the characters as incapable of improving their lots and showing them to be victims of circumstances beyond their control aroused the ire of playwright Bertolt Brecht (1898-1956) in the 1920s. Brecht, dedicated to the changing of societal conditions via the theater, harshly condemned Naturalism's "naive" and "criminal" instincts and its propensity for pitying the disadvantaged and underprivileged while, at the same time, conveying the notion that their fate was "natural" and hence inevitable.

Holz's comedy *Sozialaristokraten* (*Social Aristocrats* [1896]) deviated from the lower middle-class family setting of *Die Familie Selicke* and abandoned its presentation of a *tranche de vie* (slice of life) in that it provided a satirical portrait of the contemporaneous intellectuals in general, and the literati of the *Friedrichshagener Dichterkreis* in particular. His ambitious attempt to provide an incisive analysis of the epoch by means of a number of plays — each of which was to be set in a different social milieu — failed to materialize. *Sozialaristokraten* is a Naturalistic comedy in its exploration of a specific milieu — that of intellectuals — and the rendition of various dialects. As in *Die Familie Selicke*, these dialects function as sociolects and embody the mimetic principle of making thought patterns and behavior transparent; the comedy also satirically exposes the adherents of the Nietzschean "superman" and of anarchism (derived from Max Stirner [1806-1856] and Mikhail Bakunin [1814-1876]) — notions that run counter to Naturalism but were espoused by the Friedrichshagen writers who broke with the movement's social orientation. Whereas Holz depicts the "social aristocrats" primarily as somewhat harmless and trendy fellow travelers, today the comedy is also perceived as a warning against the dangers of nationalism, racism, and anti-Semitism because of the depicted intellectuals' unprincipled susceptibility that leads them to embrace anti-democratic and anti-semitic ideologies for the sake of attracting public attention.

Holz's later works, especially his poetic experiments with words and rhythms that resulted in *Phantasus* (first published in 1898), a frequently rewritten and almost never-ending poem of 1,556 pages (3 volumes in the 1925 edition) on which he worked from 1898 to 1916, hardly corresponded to Naturalism. Whereas Holz's earlier verse in the vein of Naturalism was couched in traditional form, *Phantasus* — the first poems under this title appeared in *Buch der Zeit* — is anything but traditional. In his *Revolution der Lyrik* (*Revolution of Poetry* [1899]), Holz postulated that it was the task of Naturalistic poetry to express the internal rhythm of that which was being conveyed. Hence *Phantasus* is without rhyme or stanza. Meter is lacking as well, replaced by rhythm arrayed in a balanced way on either side of an imaginary central point, the *Längsachse*, which was intended to force the reader to read rhythmically. Although the central figure of the poet hungering in his attic stems from Holz's Naturalistic phase, *Phantasus* is both indebted to and indicative of Impressionism and other currents that, as early as the nineties, began to replace Naturalism.

B. Gerhart Hauptmann

Holz's significance for German Naturalism was eventually overshadowed by that of Gerhart Hauptmann whose artistic range encompassed all literary genres but especially the drama and prose fiction. Born on 15 November 1862 in Bad

Salzbrunn in the then eastern German province of Silesia (now part of Poland), he died on 6 June 1946 in his house Wiesenstein in the Silesian village of Agnetendorf. During the eighty-three years of his life he witnessed the turbulent phases of modern German history from the victory over France and the *Reichsgründung* in 1871 — his most vivid childhood memories — to the destruction of Dresden in the Second World War, the defeat of Nazi Germany, and the very beginnings of life in Germany after the Second World War. Following several desultory attempts to acquire the necessary schooling for a vocational livelihood and to begin a career as a sculptor, Hauptmann, who in 1885 settled in Berlin (from 1885 to 1889 he and his family lived in Erkner near Berlin), joined the Berlin Naturalists whose leading figure he was to become within a few years. Hauptmann's creativity soon overcame the confines of Naturalism; in 1912, the year in which he turned fifty, he was awarded the Nobel Prize for Literature — an international recognition of the dominant place he occupied in German letters. His public and representational role during the Weimar Republic was uncontested — Thomas Mann, perhaps not without irony — called him "King of the Republic" in 1922. Hauptmann succeeded in this role because his formerly anti-establishment works had lost their sting; his subsequent, dubious accommodation to the Nazis who claimed him as one of their own cast a shadow over his reputation — particularly among those writers who, like Thomas and Heinrich Mann and Brecht, were forced into exile.

Before making his mark in the theater, Hauptmann made a significant contribution to Naturalistic prose fiction not with a major novel but with his novella *Bahnwärter Thiel* (1888). First published in *Die Gesellschaft*, it was immediately hailed as a major achievement in prose fiction. The novella has received continuous popular and critical acclaim as Hauptmann's first masterpiece. True to the tenets of Naturalism, Thiel belongs to the working class — although he lives in a rural environment far removed from the modern technology and social tensions of the big city to which the express trains provide a link. Hereditary factors also play a (minor) role, but, as will be seen, the tragic events proceed not only from characters doomed by heredity. In addition, Hauptmann employs a realistic narrative style; however, in contrast to Holz and Schlaf in *Papa Hamlet*, he relies on a quasi-authorial narrator that detracts from the narrative's objectivity. Moreover, *Bahnwärter Thiel* is rich in symbolism, and spectacular and demonized nature plays a fateful role. Hauptmann's real concern was the psychopathological dimension — in 1888 he studied in Zurich under the psychiatrist Auguste Forel (1848-1931) — which is evident in the psychological aberrations of protagonist Thiel.

Thiel is torn between two women. He idolizes the memory of his first wife, the ethereal Minna. At night his signalman's booth deep in the forest becomes a shrine for her worship, and in his visions he sees the dead woman reappear in person. Quite the opposite of Minna is his very earthy second wife, the robust and domineering Lene, who holds him in sexual thralldom to her ample physical charms and whose domain is the humble dwelling of the Thiels in the village. Thiel's love for Minna had been more spiritual than physical — a relationship given corporeal form in the sickly Tobias, their son, whose development has been retarded. As Tobias and Thiel come to share a close relationship, Lene, now the mother of a healthy new baby, makes life brutally miserable for her stepson. Although Thiel, who is enslaved to Lene's sexuality, knows of her brutality, he does not interfere. After all, he has his refuge in his job and in his signalman's booth, a world from which he rigorously excludes Lene.

Unfortunately, the two worlds come together when Lene begins working on a plot of land near the tracks and near his booth. When Thiel goes to carry out his signalman's duties for the onrushing Silesian Express and leaves Tobias with Lene, Tobias is killed by the train. Thiel breaks mentally. Shortly thereafter he murders both Lene and the baby, after which he is taken to the psychiatric ward of the Charité hospital in Berlin, still clutching Tobias's brown cap, which he regards with the tenderness and solicitude that characterized him before the death of his son.

Bahnwärter Thiel, with its mystic evocation of nature and its nature (and color) symbolism, looks back to early nineteenth-century Romanticism, but not quite so much as it looks ahead to a kind of Naturalism that had been anticipated by Büchner. Büchner's influence is evident in both the psychopathological aspect of *Bahnwärter Thiel* and the close attention to the lot of "simple" people. Both elements are reminiscent of Büchner's novella *Lenz* (1839), whereas the tragic accident is prefigured by the motif of the color red that is associated with blood in the manner of Büchner's drama *Woyzeck* (not published until 1879).

Far more controversial than *Bahnwärter Thiel* with its mixture of traditional and innovative elements was Hauptmann's "social drama" *Vor Sonnenaufgang*. The play appeared in print in August 1889 before it was produced by the *Freie Bühne* in October of the same year. Hence it was known to friend and foe, and the battle lines were drawn on opening night. Although the *Freie Bühne* had been explicitly founded with the intent of producing "modern" plays not subject to censorship, the great majority of its supporting members — for the most part bourgeois intellectuals and professionals — were clearly not prepared for Hauptmann's brand of modernism. Accustomed to the noncontroversial and rather insipid contemporary fare of the Francophile Paul Lindau (1839-1919) or the "well-made plays" of Victorien Sardou (1831-1908) and his ilk, the audience reacted with outrage when in act 5 of *Vor Sonnenaufgang* the protracted moaning of a woman giving birth to a stillborn child offstage was being heard. A gynecologist threw his forceps on the stage, and in the resulting tumult the actors could hardly continue playing. But what proved to be even more provocative than the taboo subjects of sex, conception, and childbirth was the figure of Alfred Loth.

Loth combines various — and perhaps irreconcilable — traits such as Christian charity, humanistic rationality, and revolutionary impulses derived from socialism, but also the heroic Teutonic ideology of Felix Dahn (1834-1912), popular author of historical novels. He visits a village in Silesia in order to study the condition of the coal miners with the eventual aim of redressing social injustices. The miners, representatives of the proletariat, never appear on stage, however, and the planned study never gets written because Loth coincidentally meets Hoffmann, a former friend from his university days, now an engineer. Hoffmann has married the oldest daughter of farmer Krause, who has acquired great wealth on account of the coal — in the 1880s the chief source of energy — that was found under the fields he formerly tilled. Now totally deranged because of his alcoholism, Krause has sunk so low as to approach his younger daughter Helene, who so far has escaped his debilitating influence, with incestuous intent. His second wife displays all the ill breeding and gross ostentation of the parvenu; she satisfies her sexual appetite by trysts with her nephew, an equally ill-mannered, ignorant, and brutal lout.

But Hoffmann, whose wife is also an alcoholic, has adjusted to the sordid milieu of moral degradation and crass materialism that characterizes the Krause family. As the socialist writer Franz Mehring (1846-1919) pointed out, the socio-economic circumstances and rural habitat of the Krauses are not typical of the capitalist family of the *Gründerzeit*; rather, Hoffmann corresponds more closely to the mold of the capitalist entrepreneur. Ever the opportunist, he has abandoned his youthful ideas of social justice and become a staunch defender of laissez-faire capitalism and the prevailing authoritarian order of the Empire. In act 3, Hoffmann accuses Loth of being a muckraker who incites the miners to riot; the majority of the audience at the *Freie Bühne* enthusiastically applauded the actor who played Hoffmann, and the actor who played Loth — considered to be a spokesman for Hauptmann's pro-socialist and anti-capitalist sentiments — was booed. The scene resembled a parliamentary debate, one observer remarked, rather than a theater performance. Conversely, when *Vor Sonnenaufgang* was staged at the *Freie Volksbühne* in November 1890, the audience consisting mostly of workers cheered the actor representing Loth.

Loth is the quintessential but misnamed "Bote aus der Fremde" (messenger from afar) of Naturalistic drama, that is, a figure who encounters an unfamiliar environment and by his presence exposes its flaws. He has remained a vexing problem for critics and has been condemned as a narrow-minded ideologue, a doctrinaire utopian, and even a coward. Loth remains essentially a bourgeois intellectual who sympathizes with the downtrodden miners but merely uses them as an object of study with the goal of bettering their condition. His real reformatory zeal is evident in other areas, that is, those of alcoholism and heredity. Helene, Krause's younger daughter, has taken the unprecedented step of declaring her love for him; but Loth leaves her because of his conviction that the effects of alcohol extend to the third and fourth generation. This pronouncement Loth had delivered with the force of a biblical injunction (Exodus 20:5: "visiting the iniquity of the fathers upon the children unto the third and fourth generation") before he realized that Helene was a potential victim of alcoholism. Often construed as a callous and selfish act, Loth's fierce determination to transmit his vigor and health — inherited from his forefathers — "both unsullied and undiminished to any progeny" that he might sire may also be interpreted as an act of unselfishness in which he subordinates his desire for personal happiness to what he perceives to be his responsibility to society as a whole. In such a reading Helene, who commits suicide offstage upon finding Loth's farewell note, is a victim of heredity, milieu, and upbringing — all of which make it impossible for her to escape her predicament that, in true Naturalistic fashion, has been predetermined. Her suicide merely demonstrates the utter hopelessness of the situation in which the members of the Krause family find themselves and the evolutionary dead end at which they have arrived. Admittedly, Hauptmann stacks the deck in favor of social Darwinism by references to a three-year old alcoholic, the first son of Krause's older daughter. But, surprisingly, Loth's much ballyhooed theory of the genetically transmitted susceptibility to alcohol, which Hauptmann derived from contemporaneous sources, has been vindicated to some extent: children born of alcoholic mothers who drink heavily during pregnancy have been found to suffer from a high incidence of physical and mental impairment.

After *Vor Sonnenaufgang* Hauptmann wrote in quick succession those plays for which he is famous — on an average almost a play per year during the last decade of the nineteenth century and the first decade of our century. *Vor Sonnenaufgang* was followed by *Das Friedensfest* (*A Family Catastrophe* [1890]), a family drama in the tradition of Ibsen; *Einsame Menschen* (*Lonely Lives* [1891]), a drama featuring a weak-willed male protagonist who finds himself in a triangular situation between a traditional and an emancipated woman and commits suicide in the end; and *Die Weber* (*The Weavers* [1892]), often proclaimed the climax of Hauptmann's Naturalistic drama.

First staged at the private *Freie Bühne* in 1893, the play was pro-hibited from being performed on public stages. But after a trial that attracted wide attention, *Die Weber* opened at the public *Deutsches Theater* in Berlin in 1894. This event manifests the gradual accep-tance of Naturalism in Berlin, capital of the Empire and residence of Wilhelm II (1859-1941), who had ascended to the throne in 1888. Emperor Wilhelm II had dismissed Chancellor Bismarck in 1890, and he engaged in the somewhat bi-

Gerhart Hauptmann ca. 1904.
Caricature by Arpad Schmidhammer

zarre attempt to reinstitute the divine rights of monarchs in an age of industri-alization. Not necessarily opposed to the social aspirations of the Social Democrats, Wilhelm II loathed the use of art as a vehicle for social criticism. He preferred the decorative and monumental style in painting and sculpture and considered Naturalism *Rinnsteinkunst* (gutter art). But the Emperor's personal preferences in matters of art and literature that were shared to a significant extent by the bourgeois reading and theater-going public were insufficient to prevent the arrival and acceptance of Naturalism and its chief representative, Hauptmann. In the 1890s there emerged an uneasy coexistence of the different camps; it has been suggested that Hauptmann was accorded the role of emperor in the realm of letters, albeit an emperor who represented unofficial, socially aware, modern, and anti-classical art.

In fact, the version of *Die Weber* in standard German, which had been preceded by an "authentic" version in Silesian dialect, provided a perfect example of a "social" drama in its depiction of the Silesian weavers' plight in the 1840s and their struggle against their exploiters that had elicited a number of contemporaneous literary responses, among them that by Heine. Reminiscent of the miners' strike in Zola's social novel *Germinal* (1885), the drama did not lack relevance in the nineties; as the sociological and economic sources that Hauptmann drew on attested, the misery of the weavers in the marginal Silesian cottage industry had continued unabated for nearly half a century. Curiously, both the censors — whose efforts to bar the play from public performance eventually failed — and critics who shared Hauptmann's social views, tended to regard *Die Weber* as tendentious and revolutionary in spirit. True, in contrast to *Vor Sonnenaufgang*, *Die Weber* does not feature an individual protagonist in the traditional sense nor, for that matter, a conventional plot and its resolution. In *Vor Sonnenaufgang*, Loth and his amorous involvement with Helene are in the foreground, and the miners, the subject of Loth's abortive study, never appear on stage; however, in *Die Weber* the weavers themselves act as a kind of collective protagonist. Furthermore, Hauptmann depicts segments of a complex historical process — from showing the economic roots of the weavers' exploitation in act 1, where they deliver their wares and are arbitrarily recompensed with starvation wages, to their revolutionary actions in act 5. Unlike *Vor Sonnenaufgang* with its traditional "closed" five-act structure culminating in the climactic scene of Helene's declaration of love and ending in catastrophe, *Die Weber* tends to correspond to the "open" form of drama that dispenses with a tight structure and a linear plot development. But the emotional weavers' song that connects the acts and the heightening of social tensions and revolutionary energy in the play run counter to the dispassionate display of patterns of behavior that Brecht, who selectively and critically borrowed from such predecessors as Shakespeare, the Storm and Stress dramatist Jakob Michael Reinhold Lenz (1751-1792), and Büchner, was to develop in the 1920s in his "epic theater."

Actually, whereas contemporaneous critics tended to either applaud or decry the presumably revolutionary tendency of *Die Weber*, Brecht attacked Hauptmann's depiction of a milieu that seems to be the result of fate and impervious to change through human effort. Particularly the figure of Hilse, an old weaver who makes his appearance in act 5, does not support the claim of the play's revolutionary tendencies. Hilse refuses to participate in the weavers' uprising; ironically, he is killed by a stray bullet fired by one of the Prussian soldiers called in to restore "law and order." Without doubt, Hilse is an innocent victim. But it is by no means clear what his death signifies; the broad spectrum of critical opinion ranges from those who see in Hilse's death Hauptmann's endorsement of revolutionary action as a means to achieve social justice to those who postulate the precise opposite, that is, Hauptmann's rejection of revolutionary movements. The ambivalence of

Die Weber, whose author was moved by social compassion rather than revolutionary fervor, is not evident, for example, in Brecht's play *Die heilige Johanna der Schlachthöfe* (*Saint Joan of the Stockyards* [1932]). Shortly before her death the protagonist Joan Dark formulates her hard-won insight: "Only force helps where force rules, and / only men help where men are."

But Brecht's criticism of the fatalistic attitude predominating in Naturalistic dramas misses its mark when applied to Hauptmann's *Der Biberpelz* (*The Beaver Coat* [1893]). The play, often hailed as one of the best German comedies, features a clever and resourceful washerwoman, Frau Wolff, who, in accordance with the Naturalistic practice of rendering speech patterns realistically, speaks Berlin dialect. By selling stolen goods, among them the beaver coat, she hopes to obtain the means to move ahead in the world. Frau Wolff's desire for social mobility via overtly criminal means is perhaps not fundamentally different from more respectable variants to attain social status based on the materialism and acquisitiveness of the period — the play takes place during the last years of the Bismarck era in the late 1880s. But Frau Wolff's criminal tendencies are counterbalanced by traits of genuine compassion; moreover, her misdeeds pale in comparison to the bungling of the vainglorious, authoritarian, and narrow-minded bureaucrat von Wehrhahn (roughly translated: strutting cock), who is more interested in exposing suspected democrats and liberal intellectuals than in catching criminals. Ironically, von Wehrhahn expressly praises Frau Wolff as an honest soul in the end. This ending signals that an inversion of the customary moral value system has taken place: it is no longer the individual with amoral and criminal inclinations who poses a threat to a society bent on promoting justice; rather, society (or its representatives such as von Wehrhahn) has become a threat to those individuals who, like the bourgeois intellectual Dr. Fleischer in the play, seek a just order.

Hauptmann continued writing some plays in the Naturalistic vein well into the twentieth century, when Naturalism was no longer a dominant force. In *Fuhrmann Henschel* (*Drayman Henschel* [1899]) the protagonist commits suicide after he has broken the solemn vow he made to his first wife before her death and has married a sexually attractive but domineering woman. She proves to be his downfall in a milieu that is characterized by illness, alcoholism, and moral degradation. In *Rose Bernd* (1903) the female protagonist, who is sexually exploited by several men, commits perjury and kills her illegitimate child but achieves a reconciliation with her fiancé. In the tragicomedy *Die Ratten* (*The Rats* [1911]) the rats are indicative of the undermining of the foundations of a society that was to collapse at the end of the First World War. But it is even more compelling to view *Vor Sonnenuntergang* (*Before Sunset* [1932]) as marking the end of an epoch. Although indebted to Goethe — in 1932 the one hundredth anniversary of Goethe's death was commemorated — rather than to Naturalism, the drama's title pointedly refers to *Vor Sonnenaufgang* (literally translated by James Joyce (1882-1941) as "Before Sunrise"). In *Vor Sonnenuntergang*, the seventy-year-old protagonist Clausen — Hauptmann turned seventy in 1932 — commits suicide in the fifth act (not performed at the premiere) after his greedy children, who fear for their inheritance because of the protagonist's love of a much younger woman, have succeeded in having him certified mentally incompetent. This ''new King Lear,'' which may be interpreted both as an assertion of the rights of, in today's terminology, ''gray panthers'' or in terms of the denial of their rights, premiered at the Berlin *Deutsches Theater* in February 1932. The play was directed by Max Reinhardt and featured star actors Werner Krauß (1884-1959) and Helene Thiemig (1889-1974). Considered to be not only the last significant premiere of one of Hauptmann's plays but also the last important theatrical event of the Weimar Republic, this premiere retrospectively gained poignancy because of the imminent usurpation of power by the Nazis — ruthless representatives of a new order that represented a far more serious threat to the bourgeois intellectual and moral values professed by Clausen than that posed by Clausen's children.

His reputation as the foremost dramatist of German Naturalism notwithstanding, Hauptmann began writing non-Naturalistic dramas at a comparatively early stage in his career. Notably *Die versunkene Glocke* (*The Sunken Bell* [1897]), a Neo-Romantic ''German fairy-tale drama'' in verse that turned out to be Hauptmann's most popular play, constitutes a radical departure from Naturalism by abandoning all attempts at mimetic representation and resorting to a fairy-tale world. Yet Hauptmann did not consider Naturalistic and non-Naturalistic modes as mutually exclusive. In both the play that became known under the title *Hanneles Himmelfahrt* (*Hannele* [1894, 1896]) and the ''glass-works fairy tale'' *Und Pippa tanzt!* (*And Pippa Dances!* [1906]), a contrast is established between the real world, whose inhabitants tend to speak in dialect, and the ideal world, whose denizens prefer to speak in standard German. In *Hannele* the feverish hallucinations of a poor, dying girl transfigure the grim reality of the poorhouse — Hauptmann shared his contemporaries' interest in the reconstruction of dreams — and in *Pippa*, Hauptmann's private mythology, inspired by Silesian legends, finds expression in the clash between the representatives of the instinctual-animalistic nether world and those of the higher order devoted to the spirit.

C. Hermann Sudermann

Apart from the dominant figures of Hauptmann and, to a lesser extent, Holz, some other writers contributed to the body of Naturalistic plays. Hermann Sudermann (1857-1928), of rural East Prussian origins (now in the Lithuanian Soviet Republic), was acknowledged by James Joyce in his essay *Drama and Life* (1900) as a representative of the ''new school'' of drama and appreciated by George Bernard Shaw (1856-1950). There is a curious contrast between the popular success of Sudermann's works — both his prose fiction, among them the novels *Frau Sorge* (*Dame Care* [1887]) and *Der Katzensteg* (*Regina, or The Sins of the Fathers* [1889]) and the dramas — and the lack of esteem in which he was and is held by German critics and literary historians. Sudermann's *Die Ehre* (*Honor* [1890]) opened in November 1889 in the Berlin *Lessingtheater*, a few weeks after the premiere of *Vor Sonnenaufgang*. But whereas the latter play was embattled and only eventually accepted by the public at large, the former proved to be a veritable hit; Sudermann was praised as the first dramatist who succeeded with Naturalistic plays outside of Berlin. The staying power of the play is evidenced by several film versions (twice in 1913, 1926, 1968); other dramas by Sudermann likewise served repeatedly as the bases for films.

Die Ehre avoids shocking the bourgeois audience's sensibilities as *Vor Sonnenaufgang* had done. Sudermann adapts the literary motif of the "fallen woman's" lost honor to the conditions of the *Gründerzeit*. From the eighteenth-century *bürgerliches Trauerspiel* (bourgeois tragedy) to the first part of Goethe's *Faust* (1808) and Friedrich Hebbel's renewal of the bourgeois tragedy in *Maria Magdalena* (1844), the loss of female honor, initially the result of an aristocratic male's transgression against a bourgeois female victim, inevitably led — as the genre classification implies — to tragedy. But in the second half of the nineteenth century French plays, which were widely produced in Germany, relativized the concept of honor. For example, in Sardou and Emile de Najac's popular comedy *Divorçons!* (*Let's Get a Divorce* [1880]) the woman's honor is no longer an issue; rather, in a witty dialogue a cuckolded husband's honor is said to be retroactively restored by his divorce from his wife. In a somewhat similar vein, in *Die Ehre* the "fallen woman" Alma, vivacious and pretty but from a lower-class family, engages without remorse in a liaison with the carefree son of her brother Robert's employer, owner of a coffee import firm. Robert, defender of his sister's virtue against a seducer of socially superior standing in the fashion of his literary forbears, seeks an honorable solution, that is, he demands that his sister's lover marry her or else he threatens to challenge him to a duel. But he is rebuffed by his employer, who cynically explains to him that, because of his socially inferior origins, he is not entitled to act in the name of honor; furthermore, his own family disavows him in gladly accepting monetary compensation from his employer for his sister's "shame." So far the gist of the play appears to be a frivolous anticipation of Brecht and Kurt Weill's (1900-1950) famous line from the second finale of *Die Dreigroschenoper* (*The Threepenny Opera* [1929]), "Food is the first thing. Morals follow on," that posits that the poor are not in a position to quibble about such concepts as honor as long as they lack the necessities of life. However, in an ironic twist the raisonneur of the play, a count who serves as the author's mouthpiece, not only argues that the concept of honor is a salable commodity, he proceeds to demonstrate the truth of his thesis. Robert's employer, who is at the point of disowning his daughter because she wants to marry Robert, rapidly changes his mind when he learns that Robert has become the partner and sole heir of the wealthy count.

The wealthy and the poor are, then, alike in either ignoring or merely paying lip service to the concept of honor — hardly a stinging indictment of the capitalist order. Such lack of aggressiveness without doubt facilitated the acceptance of the play whose Naturalism consisted essentially in the depiction of the milieu of the poor. In the scenes taking place among the rich, Sudermann relied on the model of the French well-made play with its dose of theatrical and melodramatic effects.

In *Heimat* (*Magda* [1893]) Sudermann chose an issue of considerable import and progressive thrust: the right of the female artist — a singer — to determine her own life independently and free from parental pressures and societal conventions restricting the emancipation of women, a social issue that was viewed sympathetically by the Naturalists. Despite Sudermann's reliance on melodramatic elements, *Heimat* secured him considerable international recognition; the best known actresses of the time such as Eleonora Duse (1859-1924) and Sarah Bernhardt (1844-1923) were eager to play the role of Magda, the female protagonist. Sudermann's international recognition notwithstanding, in 1917 the influential Berlin theater critic Alfred Kerr (1867-1948) wrote scathingly that Sudermann's works lacked authenticity; instead, they displayed false emotions, false passions, and false simplicity. Kerr's verdict is indicative of the divergence between the critical opinion on Sudermann on the one hand and his popular success on the other.

D. Max Halbe

Max Halbe (1865-1944) hailed from the then eastern territories of the Empire near Danzig (today: Gdansk); in the 1930s he began interpreting his work in terms of the Nazi ideology of *Blut und Boden* (blood and soil). He is largely forgotten today, but in the 1890s he succinctly formulated the experience of youth that rebelled against the old order in the titles of two of his plays: *Freie Liebe* (*Free Love* [1890]) and *Jugend* (*Youth* [1893]). *Freie Liebe* depicts the clash between the moral values of the old generation and those of the young, represented by a writer and his common-law wife Elise who is of proletarian origin and has socialist leanings. Elise is not necessarily an emancipated woman, but her desire to become educated is presented in an entirely positive light. Such a stance corresponds to the generally supportive attitude of the predominantly male Naturalistic dramatists towards the women's question that, for example, is also articulated in both *Vor Sonnenaufgang* and *Einsame Menschen*. Furthermore, Halbe is at pains to distinguish Elise's serious, if unsanctioned, union from the more frivolous varieties of "free love" practiced in the Bohemian circles for which Munich's artists' district Schwabing provided the model. The play ends on a somewhat sinister note: the young couple has to flee from the authorities who do not tolerate dissent from the prevailing norm of marriage.

Jugend opened in April 1883 in the Berlin *Residenztheater* and turned out to be an immediate and long-lasting success that Halbe was never able to repeat. The play's success is due to its advocating the rights of youth, particularly those of the unhampered expression of feelings and of engaging in free love. Halbe's programmatic title *Jugend* relates the play to the aspirations of a young generation of artists who opposed the monumental and historicizing painting, sculpture, and architecture of the *Gründerzeit*, voiced their dissent in the journal *Jugend*

(1896-1910), and gave rise to the term *Jugendstil.* Halbe's *Jugend* shares with Frank Wedekind's drama *Frühlings Erwachen (Spring Awakening* [1894]), a play that was not performed until 1906, its indictment of the repressive world of adults. The perception of the crushing weight of parental narrow-mindedness and institutional rigidity that stifles all attempts of youthful rebellion in Wedekind's play is only slightly mitigated by its grotesque and, conceivably, optimistic ending; conversely, in *Jugend* the old order, represented by an orthodox Catholic priest, is somewhat melodramatically restored in a fashion that thoroughly discredits it and reduces its claims to absurdity. Annchen, the heroine who displays "naive sensuality," is accidentally killed by an animal-like creature who intended to kill her lover Hans. In depicting the student Hans as a *moderner Stimmungsmensch* (modern, sensitive man) with touches of nervousness, Halbe created a character who corresponds more closely to Impressionism than Naturalism and is a far cry from the serious, socially conscious, but single-minded Loth in *Vor Sonnenaufgang.* Halbe's tendency to break the mold of Naturalism is also evident in *Der Strom* (*The Stream* [1903]), a drama about the enmity among brothers that, according to his own retrospective reading, transcends Naturalistic materialism and the scientific reproduction of reality and introduces metaphysical questions concerning crime and punishment.

Conclusion

As has been noted in the foregoing discussion, even the chief representatives of Naturalism such as Hauptmann and Holz eventually turned away from Naturalistic modes of representation. Naturalism was a comparatively short-lived phenomenon that began in 1882 with a theoretical prelude in which the Harts played a significant role. When literary publications appeared, poetry became the dominant genre around 1885, but prose fiction soon assumed the leading role until 1889-1890, when Hauptmann and other dramatists came to the fore and Berlin became the unchallenged center of German Naturalism for the next decade or so. But as early as 1891 the versatile Viennese writer Hermann Bahr (1863-1934) published his pamphlet entitled *Die Überwindung des Naturalismus (Beyond Naturalism* [1894]), in which he posited that Naturalism would be replaced by a "nervous Romanticism," a "mysticism of the nerves," and assigned to Naturalism the function of an *entr'acte* between the old and the new. Bahr's negative assessment has been echoed by many critics who tend to privilege the counter-movements to Naturalism, such as Neo-Romanticism, Impressionism, and *Jugend-stil,* that began to develop almost simultaneously with the breakthrough of Naturalism. Even though the canon of Naturalistic works — apart from Hauptmann — is small, the Naturalists' vigorous attack on widely read authors such as Heyse who failed to provide new impulses, their rediscovery and adaptation of indigenous literary traditions such as those of the Storm and Stress and Young Germany, and their discovery of new literary subjects such as the big city, wage slavery, the milieu of the poor, generational conflicts, and women's emancipation, invigorated and enriched literature and became part of the literary tradition. This can readily be seen in the adoption of Naturalistic topics by widely divergent literary movements — Expressionism at the beginning of our century and the literature of the Workday World *(Literatur der Arbeitswelt)* in the 1960s. If the strict mimetic representation of *konsequenter Naturalismus* did not find many imitators, its inventors opened the door for future experimentation that would not be restricted by Naturalistic theory.

About the Authors

Judith Aikin, Professor of German at the University of Iowa, is the author of *German Baroque Drama* (Twayne, 1982) and *Scaramutza in Germany: The Dramatic Works of Caspar Stieler* (Pennsylvania State University Press), as well as numerous articles, most of them on drama and opera in seventeenth- and eighteenth-century Germany. Her recent studies include articles on the composer Heinrich Schütz and his vocal music projects with the poets Martin Opitz and Augustus Buchner. She is currently writing a book on the development of verse forms for early German opera.

Gabrielle Bersier is Associate Professor of German at Indiana University-Indianapolis. She studied in Fribourg (Switzerland), London, Mainz, and Madison, Wisconsin, where she received her doctorate in 1979. She is the author of *Wunschbild und Wirklichkeit. Deutsche Utopien im 18. Jahrhundert* (1981) and articles on German Enlightenment, Enlightenment state novel, Jacobinism, utopian travel fiction, Gessner, Goethe, and Wieland. She is currently writing a monograph on Goethe's post-classical works of the Napoleonic years.

Christopher R. Clason attended the University of California at Los Angeles, Santa Barbara, and Davis, from which he received the Ph.D. in German literature. He was a Germanistic Society of America fellow at Georg August Universität, Göttingen, from 1984 to 1985. He is currently revising his dissertation, "E.T.A. Hoffmann's *Kater Murr*: Feline Characteristics and their Literary Expression." His research interests include German poetry, German Romanticism, and Poetic Realism. After having taught at Duquesne University from 1987 to 1990, he is now Assistant Professor of German at Oakland University.

Albrecht Classen received his doctorate from the University of Virginia in 1986, where he taught for one year before being appointed Assistant Professor at the University of Arizona. In addition to numerous scholarly articles, he has published a monograph on Oswald von Wolkenstein (*Zur Rezeption norditalienischer Kultur des Trecento im Werk Oswalds von Wolkenstein* [1987]), a study on Wolfram von Eschenbach's *Titurel* (*Utopie und Logos. Vier Studien zu Wolframs von Eschenbachs "Titurel"* [1990]), and a book on the late medieval lyric autobiography in Europe (*Die autobiographische Lyrik des europäischen Spätmittelaters...* [1991]). He has also edited two volumes (1989, 1991) of proceedings from the International Congress on Medieval Studies in Kalamazoo, Michigan. A translation of the Middle High German novella *Moriz von Craûn* will soon be published by

About the Authors

Reclam Verlag in Germany. Presently, he is working on a monograph on the German chapbook.

Robert C. Holub is Professor of German at the University of California at Berkeley. His most important publications are *Heinrich Heine's Reception of German Grecophilia: The Function and Application of the Hellenic Tradition in the First Half of the Nineteenth Century* (1981), *Reception Theory: A Critical Introduction* (1984), and *Reflections on Realism: Paradox, Norm, and Ideology in Nineteenth-Century German Prose* (1991). He is editor of *Teoria della ricezione* (1989), and co-editor with Jost Hermand of *Heinrich Heine: Poetry and Prose* (1982) and *The Romantic School and other Essays* (1985).

Lee B. Jennings is Professor of German and Head of the Department of German at the University of Illinois at Chicago. He received his Ph.D. in 1955 from the University of Illinois at Urbana-Champaign and has held positions at Harvard University, the University of California, Los Angeles, and the University of Texas at Austin. His main area of interest is German literature of late Romanticism and early Realism, as well as fantasy, the grotesque, and psychoanalytical approaches to literature. He has published books on the grotesque in German post-Romantic literature (*The Ludicrous Demon: Aspects of the Grotesque in German Post-Romantic Prose*, 1963) and on Justinus Kerner (*Justinus Kerners Weg nach Weinsberg [1809-1819]: Die Entpolitisierung eines Romantikers*, 1982), as well as numerous articles on E.T.A. Hoffmann, Gottfried Keller, Eduard Mörike, and other authors of the period.

Nancy Kaiser received her Ph.D. in German Literature from Yale University in 1980. Since then she has been at the University of Wisconsin-Madison, where she is on the faculty in the German Department and the Women's Studies Program. Professor Kaiser's publications include essays on German Realism, German and English Romantic women writers, and aspects of German literature since the Enlightenment. She is the author of *Social Integration and Narrative Structure. Patterns of Realism in Auerbach, Freytag, Fontane, and Raabe* (1986), and co-editor with David Wellbery of *Traditions of Experiment from the Enlightenment to the Present* (1992). She has also co-edited (with Peter Böthig) *elsewhere/anderswo. Texte von Feministinnen aus den USA* (1992). Her most recent articles concern nineteenth-century German literature, particularly women's issues.

Richard H. Lawson is Professor Emeritus of German at the University of North Carolina at Chapel Hill. He is the author of numerous articles on *Tatian, Otfrid, Das Hildebrandslied*, Old Alemannic, Gothic, and Middle High German. His recent books include *Günther Grass, Franz Kafka*, and *Survey of German Literature* (with Kim Vivian and Frank Tobin).

Siegfried Mews is Professor of German and chair of the Department of Germanic Languages at the University of North Carolina at Chapel Hill. His publications include editions of works by Zuckmayer and Brecht, edited volumes on Brecht and Grass, and monographs on Zuckmayer and Plenzdorf. He recently was executive director of the South Atlantic Modern Language Association and editor of *South Atlantic Review.*

Frank Tobin is Professor of German at the University of Nevada, Reno. He received his Ph.D. from Stanford University in 1967. His publications include books on Hartmann and Meister Eckhart and numerous articles on medieval German literature and religious thought. He is co-editor with Kim Vivian and Richard H. Lawson of *Survey of German Literature.*

John Van Cleve is Professor of German at Mississippi State University. His publications include two books: *Harlequin Besieged: The Reception of Comedy in Germany during the Early Enlightenment* and *The Merchant in German Literature of the Enlightenment.* He has published articles on Gellert, Goethe, and Lenz, among others.

Kim Vivian received his doctorate from the University of California, Santa Barbara. He studied for two years at Georg August Universität in Göttingen and was twice a recipient of a grant from the Deutscher Akademischer Austauschdienst (DAAD). He has written articles on Goethe, Herder, and Rousseau. He is co-editor with Roselinde Konrad of *Mosaik: Deutsche Literatur* and with Frank Tobin and Richard Lawson of *Survey of German Literature.*

Books For Further Reading

1. The Early Middle Ages: Gothic and Old High German

Bostock, John Knight. *A Handbook on Old High German Literature.* 2nd ed. rev. by K.C. King and D.R. McLintock. Oxford: Clarendon Press, 1976.

Friedrichsen, George W.S. *The Gothic Version of the Epistles.* London: Oxford UP, 1939.

——. *The Gothic Version of the Gospels.* London: Oxford UP, 1926.

Lloyd, Albert L. *The Manuscripts and Fragments of Notker's Psalter.* Giessen: Schmitz, 1958.

McKenzie, Donald A. *Otfrid von Weissenburg: Narrator or Commentator?* New York: AMS Press, 1967.

Miller, C. "The Old High German and Old Saxon Charms." Diss., Washington University, St. Louis, 1963.

Mullins, Sister Patrick Jerome. *The Spiritual Life According to Saint Isidore of Seville.* Washington: Catholic University of America Press, 1940.

Murdoch, Brian O. *Old High German Literature.* Boston: Twayne, 1983.

Norman, Frederick. *Three Essays on the "Hildebrandslied."* Ed. A. T. Hatto. London: Institute of Germanic Studies, 1973.

Ortberg, K. *The Old High German "Isidor" and its Relationship to the Extant Manuscripts (8th-12th Cent.) of Isidore's "De Fide Catholica."* Göppingen: Kümmerle, 1979.

Thompson, E.A. *The Visigoths in the Time of Ulfila.* Oxford: UP, 1966.

Van Zeller, Hubert. *The Holy Rule: Notes on St. Benedict's Legislation for Monks.* New York: Sheed and Ward, [1958].

Waterman, John T. *A History of the German Language.* Seattle-London: Univ. of Washington Press, 1966. 2nd ed. 1976, reissued Prospect Heights, Il.: Waveland Press, 1991.

Weringha, Juw von. *Heliand and Diatessaron.* Assen: Van Gorcum, 1965.

2. Middle High German

Batts, Michael. *Gottfried von Strassburg.* New York: Twayne, 1971.

Bäuml, Franz. *Medieval Civilization in Germany, 800-1273.* New York: Praeger, 1969.

Bekker, Hugo. *The "Nibelungenlied." A Literary Analysis.* Toronto: University of Toronto Press, 1971.

Clark, James M. *The Great German Mystics.* Oxford: UP, 1949. 2nd. ed. 1969.

Gentry, Frank. *Triuwe and Vriunt in the "Nibelungenlied."* Amsterdam: Rodopi 1975.

Haymes, Edward. *The "Nibelungenlied." History and Interpretation.* Urbana: Univ. of Illinois Press, 1986.

Jones, George F. *Walther von der Vogelweide.* New York: Twayne, 1968.

Mcconnell, Winder. *The "Nibelungenlied."* Boston: Twayne, 1984.

Mowatt, D.G., and Hugh Sacker. *The "Nibelungenlied." An Interpretative Commentary.* Toronto: University of Toronto Press, 1967.

Poag, James. *Wolfram von Eschenbach.* New York: Twayne, 1972.

Sacker, Hugh. *An Introduction to Wolfram's "Parzival."* Cambridge: UP, 1963.

Sayce, Olive. *Poets of the "Minnesang."* Oxford: UP, 1967.

Simon, Eckehard. *Neidhart von Reuental.* New York: Twayne, 1975.

Tobin, Frank. "Gregorius and Fallen Man." *Germanic Review* 50 (1975), 85-98.

———. "Hartmann's '*Erec*': The Perils of Young Love." *Seminar* 14 (1978), 1-14.

———. *Meister Eckhart. Thought and Language.* Philadelphia: Univ. of Pennsylvania Press, 1986.

Thomas, J. W. *The Strassburg Alexander and the Munich Oswald.* Columbia: Camden House, 1989.

———. *The Best Novellas of Medieval Germany.* Columbia: Camden House, 1984.

Waterman, John T. *A History of the German Language.* Seattle-London: Univ. of Washington Press, 1966. 2nd ed. 1976, reissued Prospect Heights, Il.: Waveland Press, 1991.

3. Late Middle High German, Renaissance, and Reformation

Bernstein, Eckhard. *German Humanism.* Boston: Twayne, 1983.

Burger, Heinz Otto. *Renaissance, Humanismus, Reformation. Deutsche Literatur im europäischen Kontext.* Frankfurter Beiträge zur Germanistik, 7. Bad Homburg v.d.H./Berlin/Zurich: Gehlen, 1969.

Classen, Albrecht. *Die autobiographische Lyrik des europäischen Spätmittelalters. Studien zu Hugo von Montfort, Oswald von Wolkenstein, Antonio Pucci, Charles d'Orléans, Thomas Hoccleve, Michel Beheim, Hans Rosenplüt und Alfonso Alvarez de Villasandino.* Amsterdamer Publikationen zur Sprache und Literatur, 91. Amsterdam/Atlanta,: Editions Rodopi, 1991.

Ertzdorff, Xenja von. *Romane und Novellen des 15. und 16. Jahrhunderts in Deutschland.* Darmstadt: Wissenschaftliche Buchgesellschaft, 1989.

Frey, Winfried, Walter Raitz, Dieter Seitz, et al, eds. *Einführung in die deutsche Literatur des 12. bis 16. Jahrhunderts.* Vol. 2: *Patriziat und Landesherrschaft – 13.-15. Jahrhundert.* Vol. 3: *Bürgertum und Fürstenstaat – 15./16. Jahrhundert.* Opladen: Westdeutscher Verlag, 1981/1982.

Jones, George Fenwick. *Oswald von Wolkenstein.* Boston: Twayne, 1973.

——. "Germany." In: *The Current State of Research in Fifteenth-Century Literature: Germania-Romania,* ed. William C. McDonald. Göppinger Arbeiten zur Germanistik, 442. Göppingen: Kümmerle, 1986, 29-48.

Kemper, Hans-Georg. *Deutsche Lyrik der frühen Neuzeit.* Vol. 1: Epochen- und Gattungsprobleme. Reformationszeit. Tübingen: Niemeyer, 1987.

Könneker, Barbara. "Deutsche Literatur im Zeitalter des Humanismus und der Reformation." In: *Renaissance und Barock* (II. Teil), ed. August Buck et al. Neues Handbuch der Literatur wissenschaft, 10. Frankfurt a. M.: Akademische Verlagsanstalt, 1972, 145-176.

McDonald, William C. *"Whose Bread I Eat": The Song-Poetry of Michel Beheim.* Göppinger Arbeiten zur Germanistik, 318. Göppingen: Kümmerle, 1981.

Schade, Richard Erich. *Studies in Early German Comedy. 1500-1650.* Studies in German Literature, Linguistics, and Culture, 24. Columbia, S.C.: Camden House, 1988.

Van Cleve, John. *The Problem of Wealth in the Literature of Luther's Germany.* Studies in German Literature, Linguistics, and Culture, 55. Columbia, S.C.: Camden House, 1991.

Walz, Herbert. *Deutsche Literatur der Reformationszeit. Eine Einführung.* Darmstadt: Wissenschaftliche Buchgesellschaft, 1988.

Waterman, John T. *A History of the German Language.* Seattle-London: Univ. of Washington Press, 1966. 2nd ed. 1976, reissued Prospect Heights, Il.: Waveland Press, 1991.

4 Baroque

Aikin, Judith P. *German Baroque Drama.* Boston: Twayne, 1982.

Browning, Robert M. *German Baroque Poetry. 1618-1723.* University Park, PA: Penn State UP, 1971.

Capua, A.G. de. *German Baroque Poetry: Interpretive Readings.* Albany: SUNY Press, 1973.

Daly, Peter M. *Literature in the Light of the Emblem: Structural Parallels between the Emblem and Literature in the Sixteenth and Seventeenth Centuries.* Toronto: UP, 1979.

Gillespie, Gerald. *German Baroque Poetry.* Boston: Twayne, 1973.

Hoffmeister, Gerhart, ed. *German Baroque Literature: The European Perspective.* New York: Ungar, 1983.

Newman, Jane O. *Pastoral Conventions: Poetry, Language, and Thought in Seventeenth-Century Nuremberg.* Baltimore: Johns Hopkins, 1990.

Pascal, Roy. *German Literature in the Sixteenth and Seventeenth Centuries: Renaissance – Reformation – Baroque.* New York: Barnes & Noble, 1968.

Skrine, Peter. *The Baroque: Literature and Culture in Seventeenth-Century Europe.* London: Methuen, 1978.

Wagener, Hans. *German Baroque Novel.* Boston: Twayne, 1971.

Warnke, Frank. *Versions of Baroque. European Literature in the Seventeenth Century.* New Haven: Yale UP, 1972.

5 Enlightenment

Brown, F. Andrew. *Gotthold Ephraim Lessing.* Boston: Twayne, 1971.

Bruford, Walter Horace. *Germany in the Eighteenth Century: The Social Background of the Literary Revival.* Cambridge: UP, 1971.

Hardin, James and Christoph Schweitzer. Eds. *German Writers from the Enlightenment to Sturm und Drang 1720-1764.* Dictionary of Literary Biography vol. 97. Detroit: Gale Research, 1990.

Heitner, Robert. *German Tragedy in the Age of Enlightenment.* Berkeley and Los Angeles: Univ. of California Press, 1963.

Kimpel, Dieter. *Der Roman der Aufklärung.* Stuttgart: Metzler, 1967.

McCarthy, John A. *Christoph Martin Wieland.* Boston: Twayne, 1979.

Menhennet, Alan. *Order and Freedom: Literature and Society in Germany from 1720 to 1805.* London: Weidenfeld and Nicholson, 1973.

6 Storm and Stress

Bruford, Walter H. *Germany in the Eighteenth Century: The Social Background of the Literary Revival.* Cambridge: UP, 1971.

——. *Theater, Drama, and Audience in Goethe's Germany.* London: Routledge & Paul, 1950.

Closs, August. *The Genius of the German Lyric: An Historical Survey of its Formal and Metaphysical Values.* Philadelphia: Dufour, 1962 (first published   1938).

Engall, James. *The Creative Imagination: Enlightenment to Romanticism.* Cambridge and London: Harvard UP, 1981.

Grimminger, Rolf, ed. *Deutsche Aufklärung bis zur französischen Revolution, 1600-1789.* Hansers Sozialgeschichte der deutschen Literatur, vol. 3. Munich: Hanser, 1980. (see particularly: "Drama" by Jochen Schulte-Sasse, pp. 423-499, "Geniekult im Sturm und Drang" by Gerhard Sauder, pp. 327-340, "Lyrik in der zweiten Hälfte des 18. Jahrhunderts" by Wolfgang

Promies, pp. 569-604, "Roman" by Rolf Grimmiger, pp. 635-715, and "Von der Wanderbühne zum Hof-und Nationaltheater" by Reinhart Meyer, pp. 186-218)

Hardin, James and Christoph Schweitzer. Eds. *German Writers in the Age of Goethe: Sturm und Drang to Classicism.* Dictionary of Literary Biography vol. 94. Detroit: Gale Research, 1990.

Hinck, Walter, ed. *Sturm und Drang.* Kronberg: Athenäum, 1978.

Huyssen, Andreas. *Drama des Sturm und Drang.* Munich: Winkler, 1980.

———. "Sturm und Drang." In: *Geschichte der deutschen Lyrik,* ed. Walter Hinderer. Stuttgart: Reclam, 1983. Pp. 177-201.

Kistler, Mark O. *Drama of the Storm and Stress.* New York: Twayne, 1969.

Kließ, Werner. *Sturm und Drang.* Friedrichs Dramatiker des Welttheaters, vol. 25. Velber bei Hannover: Friedrich, 1966.

Lange, Victor. *The Classical Age of German Literature 1740-1815.* NY: Holmes & Meier, 1982.

Menhennet, Alan. *Order and Freedom. Literature and Society in Germany from 1720 to 1805.* New York: Basic Books, 1974.

Pascal, Roy. *The German Sturm und Drang.* Manchester: UP, 1953.

Prawer, Siegbert Salomon. *German Lyric Poetry: A Critical Analysis of Selected Poems from Klopstock to Rilke.* New York: Barnes & Noble, 1965.

Sturm und Drang: Erläuterungen zur deutschen Literatur. Berlin: Volk und Wissen, 1978.

7. Classicism

Atkins, Stuart P. *Goethe's "Faust": A Literary Analysis.* 3rd ed. Cambridge, Mass.: Harvard UP, 1969.

Bennett, Benjamin. *Modern Drama and German Classicism. Renaissance from Lessing to Brecht.* Ithaca, NY: Cornell UP, 1979.

Berghahn, Klaus L., ed. *Die Weimarer Klassik. Paradigma des Methodenpluralismus in der Germanistik.* Kronberg/Czech.: Scriptor, 1976.

———. *Schiller. Ansichten eines Idealisten.* Frankfurt: Athenäum, 1986.

Boerner, Peter, and Sidney Johnson, eds. *Faust through Four Centuries: Retrospect and Analysis.* Tübingen: Niemeyer, 1989.

Borchmeyer, Dieter. "Weimar im Zeitalter der Revolution und der Napoleonischen Kriege." In: *Geschichte der deutschen Literatur vom 18. Jahrhundert bis zur Gegenwart,* vol. 1, ed. Victor Zmegac. Königstein/Czech.: Athenäum, 1984.

Brown, Jane K. *Goethe's "Faust." The German Tragedy.* Ithaca, NY: Cornell UP, 1986.

Bruford, Walter H. *Culture and Society in Classical Weimar 1775-1806*. London: Cambridge UP, 1965.

——. *Germany in the Eighteenth Century: The Social Background of the Literary Revival*. Cambridge: UP, 1971.

——. *Theater, Drama, and Audience in Goethe's Germany*. London: Routledge & Paul, 1950.

Carlson, Marvin A. *Goethe and the Weimar Theater*. Ithaca, NY: Cornell UP, 1978.

Eissler, Kurt Robert. *Goethe. A Psychoanalytic Study. 1775-1786*. Detroit: Wayne State UP, 1963.

Friedenthal, Richard. *Goethe. His Life and Times*. Cleveland: The World Publishing Co., 1965.

Glaser, Horst Albert. *Zwischen Revolution und Restauration: Klassik und Romantik: 1786-1815*. Deutsche Literatur: Eine Sozialgeschichte, vol. 5. Reinbek bei Hamburg: Rowohlt, 1980

Graham, Ilse. *Goethe. A Portrait of the Artist*. Berlin/NY: de Gruyter, 1977.

——. *Schiller. A Master of the Tragic Form. His Theory in His Practice*. Pittsburgh: Duquesne UP, 1975.

Grimm, Reinhold, and Jost Hermand, eds. *Our Faust? Roots and Ramifications of a Modern German Myth*. Madison: Univ. of Wisconsin Press, 1987.

Hardin, James and Christoph Schweitzer. Eds. *German Writers in the Age of Goethe: 1789-1832*. Dictionary of Literary Biography vol. 90. Detroit: Gale Research, 1989.

Koopman, Helmut. *Friedrich Schiller*. Stuttgart: Metzler, 1966.

Lukács, Georg. *Goethe and His Age*, tr. Robert Anchor. NY: Grosset & Dunlap, 1968.

Passage, Charles E. *Friedrich Schiller*. NY: Ungar, 1975.

Prawer, Siegbert Salomon. *German Lyric Poetry: A Critical Analysis of Selected Poems from Klopstock to Rilke*. New York: Barnes & Noble, 1965.

Prudhoe, John. *The Theater of Goethe and Schiller*. Oxford: Blackwell, 1973.

Reed, Terence James. *The Classical Centre. Goethe and Weimar 1775-1832*. London: Croom Helm, 1980.

Simons, John D. *Friedrich Schiller*. Boston: Twayne, 1981.

Ugrinsky, Alexej, ed. *Friedrich von Schiller and the Drama of Human Existence*. New York: Greenwood, 1988.

Unger, Richard. *Friedrich Hölderlin*. Boston: Twayne, 1984.

Wiese, Benno von. *Friedrich Schiller*. 4th ed. Stuttgart: Metzler, 1978.

8 Romanticism

Blackall, Eric A. *The Novels of the German Romantics.* Ithaca and London: Cornell UP, 1985.

Brown, Marshall. *The Shape of German Romanticism.* Ithaca and London: Cornell UP, 1979.

Engall, James. *The Creative Imagination: Enlightenment to Romanticism.* Cambridge and London: Harvard UP, 1981.

Furst, Lilian R. *Romanticism.* London: Methuen, 1969.

Glaser, Horst Albert. *Zwischen Revolution und Restauration: Klassik und Romantik: 1786-1815.* Deutsche Literatur: Eine Sozialgeschichte, vol. 5. Reinbek bei Hamburg: Rowohlt, 1980.

Hughes, Glyn Tegai. *Romantic German Literature.* New York: Holmes and Meier, 1979.

Pohlheim, Karl Konrad, ed. *Der Poesiebegriff der deutschen Romantik.* Paderborn: Schöningh, 1972.

Prawer, Siegbert, ed. *The Romantic Period in Germany: Essays.* New York: Schocken, 1970.

Steffan, Hans, ed. *Die deutsche Romantik: Poetik, Formen und Motive.* Göttingen: Vandenhoeck und Ruprecht, 1967.

Thalmann, Marianne. *The Literary Sign Language of German Romanticism.* Detroit: Wayne State UP, 1972.

Tymns, Ralph. *German Romantic Literature.* London: Methuen, 1955.

Walzel, Oskar. *German Romanticism.* New York: Ungar, 1932 (rpt. 1965).

Wernaer, Robert M. *Romanticism and the Romantic School in Germany.* New York: Haskell House, 1966.

Wiese, Benno von. *Deutsche Dichter der Romantik: Ihr Leben und Werk.* Berlin: Schmidt, 1971.

9 Young Germany

Behrens, Wolfgang W., et al. *Der literarische Vormärz.* Munich: List, 1973.

Bock, Helmut, et al. *Streitpunkt Vormärz: Beiträge zur Kritik bürgerlicher und revisionistischer Erbeauffassungen.* Berlin: Akademie-Verlag, 1977.

Butler, Eliza Marian. *The Saint-Simonian Religion in Germany: A Study of the Young German Movement.* Cambridge: UP, 1926.

Dietze, Walter. *Junges Deutschland und deutsche Klassik: Zur Ästhetik und Literaturtheorie des Vormärz.* Berlin: Rütten & Loening, 1957.

Gieger, Ludwig. *Das junge Deutschland: Studien und Mitteilungen.* Berlin: Schottlaender, 1907.

Hoemberg, Walter. *Zeitgeist und Ideenschmuggel: Die Kommunikationsstrategie des Jungen Deutschland.* Stuttgart: Metzler, 1975.

Houben, Heinrich Hubert. *Jungdeutscher Sturm und Drang: Ergebnisse und Studien.* Leipzig: Brockhaus, 1911.

Koopmann, Helmut. *Das junge Deutschland: Analyse seines Selbstverständnisses.* Stuttgart: Metzler, 1970.

Kruse, Joseph A., and Bernd Kortländer, eds. *Das junge Deutschland.* Hamburg: Hoffmann und Campe, 1987.

Mattenklott, Gerd, and Klaus Scherpe, eds. *Demokratisch-revolutionäre Literatur in Deutschland: Vormärz.* Kronberg/Czech.: Scriptor, 1974.

Rosenberg, Rainer. *Literaturverhältnisse im deutschen Vormärz.* Berlin: Akademie-Verlag, 1975.

Sagarra, Eda. *Tradition and Revolution: German Literature and Society 1830-1900.* New York: Basic Books, 1971.

Sammons, Jeffrey L. *Six Essays on the Young German Novel.* Chapel Hill: Univ. of North Carolina Press, 1972.

Stein, Peter. *Epochenproblem "Vormärz" (1815-1848).* Stuttgart: Metzler, 1974.

10. Biedermeier

Bennett, Edwin K. *The German Novella.* Cambridge: UP, 1961.

Blackall, Eric A. *Adalbert Stifter: A Critical Study.* Cambridge: UP, 1948.

Burkhard, Arthur. *Franz Grillparzer in England and America.* Vienna: Bergland, 1961.

Fehr, Karl. *Jeremias Gotthelf (Albert Bitzius).* Stuttgart: Metzler, 1985.

Hein, Alois. *Adalbert Stifter: Sein Leben und seine Werke.* Vienna: Krieg, 1952.

Hermand, Jost. *Die literarische Formenwelt des Biedermeiers.* Giessen: Schmitz,   1958.

——, and Manfred Windfuhr, eds. *Zur Literatur der Restaurationsepoche 1815-1848.* Stuttgart: Metzler, 1970.

Heselhaus, Clemens. *Annette von Droste-Hülshoff: Werk und Leben.* Düsseldorf: Bagel, 1971.

Mare, Margaret. *Eduard Mörike: The Man and the Poet.* London: Methuen, 1957.

——. *Annette von Droste-Hülshoff.* Lincoln: Univ. of Nebraska Press, 1965.

Martens, Wolfgang. *Bild und Motiv im Weltschmerz: Studien zur Dichtung Lenaus.* Cologne: Böhlau, 1957.

Mayer, Birgit. *Eduard Mörike.* Stuttgart: Metzler, 1987.

Maync, Harry. *Eduard Mörike: Sein Leben und Dichten.* 5th ed, Stuttgart: Cotta, 1944.

Meyer, Herbert. *Eduard Mörike.* Stuttgart: Metzler, 1950.

Morgan, Mary E. *Annette von Droste-Hülshoff: A Woman of Letters in a Period of Transition.* New York: Lang, 1980.

——. *Annette von Droste-Hülshoff: A Biography.* New York: Lang, 1984.

Muschg, Walter. *Jeremias Gotthelf: Eine Einführung in seine Werke.* Bern: Francke, 1960.

Naumann, Walter. *Franz Grillparzer: Das dichterische Werk.* Stuttgart: Kohlhammer, 1967.

Neubuhr, Elfriede. *Begriffsbestimmung des literarischen Biedermeier.* Darmstadt: Wissenschaftliche Buchgesellschaft, 1974

Politzer, Heinz. *Franz Grillparzer oder das abgründige Biedermeier.* Vienna: Molden, 1972.

Prawer, Siegbert Salomon. *German Lyric Poetry: A Critical Analysis of Selected Poems from Klopstock to Rilke.* New York: Barnes & Noble, 1965.

Roedl, Urban. *Adalbert Stifter: Geschichte seines Lebens.* 2nd ed. Bern: Francke, 1958.

Schmidt, Hugo. *Nikolaus Lenau.* New York: Twayne, 1971.

Schneider, Ronald. *Annette von Droste-Hülshoff.* Stuttgart: Metzler, 1977.

Sengle, Friedrich. *Biedermeierzeit: Deutsche Literatur im Spannungsfeld zwischen Restauration und Revolution 1815-1848.* Stuttgart: Metzler, 1971-1980.

Slessarev, Helga. *Eduard Mörike.* New York: Twayne, 1970.

Swales, Martin W. *The German "Novelle."* Princeton: UP, 1977.

——, and Erika Swales. *Adalbert Stifter: A Critical Study.* Cambridge: UP, 1984.

Thompson, Bruce. *Franz Grillparzer.* Boston: Twayne, 1981.

Waidson, H.M. *Jeremias Gotthelf: An Introduction to the Swiss Novelist.* Oxford: Blackwell, 1953.

Wells, G.A. *The Plays of Grillparzer.* London: Pergamon, 1965.

Wiese, Benno von. *Eduard Mörike.* Tübingen and Stuttgart: Wunderlich, 1950.

Yates, Douglas. *Franz Grillparzer: A Critical Biography.* Oxford: Blackwell, 1946.

Yates, W.E. *Grillparzer: A Critical Introduction.* Cambridge: UP, 1972.

11. Realism

Auerbach, Erich. *Mimesis.* Trans. W. Trask. Princeton: UP, 1968.

Aust, Hugo. *Literatur des Realismus.* Sammlung Metzler, 157. Stuttgart: Metzler, 1981.

Bark, Joachim. "Bürgerlicher Realismus. Biedermeier-Vormärz." *Bürgerlicher Realismus.* Stuttgart: Klett, 1984. Pp. 78-146.

Begriffsbestimmung des literarischen Realismus. Ed. Richard Brinkmann. Wege der Forschung, 212. Darmstadt: Wissenschaftliche Buchgesellschaft, 1969.

Berman, Russell. *The Rise of the Modern German Novel: Crisis and Charisma.* Cambridge: Harvard UP, 1986.

Bernd, Clifford. *German Poetic Realism.* Boston: Twayne, 1981.

Boeschenstein, Hermann. *German Literature of the Nineteenth Century.* New York: St. Martin's Press, 1969.

Bramstedt, Ernest K. *Aristocracy and the Middle Classes in Germany: Social Types in German Literature 1830-1900.* 1937; rpt. Chicago: University of Chicago Press, 1964.

Bucher, M. ed. *Realismus und Gründerzeit: Manifeste und Dokumente zur deutschen Literatur 1848-1880.* 2 vols. Stuttgart: Metzler, 1976.

Cowen, Roy. *Der Poetische Realismus.* Munich: Winkler, 1985.

Frederiksen, Elke, ed. *Die Frauenfrage in Deutschland 1865-1915.* Stuttgart: Reclam, 1981.

Holub, Robert C. *Reflections of Realism: Paradox, Norm, and Ideology in Nineteenth-Century German Prose.* Detroit: Wayne State Press, 1991.

Huyssen, Andreas, ed. *Bürgerlicher Realismus.* Stuttgart: Reclam, 1974.

Kaiser, Nancy. *Social Integration and Narrative Structure: Patterns of Realism in Auerbach, Freytag, Fontane, and Raabe.* Bern: Lang, 1986.

Kinder, Hermann. *Poesie als Synthese: Ausbreitung eines deutschen Realismusverständnisses in der Mitte des 19. Jahrhunderts.* Frankfurt/M.: Athenäum, 1973.

Martini, Fritz. *Deutsche Literatur im bürgerlichen Realismus 1848-1898.* 4th edition. Stuttgart: Metzler, 1981.

McInnes, Edward. *Das deutsche Drama des 19. Jahrhunderts.* Berlin: Erich Schmidt Verlag, 1983.

Müller-Seidel, Walter. *Theodor Fontane. Soziale Romankunst in Deutschland.* Stuttgart: Metzler, 1975.

Plumpe, Gerhard, ed. Theorie des bürgerlichen Realismus. Eine Textsammlung. Stuttgart: Reclam, 1985.

Sagarra, Eda. *Tradition and Revolution: German Literature and Society 1830-1890.* New York: Basic Books, 1971.

Sammons, Jeffrey L. *Wilhelm Raabe: The Fiction of the Alternative Community.* Princeton: Princeton University Press, 1987.

Sammons. *The Shifting Fortunes of Wilhelm Raabe. A History of Criticism as a Cautionary Tale.* Columbia: Camden House, 1991.

Silz, Walter. *Realism and Reality: Studies in the German Novella of Poetic Realism.* Chapel Hill: University of North Carolina, 1954.

Stern, J.P. *On Realism*. London/Boston: Routledge and Kegan Paul, 1973.

Widhammer, Helmuth. *Die Literaturtheorie des deutschen Realismus (1848-1860)*. Sammlung Metzler, 152. Stuttgart: Metzler, 1977.

———. *Realismus und klassistische Tradition: Zur Theorie der Literatur in Deutschland 1848-1860*. Tübingen: Niemeyer, 1972.

———, and Hans-Joachim Ruckhäberle, eds. *Roman und Romantheorie des deutschen Realismus*. Kronberg/Ts.: Athenäum, 1977.

12. Naturalism

Hardin, James, ed. *German Fiction Writers, 1885-1913*. Part I: A-L, Part II: M-Z. Hardin. Dictionary of Literary Biography, vol. 66. Detroit: Gale Research, 1988.

Hardin and Donald Daviau, eds. *Austrian Fiction Writers, 1875-1913*. Dictionary of Literary Biography volume 81. Detroit: Gale Research, 1989.

Marshall, Alan. *The German Naturalists and Gerhard Hauptmann. Reception and Influence*. Frankfurt am Main: Lang, 1982.

Maurer, Warren R. *The Naturalist Image of German Literature. A Study of the German Naturalists' Appraisal of Their Literary Heritage*. Munich: Fink, 1972.

McInnes, Edward. *German Social Drama 1840-1900: From Hebbel to Hauptmann*. Stuttgart: Heinz, 1976.

Osborne, John. *The Naturalist Drama in Germany*. Manchester: UP, 1971.

Pascal, Roy. *From Naturalism to Expressionism. German Literature and Society 1880-1918*. London: Weidenfeld and Nicholson, 1973.

Sagarra, Eda. *Tradition and Revolution. German Literature and Society 1830- 1890*. London: Weidenfeld and Nicholson, 1971.

[Siegfried Mews gratefully acknowledges the assistance of Roger Russi in compiling this section.]

INDEX

332

Index